DATE DUE

DEMCO 128-5046

SOMETHING ABOUT THE AUTHOR®

Something about
the Author *was named
an "Outstanding
Reference Source,"
the highest honor given
by the American
Library Association
Reference and User
Services Association.*

ISSN 0276-816X

SOMETHING ABOUT THE AUTHOR®

Facts and Pictures about Authors
and Illustrators of Books for Young People

EDITED BY
ALAN HEDBLAD

VOLUME 106

GALE GROUP

Detroit
San Francisco
London
Boston
Woodbridge, CT

STAFF

Editor: Alan Hedblad
Associate Editor: Melissa Hill
...atures Coordinator: Motoko Fujishiro Huthwaite

... ...ara L. Constantakis, Catherine Goldstein, Maria Job, Arlene M. Johnson
Editorial Assistant: Erin E. White

Editorial Technical Specialist: Karen Uchic

Managing Editor: Joyce Nakamura
Publisher: Hal May

Research Manager: Victoria B. Cariappa
Project Coordinator: Cheryl L. Warnock
Research Associates: Patricia Tsune Ballard, Tamara C. Nott, Wendy K. Festerling, Tracie A. Richardson,
Corrine A. Stocker, Robert Whaley
Research Assistant: Patricia L. Love

Permissions Manager: Maria L. Franklin
Permissions Associates: Sarah Chesney, Edna Hedblad, Michele Lonoconus

Production Director: Mary Beth Trimper
Production Assistant: Deborah Milliken

Graphic Artist: Gary Leach
Image Database Supervisor: Randy Bassett
Imaging Specialists: Robert Duncan, Michael Logusz
Imaging Coordinator: Pamela A. Reed

While every effort has been made to ensure the reliability of the information presented in this publication, Gale Research does not guarantee the accuracy of the data contained herein. Gale accepts no payment for listing; and inclusion of any organization, agency, institution, publication, service, or individual does not imply endorsement of the editors or publisher. Errors brought to the attention of the publisher and verified to the satisfaction of the publisher will be corrected in future editions.

Library of Congress Catalog Card Number 72-27107

ISBN 0-7876-3215-5
ISSN 0276-816X

Printed in the United States of America

10 9 8 7 6 5 4 3 2 1

Contents

Authors in Forthcoming Volumes vii
Introduction ix
Acknowledgments xi

Authors in Forthcoming Volumes

Below are some of the authors and illustrators that will be featured in upcoming volumes of *SATA*. These include new entries on the swiftly rising stars of the field, as well as completely revised and updated entries (indicated with *) on some of the most notable and best-loved creators of books for children.

*Verna Aardema: Aardema is well known for her retellings of African stories and tall tales, including the Caldecott Medal-winner *Why Mosquitoes Buzz in People's Ears,* and *Who's in Rabbit's House?,* which received a Lewis Carroll Shelf Award. Her recent efforts include *Borreguita and the Coyote,* illustrated by Petra Mathers, and *This for That: A Tonga Tale,* illustrated by Victoria Chess.

Fleur Beale: A writer of young-adult novels set in her native New Zealand, Beale is credited with producing realistic, fast-paced stories that have wide appeal for teens, particularly reluctant male readers.

Nic Bishop: Author and photographer Bishop has garnered favorable critical attention for *The Secrets of Animal Flight,* which explains the mechanics of the flight of birds, bats, and insects in clear prose, accentuated with his full-color, stop-action photographs.

Kathy Eldon: Eldon's son Dan, a talented freelance photojournalist, was stoned to death at the age of twenty-two while on an assignment in Somalia. Eldon compiled *The Journey is the Destination,* a collection of Dan's writings, drawings, and photographs that pays tribute to his short yet accomplished life.

*Nikki Giovanni: A celebrated African-American poet with a body of work that spans three decades, Giovanni continues to create poems that express strong racial pride and respect for family. Her most recent book for children is *The Sun Is So Quiet.*

Daniel Kirk: Author and illustrator Kirk has several well-received picture books to his credit, including *Breakfast at the Liberty Diner* and *Trash Trucks!* He also provided the illustrations for a 1995 reinterpretation of Margaret Wise Brown's classic *The Diggers.*

*Elizabeth Levy: From children's chapter and picture books to young-adult novels and mystery series, Levy's large body of work encompasses a wide range of reading levels and genres. Her most recent works include new installments of her popular "Something Queer" series, the young-adult thriller *The Drowned,* and the picture book *Cleo and the Coyote.*

*Jerry Pinkney: Regarded as one of the most gifted contemporary American illustrators for children, Pinkney is credited with being instrumental in bringing multicultural subjects, especially those regarding African Americans, to the picture-book genre. He recently received two Caldecott Honor Awards, for *The Talking Eggs* by Robert D. San Souci and *John Henry* by Julius Lester, as well as a Coretta Scott King Award for *Minty: A Story of Young Harriet Tubman.*

Ching Yeung Russell: Russell's several novels for young readers, including *Lichee Tree* and the award-winning *First Apple,* are set in the small, rural Chinese town of her youth.

Nava Semel: Semel's works draw heavily upon her experiences growing up as the daughter of Holocaust refugees in postwar Israel.

David Shannon: Shannon's illustrations have graced the pages of the works of such well-known authors as Isaac Asimov, Jane Yolen, and Robert D. San Souci. He has also illustrated his own texts, including the critically acclaimed *The Amazing Christmas Extravaganza* and the award-winning *No, David!*

*Todd Strasser: A prolific author of fiction for preteens and teenagers, Strasser has added several volumes to his award-winning "Help, I'm Trapped!" series. Another recent effort, *Hey Dad, Get a Life!,* was named an ALA Notable Book.

Introduction

Something about the Author (*SATA*) is an ongoing reference series that examines the lives and works of authors and illustrators of books for children. *SATA* includes not only well-known writers and artists but also less prominent individuals whose works are just coming to be recognized. This series is often the only readily available information source on emerging authors and illustrators. You'll find *SATA* informative and entertaining, whether you are a student, a librarian, an English teacher, a parent, or simply an adult who enjoys children's literature.

What's Inside SATA

SATA provides detailed information about authors and illustrators who span the full time range of children's literature, from early figures like John Newbery and L. Frank Baum to contemporary figures like Judy Blume and Richard Peck. Authors in the series represent primarily English-speaking countries, particularly the United States, Canada, and the United Kingdom. Also included, however, are authors from around the world whose works are available in English translation. The writings represented in *SATA* include those created intentionally for children and young adults as well as those written for a general audience and known to interest younger readers. These writings cover the entire spectrum of children's literature, including picture books, humor, folk and fairy tales, animal stories, mystery and adventure, science fiction and fantasy, historical fiction, poetry and nonsense verse, drama, biography, and nonfiction.

Obituaries are also included in *SATA* and are intended not only as death notices but also as concise overviews of people's lives and work. Additionally, each edition features newly revised and updated entries for a selection of *SATA* listees who remain of interest to today's readers and who have been active enough to require extensive revisions of their earlier biographies.

New Autobiography Feature

Beginning with Volume 103, *Something about the Author* will feature three or more specially commissioned autobiographical essays in each volume. These unique essays, averaging about ten thousand words in length and illustrated with an abundance of personal photos, present an entertaining and informative first-person perspective on the lives and careers of prominent authors and illustrators profiled in *SATA*.

Two Convenient Indexes

In response to suggestions from librarians, *SATA* indexes no longer appear in every volume but are included in alternate (odd-numbered) volumes of the series, beginning with Volume 57.

SATA continues to include two indexes that cumulate with each alternate volume: the Illustrations Index, arranged by the name of the illustrator, gives the number of the volume and page where the illustrator's work appears in the current volume as well as all preceding volumes in the series; the Author Index gives the number of the volume in which a person's biographical sketch, autobiographical essay, or obituary appears in the current volume as well as all preceding volumes in the series.

These indexes also include references to authors and illustrators who appear in Gale's *Yesterday's Authors of Books for Children, Children's Literature Review,* and *Something about the Author Autobiography Series.*

Easy-to-Use Entry Format

Whether you're already familiar with the *SATA* series or just getting acquainted, you will want to be aware of the kind of information that an entry provides. In every *SATA* entry the editors attempt to give as complete a picture of the person's life and work as possible. A typical entry in *SATA* includes the following clearly labeled information sections:

- *PERSONAL:* date and place of birth and death, parents' names and occupations, name of spouse, date of marriage, names of children, educational institutions attended, degrees received, religious and political affiliations, hobbies and other interests.

- *ADDRESSES:* complete home, office, electronic mail, and agent addresses, whenever available.

- *CAREER:* name of employer, position, and dates for each career post; art exhibitions; military service; memberships and offices held in professional and civic organizations.

- *AWARDS, HONORS:* literary and professional awards received.

- *WRITINGS:* title-by-title chronological bibliography of books written and/or illustrated, listed by genre when known; lists of other notable publications, such as plays, screenplays, and periodical contributions.

- *ADAPTATIONS:* a list of films, television programs, plays, CD-ROMs, recordings, and other media presentations that have been adapted from the author's work.

- *WORK IN PROGRESS:* description of projects in progress.

- *SIDELIGHTS:* a biographical portrait of the author or illustrator's development, either directly from the biographee—and often written specifically for the *SATA* entry—or gathered from diaries, letters, interviews, or other published sources.

- *FOR MORE INFORMATION SEE:* references for further reading.

- *EXTENSIVE ILLUSTRATIONS:* photographs, movie stills, book illustrations, and other interesting visual materials supplement the text.

How a SATA Entry Is Compiled

A *SATA* entry progresses through a series of steps. If the biographee is living, the *SATA* editors try to secure information directly from him or her through a questionnaire. From the information that the biographee supplies, the editors prepare an entry, filling in any essential missing details with research and/or telephone interviews. If possible, the author or illustrator is sent a copy of the entry to check for accuracy and completeness.

If the biographee is deceased or cannot be reached by questionnaire, the *SATA* editors examine a wide variety of published sources to gather information for an entry. Biographical and bibliographic sources are consulted, as are book reviews, feature articles, published interviews, and material sometimes obtained from the biographee's family, publishers, agent, or other associates.

Entries that have not been verified by the biographees or their representatives are marked with an asterisk (*).

Contact the Editor

We encourage our readers to examine the entire *SATA* series. Please write and tell us if we can make *SATA* even more helpful to you. Give your comments and suggestions to the editor:

BY MAIL: Editor, *Something about the Author,* The Gale Group, 27500 Drake Rd., Farmington Hills, MI 48331-3535.

BY TELEPHONE: (800) 347-GALE

BY FAX: (248) 699-8065

Acknowledgments

Grateful acknowledgment is made to the following publishers, authors, and artists whose works appear in this volume.

ADLER, DAVID A. Maione, Heather Harms, illustrator. From an illustration in *Wacky Jacks,* by David A. Adler. Random House, Inc., 1994. Illustrations copyright © 1994 by Heather Harms Maione. Reproduced by permission of Random House, Inc. / Ritz, Karen, illustrator. From a cover of *A Picture Book of Anne Frank,* by David A. Adler. Holiday House, Inc., 1993. Illustrations copyright © 1993 by Karen Ritz. Reproduced by permission of Holiday House, Inc. / O'Malley, Kevin, illustrator. From an illustration in *Chanukah,* by David A. Adler. Lothrop, Lee & Shepard Books, 1997. Illustrations copyright © 1997 by Kevin O'Malley. Reproduced by permission of Lothrop, Lee & Shepard Books, an imprint of Morrow Junior Books, a division of William Morrow & Company, Inc. / Widener, Terry, illustrator. From an illustration in *Lou Gehrig: The Luckiest Man,* by David A. Adler. Gulliver Books, 1997. Text © 1997 by David A. Adler. Illustrations © 1997 by Terry Widener. Reproduced by permission of Harcourt, Inc. / Adler, David A., photograph by Walter Paisol. Reproduced by permission of David A. Adler.

ALDA, ARLENE. From a cover of *Arlene Alda's 1 2 3,* by Arlene Alda. Tricycle Press, 1998. Copyright © 1999 by Arlene Alda. Reproduced by permission of Tricycle Press, P. O. Box 7123, Berkeley, CA 94707.

ANDERSON, POUL. All images reproduced by permission of Poul Anderson.

BABBITT, NATALIE. Babbitt, Natalie, illustrator. From a cover of her *The Devil's Other Storybook.* Farrar, Straus & Giroux, Inc. Copyright © 1987 by Natalie Babbitt. Reproduced by permission of Farrar, Straus & Giroux, Inc. / Natalie Babbitt, photograph by Steve Adams Photography. Reproduced by permission.

BELBIN, DAVID. Belbin, David, photograph by Sue Dymoke. Reproduced by permission of David Belbin.

BERNARD, PATRICIA. Bernard, Patricia, photograph. Reproduced by permission.

BERTRAND, DIANE GONZALES. DeLange, Alex Pardo, illustrator. From a postcard for the book *Sip, Slurp, Soup, Soup, Caldo, Caldo, Caldo,* by Diane Gonzales Bertrand. Pinata Books, 1996. Reproduced by permission of Arte Público Press—University of Houston. / Bertrand, Diane Gonzales, photograph. Reproduced by permission.

BOYES, VIVIEN. Boyes, Vivien, photograph. Reproduced by permission.

BRANFORD, HENRIETTA. Leister, Bryan, illustrator. From a jacket of *Fire Bed & Bone,* by Henrietta Branford. Candlewick Press, 1998. Jacket illustration copyright © 1998 by Bryan Leister. Reproduced by permission of Walker Books Ltd. Published in the U.S. by Candlewick Press, Inc., Cambridge, MA. / Branford, Henrietta, photograph by Paul Carter. Reproduced by permission of Paul Carter.

BUELL, JANET. From a cover of *Ancient Horsemen of Siberia,* by Janet Buell. Sovfoto/Novosti. Twenty-First Century Books, 1998. Reproduced by permission of Millbrook Press. / Buell, Janet, photograph. Reproduced by permission.

BUTTERWORTH, NICK. From an illustration in *My Mom Is Excellent,* by Nick Butterworth. Candlewick Press, 1989. Copyright © 1989 by Nick Butterworth. Reproduced by permission of Walker Books Ltd. Published in the U.S. by Candlewick Press, Inc., Cambridge, MA. / From an illustration in *Jasper's Beanstalk,* by Nick Butterworth and Mick Inkpen. Aladdin Paperbacks, 1993. Copyright © 1993 by Nick Butterworth and Mick Inkpen. Reproduced by permission of Hodder & Stoughton Limited. In the U. S. by Simon & Schuster Books for Young Readers, an imprint of Simon & Schuster Children's Publishing Division. / From a cover of *Jingle Bells,* by Nick Butterworth. Orchard Books, 1998. Reproduced by permission of Orchard Books, New York. In the U. K. by HarperCollins Publishers Ltd. / Butterworth, Nick, photograph. Reproduced by permission.

CHENG, CHRISTOPHER. Woolman, Steven, illustrator. From a promotional piece for *One Child,* by Christopher Cheng. Era Publications, 1997. Reproduced by permission. / Cheng, Christopher, photograph by Mary Jo Corso. Reproduced by permission of Christopher Cheng.

COHEN, MIRIAM. Hoban, Lillian, illustrator. From an illustration in *Will I Have a Friend?,* by Miriam Cohen. Aladdin

WESLEY, VALERIE WILSON. From a cover of *Where Do I Go from Here?,* by Valerie Wilson Wesley. Scholastic Inc., 1993. Cover illustrations copyright © 1993 by Scholastic Inc. Reproduced by permission.

WOODRUFF, ELVIRA. Gammell, Stephen, illustrator. From an illustration in *The Wing Shop,* by Elvira Woodruff. Holiday House, 1991. Illustrations copyright © 1991 by Stephen Gammell. Reproduced by permission of Holiday House, Inc. / Dooling, Michael, illustrator. From an illustration in *The Memory Coat,* by Elvira Woodruff. Scholastic Press, 1998. Illustrations copyright © 1999 by Michael Dooling. Reproduced by permission of Scholastic Press, a division of Scholastic Inc.

WORMSER, RICHARD. From a jacket of *Hoboes: Wandering in America, 1870-1940,* by Richard Wormser. Walker and Company, 1994. Jacket photograph courtesy of The Library of Congress. Reproduced by permission. / From a jacket of *American Childhoods: Three Centuries of Youth at Risk,* by Richard Wormser. Walker and Company, 1996. Jacket photographs © 1993 Lina Pallotta, Impact Visuals (top); Street Arabs in Area of Mulberry Street, The Jacob A. Riis Collection, #123, Museum of the City of New York (bottom). Reproduced by permission of Walker and Company.

YE, TING-XING. Ye, Ting-Xing, photograph by Peter McEwan. Reproduced by permission of Ting-Xing Ye.

SOMETHING ABOUT THE AUTHOR

ADLER, David A. 1947-

Personal

Born April 10, 1947, in New York, NY; son of Sidney
G. (a businessman and teacher) and Betty (a psychiatric
social worker; maiden name, Straus) Adler; married
Renee Hamada (a psychologist), April 8, 1973; children:
Michael, Eddie, Eitan. *Education:* Queens College of the
City University of New York, B.A., 1968; New York
University, M.B.A., 1971; doctoral study, 1971-72.
Religion: Jewish. *Hobbies and other interests:* Travel,
reading, photography, political memorabilia, baseball,
art.

Addresses

Agent—c/o Writers House, 21 West 26th St., New York,
NY 10010.

Career

New York City, math teacher, 1968-77; children's
author, 1972—; Jewish Publication Society, New York
City, editor, 1978-90. American Committee for Shaare
Zedek Hospital, member of board of directors; Hebrew
Academy of the Five Towns and Rockaway (HAFTR),
member of board of trustees; Jewish Publication Society,
member of publication committee. Professional artist
whose drawings and cartoons have appeared in magazines and newspapers. *Exhibitions:* Art work has been
displayed in public exhibitions in New York and Florida.
Works represented in private collections in the United

David A. Adler

1

States and Europe. *Member:* Society of Children's Book Writers and Illustrators, PEN, Authors Guild.

Awards, Honors

Outstanding Science Trade Book for Children, National Science Teachers Association and Children's Book Council (NSTA-CBC), 1976, for *3D, 2D, 1D;* Children's Book Showcase, CBC, 1977, for *A Little at a Time;* Notable Book, American Library Association (ALA), 1981, for *A Picture Book of Jewish Holidays;* Best Books, New York Public Library, 1983, for *Bunny Rabbit Rebus;* Honor Book, Carter G. Woodson Award, National Council for the Social Studies, 1985, for *Our Golda: The Story of Golda Meir;* Sydney Taylor Book Award, Association of Jewish Libraries, 1987, for *The Number on My Grandfather's Arm;* Children's Book of the Year, Child Study Book Committee, for *Thomas Jefferson: Father of Our Democracy,* 1988, *Cam Jansen and the Triceratops Pops Mystery,* and *Jackie Robinson: He Was the First;* Best Books, Society of School Librarians International, for *A Picture Book of Abraham Lincoln,* 1989, *Jackie Robinson: He Was the First,* and *A Picture Book of Martin Luther King, Jr;* Best Books, *Parents* magazine, 1989, for *Happy Hanukkah Rebus,* and 1990, for *A Picture Book of Helen Keller;* Notable Book, ALA, and 100 Titles for Reading and Sharing, New York Public Library, both 1997, Lemme Book Award and Patterson Award, both 1998, Honor Book, *Boston Globe/Horn Book,* Gold Medal Book, *Parents* magazine, and Best Books, *New York Times,* all for *Lou Gehrig: The Luckiest Man;* Parents Choice Picture Book Award, 1998, for *Shape Up!;* Parents Choice Honor Book, 1998, for *A Picture Book of Amelia Earhart;* Children's Choice Awards, International Reading Association and Children's Book Council (IRA-CBC), for *Roman Numerals, Cam Jansen and the Mystery of the Monster Movie, The Fourth Floor Twins and the Fish Snitch Mystery, . . . and the Skyscraper Parade, My Dog and the Knock Knock Mystery, . . . and the Birthday Mystery, Remember Betsy Floss and Other Colonial American Riddles,* and *Happy Thanksgiving Rebus;* Notable Children's Trade Book in the Field of Social Studies, National Council for the Social Studies and Children's Book Council (NCSS-CBC), for *Our Golda: The Story of Golda Meir, Martin Luther King, Jr.: Free at Last, A Picture Book of Martin Luther King, Jr., . . . Eleanor Roosevelt, . . . Anne Frank, . . . Sojourner Truth, We Remember the Holocaust, One Yellow Daffodil, Hilde and Eli, Children of the Holocaust,* and *Child of the Warsaw Ghetto;* Pick of the List, American Booksellers Association, for *Cam Jansen and the Mystery of the Gold Coins, . . . Monster Movie, . . . Carnival Prize, The Fourth Floor Twins and the Fish Snitch Mystery, . . . Fortune Cookie Chase, A Picture Book of Abraham Lincoln, . . . of George Washington,* and *Happy Thanksgiving Rebus;* Notable Book for a Global Society, IRA, for *One Yellow Daffodil;* citation on First Biannual List of Outstanding Children's Books, ALA, for *Our Golda: The Story of Golda Meir;* Best Books, Child Study Children's Book Committee at Bank Street College, for *Jackie Robinson: He Was the First* and *Cam Jansen and the Mystery at the Haunted House;*

Helen Keating Ott Award, Church and Synagogue Library Association, for promoting high moral and ethical values through children's literature.

Writings

PICTURE BOOKS

A Little at a Time, illustrated by N. M. Bodecker, Random House, 1976.

The House on the Roof: A Sukkot Story, illustrated by Marilyn Hirsh, Bonim, 1976.

The Children of Chelm, illustrated by Arthur Friedman, Bonim, 1979.

You Think It's Fun to Be a Clown!, illustrated by Ray Cruz, Doubleday, 1980.

My Dog and the Key Mystery, illustrated by Byron Barton, F. Watts, 1982.

Bunny Rabbit Rebus, illustrated by Madelaine Gill Linden, Crowell, 1983.

My Dog and the Knock Knock Mystery, illustrated by Marsha Winborn, Holiday House, 1985.

. . . Green Sock Mystery, illustrated by Dick Gackenbach, Holiday House, 1986.

. . . Birthday Mystery, illustrated by Gackenbach, Holiday House, 1987.

I Know I'm a Witch, illustrated by Sucie Stevenson, Holt, 1988.

Malke's Secret Recipe: A Hanukkah Story, illustrated by Joan Halpern, Viking, 1989.

Happy Hanukkah Rebus, illustrated by Jan Palmer, Viking, 1989.

Happy Thanksgiving Rebus, illustrated by Palmer, Viking, 1991.

The Rabbi and His Driver, HarperCollins, 1993.

One Yellow Daffodil: A Hanukkah Story, illustrated by Lloyd Bloom, Gulliver, 1995.

Chanukah in Chelm, illustrated by Kevin O'Malley, Lothrop, Lee and Shepard, 1997.

Shape Up!, illustrated by Nancy Tobin, Holiday House, 1998.

The Babe and I, illustrated by Terry Widener, Harcourt, 1999.

How Tall, How Short, How Far Away, illustrated by Nancy Tobin, Holiday House, 1999.

RIDDLE BOOKS

The Carsick Zebra and Other Animal Riddles, illustrated by Tomie dePaola, Holiday House, 1983.

The Twisted Witch and Other Spooky Riddles, illustrated by Victoria Chess, Holiday House, 1985.

The Purple Turkey and Other Thanksgiving Riddles, illustrated by Marylin Hafner, Holiday House, 1986.

Remember Betsy Floss and Other Colonial American Riddles, illustrated by John Wallner, Holiday House, 1987.

Wild Pill Hickok and Other Old West Riddles, illustrated by Glen Rounds, Holiday House, 1988.

The Dinosaur Princess and Other Prehistoric Riddles, illustrated by Loreen Leedy, Holiday House, 1988.

A Teacher on Roller Skates, and Other School Riddles, illustrated by John Wallner, Holiday House, 1989.

Calculator Riddles, illustrated by Cynthia Fisher, Holiday House, 1995.

BIOGRAPHY

Our Golda: The Story of Golda Meir, illustrated by Donna Ruff, Viking, 1984.

Martin Luther King, Jr.: Free at Last, illustrated by Robert Casilla, Holiday House, 1986.

Thomas Jefferson: Father of Our Democracy, illustrated by Jacqueline Garrick, Holiday House, 1987.

George Washington: Father of Our Country, illustrated by Garrick, Holiday House, 1988.

Jackie Robinson: He Was the First, illustrated by Robert Casilla, Holiday House, 1989.

A Picture Book of Martin Luther King, Jr., illustrated by Casilla, Holiday House, 1989.

A Picture Book of Abraham Lincoln, illustrated by John and Alexandra Wallner, Holiday House, 1989.

A Picture Book of George Washington, illustrated by J. and A. Wallner, Holiday House, 1989.

A Picture Book of Helen Keller, illustrated by J. and A. Wallner, Holiday House, 1990.

A Picture Book of Thomas Jefferson, illustrated by J. and A. Wallner, Holiday House, 1990.

A Picture Book of Benjamin Franklin, illustrated by J. and A. Wallner, Holiday House, 1990.

Thomas Alva Edison: Great Inventor, illustrated by Lyle Miller, Holiday House, 1990.

Christopher Columbus: Great Explorer, illustrated by Miller, Holiday House, 1991.

A Picture Book of Eleanor Roosevelt, illustrated by Robert Casilla, Holiday House, 1991.

A Picture Book of John F. Kennedy, illustrated by Casilla, Holiday House, 1991.

A Picture Book of Christopher Columbus, illustrated by John and Alexandra Wallner, Holiday House, 1991.

Benjamin Franklin: Printer, Inventor, Statesman, illustrated by Lyle Miller, Holiday House, 1992.

A Picture Book of Harriet Tubman, illustrated by Samuel Byrd, Holiday House, 1992.

A Picture Book of Simon Bolivar, illustrated by Robert Casilla, Holiday House, 1992.

A Picture Book of Florence Nightingale, illustrated by John and Alexandra Wallner, Holiday House, 1992.

A Picture Book of Jesse Owens, illustrated by Robert Casilla, Holiday House, 1992.

A Picture Book of Frederick Douglass, illustrated by Samuel Byrd, Holiday House, 1993.

A Picture Book of Anne Frank, illustrated by Karen Ritz, Holiday House, 1993.

A Picture Book of Rosa Parks, illustrated by Robert Casilla, Holiday House, 1993.

A Picture Book of Sitting Bull, illustrated by Samuel Byrd, Holiday House, 1993.

A Picture Book of Sojourner Truth, illustrated by Gershom Griffith, Holiday House, 1994.

A Picture Book of Robert E. Lee, illustrated by John and Alexandra Wallner, Holiday House, 1994.

A Picture Book of Jackie Robinson, illustrated by Robert Casilla, Holiday House, 1994.

A Picture Book of Paul Revere, illustrated by John and Alexandra Wallner, Holiday House, 1995.

A Picture Book of Patrick Henry, illustrated by J. and A. Wallner, Holiday House, 1995.

A Picture Book of Davy Crockett, illustrated by J. and A. Wallner, Holiday House, 1996.

A Picture Book of Thomas Alva Edison, illustrated by J. and A. Wallner, Holiday House, 1996.

Lou Gehrig: The Luckiest Man, illustrated by Terry Widener, Harcourt, 1997.

A Picture Book of Thurgood Marshall, illustrated by Robert Casilla, Holiday House, 1997.

A Picture Book of Louis Braille, illustrated by John and Alexandra Wallner, Holiday House, 1997.

A Picture Book of Amelia Earhart, illustrated by Jeff Fisher, Holiday House, 1998.

A Picture Book of George Washington Carver, illustrated by Dan Brown, Holiday House, 1999.

"CAM JANSEN" MYSTERY SERIES; ILLUSTRATED BY SUSANNA NATTI

Cam Jansen and the Mystery of the Stolen Diamonds, Viking, 1980.

. . . and the Mystery of the U. F. O., Viking, 1980.

. . . and the Mystery of the Dinosaur Bones, Viking, 1981.

. . . and the Mystery of the Television Dog, Viking, 1981.

. . . and the Mystery of the Gold Coins, Viking, 1982.

. . . and the Mystery of the Babe Ruth Baseball, Viking, 1982.

. . . and the Mystery of the Circus Clown, Viking, 1983.

. . . and the Mystery of the Monster Movie, Viking, 1984.

. . . and the Mystery of the Carnival Prize, Viking, 1984.

. . . and the Mystery at the Monkey House, Viking, 1985.

. . . and the Mystery of the Stolen Corn Popper, Viking, 1986.

. . . and the Mystery of Flight 54, Viking, 1989.

. . . and the Mystery at the Haunted House, Viking, 1992.

Cam Jansen Activity Book, Viking, 1992.

. . . and the Chocolate Fudge Mystery, Viking, 1993.

. . . and the Triceratops Pops Mystery, Viking, 1995.

Young Cam Jansen and the Missing Cookie, Viking, 1996.

Young Cam Jansen and the Dinosaur Game, Viking, 1996.

Cam Jansen and the Ghostly Mystery, Viking, 1996.

Young Cam Jansen and the Lost Tooth, Viking, 1997.

Cam Jansen and the Scary Snake Mystery, Viking, 1997.

Young Cam Jansen and the Ice Skate Mystery, Viking, 1998.

Cam Jansen and the Catnapping Mystery, Viking, 1998.

Young Cam Jansen and the Baseball Mystery, Viking, 1999.

Cam Jansen and the Barking Treasure Mystery, Viking, 1999.

"JEFFREY'S GHOST" ADVENTURE SERIES; ILLUSTRATED BY JEAN JENKINS

Jeffrey's Ghost and the Leftover Baseball Team, Holt, 1984.

. . . and the Fifth-Grade Dragon, Holt, 1985.

. . . and the Ziffel Fair Mystery, Holt, 1987.

"FOURTH FLOOR TWINS" ADVENTURE SERIES; ILLUSTRATED BY IRENE TRIVAS

The Fourth Floor Twins and the Fortune Cookie Chase, Viking, 1985.

. . . and the Fish Snitch Mystery, Viking, 1985.

. . . and the Disappearing Parrot Trick, Viking, 1986.

. . . and the Silver Ghost Express, Viking, 1986.

... and the Skyscraper Parade, Viking, 1987.
... and the Sand Castle Contest, Viking, 1988.

"T. F. BENSON" MYSTERY SERIES

T. F. Benson and the Funny-Money Mystery, Bantam, 1992.
... and the Dinosaur Madness Mystery, Bantam, 1992.
... and the Jewelry Spy Mystery, Bantam, 1992.
... and the Detective Dog Mystery, Bantam, 1993.

"HOUDINI CLUB MAGIC MYSTERY" SERIES; ILLUSTRATED BY HEATHER HARMS MAIONE

Onion Sundaes, Random House, 1994.
Wacky Jacks, Random House, 1994.
Lucky Stars, Random House, 1996.
Magic Money, Random House, 1997.

"ANDY RUSSELL" SERIES; ILLUSTRATED BY WILL HILLENBRAND

The Many Troubles of Andy Russell, Harcourt, 1998.
Andy and Tamika, Harcourt, 1999.
School Trouble for Andy Russell, Harcourt, 1999.

NONFICTION

Base Five, illustrated by Larry Ross, Crowell, 1975.
3D, 2D, 1D, illustrated by Harvey Weiss, Crowell, 1975.
Roman Numerals, illustrated by Byron Barton, Crowell, 1977.
Redwoods Are the Tallest Trees in the World, illustrated by Kazue Mizumura, Crowell, 1978.
3-2-1 Number Fun, Doubleday, 1981.
A Picture Book of Jewish Holidays, illustrated by Linda Heller, Holiday House, 1981.
Calculator Fun, illustrated by Arline and Marvin Oberman, F. Watts, 1981.
A Picture Book of Passover, illustrated by Linda Heller, Holiday House, 1982.
A Picture Book of Hanukkah, illustrated by Heller, Holiday House, 1982.
Hyperspace!: Facts and Fun from All over the Universe, illustrated by Fred Winkowski, Viking, 1982.
Our Amazing Ocean, illustrated by Joseph Veno, Troll, 1983.
All about the Moon, illustrated by Raymond Burns, Troll, 1983.
World of Weather, illustrate by Burns, Troll, 1983.
Wonders of Energy, illustrated by Lewis Johnson, Troll, 1983.
Amazing Magnets, illustrated by Dan Lawler, Troll, 1983.
All Kinds of Money, illustrated by Tom Huffman, F. Watts, 1984.
Prices Go Up, Prices Go Down: The Laws of Supply and Demand, illustrated by Huffman, F. Watts, 1984.
A Picture Book of Israel, Holiday House, 1984.
Inflation: When Prices Go Up, Up, Up, illustrated by Tom Huffman, F. Watts, 1985.
Banks: Where the Money Is, illustrated by Huffman, F. Watts, 1985.
The Number on My Grandfather's Arm, photographs by Rose Eichenbaum, Union of American Hebrew Congregations, 1987.
The Children's Book of Jewish Holidays, illustrated by Dovid Sears, Mesorah, 1987.

We Remember the Holocaust, Holt, 1989.
You Breathe In, You Breathe Out: All about Your Lungs, illustrated by Diane Paterson, F. Watts, 1991.
Hilde and Eli, Children of the Holocaust, illustrated by Karen Ritz, Holiday House, 1994.
Child of the Warsaw Ghetto, illustrated by Ritz, Holiday House, 1995.
Fraction Fun, illustrated by Nancy Tobin, Holiday House, 1996.
(Editor) *The Kids' Catalog of Jewish Holidays,* Jewish Publication Society, 1996.
Easy Math Puzzles, illustrated by Cynthia Fisher, Holiday House, 1997.
Hiding from the Nazis, illustrated by Karen Ritz, Holiday House, 1997.

OTHER

Hanukkah Fun Book: Puzzles, Riddles, Magic, and More, Bonim, 1976.
Passover Fun Book: Puzzles, Riddles, Magic, and More, Bonim, 1978.
Hanukkah Game Book: Games, Puzzles, Riddles, and More, Bonim, 1978.
The Bible Fun Book: Puzzles, Riddles, Magic, and More, Bonim, 1979.
Finger Spelling Fun, illustrated by Dennis Kendrick, F. Watts, 1980.
A Children's Treasury of Chasidic Tales, illustrated by Arie Haas, Mesorah, 1983.
Eaton Stanley and the Mind Control Experiment (young adult fiction), illustrated by Joan Drescher, Dutton, 1985.
Benny, Benny, Baseball Nut (young adult fiction), Scholastic, 1987.
Jewish Holiday Fun, Kar-Ben, 1987.
Rabbit Trouble and the Green Magician (young adult fiction), illustrated by Giora Carmi, Weekly Reader Books, 1987.
Brothers in Egypt, Dreamworks, 1998.
My Writing Day, photographs by Nina Crews, R. C. Owen, 1999.

Adler's works have been translated into Swedish, Danish, Dutch, Spanish, Hebrew, Japanese, Chinese, German, and Braille.

Work in Progress

Gertrude Ederle: America's Champion Swimmer, a picture book biography, illustrated by Terry Widener, and *Mama Played Baseball,* both for Harcourt; *A Picture Book of Sacagawea, Heroes of the Revolution, The Abolitionists, Money Madness,* and *The Courage of Janusz Korczak,* all for Holiday House; *Young Cam Jansen and the Pizza Shop Mystery* and "First Chapter Books," both for Viking.

Sidelights

David A. Adler is the prolific and award-winning author of well over one hundred titles for young readers. His subjects include biography, puzzles and riddles, Holocaust studies, Jewish holidays, adventure stories, and mysteries. His popular "Cam Jansen" series about a ten-year-old girl who plays detective is growing quickly, and his picture-book biographies have featured personalities from George Washington to Thurgood Marshall. Adler excels at beginning chapter-books as well as picture books for older readers, and his ability to present the issues of the Holocaust in a manner assimilable for primary-grade children has won him fans with teachers and students alike.

One of six children, Adler was raised in New York City. As a youngster he was known as the family artist; he continues to paint in the spare time afforded him by a busy writing schedule and has had several exhibitions of his work. He also loved stories and storytelling as a youngster, and often invented tales for his younger siblings. A self-confessed daydreamer in school, he enjoyed fantasizing about possible future careers—baseball player, actor, artist, lawyer—more than doing his class work. Such an active imagination led one educator to speculate that perhaps the young Adler would turn out to be a writer.

It was an accurate prophecy, though it would not come about until after Adler had himself taken up a career in education. Mathematics was always a strong subject for him, and he majored in economics at Queens College of the City University of New York. Upon graduation, he began teaching math in an intermediate school. At the same time, he completed a master's degree in business administration and then went on for his doctorate. At this point, however, serendipity intervened. Inspired by a nephew who kept asking him questions, Adler wrote his first children's book, *A Little at a Time,* and sent it off to a publisher, little realizing how difficult it can be to publish a work. But Adler's benighted optimism paid off; the book was purchased by Random House and ultimately won a Showcase Award from the Children's Book Council. Encouraged by this initial success, Adler saw the possibilities for a career in writing. His doctoral studies were put on hold as he started a second book and continued to teach math. Five years after publication of his first book, Adler quit teaching to devote himself full time to writing.

Adler's many and varied interests have informed his writing, which spans a wide spectrum of topics in both fiction and nonfiction. As he once told *SATA:* "I find my fiction to be a wonderful release from all the painstaking research I must do for nonfiction, which is why I try to alternate between fiction and nonfiction." By far the largest area of concentration for Adler has been biographies, with almost forty to his credit. His popular picture-book biographies are used in schools and libraries, and have been translated into several languages. "The picture-book biographies may be short," Adler once told *SATA,* "but that makes them very difficult to write." Adler often weaves in the history of an era with his biographies, as with his *A Picture Book of Simon Bolivar.* With this work Adler had to add some general history of South America so that the young reader would have context for the biography, and all this in under fifty pages, including illustrations.

Young Herman Foster uses magic tricks to find out how the classroom pet hamster disappeared in **Wacky Jacks,** *a title from Adler's "Houdini Club Magic Mystery" series. (Illustrated by Heather Harms Maione.)*

Adler's first biography, *Our Golda: The Story of Golda Meir,* recounts the life of the one-time leader of Israel and became a Carter G. Woodson Award Honor Book. Further subjects include political leaders both contemporary and historical, such as Martin Luther King Jr., John F. Kennedy, George Washington, Thomas Jefferson, and Eleanor Roosevelt; inventors and explorers such as Christopher Columbus, Amelia Earhart, Thomas A. Edison, and Louis Braille; and sports stars such as Jackie Robinson and Lou Gehrig. Reviewing Adler's *Lou Gehrig: The Luckiest Man,* a reviewer for *Publishers Weekly* noted that "Adler brings his subject into clear focus as he concisely tracks the legendary first baseman's childhood and career, tragically shortened by the disease that now bears his name." The reviewer concluded that Adler's book was a "gracious tribute to a stalwart, modest and tirelessly optimistic man." Ilene Cooper, in a boxed *Booklist* review of the same book, applauded both illustrations and text which "crisply and concisely" cover the high points of Gehrig's career, while Janice M. Del Negro concluded in *Bulletin of the Center for Children's Books:* "as beginning biographies go, this one is a home run."

Another sports great, Jackie Robinson, is featured in *A Picture Book of Jackie Robinson.* As with other Adler biographies, the Robinson story serves double duty, telling the story of one man's life, but also giving the larger context. In this case, Adler "tells how a courageous man and outstanding athlete desegregated major league baseball," according to a *Kirkus Reviews* contributor. The fifth child of Georgia sharecroppers, Robinson went on to be a star high-school athlete in California where the family moved after Robinson's father left them. After playing professional football in Hawaii, Robinson joined the military during World War II, then played baseball in the all-black leagues after the war until scouts for the Brooklyn Dodgers spotted him and brought him to the majors in 1947. Defying the race barrier and some racist fans, Robinson won Rookie of the Year and played for eight successful seasons before retiring. The writer for *Kirkus Reviews* concluded that Adler's biography was "easily read and educational," and that it was a "fine addition to this notable series."

Tom S. Hurlburt noted in *School Library Journal* that Adler's biography was a "sound introduction to a significant figure."

The pioneering aviator Amelia Earhart gets the Adler treatment in *A Picture Book of Amelia Earhart.* Earhart grew up in an era when girls were not expected to participate in such "masculine" endeavors as flying. Adler traces Earhart's life from childhood, when she was already engaging in "activities typically enjoyed by boys and wore bloomers that were a departure from the dress expected of ladies," as Cheryl Cufari commented in *School Library Journal.* "Readers glean a sense of Earhart's courage and determination," Cufari added, with Adler's recounting of her solo flights across the Atlantic and her subsequent fatal round-the-world trip. *Booklist* contributor Carolyn Phelan noted that *A Picture Book of Amelia Earhart* was a "useful addition to the series."

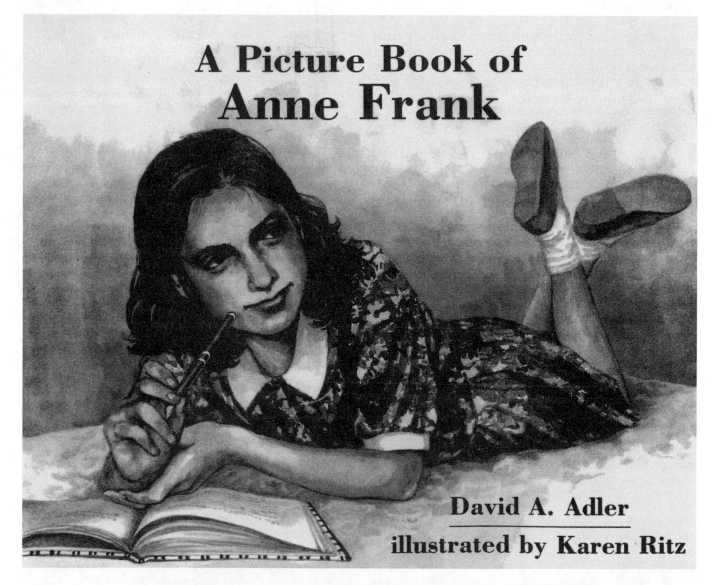

Adler has penned a biography of Anne Frank that documents the life of the Holocaust victim in text appropriate for young readers. (Cover illustration by Karen Ritz.)

Somewhat harder-hitting was Adler's biography of Anne Frank. Cufari, writing again in *School Library Journal,* remarked that "the life of Anne Frank serves as a microcosm of the experiences of millions of Jews who met tragedy, torture, and death during the Holocaust," and that Adler presents an "excellent entry-level introduction to this historical figure, her family, and the climate of the times." For this book, Adler thoroughly researched German history following the First World War and the rise of Adolf Hitler. He also researched "the refusal of the world to accept refugees of extreme persecution, vital information about the Second World War, and the horrible truth about the death camps," as he once told *SATA.* Cufari concluded that "emotions are well expressed in this sensitive and age-appropriate portrait," while Betsy Hearne commented in *Bulletin of the Center for Children's Books* that Anne Frank's story itself "is, of course, inherently dramatic, with suspense and tragedy that cannot fail to touch children and broaden their empathy."

For his biography of Anne Frank, Adler worked with the illustrator Karen Ritz. The two have teamed up for several other Holocaust-related titles, including *Hilde and Eli, Children of the Holocaust, Child of the Warsaw Ghetto,* and *Hiding from the Nazis.* Hilde Rosenzweig and Eli Lax are real names with which Adler tells the story of the 1.5 million Jewish children murdered under the aegis of Hitler's Final Solution. Hilde, 18, and her mother, were gassed on a train, and Eli, from Czechoslovakia, died at Auschwitz. Their stories are related by siblings and relatives who survived the Holocaust, in what a *Kirkus Reviews* contributor called a "sensitive but unsentimental account." Roger Sutton of *Bulletin of the Center for Children's Books* remarked that "Adler explains simply the facts of their lives and the concurrent events of the Nazi rise and World War II that determined their fate." Adler again funnels "a vast, horrific subject through the true experiences of one Jewish child" in *Hiding from the Nazis,* according to a reviewer for *Publishers Weekly.* Four-year-old Lore Baer was sent into hiding in Holland to avoid the Nazis and lived with a Christian family for two years, growing as close to the them as she was to her own family. The *Publishers Weekly* critic went on to note that "readers will gain an understanding of both the events and their impact on children" from Adler's book, while a writer for *Kirkus Reviews* concluded: "So real and clearly explained is Lore's anxiety that to younger readers the events that compelled it will not seem remote at all."

Adler has also written books on general Jewish themes, especially dealing with Jewish holidays and customs. Two Hanukkah tales are *One Yellow Daffodil* and *Chanukah in Chelm.* The former is a "simple but powerful story," according to Jane Marino writing in *School Library Journal,* about two children who help a man overcome horrible memories of the Holocaust by celebrating Hanukkah with their family. Marino went on to note that "Adler's heartfelt text speaks of his own belief in the miracle of Hanukkah," while Kay Weisman remarked in *Booklist* that Adler's story also "lends itself to sharing on Holocaust Remembrance Day." Chelm, a town famous in Jewish folklore for its muddled citizenry, serves as the setting for Adler's original tales in *Chanukah in Chelm,* which has, according to *Horn Book* reviewer Susan P. Bloom, "more than enough broad humor, especially in comic-bubble commentary, to have youngsters groaning appropriately."

In addition to nonfiction biographies and storybooks, Adler also has penned a score of riddle and puzzle books, some employing mathematics as their thematic material. But equally popular are Adler's series readers built around mysteries and adventures. These easy chapter-books have made Adler's a household name to many. His best-known series features Cam Jansen, a girl with what Adler called "a sense of adventure;" a girl who is "headstrong" and who has a "fearless nature." Adler has adapted this series as both a chapter-book series and a beginning-to-read series featuring a younger Cam. Employing a photographic memory, both young and somewhat older Cam Jansen manage to solve small mysteries at school or at home; solutions also often come with deductive reasoning. Typical of the chapter-books is *Cam Jansen and the Catnapping Mystery,* in which Cam, her parents, and friend Eric are going to meet an aunt and Cam ends up solving the mystery of who kidnapped Little Tiger the cat. Kit Vaughan

Adler profiles the boyhood and career of baseball legend Lou Gehrig, and traces his battle with the deadly disease that carries his name. (From Lou Gehrig: The Luckiest Man, *illustrated by Terry Widener.)*

CHELM SWEET CHELM

Is that herring I'm hearing, or smelt I smell?

The simplest preparations for Chanukah unwind into a complicated series of mishaps in a tale based on the Jewish folk story of the witless inhabitants of Chelm. (From Chanukah in Chelm, *written by Adler and illustrated by Kevin O'Malley.)*

concluded in *School Library Journal* that this was "another fine mystery for beginning chapter-book readers." Reviewing his beginning-readers' titles *Young Cam Jansen and the Dinosaur Game* and *Young Cam Jansen and the Missing Cookie, Booklist* contributor Carolyn Phelan noted that just like Adler's books for slightly older readers, "these appealing minimysteries will find a ready audience."

Other series are the "Houdini Club" magic mystery series and the "Andy Russell" series. Herman "Houdini" Foster, aspiring magician, uses his tricks to solve mysteries such as the disappearance of the classroom pet, Alfred the hamster, in the second title of the series, *Wacky Jacks.* Included in each book is an actual magic trick with step-by-step instructions on how to perform it. Lesley McKinstry, writing in *School Library Journal,* concluded: "with its numerous black-and-white illustrations and simple text and sentence structure, this title will appeal to reluctant readers." Charlene Strickland

noted in *Wilson Library Bulletin* that "each short, chatty chapter ends with a cliff-hanging sentence, sure to entice the reader into the next." Missing pets are also at the heart of Adler's first title of the "Andy Russell" beginning chapter-book series, *The Many Troubles of Andy Russell.* But the missing gerbils are only part of Andy's problems both at home and at school. *Booklist* reviewer Shelle Rosenfeld noted: "kids will no doubt relate to Andy's snowballing troubles, both great and small, and appreciate the simple humor," while a critic for *Publishers Weekly* concluded that though Andy solves the problems this time, there was little doubt he would get into hot water again soon, and "readers will likely be standing by when he does."

Adler recently told *SATA:* "I've always been a dreamer. A few years ago I was at Open School Night for my middle son. His fourth-grade teacher was the same one my eldest son had seven years earlier and was the same teacher I had sometime in the 1950s. The teacher looked at me, smiled, and then told the roomful of parents, 'A long time ago, when I just started teaching, David was in my class.' She smiled again and said, 'I went to the principal and asked, "What should I do with Adler? He's always dreaming." "Leave him alone," the principal answered, "Maybe one day he'll be a writer.'" That's her story, not mine. But I know I *did* dream through much of my early school years and I *did* become a writer. Dreamers become writers, and for me, being a published writer is a dream come true.

"In my office I have this sign, 'Don't Think. Just Write!', and that's how I work. I try not to worry about each word, even each sentence or paragraph. For me, stories evolve. Writing is a process. I rewrite each sentence, each manuscript, many times. And I work with my editors. I look forward to their suggestions, their help in the almost endless rewrite process.

"I begin my fiction with the main character. The story comes later. Of course, since I'll be spending a lot of time with each main character, why not have him or her be someone I like? Andy Russell is based, loosely, on a beloved member of my family. He's fun to write about, and the boy who inspired the character is even more fun to know. Cam Jansen is based even more loosely on a classmate of mine in the first grade who we all envied because we thought he had a photographic memory. Now, especially when my children remind me of some promise they said I made, I really envy Cam's amazing memory. I have really enjoyed writing about Cam Jansen and her many adventures.

"Well, it's time to get back to dreaming, and to writing, my dream of a job."

Works Cited

Bloom, Susan, review of *Chanukah in Chelm, Horn Book,* September-October, 1997, p. 584.

Cooper, Ilene, review of *Lou Gehrig: The Luckiest Man, Booklist,* May 15, 1997, p. 1575.

Cufari, Cheryl, review of *A Picture Book of Amelia Earhart, School Library Journal,* April, 1998, p. 112.

Cufari, review of *A Picture Book of Anne Frank, School Library Journal,* May, 1993, pp. 92-93.

Del Negro, Janice M., review of *Lou Gehrig: The Luckiest Man, Bulletin of the Center for Children's Books,* April, 1997, p. 270.

Hearne, Betsy, review of *A Picture Book of Anne Frank, Bulletin of the Center for Children's Books,* March, 1993, p. 204.

Review of *Hiding from the Nazis, Kirkus Reviews,* October 15, 1997, p. 1578.

Review of *Hiding from the Nazis, Publishers Weekly,* October 20, 1997, p. 76.

Review of *Hilde and Eli, Children of the Holocaust, Kirkus Reviews,* November 15, 1994, p. 1521.

Hurlburt, Tom S., review of *A Picture Book of Jackie Robinson, School Library Journal,* December, 1994, p. 94.

Review of *Lou Gehrig: The Luckiest Man, Publishers Weekly,* February 24, 1997, p. 91.

Review of *The Many Troubles of Andy Russell, Publishers Weekly,* August 17, 1998, p. 73.

Marino, Jane, review of *One Yellow Daffodil: A Hanukkah Story, School Library Journal,* October, 1995, p. 34.

McKinstry, Lesley, review of *Wacky Jacks, School Library Journal,* February, 1998, p. 96.

Phelan, Carolyn, review of *A Picture Book of Amelia Earhart, Booklist,* April 15, 1998, p. 1447.

Phelan, review of *Young Cam Jansen and the Dinosaur Game* and *Young Cam Jansen and the Missing Cookie, Booklist,* August, 1996, pp. 1909-10.

Review of *A Picture Book of Jackie Robinson, Kirkus Reviews,* November 15, 1994, pp. 1521-22.

Rosenfeld, Shelle, review of *The Many Troubles of Andy Russell, Booklist,* August, 1998, p. 2002.

Strickland, Charlene, "Chapter One," *Wilson Library Bulletin,* June, 1995, pp. 116-17.

Sutton, Roger, review of *Hilde and Eli, Children of the Holocaust, Bulletin of the Center for Children's Books,* November, 1994, p. 79.

Vaughan, Kit, review of *Cam Jansen and the Catnapping Mystery, School Library Journal,* January, 1999, p. 79.

Weisman, Kay, review of *One Yellow Daffodil: A Hanukkah Story, Booklist,* November 1, 1995, p. 476.

For More Information See

BOOKS

Sixth Book of Junior Authors and Illustrators, H. W. Wilson, 1989, pp. 6-7.

PERIODICALS

Appraisal, winter, 1999, p. 6.

Booklist, November 15, 1994, p. 600; November 1, 1995, p. 466; December 15, 1996, p. 722; September 1, 1997, p. 127; November 1, 1997, p. 463.

Bulletin of the Center for Children's Books, May, 1996, p. 291; December, 1997, p. 116.

Kirkus Reviews, April 1, 1999, p. 530.

New York Times Book Review, February 28, 1993, p. 22; November 12, 1995, p. 31; June 8, 1997, p. 27.

Publishers Weekly, October 6, 1997, p. 52.

School Library Journal, December, 1994, p. 115; July, 1996, p. 56; November, 1996, p. 95; March, 1997, p. 170.

—Sketch by J. Sydney Jones

*　　　*　　　*

ALDA, Arlene 1933-

Personal

Born March 12, 1933, in Bronx, NY; daughter of Simon (a lithographer) and Jeanette (a seamstress; maiden name, Kelman) Weiss; married Alan Alda (an actor, writer, and director), March 15, 1957; children: Eve, Elizabeth, Beatrice. *Education:* Received degree from Hunter College (now Hunter College of the City University of New York), 1954.

Addresses

Home—Los Angeles, CA. *Agent*—Amy Berkower, Writers House Inc., 21 West 26th St., New York, NY 10010.

Career

Musician, photographer, children's book author. Houston Symphony, Houston, TX, assistant first clarinetist, 1956-57; photographer, 1967—; writer, 1980—. Performed with National Orchestral Association in New York City, and with suburban orchestras. Taught orchestral music in Manhattan; worked as private clarinet instructor. *Exhibitions:* Nikon House, New York City. *Member:* Phi Beta Kappa.

Awards, Honors

Fulbright scholarship for music study in Germany, 1954-55; New Jersey Institute of Technology award, 1983, for *Matthew and His Dad;* Notable Books for Children, American Library Association, 1999, for *Arlene Alda's 1 2 3: What Do You See?*

Writings

FOR CHILDREN

Hold the Bus: A Counting Book from 1 to 10, illustrated by Dan Regan, WhistleStop, 1996.
Hurry Granny Annie, illustrated by Eve Aldridge, Tricycle, 1999.

FOR CHILDREN; SELF-ILLUSTRATED WITH PHOTOGRAPHS

Arlene Alda's ABC Book, Celestial Arts, 1981, reissued by Tricycle, 1993.
Sonya's Mommy Works, Messner, 1982.
Matthew and His Dad, Little Simon, 1983.
Sheep, Sheep, Sheep, Help Me Fall Asleep, Delacorte, 1992.
Pig, Horse, or Cow, Don't Wake Me Now, Doubleday, 1994.
Arlene Alda's 1 2 3: What Do You See?, Tricycle, 1998.

OTHER

On Set: A Personal Story in Photographs and Words, Simon & Schuster, 1981.
(Contributor) *Women of Vision: Photographic Statements of Twenty Women Photographers,* Unicorn Publishing, 1982.
(With husband, Alan Alda) *The Last Days of M*A*S*H*,* Unicorn Publishing, 1983.

Sidelights

Before marrying Alan Alda in 1957, children's author and photographer Arlene Alda was an accomplished clarinetist who began playing in high school, studied music in Europe on a Fulbright scholarship, and then joined the Houston Symphony. Although she essentially gave up her professional music career to raise her children, she supported her struggling young husband in the early days of his acting career by giving private

Author of *Arlene Alda's ABC*
Arlene Alda's
1 2 3

What Do *You* See?

In Arlene Alda's concept book, illustrated with her photographs, the numerals from one to ten are discernible within the contours of objects and animals.

clarinet lessons and playing in obscure suburban orchestras.

According to an article in *McCall's* magazine, both Aldas believe that "for a relationship to work happily, you need two whole, self-fulfilled people." In 1967, Arlene Alda took a course in photography, and the venture proved successful. Since her first efforts in the medium, Alda has gone on to exhibit her work in galleries, to contribute photographs to national magazines, and to write books that showcase her photos. For one project, the film *The Four Seasons,* the entire Alda family contributed their talents. Alan Alda wrote, directed, and starred in the film, while the two youngest daughters acted in it. With the assistance of the eldest daughter, Arlene Alda supplied wacky vegetable photographs to appear as the work of an obsessive photographer. She remained on the set during the film's shooting and snapped pictures documenting its making. She eventually published her behind-the-scenes observations as *On Set: A Personal Story in Photographs and Words.*

Alda's books for children showcase her photography. Some reviewers have expressed a particular fondness for her pictures of animals. "Alda clearly possesses the skills to bring out every endearing quality of her animal subjects," claimed a reviewer in *Publishers Weekly.* In *Arlene Alda's ABC,* Alda discerns the shape of letters of the alphabet in her photos of ordinary objects; for example, the letter A may be detected in her photograph of a yellow sawhorse. The book "contributes a fresh look at commonplace, usually unnoticed things we find around us," according to reviewer Janice Del Negro in *Booklist*. The photographs in *Arlene Alda's 1 2 3* depict the shapes of the numbers one through ten within the contours of objects and animals; for example, the number four is found in a flamingo's crossed legs. In her *Horn Book* review of *Arlene Alda's 1 2 3: What Do You See?*, Lolly Robinson remarked: "As she did in *Arlene Alda's ABC*, the photographer has kept the images and the format simple and accessible." Patricia Pearl Dole, a reviewer for *School Library Journal*, praised the "great imagination" exhibited in these photos, calling *Arlene Alda's 1 2 3* "a unique, challenging concept book."

In other works for children, Alda incorporates a simple, rhyming text to accompany her photos of animals as seen from a child's viewpoint. In *Sheep, Sheep, Sheep, Help Me Fall Asleep*, a child who cannot go to sleep closes her eyes and begins a search for some sheep to count to help her in her pursuit. Instead she finds a bevy of other animals. When she finally comes upon some sheep, more and more sheep appear, and the book becomes a counting exercise. "Alda's breezy rhyming text and arresting photographs make this a most engaging bedtime read-aloud," suggested a critic in *Publishers Weekly*. Likewise, in *Pig, Horse, or Cow, Don't Wake Me Now*, Alda's rhyming text recounts the early morning chain reaction of waking on a farm, beginning with a peacock and ending with a reluctant boy. "Early risers and sleepyheads will . . . have fun identifying the barnyard friends," claimed Mary Harris Veeder in *Booklist*.

Works Cited

Del Negro, Janice, review of *Arlene Alda's ABC*, *Booklist*, January 1, 1994, p. 829.

Dole, Patricia Pearl, review of *Arlene Alda's 1 2 3: What Do You See?*, *School Library Journal*, December, 1998, p. 98.

Review of *Pig, Horse, or Cow, Don't Wake Me Now*, *Publishers Weekly*, October 10, 1994, p. 69.

Robinson, Lolly, review of *Arlene Alda's 1 2 3: What Do You See?*, *Horn Book*, November, 1998, pp. 708-10.

Review of *Sheep, Sheep, Sheep, Help Me Fall Asleep*, *Publishers Weekly*, November 16, 1992, p. 60.

Veeder, Mary Harris, review of *Pig, Horse, or Cow, Don't Wake Me Now*, *Booklist*, October 15, 1994, p. 434.

For More Information See

PERIODICALS

Booklist, November 1, 1992, p. 518.

Kirkus Reviews, November 15, 1994, p. 1522.

School Library Journal, January, 1993, p. 73; December, 1994, p. 71.*

Autobiography Feature

Poul Anderson

1926-

Being asked to contribute to this series was a quite unexpected honor. Even more is it a danger, the risk of boring you. Still, if the life has been quiet, the times have been otherwise, and of course everybody's experience of history is unique. I'll offer a few comments, too. Better crotchety than dull.

Some of my ancestors and living kinfolk would have much more interesting stories to tell, but that is matter for a whole book, or several books. Here I'll simply declare that the lineage of my parents was basically Danish, without going into the complications which lurk behind that "basically," except to observe that one branch has been American for more than a hundred years. My father, Anton William Andersen, was born over here but educated in Denmark. He was the son of a sea captain and no relation to the great Hans Christian. He disliked his first name and never used it, being Will or Willy to his friends. During World War One he came back to join the United States Army. There he grew tired of explaining the spelling of his surname and Anglicized it to Anderson.

A literary tradition exists on the other side; my mother, Astrid Hertz, was descended from both Carsten Hauch and Henrik Hertz. Her own father was a physician in Copenhagen, where she was born. After a series of jobs and experiences more varied than was usual for a respectable young lady in those days, she crossed the Atlantic to work as a secretary in what was then the Danish legation in Washington. By a most unlikely chance, she met Will Anderson again. They had gone to the same school in the old country but afterward lost touch with each other. Since his discharge from the army he had stayed on in America, working as a civil engineer. Now they started dating, and early in 1926 they were married. I was born on 25 November of that year, in Bristol, Pennsylvania.

Since he had promised her that she could name their first baby, I am called after her father, Poul. The middle name she made William. That first name is a version of "Paul" and I might have Anglicized too, except that in grade school the teachers kept telling me I wasn't spelling my own name right, and I got my back up about it. The proper pronunciation is not an Anglo-Saxon noise; it falls about midway between "powl" and "pole." I'll answer to anything.

Mother's parents came over for the occasion of my birth, and Grandfather was the attending doctor when this happened, at home. She herself was the anesthesiologist. He gave her a cloth soaked in chloroform to hold to her nose when the pains got bad. As consciousness dimmed, her hand naturally fell, so she could not get an overdose. I realize that this wouldn't always work.

Everybody in the apartment building, and quite a few from elsewhere, had to come see the new baby. One person who went "kitchy-kitchy-koo" had a bad cold, which I caught. Grandfather wrote a prescription for an anticongestant which the American druggist misread; it nearly killed me. Much worse was that the illness led to chronic otitis media. This condemned me to many years of recurrent torture, when the middle ear would fill up until the drums ruptured. As a result, I am hard of hearing and was disqualified for military service later on. It seemed that the trouble had finally burned itself out sometime in my

Poul Anderson

thirties, but in my fifties it recurred in the form of mastoiditis on the left side. Death was the least unpleasant of the possibilities which surgery averted. Now I seem all right; but whenever there is the slightest doubt about my state of health, I don't go near any infant.

About the age of six or so, I caught chorea, St. Vitus' dance. It took me years to get my coordination back; I remember how hard it was to master the riding of a bicycle at the venerable age of eleven. I'm still somewhat of a klutz, though I can do most things reasonably well.

This medical history is only worth mentioning, first, as a period piece, since it is happily much less common nowadays; second, as a warning to new parents, since the fact remains that such natural enemies of humankind as the tiger were trivial compared to those natural enemies that swarm everywhere around us to this day; third, because it doubtless had something to do with making my childhood and adolescence as solitary as they were.

Needless to say, it was only a single factor, and not the main one. Most of what I am came from within myself. Besides, I don't want to do an Eeyore number. On the whole, if you consider 99 percent of the human beings who have ever existed, I have been fantastically fortunate in my life. And I'll match my good luck with that of anybody else in the upper 1 percent.

I was less than a year old when a change of job for my father took the family to Port Arthur, Texas. There he advanced to chief estimator at the Texaco plant, and there, in 1930, my brother was born. It was Dad's turn to name a child, and the event caught him flat-footed. He called his engineers into conference. They came up with John Jerome.

Port Arthur lies near the Louisiana border, on the fringe of the bayou country. It is, therefore, Deep South rather than West, although amply supplied with Texas pridefulness. It was already an industrially progressing city, and canals from the Gulf had made it a seaport. We'd often see a ship apparently steaming over the flat hinterland. Summers are hot and humid; air conditioning and mosquito control were then in the future. Occasionally the waters overflowed. A kayak that my father had built got its first trial in our backyard, while a neighbor boy made a pet of a small alligator he had found in his.

After a few years my parents had saved enough money to build their own house in a suburb. Dad took a hand in the design, using his engineering skill and nautical background to make it a marvel of compactness without being cramped. Behind it was a cottage for servants, generally a maid and her man-of-all-work husband. You didn't have to be rich in those times to afford such a standard of living. Nowadays the government takes too much, before you even see it.

The suburb was a wonderland for boys, full of trees to climb and vacant lots to romp in. Once a pile of bricks lay for weeks next door; we made castles out of it and burrows in it, at considerable risk to our necks. Clay soil could be molded into figures which the sun baked dry. My parents had a good-sized boat, which Dad had built himself, and we were often out on the water, sometimes for a weekend across the state line. The Yacht Club was a fine site for crabbing or for holding a barbecue. On vacations we'd get as far afield as Carlsbad Caverns or the Ozarks—or Europe, about which more later.

The single drawback, but it enormous, was school. "The twelve-year sentence," somebody has called it. Most of that time stands in my memory as utter emptiness, a purgatory of boredom. I endured it quietly and kept my resentment to myself, aside from the rebellious things that all little boys were expected to say. Now and then a good teacher lit a torch for me, but this was rare.

Doubtless a majority of people have experienced school otherwise. Doubtless a great deal of what I suffered was my fault. There were opportunities, especially social, of which I never took advantage. Once past the cruel small-boy stage of life, hardly anybody ever tried to make trouble for me, and many made efforts to be friendly.

Perhaps this introversion was in part an inheritance from my father. He was a big, handsome man, popular because he was affable toward everybody except those few whom experience caused him to decide were humanly worthless. However, he was not what you would call very sociable. Most of his spare time he spent with his wife and children, or reading, or making things in his workshop. He was good with his hands, also as an artist; he used to draw delightful cartoons for us boys. Some chairs he made for the house were beautiful. One, though, was slyly designed to be uncomfortable; that was the one he offered unwelcome visitors. He had perhaps three or four friends who were close. Those were close indeed, and the friendships outlasted his death.

I've tended to be like that. As a kid, I had only a single real friend, but we were inseparable. The circle of other boys with whom I got along reasonably well was small. We used to model animals out of clay and with them enact long stories. In that sort of game, I could be a leader. A recurring motif was a kind of perpetual cold war between Animal Land and School Land.

Otherwise my physical handicaps caused me to make a poor showing and, during high school, develop a special hatred for physical education. As grade-schoolers, we boys played marbles for keeps, and I was no good at that either. Finally I devised some punchboards and sold chances, one marble per chance, ten to the winner. I soon had more than anybody else. Then others started doing likewise. And then the teachers noticed, and found out who it was that had turned Tyrrell School into a gambling hell.

My brother John was much more normal in every way. A great deal of our mother's lively, outgoing personality was, and is, in him.

Though a mild amount of rampaging was allowed boys, especially at Hallowe'en, they and the girls were raised in the strict code of manners of the old South. You said "Yes, sir" and "Yes, ma'm" to your elders, you rose when a lady entered the room, you never used bad language in her presence, and it was taken for granted that when you, a boy, grew up you would provide for, protect, and honor your own womenfolk.

The exception was black people. Any snot-nosed white kid called any "colored" person of any age by his or her first name. Segregation and subordination were the natural order of things. Yet there was no conscious oppression. If boys of the same race didn't go to school together, they did often play together, at least until puberty set in. White adults felt responsible for the well-being of any blacks who worked for them. Once I heard my father and some friends vow that any Ku Klux Klansman who showed up in town would leave it on a rail, attired in tar and feathers. Otherwise all thought of lynching horrified them.

Young Poul with parents, Astrid (nee Hertz) and Anton Anderson, 1927.

Affection frequently developed between the races. The day after my father's death, old Jack, caretaker at the Yacht Club, somehow made his way out to our suburb, knocked on our back door, told Mother how sorry he was, and asked if there was anything he could do for her—chop some wood, maybe? I'll agree now that the system was wrong, but never that it was evil.

People in that milieu were generally religious. My parents were not, and didn't attend church; they didn't even have John or me baptized. Nonetheless they arranged for us to go to Sunday school. Later, in Minnesota, we got Wednesday school, on a released-time program that the courts have probably since forbidden. The church happened to be Episcopalian. The idea was to expose us to that part of the heritage of our civilization. I'm glad it happened. Some schools also had prayers or the like. From the age of twelve, if not earlier, I was an agnostic, but I don't remember that these practices hurt any sensitive little soul in me, nor do I see where they violated any rights of mine.

Now John and I were not entirely assimilated to the culture around us. Our parents took care to keep the family bilingual, another deed for which we remain ever grateful. We celebrated Christmas in the Danish style, emphasis on the eve rather than the day. With the selflessness typical of American husbands in that era of male chauvinist piggery, Dad gave his wife several trips back to the old country to visit her folks there, and she took us children along. So we came to address and think of her as Mor, Danish for "Mother."

I sometimes wonder what our lives would have become if they had continued like this. Surely Dad would have gone far, as his associates did. But one fall day in 1937 turned chilly. He started back home to get his overcoat. On the way, his car collided with another. Both drivers were instantly killed.

Long afterward, Mor confessed that, though she tried to keep on doing well by us, for a while she was an automaton. Will Anderson had been the only man in her life. He always would be. Over the years she declined more than one offer of marriage. Grief went away at last, but love never did.

The couple had always considered it a sacred obligation to see their children through college, and had been putting money aside for this. Dad's attitude toward his wife was equally old-fashioned; he carried plenty of insurance. Taxes and inflation had not yet made thrift impossible, so the savings account was in good shape too. Mor was not left rich, but she wasn't badly off.

For several months she tried to carry on in Port Arthur. It was hopeless. The place was too haunted. She longed to go back to Denmark, where she had many friends and relatives, some of them in influential positions. Why not settle there? In the spring of 1938 she put the three of us on a train to upstate New York, where a friend of hers had an artist husband and a son about my age. We spent a while with them before crossing the Atlantic. I was now old enough that I well remember the scenic Hudson valley, and my introduction to Mary Poppins and Oz.

The whole trip stands pretty clear before me. Our passage was on a German liner—third class, though plenty luxurious for the likes of us—which set us off at Bremen, where we overnighted. Soldiers and Nazi functionaries were everywhere; a huge poster reminded people to make sure their gas masks were in order; in a beautiful park where swans swam on a pond, an official bulletin board displayed the International Jew plotting to rob the world.

Denmark, to which we proceeded by rail, was like another planet. If I am not being sentimental, it was still more charming then than now. Everybody was so cheerful and *decent*—including an aunt of mine who had been a Communist since 1917 and her current lover. Grandfather was dead but Grandmother remained very much alive, a tall and imposing lady with a mane of white hair. Mor's cousin Jens was a fabulous Dionysian figure. Cousins of about my own age were a lot more fun than any kids in Texas. All of these persons would later be active in resisting the Nazi occupation, but that was for the future; this was the last golden summer.

For several generations the family had had a lease on an eighteenth-century fisher cottage on the Sound near Elsinore, and there we spent a good deal of the time. Perhaps its accumulation of things my forebears had cherished, within walls older still, had more to do with nourishing a sense of history and tradition in me than did the well-known places which every tourist saw. (Long afterward, when the lease had been lost, I would be the last of us to spend a night there.) We explored Copenhagen itself, of course, and quite a bit of serene rural Denmark, and southern Sweden. I've never gotten this out of my system, nor wanted to.

But ... it was becoming too obvious that war was on the way. Mor was long since a naturalized American. What concerned her more, though, was that her sons were American born. In fall we returned.

Not to Port Arthur. Not ever, except on a visit or two. While we still had money, it wasn't a lifetime's worth. Through her connections abroad, Mor had gotten back her former secretarial job at the Danish legation. She rented a house in nearby Silver Spring, Maryland. After a while her own mother came over to live with us.

By and large, this became a rather happy time for me. The local junior high school was excellent. The faculty were relaxed and amiable, and believed in encouraging individual potentialities. Simultaneously, they upheld a proud academic standard. Both these features made school, on the whole, actually enjoyable. I soon became close friends with a classmate, Neil Waldrop; we could talk to each other, and about stuff like astronomy and evolutionary biology. Rock Creek Park was grand for a Saturday ramble and amateur geologizing. The Smithsonian was an Aladdin's cave of wonders.

It was different for my brother John. He had adored his father, whose death came at his vulnerable age of seven. Now he didn't get along with Grandmother, Mor's job took most of her time and energy, he had no friends in his grade school. One day Mor came home to see him sitting on the steps in his cowboy suit, aiming his cap pistol at the empty air and saying, "Bang, bang, bang," while tears poured down his face. She decided the time was overpast for getting out of this situation. But where to?

California was a possibility. A friend of her youth had gotten married in the San Diego area, to a businessman who had made himself a fortune. He offered to invest Mor's money for her. Had she accepted, she too would undoubtedly have become wealthy, and John and I would have grown up surrounded by worldly goods and left-wing ideology.

This is as convenient a place as any for some remarks on politics. We have to make an effort, these days, to put ourselves in the minds of people of goodwill, back in 1917 and after. They had seen the grimness of working-class lives. My medical grandfather never presented many a bill, because he knew the patient couldn't afford it; and he would hear workers trudging to the job before sunrise and back after sunset. The vast improvement since is almost entirely due to better technology and to whatever degree government has kept hands off, but that was not generally foreseeable then. Additionally, his generation and his children's witnessed the mass lunacy that was World War One. They were ripe to believe that the October Revolution was the red dawn of a new day. The Edwardian Enlightenment was ironically conducive to that; it amounted to a faith in human rationality, and Marxism claims to be founded on fact and reason.

Mor never became a Communist, but a sister of hers and various friends did, and others were fellow travelers, including the lady now in San Diego. My parents were Democrats, like practically everybody else in the South. They thought the New Deal was actually doing something to relieve the Depression. As a matter of course, I was raised under this idea. I don't know what intensive exposure to the real Left would have done, though it seems plausible that I'd have ended up as a flaming Tory.

In the event, Mor made a different decision. It was to prove financially disastrous. Yet she always believed afterward that it was beneficial for her sons and this was profit enough. Her brother Jakob Hertz—Jack, he called himself—had immigrated too, done well as an engineer, and now for some reason got the notion that he wanted to be a farmer. His wife had kinfolk in southern Minnesota. He wrote to Mor, proposing that they buy adjacent properties, both of which he would operate. Mainly she saw

"Mor (Danish for mother)," Anderson's mother, 1971.

this as a wholesome environment which might heal John. She agreed.

First, after she quit her job, we made a cross-country auto trip. I suspect she meant it as a last fling at freedom. Passing through such marvels as Yellowstone, we ended in a cottage on the ocean shores of Washington state, an area with which I have ever since been in love. There Grandmother said good-bye, took a bus to New York, and thence sailed home to Denmark. It had not worked out, her joining the household. She was a gallant old soul nonetheless; afterward she personally defied and once even outwitted the Germans; it is well for me to recall that she revisited us after the war, and later Mor visited her before her death, and those were happy times.

We three drove back to Minnesota. There Mor bought her farm, forty acres of plowland, pasture, and second-growth woods. It had no buildings, so while the house and barn and the rest were under construction we spent several months, 1939-40, in Northfield. That's a middle-sized town south of Minneapolis, partly a farmer's market, partly the home of two colleges, Carleton and St. Olaf. Carleton in particular enjoys an international reputation. Northfield is thus an odd, pleasant mixture of Academe and Demos. We acquired friends in both.

We boys were enrolled in its schools. Later, living in the countryside, we should technically have gone to its high school. Concerned for our education, Mor pulled wires to keep us where we were. It meant long bus rides, but is another deed for which we are grateful.

I want to be fair to Northfield High School. It was the best in a wide radius, offering such subjects as physics, chemistry, mathematics through advanced algebra and solid geometry, Latin and living foreign languages, one good course each in world history and sociology. (The ignorance of these last two nowadays, especially among college graduates, is appalling, and goes far toward explaining the Totentanz that has been postwar American politics.) The faculty were dedicated and generally kindly. The student body was amiable. I learned more than I realized at the time.

Yet those years are pretty bad in my memory. I was a total social misfit. It didn't help that the war came along, gasoline was rationed, and I couldn't get into town on my own even if time had permitted after my farm chores or if, for that matter, I had wanted to. My grades were excellent and my deportment got me a name for prissiness among the other boys. They hadn't heard me out on the farm, swearing at a horse or cow or balky piece of machinery; there I earned a certain admiration from hardened men. As for school, except for the occasional fire-kindling teacher, it was something to be outlived.

I regret having to include my English classes. The teachers meant well, and they did get the mechanics of the language firmly into my head, but they were old maids, some nice, some waspish, and their idea of introducing us to literature was to lay a piece of work out on a dissecting table. It took me years afterward to discover that Shakespeare, for instance, is fun; and to this day I generally look upon literary critics as being old maids, of whatever sex.

Let me repeat, the basic misery of those years I brought largely on myself; and it is largely in retrospect that I see how wretched they were. During them, that was just the way life was, and at least I was not in a concentration camp or anything like that. John, always more normal, soon regained emotional equilibrium, went through the same school, and had a generally fine time.

Anyway, I had my private world to retreat to, the world of books and, specifically, science fiction.

I'd kept in touch by mail with my Silver Spring schoolmate Neil Waldrop. Shortly after my arrival in Minnesota, he sent me a bundle of magazines. They seemed to be terrible pulp trash, and I didn't intend to read them, but fell sick abed for a few days and had nothing else. Immediately I was hooked. *Thrilling Wonder Stories; Startling Stories; Amazing Stories;* above all, the cerebral *Astounding Science Fiction . . . .*

As a kid, I'd been a great fan of such imaginative comic strips as "Popeye" and "Alley Oop"—the splendid creations of Segar and Hamlin, not the zombie imitations which have succeeded. I've mentioned Oz and Mary Poppins, and there was also Dr. Dolittle. (They tell me you can't get him anymore. Those books have been banned as racist by the people who so bravely defend the rights of pornographers.) Later came Jules Verne, H. Rider Haggard, Sax Rohmer, a bit of H. G. Wells. And of course stars, planets, dinosaurs, atoms, the whole stuff of science had always been magical. Now here were these magazines, which offered stories of this kind every month!

I spent much of my tiny allowance on subscriptions. These didn't give me enough science fiction, so I started writing my own, in longhand. Neil did likewise for a while, and we'd exchange manuscripts for mutual comments, but presently he stopped and I went on alone, writing for nobody but myself. I didn't intend to make a career of this, but I did daydream about moonlighting at it and perhaps, someday, seeing words of mine in print, right up there with the words of Robert Heinlein, Isaac Asimov, or A. E. van Vogt.

Meanwhile there was reality to get through. I don't want to say anything against my uncle Jack. Suffice it that Pearl Harbor happened, and he went into war industry in Minneapolis, and his wife Jenny must needs take over their farm. She was a dear person, energetic and conscientious, but she and Mor were left essentially alone, dependent on the goodwill of neighbors to keep going.

About one of these, a relative on whom they had counted, I certainly do want to say something, but there might be a legal hazard in that, even at this late date. Enough that he appointed himself an enemy. The rest of the men around were, on the whole, okay. Mor did have to give one of them the knee once, when he got grabby; but he learned his lesson and made no more trouble of that kind. The others never did at all. Their wives were unfailingly kind and helpful.

If these people tended to bore the Anderson family in social situations, quite likely this was our fault. In their ways, they were actually apt to be colorful individualists. I have since encountered far more sheep-like conformity in the thinking of academics and journalists. Nonetheless, we never fitted very well into the community.

We could not isolate ourselves from it. People needed each other to a degree that scarcely exists anymore. For instance, men and boys of the neighborhood got together for such jobs as haying and threshing, farm by farm, while their women prepared communal meals. When a blizzard closed roads, you checked around to make sure nobody was in trouble. It wasn't exactly a pioneer situation, but it was the last remnant of the old yeomanry.

That's long gone. Mor went broke because forty acres are too little to support the equipment you need. Also she, as a widow, had to pay for much of her help—and weren't most of our hired men a succession of weirdos! We were basically chicken farmers, and our dear government slapped wartime price controls on eggs while letting the cost of feed soar.

She never said much afterward about that struggle. It is only my thinking about it that has put me in awe of her. She was worse than alone, she was saddled with a pair of teenage boys, as sullen and selfish as is usual at that age— or perhaps more so, since the war denied us many of the outlets now taken for God-given rights. In any case, school, together with the long commute to and fro, limited what we could do to help.

Those years weren't altogether bad. They may have forced upon us a certain discipline which has stood us in good stead. She always thought so. For my part, I am not sorry to have made the acquaintance of different kinds of animals, and winter and hard labor, and men and women who earned their livings with their hands. Though I would not willingly go back, it is well to have been there.

By 1944, though, Mor was at the end of her resources. The farm had consumed all her money except for the hallowed education fund. Through a friend on the Carleton College faculty, she got a job at its library, which she held until she reached retirement age. Meanwhile, she got rid of the farm.

She became a hell of a great librarian. She mastered the skills fast and, with her background in foreign languages and history, was often the best researcher on hand. Lacking the degree, she could only go so far in grade. Some of academe's characteristic, vicious infighting sometimes touched her peripherally. Otherwise, the students and most of the faculty loved her. Not that she was a sweet little old lady—no, always a salty character.

Well, this is getting ahead of the story. After high school graduation in 1944, I tried to enlist in the army—were we not in a glorious crusade which our leaders assured us would bring peace forever after?—but was turned down because of my scarred eardrums. A routine draft call later that year had the same result.

Carleton College had offered me a small scholarship, on the basis of my high school grades, but I chose to enroll at the University of Minnesota. This was because its Institute of Technology offered an almost 100 percent scientific program. (A year of engineering English was required. So was a quarter of literary English, where I breezed through the reading of a few novels and the twaddle I was supposed to write about them. As electives I took some Spanish and some philosophy of science, the latter taught by the brilliant, hard-boiled logical positivist Herbert Feigl.) My aim was to become a physicist.

Suddenly I was free. The old maids and soft young faces of high school were behind me. I was among men, and men whose trade was knowledge. They regarded me as an adult, willingly gave help if asked but never volunteered any, always taking for granted that I was responsible for myself. Minneapolis was a much less interesting city than it has since become, but it was my first city to run about in on my own. Less among classmates than among chance acquaintances out of the entire student body, I made new friends and with them, for the first time, began really deep-going exploration of things that really mattered.

Not that life became uproarious. Aside from an occasional beer bust or the like, it stayed pretty quiet. For the first couple of years I went home most weekends to help out on the farm, till Mor found a buyer. I avoided extracurricular activities. If nothing else was happening, and it usually wasn't, I'd spend my evenings reading, or else writing stories. Regardless, and never mind any missed opportunities, this was a splendid time for me.

The war ended, for the nonce, at Hiroshima and Nagasaki. As a reader of science fiction, perhaps I understood a little better than most folk what this meant. But I don't claim any prophetic insights, and in fact the world has gone down ways that nobody predicted. I suspect it always will.

Abruptly campus was flooded with veterans enrolling on GI benefits. They were generally fine guys, for whom I felt a certain wistful admiration, though they hardly ever boasted of their combat doings. They did, however, overcrowd my classes. It seemed as if everybody wanted to be a nuclear physicist. This was one reason why I moved over more toward astronomy. Another was a growing realization that not only was I awkward in the laboratory, I lacked any mathematical gift. It was easy to learn theorems that somebody else had proven, but where it came to creating a demonstration for myself, I wasn't much.

Unfortunately for me, Minnesota had only a minor astronomy department. Its head, Willem Luyten, was a first-rank scientist, but what he could offer students was quite limited.

Meanwhile, as it happened, Neil Waldrop came to Minnesota in 1946, enrolling in its excellent premedical school. We spent many delighted hours together. Out of conversations about the atomic bomb came the idea for a story, which I thereupon wrote. He said it merited submitting for publication. I borrowed Mor's typewriter, put the thing in proper form, and sent it to *Astounding*— giving Neil a shared byline, since the basic notion had been his.

Months passed. I went off to a summer job in the north woods. I was back at school that fall before a letter came. John Campbell, the editor, had *read* "Tomorrow's Children." He wanted to *buy* and *print* it. That kind of experience comes one to a lifetime.

This first effort of mine appeared in the spring of 1947. In the following year or so I wrote and sold a couple more, for what was then fairly good money. This may have been a factor causing me to run out of academic steam. More and more, my attention went to other things than studies. I did graduate in 1948 "with distinction," my college's equivalent of "cum laude," but my heart was no longer entirely in it.

Another factor has already been mentioned, the slow and reluctant realization that I could never be more than a second-rate scientist. A third, doubtless the main one, was a whole new direction that my life had taken.

This came about through science fiction. Its influence on quite a few lives has been enormous. In some cases the results have been unhealthy, but generally they are straightforward and beneficent. By casting glamour over science and technology, it has recruited many a young person into these fields, and helped him or her get through long, unglamorous years of study and apprenticeship. I have this admission from a number of them, some world-famous, and certainly the influence was there upon me, though in my case it worked itself out along different lines.

Before Pearl Harbor, several boys and a couple of adults, enthusiasts of the literature, had founded what they called the Minneapolis Fantasy Society. Like other such fan groups, it held meetings to discuss its favorite subject, and it put out a mimeographed amateur magazine to exchange for similar publications. Presently most of the members went into uniform, and when they came back they were no longer boys but young men. Just the same, they were as avid for science fiction as ever, and late in 1947 they reconstituted the MFS. Some had died or moved elsewhere, but some new people joined. I was among these.

A letter of mine, published in a professional magazine, led to my being invited to a meeting. What an evening that was! I met a god of mine, Clifford D. Simak, who turned out to be a warm human being. I met a whole clutch of kindred spirits, more or less my age, and after the meeting we went out for beer and talk till the bars closed, and then for coffee and talk, and I rolled back to my lodgings at sunrise full of new worlds and exploding stars.

Thereafter I was a regular member and made friendships, which time and long separations have not dimmed in

Anderson's wife, Karen Anderson, about 1963.

the least. Whenever we get together again, all too seldom these years, it is as if we had never been apart. Doubtless the best known of these comrades of mine, today, is Gordon R. Dickson, who has long since realized the ambition he had borne since childhood, to be a writer. Especially influential on me was an older man, already a husband and father, Kenneth Gray. We used to sit up half the night at his house, arguing. Self-taught, he knew more history than most professors of the subject, and military service had taken him into far and strange corners of the world. His political conservatism gave my left liberalism of that time a salutary kick in the guts. There were others, most of whom have gone on to distinguish themselves in their chosen fields, but the list would grow too long.

The list of women would not. They were precious few in our circle. Any who appeared and were attractive and intelligent were quickly snapped up by some fellow. I've scant patience with today's paranoid feminism, but it seems undeniable that education and expectations in those days turned most girls into bores. Matters have improved enormously since then.

MFS activities were more than simply fannish. In fact, soon we lost interest in fandom per se, though not in science fiction. We stopped having regular meetings or issuing publications, and "MFS" became a shorthand phrase for a group of people who saw a lot of each other.

Parties, picnics, cross-country junkets ... softball on summer Sundays, rough touch football in the autumn ... our favorite downtown bar, where you could nearly always find somebody ... the German Dinner Club ... the confidences and desperations of youth.... Those were not years of pure bliss, especially not for Gordy and myself, as hand-to-mouth as we were living. We suffered our disappointments in love, the manifold frustrations of being poor, the sight of our work in sleezy paperbacks ineptly copyedited, for in those days a science fiction writer was at the absolute bottom of the totem pole. In just about every way, our lives since have vastly bettered. But still and all, I am glad to have had those years.

This was when I settled into a writing career in earnest. Graduating into a recession, with no money left for further studies, but being a bachelor who had never had a chance to develop expensive tastes, I thought I'd support myself by my stories while I looked around for steady employment. The search was half-hearted, and eventually petered out. I liked too much being my own boss, precarious though the living often was. Only slowly did it dawn on me that writing had, all along, been what nature cut me out to do.

Mostly I was selling to the magazines, especially *Astounding,* as it was then called (nowadays *Analog*). My early pieces there tended to be rather cold and abstract. However, for a brief span I became a mainstay of *Planet Stories,* which featured blood-and-thunder adventure yarns—along with experimental work by such people as Ray Bradbury, which nobody else would touch. And the first novel I wrote which saw print, *The Broken Sword,* is a rather passionate love story among other things. It took years to find a publisher, and meanwhile I did a juvenile book on commission, which was therefore my premier appearance at that length. Occasionally Gordy and I collaborated on a humorous "Hoka" yarn. The first few of these were run in a magazine published in Chicago, whose assistant editor, Bea Mahaffey, was gorgeous. I sometimes took the train there just to date her.

My initial science fiction convention was in Toronto, 1948. Events of this kind were then small, humbly housed, and almost entirely masculine. That was soon to change.

Restlessness grew within me. In the summer of 1949 I went with my brother John to Mesa Verde National Park, where we had jobs. Mine was behind the lunch counter, and ever since then I have felt a perhaps exaggerated sympathy for waiters and such. I quit early and hitchhiked back to Minnesota, to drive with Oliver Saari to the convention in Cincinnati.

Ollie and I traveled cross-country next year to a more professional gathering in New York. That was where I first met Isaac Asimov, L. Sprague de Camp, Willy Ley, and many another giant. All were gracious to this brash newcomer. Later that summer, John and I fared out to the Pacific coast. We looked in on the world convention in Portland, where I enjoyed a lively evening with Anthony Boucher, co-founder and co-editor of *The Magazine of Fantasy and Science Fiction.* He was to become a dear friend.

By the spring of 1951 I had enough money to go to Europe. John came too. We crossed on the old *Empress of Canada*—ah, that last night out, a full moon working its magic on the girls—and bought bicycles in Liverpool. Thence we youth-hosteled our way through a good bit of Britain and the Continent. When John went back to college in fall, I stayed on for a couple of months more, knocking around by myself or in company with chance-met Europeans.

Landing in New York, I took a few days there. One of my high hopes was to meet John W. Campbell, editor of *Astounding,* practically the single-handed creator of modern science fiction. He gave a cordial reply to my telephone call, and I spent an unforgettable afternoon in his office. Our relationship was to become close over the years. It wasn't simply that I was among his most frequent

"Building the houseboat," about 1962.

contributors, or that we struck up a lengthy and argumentative correspondence. Gradually it became clear to me that beneath that prickly exterior of his was a gentle, even shy soul. I had begun by worshipping him; I went on to admire and like him; I ended loving him. In his last years, when he was under heavy and often nasty attack from lit'ry types who considered him a reactionary and a has-been, I took every chance to defend him. He didn't bother to do that himself. I doubt he minded very much. But I damn well did.

The story's gotten ahead of itself again. Returning to Minneapolis, I began to find it more and more confining. My dream was to get back to Europe and settle down there, in some base from which to explore the entire eastern hemisphere. However, I was now pretty broke. Not only would passage money be needed, but a stake. I settled down to earn the necessary sum. Trying to save, I did scarcely any traveling in 1952, except to the world convention in Chicago.

That changed my plans.

Chicago's was the first of the big conventions, a thousand or so in attendance. Nowadays the major ones run to several times that number, and camaraderie between professionals and fans has pretty well drowned in the mob. The old bacchanalian, almost orgiastic spirit seems extinct also—this generation of young people is more sober and decorous than mine was—though at my present age that doesn't bother me, while the overcrowding does. I seldom attend any more, except an occasional regional gathering which is of humane size.

In 1952 you weren't yet overwhelmed. It was easy to get together with the individuals you wanted to be with, and to meet new persons whom you found you also wanted to be with.

Among the latter I encountered a young lady by the name of Karen Kruse. Born in Kentucky in 1932, she now lived in the Washington, D.C. area with her widowed mother and two younger brothers. While still in high school, she had founded a Sherlock Holmes society—there is considerable overlap between followers of science fiction and of the great detective—which remains active today in the capital under the thumb-to-nose name she gave it, the Red Circle. Upon graduation she had gone to work for the Army Map Service. With some money saved, she planned to enter Catholic University. She was not of that faith, but it had a fine drama department, and that was where her main interest lay, outside of science fiction and its fandom.

I took her aside for a beer and we became nearly inseparable for the rest of the long weekend, right on through the last party, where Stu Byrne sang Gilbert and Sullivan all night and we, with Tony Boucher, watched the sun rise over Lake Michigan. After going back to our respective homes, we corresponded eagerly. It was a curious courtship, but by spring we knew we were in love.

John had graduated from Carleton College and returned to Denmark on a one-year Fulbright scholarship. His field was history, with an eye to getting into the foreign service. It had been agreed that I would meet him over there when he was finished and we'd travel around, Mor joining us when she got her vacation. I was no longer exactly anxious to go, but people were counting on me. I did manage a few days in Karen's neighborhood and a few

more with her in New York, to which her mother drove us, before the *Ryndam* sailed.

Nevertheless, on the whole it became a jolly summer. John and I rented a motorcycle with a sidecar. Czech-made, it kept breaking down along the way, until we had practically rebuilt it, but it did put wheels under three persons. At first the third was a Danish friend. He hitchhiked back from the south of France, and we went north again through Switzerland to England, where Mor landed. Now it was her turn in the sidecar, going to Paris, Holland, and Denmark. That was a rainy year. I remain convinced that a motorcycle is an ingenious combination of the drawbacks of bicycle and automobile. But what the hell.

John and Mor went home in fall. Since I had not originally intended to do so, I had no ticket, and must perforce wait a while; transatlantic passages were nowhere near as available then as now. I would have gone to Norway, but fell sick. My Communist aunt tended me as lovingly, in her tiny apartment, as she had tended her mother during the old lady's long dying.

The Berlin blockade and the Korean War were recent memories, the cold war was in its deepest freeze and a hot one looked imminent. Kenny Gray had gotten me to learn the truth about the Soviet Union and its institutionalized horrors. Among the Danish Communists, neither John nor I made any bones about where our loyalties lay—and our loathings; but personal relationships stayed entirely amicable.

This may be why John realized he could never hope to get into the foreign service. It was the so-called McCarthy era. In retrospect, I must agree that this consisted largely of intellectuals screaming from the rooftops that they were afraid to speak above a whisper. Certainly no one scolded me for my 1953 story "Sam Hall," in which a fascistic American government of the future is violently overthrown. John Campbell, who bought it, was himself a political conservative. Also, Communist espionage and subversion were an ugly fact.

Even so, some cruel and costly mistakes were made. The United States lost a good spokesman in my brother. He wanted a job that would let him travel, so after his army hitch he returned to school and got his degree in geology. Among other things, he later led the first expedition ever made into the Sentinel and Heritage Mountains of Antarctica. Doing field work in Utah, he met one Linda Jones and married her. They have two daughters. Until his retirement, he was professor of his subject at Kent State University in Ohio.

But all that was far in the future. I eventually got a cancelled berth on the *Stockholm* and came back to the States myself. This wasn't to Minnesota, except for farewells. If I couldn't live abroad just yet, I wanted to try something a bit glamorous, and remembered San Francisco from a visit earlier. Besides, Tony Boucher lived and worked right across the Bay, so there was one ready-made friend. Karen felt restless too. We agreed to try our luck yonder. She went and got herself an apartment in Berkeley and a job, and was waiting when I arrived. We were married that December.

For the next several years we lived in Berkeley. In those days the town was civilized, stimulating, amiably wacky. Its climate was better than that of San Francisco, which was only a short drive away anyhow. Here our daughter Astrid was born, in 1954. She tied us down somewhat; doubtless we could have traveled more with her than we did, but in the event decided not to. She was worth it. She still is.

Among people we went around with were Tony Boucher, Reginald Bretnor, Jack Vance, and their wives. Over the years we became closely knitted to them. Besides other writers than these, those who became good friends included members of the Elves', Gnomes', and Little Men's Science Fiction, Chowder, and Marching Society, which met on alternate Friday evenings for a program of some kind followed by beer and conversation till its favorite bar closed, and often threw hellratious parties.

If it seems that our social life has been dominated by persons concerned with science fiction, this is doubtless true, but that doesn't mean it has been narrow. The average reader or writer is uncommonly aware of the real world and active in it, with an uncommonly broad range of interests and knowledge. To give a single example, Jack Vance used to hold jam sessions at his house, which was where I got some understanding and appreciation of jazz. He also taught me most of what I know about carpentry. This was when he and I were building a houseboat for the use of our families. Originally Frank Herbert was a partner in the enterprise, but he was then a newspaperman and a change of jobs caused him to move away. Jack and Frank are among the most widely traveled, as well as widely read individuals I have ever met or heard of.

Besides, Karen and I had more activities. We attended meetings of the Mystery Writers of America, where speakers told fascinating things about crime and police work. We revived the local Sherlock Holmes club. There were all sorts of lectures, movies, and other such events. Mor came out each year for a lengthy visit and charmed everybody.

It wasn't entirely fun or easy. For a while it was damned rough. The science fiction field fell on evil days, a publishing contract on which I'd counted was renegotiated to my disadvantage, sales elsewhere languished, we went into debt. Karen had lost her job soon after I came to join her, and never taken another, in part because of my Southern prejudices about the roles of man and wife. It became clear that I'd better get one.

With a background in both physics and writing, I was offered a good post as a tech writer at the Lawrence Radiation Laboratory. This required a clearance for top secret material. I told the FBI men about my Communist aunt and the rest. If that was disqualifying, I said, they should so inform me and I'd withdraw my application with no hard feelings. They said it wasn't necessarily, and later called me in for another interview. That was obviously just a fishing expedition, full of questions about people I knew scarcely or not at all. I must say the agents were courteous, and it was perhaps not nice of me to start using sesquipedalian words in order that the man with the stenotype must ask me how to spell them.

Time passed. There was no word. Karen and I got broker and broker. Finally I gave up and took another offer. I am told that this was a favorite trick of the government's.

If officialdom had no sound reason not to clear somebody, but didn't want to, it stalled him till he could wait no longer and went away. I don't think this exactly expedited defense work.

My job was at a local Department of Agriculture laboratory, as a very junior-grade chemist. Boss and co-workers were likeable, but it was intensely boring, and perhaps this is a reason why, after the nine months of probation usual in civil service, I was gently told that they couldn't use me.

By then, however, that was a deliverance. My paychecks had kept us going. Evenings and weekends I wrote. The earnings from that paid off our debts and gave us a stake. When my mild bondage ended, in 1957, we celebrated by taking Astrid and Mor on a camping trip up the north coast. Ever since, I have been a full-time freelance writer and have done pretty well financially.

The annual world science fiction convention, on Labor Day weekend if held in the United States, traditionally has some professional as its guest of honor. He or she gets a room at the hotel (these days, all expenses) in return for making a keynote speech and being accessible to the fans. In 1959 the convention took place in Detroit, and the honor fell to me.

We put Astrid in the back seat of the Morris Minor we'd bought, as part of the "tailfin rebellion" of that era, and started off. Our trip to Detroit took a couple of months, since we went by way of Tennessee, Washington, New York, and Quebec; afterward we stayed a few weeks with Mor in Minnesota, and as the first snow fell headed home via Arizona. It was a grand trek, but I'll never do that much driving again. Since, we've flown to our basic destination and rented a car.

Less and less were we content in Berkeley. Sleaze and smog were moving in. A filling station replaced the house next door. Besides, it no longer made sense to pay rent when we could be paying off a mortgage and getting a tax break to boot. Early in 1960, we started looking around.

What we eventually found was a house in Orinda. This is a suburb on the eastern flanks of the hills which wall Berkeley and Oakland. It's beautiful and peaceful; a woman can walk its unlighted streets after dark without fear. Though it's fairly well built up, the topography and the many trees give an illusion of being in the countryside, and the air on the upper slopes is always clean. The house we saw is rather small, but sufficed for three, and it stands on one of the half-acre lots for which the area is zoned. A fountain was playing in the patio. We couldn't really afford it, but love generally finds its way. Astrid has since moved to a home of her own—her husband is my colleague Greg Bear—but Karen and I are there still. We now have two grandchildren, who are, of course, incomparable.

As it happened, we moved barely in time. The 1960s' Revolt of the Idealists was getting under way. It changed our funny old Berkeley into a place humorless, dirty, and dangerous. By now the tide of neo-barbarism has receded, though local slang still bespeaks the People's Republic of Berkeley.

That decade scrubbed me free of any last traces of liberalism and, for that matter, intellectual elitism. I saw academe fawn upon the kooks and goons whom its own lies had evoked. As for the Vietnam War, its aftermath suggests to me that perhaps those of us who supported the American

"Two halves of a Hoka," Anderson (left) with fellow writer and friend, Gordon R. Dickson, about 1970.

effort had a valid point or two to make. With rare exceptions, the people who agitated for our defeat do not admit that they may have done the world a disservice, any more than the average German did after Hitler. Nowadays these leaders seem primarily concerned with saving us from the cleanliness, safety, economy, and abundance of nuclear energy.

I will agree that our government had no business squandering lives and treasure—on both sides—on a war it had no intention of winning. But there is no monstrosity of which a government is incapable. Because a few limitations on it still survive, ours can be endured, most of the time, which is more than can be said for nearly all the rest. The liberals are working hard to change this.

Aside from politics, life remained good for my family. We prospered. Science fiction became respectable, almost too much so. For some years I did a fair amount of lecturing around the country, thereby discovering that most students continued to be clean and reasonable human beings. By 1965 we were able to go abroad for several months, something we've done fairly often since then. Among experiences on this particular trip was a tour of the paleolithic sites in the Dordogne countryside such as the president of France might get if he asked politely, as well as becoming intimate with that whole lovely region. It was

courtesy of the prehistorian in charge of work there, the late François Bordes, and his wife-colleague. He was still another person we'd met through science fiction. Stories about him could go on for many pages.

We had adventures closer to home. Jerry Pournelle, afterward to become a writer himself, and I attempted to bring a sailboat down from Seattle to Los Angeles. She was a nimble twenty-footer but we were an awful pair of amateurs who hadn't even equipped her with an outboard motor. When a gale hit us off Cape Flattery, I had the helm all night, trying to keep us off a lee shore, while Jerry handled such jobs as taking in reef points. Subsequently we were stormbound, along with the entire fishing fleet, so long that Jerry ran out of time and we had to give up. But I remember things like lying becalmed in an unutterably quiet blue-and-silver dawn, and a pod of killer whales swimming by and one raising himself to look over the rail as if to say good morning....

In the pause between Gemini and Apollo, 1963-64, I got a contract to write the script of a television documentary on the space program for the United States Information Agency. The budget was miserable, but visiting the sites and meeting the people on the project was a tremendous experience. Karen and I have both been quite involved with space, as spectators and as activists. Joe Green, who works at the Cape, used to throw terrific parties for the science fiction types who, armed with press credentials, got together each time a ship was about to leave for the moon.

All three Andersons were in the Society for Creative Anachronism, from its start in a Berkeley backyard, 1966. This organization, which is now nationwide and has overseas branches, goes in for medieval combat with wooden weapons—and if you think that's effete, you haven't been on the receiving end of one—as well as costumery, music, dance, cuisine, poetry, crafts, and everything else needed to revive the Middle Ages "not as they were but as they should have been." It was fine recreation for the whole family. Despite my age, I did well enough in battle to be awarded a knighthood, while Karen served a term as head of the College of Heralds. Since Astrid moved away we haven't attended many events, but the memories are warm.

In 1972-73 I put in a stretch as president of the Science Fiction Writers of America. That proved to be a job still more hard and thankless than I had imagined. In large part this was because of internal chaos. Nobody knew what anybody else was supposed to do. Nobody could so much as find a copy of the bylaws. Such a development is quite common in service organizations staffed by volunteers, and often destroys them. I spent most of my year coaxing forth a consensus for basic structural reforms and, at the end of it, getting them voted in. My successor, Jerry Pournelle, put them into effect and started the machinery working. He deserves most of the credit for saving what has by now evolved into the most active and effective group this side of the Screen Writers' Guild. However, I'm proud of my smaller role.

Mor retired and moved to Ohio to be with John, Linda, and her young granddaughters. She still came out almost every year to us, and sometimes we visited them. Her last stay here was in 1981. Her health had generally been excellent—at the age of seventy-nine, she hiked to the bottom of the Grand Canyon and back on the same day—but now suddenly it failed, and later that year she died, as gallantly as she had always lived. Both her sons were there.

Inevitably, we have had other losses and sorrows, as well as reverses, but there have been abundant joys too, and on the whole we must reckon ourselves among the luckiest people who have ever lived. Most of this is too personal for public discussion, and in any event has little or nothing to do with my development as a writer, which I suppose this essay is mainly about.

Karen has written professionally too, a few stories and poems. I wish she'd do more. Sometimes she's given me so much in the way of ideas for a piece that I've shared the byline with her. Always she's been my co-thinker or mental spark plug or whatever you want to call a person who'll talk with you, at length and brilliantly, about whatever you have in mind. She can supply information as well, whether right out of her head—she's a lot better at languages than I am, reads more on every conceivable subject, and remembers it more clearly—or looking it up for me. As a manuscript emerges in first draft, she becomes what she calls my resident nitpicker, and has combed out countless solecisms. She's a topnotch proofreader. And, oh, yes, a great cook.

If I don't otherwise say much about my work, it's because of a feeling that it has to speak for itself. As of today, the books total about eighty. That's less impressive than it looks, when you consider how long I've been in the business. Compared to, say, Isaac Asimov, I'm a sluggard—especially as of the past decade or so. Mainly my work is classifiable as science fiction or fantasy, but it also includes historical, mystery, and juvenile fiction, science fact, journalism, essays, verse, and translations.

I've been honored with various awards and such, but am not among those writers who appeal to English departments. No sour grapes here; those who do, like Ursula LeGuin and Frank Herbert, I admire myself, and enjoy reading. It is more than enough for me to know that my following numbers in it scientists, technologists, astronauts, and others of whose doings *I* am a fan. Considering the generally masculine tone of my writing, I've been a little surprised at the high proportion of women among those readers who really like and understand it. The last time I counted, words of mine had appeared in eighteen foreign languages.

I hope I've been improving. Certainly I no longer find the production of my first several years readable, and it's lucky for me that the public in those days was tolerant. Influences upon a writer are often hard to identify, but I think I know what some of the more important ones have been for me. There were editors John Campbell and Tony Boucher, who provided all sorts of inspiration and opportunity while scarcely ever trying to dictate. Besides H. G. Wells and Olaf Stapledon in science fiction, there were the giants of the Campbell Golden Age. Towering elsewhere have been the classical Greeks, the Icelandic Eddas and sagas, the King James Bible, Shakespeare, Mark Twain, Rudyard Kipling, Robinson Jeffers, and a Dane by the name of Johannes V. Jensen. I don't mean that my stuff measures up to any of this, only that I've tried. Science, technology, history, the whole world around us and the whole universe around it, provide endlessly fascinating subject matter.

Over the years I've written in a lot of different veins, from romantic to realistic, adventurous to abstract, somber to slapstick. The last two or three novels seem to be pointed in other directions, new to me. Where this will lead I don't know, but it should be fun along the way.

Writings

FICTION

Brain Wave, Ballantine, 1954; Heinemann, 1955.

(With Gordon R. Dickson) *Earthman's Burden* (short stories), Gnome Press, 1957.

The Enemy Stars, Lippincott, 1959; Coronet, 1972.

The High Crusade, Doubleday, 1960; Corgi, 1981.

Guardians of Time (short stories), Ballantine, 1960; Gollancz, 1961.

Three Hearts and Three Lions, Doubleday, 1961; Sphere, 1974.

Tau Zero, Doubleday, 1970; Gollancz, 1971.

The Broken Sword (revised edition), Ballantine, 1971; Sphere, 1973.

Hrolf Kraki's Saga, Ballantine, 1973.

A Midsummer Tempest, Doubleday, 1974; Futura, 1975.

The Avatar, Berkeley/Putnam, 1978; Sidgwick & Jackson, 1980.

The Merman's Children, Berkeley/Putnam, 1979; Sidgwick & Jackson, 1981.

(With Gordon R. Dickson) *Hoka!,* Wallaby/Simon & Schuster, 1983.

Orion Shall Rise, Timescape/Simon &Schuster, 1983.

The Boat of a Million Years, Tor, 1989.

Harvest of Stars, Tor, 1993.

The Stars Are Also Fire, Tor, 1994.

The Fleet of Stars, Tor, 1997.

Way of the Gods, Tor, 1997.

Starfarers, Tor, 1998.

These titles are the author's selection of his best-known or representative works. A list of his extensive writings may be found in *Something about the Author,* Volume 90, Gale, 1997.

B

BABBITT, Natalie (Zane Moore) 1932-

Personal

Born July 28, 1932, in Dayton, OH; daughter of Ralph Zane (a business administrator) and Genevieve (Converse) Moore; married Samuel Fisher Babbitt (a university administrator), June 26, 1954; children: Christopher Converse, Thomas Collier II, Lucy Cullyford. *Education:* Smith College, B.A., 1954. *Politics:* Democrat.

Natalie Babbitt

Hobbies and other interests: Needlework, piano, word puzzles.

Addresses

Home—81 Benefit St., Providence, RI 02904; and 63 Seaside Ave., Dennis, MA 02638.

Career

Author and illustrator. *Member:* Authors Guild, Author's League of America, PEN (American Center).

Awards, Honors

Best Book for children ages nine to twelve, *New York Times,* 1969, for *The Search for Delicious;* Notable Book, American Library Association (ALA), 1970, Newbery Honor Book, ALA, 1971, and Honor citation, *Horn Book,* all for *Kneeknock Rise;* Children's Spring Book Festival Honor Book, *Book World,* 1971, Children's Book Showcase, Children's Book Council, Best Books, *School Library Journal,* and Edgar Allan Poe award runnerup, Mystery Writers of America, all 1972, all for *Goody Hall;* Notable Book, ALA, Best Books, *School Library Journal,* Honor citation, *Horn Book,* and National Book Award finalist, American Academy and Institute of Arts and Letters, all 1975, and Parents' Choice Award (story book category), Parent's Choice Foundation, 1987, all for *The Devil's Storybook;* Best Books, *New York Times,* 1975, Notable Book, ALA, Honor citation, *Horn Book,* Christopher Award for juvenile fiction, The Christophers, all 1976, Children's Choice, International Reading Association, United States Honor Book citation, Congress of the International Board on Books for Young People citation, and Lewis Carroll Shelf Award, all 1978, all for *Tuck Everlasting;* Notable Book, ALA, 1977, for *The Eyes of the Amaryllis;* Recognition of Merit Award, George C. Stone Center for Children's Books, 1979, for body of work; Hans Christian Andersen Medal nomination, International Board on Books for Young People, 1981; Best Books, *New York Times,* 1982, for *Herbert*

Rowbarge; Children's Literature Festival Award, Keene State College, 1993, for body of work; Blue Ribbon Book, *Bulletin of the Center for Children's Books,* 1998, and Notable Book, ALA, 1999, both for *Ouch! A Tale from Grimm.*

Writings

SELF-ILLUSTRATED VERSE

Dick Foote and the Shark, Farrar, Straus, 1967.
Phoebe's Revolt, Farrar, Straus, 1968.

SELF-ILLUSTRATED FICTION

The Search for Delicious, Farrar, Straus, 1969.
Kneeknock Rise, Farrar, Straus, 1970.
The Something, Farrar, Straus, 1970.
Goody Hall, Farrar, Straus, 1971.
The Devil's Storybook, Farrar, Straus, 1974.
Tuck Everlasting, Farrar, Straus, 1975.
The Eyes of the Amaryllis, Farrar, Straus, 1977.
Herbert Rowbarge, Farrar, Straus, 1982.
The Devil's Other Storybook, Farrar, Straus, 1987.
Nellie: A Cat on Her Own, Farrar, Straus, 1989.
Bub, or, the Very Best Thing, HarperCollins, 1994.

ILLUSTRATOR

Samuel Fisher Babbitt, *The Forty-Ninth Magician,* Pantheon, 1966.
Valerie Worth, *Small Poems,* Farrar, Straus, 1972.
Worth, *More Small Poems,* Farrar, Straus, 1976.
Worth, *Still More Small Poems,* Farrar, Straus, 1978.
Worth, *Curlicues: The Fortunes of Two Pug Dogs,* Farrar, Straus, 1980, also published as *Imp and Biscuit: The Fortunes of Two Pugs,* Chatto & Windus, 1981.
Worth, *Small Poems Again,* Farrar, Straus, 1986.
Worth, *Other Small Poems Again,* Farrar, Straus, 1986.
Worth, *All the Small Poems,* Farrar, Straus, 1987.
Worth, *All the Small Poems and Fourteen More,* Farrar, Straus, 1994.

OTHER

(Reteller) *Ouch! A Tale from Grimm,* illustrated by Fred Marcellino, HarperCollins/Michael di Capua Books, 1998.

Contributor to *Redbook, Publishers Weekly, Horn Book, New York Times Book Review, Cricket, School Library Journal, USA Today,* and *Washington Post Book World.* Babbitt's books have been translated into several languages.

Adaptations

Knee-Knock Rise (filmstrip), Miller-Brody Productions, 1975.
Tuck Everlasting (videorecording), Great Plains National Instructional Television Library, 1980.
The Eyes of the Amaryllis (full-length film), Family Home Entertainment, 1982.

Sidelights

Primarily known as a children's book writer, Natalie Babbitt is also appreciated as a gifted storyteller by adult readers. In entertaining narratives, her characters confront many basic human necessities, including the need for love and acceptance, the need to grow and make independent decisions, the need to overcome fears, and the need to believe in something unexplainable. Her originality, sense of humor, and challenging themes have earned her acclaim as a children's author. Babbitt's books have won many awards, including a Newbery Honor in 1971, a National Book Award nomination in 1974, and the Christopher Award for juvenile fiction in 1976.

Babbitt's mother encouraged the author's early interest in art and reading. Genevieve Moore read children's books aloud to her two daughters, and the three decided that Natalie would become an artist and her sister a writer. Impressed with Spanish artist Luis de Vargas's airbrushed figures of glamorous women, which were popular during the Second World War, young Babbitt imitated them using colored pencils. Discouraged by the difference between Vargas's finished drawings and her own, she was inspired by Sir John Tenniel's illustrations in *Alice in Wonderland* and decided to work with pen and ink, which became her specialty.

Babbitt received brief training in a summer fashion illustration course at the Cleveland School of Art. There she realized that she enjoyed creative drawing more than sketching alligator bags. Later, in art classes at Smith College, where she competed with other artists for the first time in her life, she saw that success as an illustrator required more than creativity. In an essay for *Something about the Author Autobiography Series* (SAAS), Babbitt explained, "It was an invaluable lesson, the best lesson I learned in four years of college: to wit, you have to work hard to do good work. I had always done what came easily, and what came easily had always been good enough. It was not good enough at Smith, and would never be good enough again."

While at Smith, she met Samuel Babbitt, whom she married in 1954. She kept busy working and raising a family of three children while her husband, an aspiring writer, wrote a novel. The many hours alone with the novel did not suit him, however, and he went back to work as a college administrator. Babbitt's sister also produced a comic novel, for which Babbitt supplied illustrations, but the project was abandoned when an editor asked for a substantial rewriting. "I learned three valuable things from observing what happened to my mother, sister, and husband with their forays into the writer's world," she said in her autobiographical essay. "You have to give writing your full attention, you have to like the revision process, and you have to like to be alone. But it was years before I put any of it to good use." After reading Betty Friedan's *The Feminine Mystique,* Babbitt realized that while her life as a homemaker had been successful, it was time to try to develop her talents. After discussions with other women making similar discoveries, she decided to pursue a career as an illustrator.

In 1966, *The Forty-Ninth Magician,* illustrated by Babbitt and written by her husband, was published with the help of Michael di Capua at Farrar, Straus & Giroux. Di Capua encouraged Babbitt to continue producing children's books even after her husband became too busy to write the stories. She began by writing *Dick Foote and the Shark* and *Phoebe's Revolt,* two picture books in which the stories are told in rhyming poetry.

Babbitt's ideas for books sometimes start with a single image, such as a mountain and what can be found behind it, or a single word. While thinking about the image or the word, she imagines characters. Their personalities allow her to see what the characters will say and what will happen in each story. The final result is often very different from her first idea.

Goody Hall started with Babbitt's thinking about the word "smuggler," yet it became a conversation with her mother. In *SAAS,* Babbitt wrote, "My mother not only

wanted things, she knew what to want—what, that is, in terms of a Great American Dream of wealth, accomplishment, and social acceptability.... Like the heroes of Horatio Alger, my mother was never afraid of hard work, and many of the things she wanted were worth wanting.... She died when I was twenty-four and not yet mature enough to have figured it all out and [to have] discussed it with her. So I put it all into my story *Goody Hall* instead."

Goody Hall is a Gothic mystery set in the English countryside. A large Victorian house decorated with "gingerbread" woodcarvings belongs to Midas Goody, whose disappearance spurs a young tutor to investigate. His encounters with an empty tomb, a gypsy, a rich youngster and his unusual mother, and other surprises lead to a happy ending when the Goody family is reunited. Though the plot, like the old house with its hints of secret passageways and hidden closets, can frighten and bewilder, "in the end we feel the way the Goodys did about their house," Jean Fritz observed in the *New York Times Book Review.*

In *The Devil's Storybook,* the title character is a trickster who is fooled as often as he tries to fool others. For example, he gives the power of speech to a goat who then annoys him with his constant complaining. In another story, the Devil sneaks into the bedroom of a pretty lady who outwits him. Babbitt's Devil is middle-aged and pot-bellied and often fails to attain his goal of causing trouble for others. "The stories are delightful in their narrative fluency," declared Paul Heins in *Horn Book.* Others noted Babbitt's humorous illustrations: "Neatly framed pen sketches of beefy peasants and roguish inmates of Hell add folktale flavor and provide further proof of this Devil's fallibility," noted Jane Abramson in *School Library Journal.*

Tuck Everlasting features a family who, upon discovering a secret spring that imparts immortality, finds out that living forever without ever growing or changing is not very pleasant. This becomes clear to a ten-year-old girl who discovers the family by accident and decides to try to help them. Tuck's explanation of the role of death in the cycle of nature "is one of the most vivid and deeply felt passages in American children's literature," *Ms.* reviewer Michele Landsberg declared. In *Children's Books and Their Creators,* Eden Edwards remarked of *Tuck Everlasting:* "The writing is economical, straightforward, and unassuming, like the Tucks, yet the result is a mysterious, subtle evocation of emotion for this family and their fate. Here, as in most of Babbitt's fiction, sophisticated ideas are presented with simplicity."

Babbitt's 1977 tale, *The Eyes of Amaryllis,* features a sea-faring family haunted by a tragic accident. After her grandmother breaks an ankle, eleven-year-old Jenny Reades must go to the ocean shore and help the elderly woman recover. Forbidden from visiting the sea by her father, Jenny looks forward to finally seeing the strong waves of the Atlantic. During the summer, the young protagonist begins to understand her grandmother's

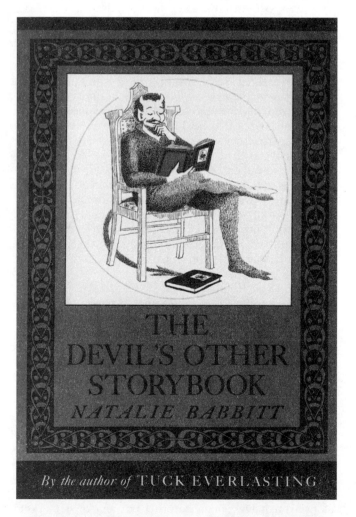

The Devil's Other Storybook, *a collection of ten tales by Babbitt featuring the Devil as protagonist, portrays Satan as a trickster figure who is equally likely to be duped himself.*

habit of searching the beach after every high tide, looking for remnants of the missing ship her husband captained over thirty years ago. Strangely, a piece of the lost ship surfaces during Jenny's stay, beginning a life-threatening series of events. Praising the use of the sea both "as an impelling atmospheric force and as an effective protagonist," *Booklist* reviewer Barbara Elleman claimed that "Babbitt wastes nary a word, deftly carving characters and events into a gripping tale." Writing in *Horn Book,* Mary M. Burns credited the book's success to "a well-wrought narrative in which a complex philosophic theme is developed through the balanced, subtle use of symbol and imagery."

Not limiting her efforts to novels for children, Babbitt entered the genre of picture books with *Nellie: A Cat on Her Own,* which she both wrote and illustrated. Created by an old woman from wood, string, and broom straws, Nellie is a marionette who thinks she cannot dance without the old woman's help. After her master dies, Big Tom, a cat, encourages Nellie to learn to dance on her own. At a midnight gathering of other cats, Nellie finds inspiration in the moonlight and learns to find joy in dancing just to please herself. Describing the picture book as a "small tale, charmingly rendered," *Horn Book* contributor Ann A. Flowers insisted that "this tale of independence achieved ... is enhanced by delicate watercolors of the dubious Nellie and competent Big Tom." Praising Babbitt's theme, Ilene Cooper wrote in a *Booklist* review, "Babbitt subtly yet surely weaves a strong message about self-reliance into this charming fantasy."

In *Bub, or, The Very Best Thing,* a picture book fantasy, a young king and queen argue about what is the very best thing for their young son. Pursuing an authoritative answer, the king and his advisors look into books, while the queen, accompanied by the child, his toy dragon, and a dog dressed as a court jester, traverse the castle, asking everyone they encounter. Finally, the cook's daughter suggests they ask the child himself, who replies "bub," which the girl interprets for adults as "love." "It's a fine book for new parents, whose point of view it reflects entirely," remarked Betsy Hearne in the *Bulletin of the Center for Children's Books.* In a *Horn Book* review, Hanna B. Zeiger declared that the author's "elegant writing style and the totally engaging characterizations in her illustrations combine to create a memorable picture book."

After her husband stopped writing, Babbitt gave up illustrating for others, with the exception of the poetry books of Valerie Worth. Published as *Small Poems, More Small Poems, Still More Small Poems, Small Poems Again,* and so forth, the collection reached eight volumes in 1994 with *All the Small Poems and Fourteen More,* which brought the total number of poems to one hundred and thirteen. "The earlier works have been widely praised, for good reason," remarked Nancy Vasilakis in a *Horn Book* review of *All the Small Poems and Fourteen More,* adding that the fourteen new poems are "every bit as worthy as their predecessors." Babbitt's illustrations were praised by Hazel Rochman in *Booklist,*

who wrote that the artist's "small ink drawings embody the realistic and make us imagine much more."

Babbitt has also written texts that have been illustrated by other artists, including her retelling *Ouch!: A Tale from Grimm,* featuring artwork by Fred Marcellino. In this story, a young man named Marco, born with a crown-shaped birthmark, grows up to marry a princess. Unfortunately, her evil father insists that Marco go down to Hell and steal three golden hairs from the devil's head, a deed the young man convinces the devil's grandmother to commit. Marco, meanwhile, returns to the kingdom to exact revenge from his evil father-in-law. "Babbitt rewrites the classic story in a casual voice infused with wry wit," wrote a reviewer in *Publishers Weekly,* concluding that "readers will likely lap up [her] intelligent retelling, mixed with a dash of sly humor."

Babbitt once commented, "I write for children because I am interested in fantasy and the possibilities for experience of all kinds before the time of compromise. I believe that children are far more perceptive and wise than American books give them credit for being." In a 1988 *Horn Book* essay, however, she expressed her concern about the ultimate effect of fantasy stories on impressionable minds. She wrote, "On a recent school visit a fifth-grader asked me if the magic spring water in *Tuck Everlasting* ... was real. 'No,' I said, 'it isn't real.' 'But,' said the fifth-grader, 'didn't you ever think that when you described it so well, as if it was real, we might believe you?' I have lain awake over that question. Are we somehow implying in our books that the unreal, the impossible, is more greatly to be desired than the real and the possible? ... I am only trying to say that we had better tread lightly." Babbitt believes writers need to be aware of how children's self-esteem can plummet when they compare themselves to fictional wizards and beauty queens: "It is absolutely true that in America anyone can grow up to be president, but the word is *can,* not *will.* We'd better be sure our children know that while luck is always a factor in how things turn out, there will be no magic, no fairy godmother, no hag on the road with her basket of charms." The author believes young readers also need to be reminded that in the real world, growth and change can take a long time to achieve.

Looking back on her published work, Babbitt recognizes that many of her own childhood memories are in the stories. The childhood experiences recalled in Babbitt's books remain meaningful into adulthood, according to Anita Moss in *Dictionary of Literary Biography,* a quality that makes her books enjoyable for readers of all ages. Michael Dirda, children's book editor for the *Washington Post Book World,* exclaimed: "As a writer, Natalie Babbitt possesses a worth beyond rubies; just say *Tuck Everlasting* or *The Search for Delicious* or *The Devil's Storybook* and any child, or former child, will instinctively cry out 'More, ma'am, please.'" A *Horn Book* commentator summarized the author-illustrator's accomplishment: "Babbitt's ... sense of humor, her wisdom and perspective on life, and her ability not to take herself too seriously—but to take what she writes and her audience very seriously—have shaped a magnificent body of work."

Works Cited

Abramson, Jane, review of *The Devil's Storybook, School Library Journal,* October, 1974, p. 102.

Babbitt, Natalie, "Metamorphosis," *Horn Book,* September, 1988, pp. 582-89.

Babbitt, Natalie, essay in *Something about the Author Autobiography Series,* Volume 5, Gale, 1988, pp. 41-52.

Burns, Mary M., review of *The Eyes of Amaryllis, Horn Book,* February, 1978, pp. 42-43.

Cooper, Ilene, review of *Nellie: A Cat on Her Own, Booklist,* October 15, 1989, pp. 447-48.

Dirda, Michael, review of *Bub, or, The Very Best Thing, Washington Post Book World,* April 3, 1994, p. 10.

Edwards, Eden, essay on Babbitt in *Children's Books and Their Creators,* edited by Anita Silvey, Houghton Mifflin, 1995, pp. 42-44.

Elleman, Barbara, review of *The Eyes of Amaryllis, Booklist,* November 15, 1977, p. 546.

Flowers, Ann A., review of *Nellie: A Cat on Her Own, Horn Book,* January-February, 1990, p. 48.

Fritz, Jean, "Teen-Age Fiction: Finding Out," *New York Times Book Review,* May 2, 1971, p. 18.

Hearne, Betsy, review of *Bub, or, The Very Best Thing, Bulletin of the Center for Children's Books,* June, 1994, pp. 312-13.

Heins, Paul, review of *The Devil's Storybook, Horn Book,* October, 1974, p. 134.

Landsberg, Michele, "The Classic Shelf: *Tuck Everlasting* by Natalie Babbitt," *Ms.,* May 11, 1990, p. 74.

Moss, Anita, in *Dictionary of Literary Biography, Volume 52: American Writers for Children since 1960: Poets, Writers, Illustrators, and Non-Fiction Authors,* Gale, 1987, pp. 22-29.

Review of *Ouch!: A Tale from Grimm, Publishers Weekly,* November 2, 1998, p. 80.

"A Rare Entity," *Horn Book,* March, 1989, pp. 133-34.

Rochman, Hazel, review of *All the Small Poems and Fourteen More, Booklist,* January 15, 1995, p. 933.

Vasilakis, Nancy, review of *All the Small Poems and Fourteen More, Horn Book,* March-April, 1995, p. 212.

Zeiger, Hanna B., review of *Bub, or, The Very Best Thing, Horn Book,* May-June, 1994, p. 305.

For More Information See

BOOKS

Children's Literature Review, Volume 53, Gale, 1999, pp. 20-39.

Twentieth-Century Children's Writers, fourth edition, St. James Press, 1995.

PERIODICALS

Booklist, February 15, 1994, pp. 1091-92.

New York Times Book Review, March 14, 1999, p. 31.

BELBIN, David 1958-

Personal

Born January 19, 1958, in Sheffield, England; son of John and Jo Belbin. *Education:* University of Nottingham, B.A. (with honors), 1980.

Addresses

Home—27 Devonshire Rd., Sherwood, Nottingham NG5 2EW, England. *Electronic mail*—dymbel@innotts.co.uk. *Agent*—Jennifer Withlen, The Rowans, 88 Hamfield Rd., Leicester LE2 1SB, England.

Career

Teacher of English, drama, and media studies in Nottingham, England, 1985-94; writer, 1994—. *Member:* Society of Authors.

Writings

FOR YOUNG ADULTS

The Foggiest, illustrated by Tim Beer, Hippo Books (London, England), 1990.

Shoot the Teacher, Scholastic (London), 1993, U.S. edition published as *Deadly Secrets,* illustrated by David Wyatt, Scholastic, 1994.

Final Cut, Scholastic, 1994.

Avenging Angel, Scholastic, 1994.

Break Point, Scholastic, 1995.

Deadly Inheritance, Scholastic, 1996.

Dark Journey, Mammoth (London), 1997.

The David Belbin Collection: Three Degrees of Murder (contains *Avenging Angel, Deadly Inheritance,* and *Final Cut*), Scholastic, 1997.

David Belbin

Haunting Time (stories), Five Leaves Press, 1998.
Love Lessons, Scholastic, 1998.
Dying for You, Scholastic, 1999.

"THE BEAT" SERIES

Missing Person, Scholastic, 1995.
Black and Blue, Scholastic, 1995.
Smokescreen, Scholastic, 1996.
Asking for It, Scholastic, 1996.
Dead White Male, Scholastic, 1996.
Losers, Scholastic, 1997.
Sudden Death, Scholastic, 1997.
Night Shift, Scholastic, 1998.
Victims, Scholastic, 1998.
Suspects, Scholastic, 1999.

FOR ADULTS

(Editor) *City of Crime* (stories), Five Leaves Press (Nottingham, England), 1997.

OTHER

Work represented in anthologies, including *Thirteen More Tales of Horror; Thirteen Again; Chilling Christmas Tales; Thirteen Murder Mysteries; Literacy World; Best Short Stories of the Year 1993,* Heinemann, 1994; *The Minerva Book of Short Stories 6,* Minerva; and *City of Crime,* Five Leaves Press. Contributor to periodicals.

Work in Progress

Fallen Angel, for "The Beat" series, publication by Scholastic expected in 2000; *Runaway Train,* for Puffin.

Sidelights

Born in Sheffield, England, David Belbin, a high school English teacher turned author, lived in Leicester, Merseyside, and Lancashire before going to university in Nottingham, where he has lived ever since. His short stories for adults have appeared regularly since 1989. His first novel for young adults, *The Foggiest,* was published in 1990 and has been translated into several languages.

According to Belbin, his biggest break came in 1993, when *Shoot the Teacher* appeared as the first title in the "Point Crime" series. Its success enabled him to become a full-time writer. In 1994, Scholastic published *Avenging Angel,* which introduced Clare Coppola, an Anglo-Italian student who sets out to find the hit-and-run driver who killed her younger brother. At the end of the book, Clare joins the police. Her career can be followed in "The Beat," an ongoing series of mysteries about young police officers.

"Young adult fiction scarcely existed when I was a teenager," Belbin told *SATA.* "I only discovered it in my mid-twenties, when I was training to be an English teacher. Excited by the work of writers like Robert Cormier and Robert Westall, I decided to have a go at writing a young adult novel of my own. This became *The Foggiest,* which was eventually published five years later, in 1990.

"I mostly write the kind of books that I would have liked to read when I was twelve or thirteen. They're often stories with twisted plots which open up the adult world and seem to appeal particularly to boys. My two most popular books, *Shoot the Teacher* and *Final Cut,* a mystery set in the film world, are examples of this. 'The Beat' is more serious, dealing with moral and social issues in a total of twelve novels [including *Avenging Angel*] about young police officers in Nottingham, where I live.

"I think that my best book—certainly the best received one—is *Love Lessons.* It is a full-length novel which examines the machinations and morality of a sexual affair between a male English teacher and a fifteen-year-old female student. I wrote the first draft as an adult novel. The young adult version took me nearly ten years and a brave editor to get right, but it turned out to be a better book for it.

"I still publish fiction for adults and am often asked what the difference is between writing for adults and writing for younger people. The answer: not much. There is less sex and swearing, sure, but there are ways of implying what you need to communicate so that the more mature reader understands what is going on. I don't use a difficult word or complicated syntax when something simpler would do the job, but neither do my favorite writers. I like a clean, considered style, not one that shows off."

For More Information See

PERIODICALS

Books for Keeps, January, 1996, p. 11; July, 1996, p. 12.
School Librarian, November, 1993, pp. 164-65.*

*   *   *

BERNARD, Patricia 1942-

Personal

Born July 6, 1942, in Melbourne, Australia; daughter of Robert and Edith Lack; married Kenneth Bernard, 1964; children: Marcelle, Shona, S'Haila, Tyru. *Education:* Attended Australian state schools. *Hobbies and other interests:* Travelling, reading, bike riding.

Addresses

Home—70 Sutherland Street, Paddington, Sydney 2021, New South Wales, Australia. *Agent*—Rachel Skinner, Rick Raftos Management.

Career

Writer and lecturer. *Member:* Australian Authors Association.

Awards, Honors

Multicultural Award for *Monkey Hill Gold;* Aurealis Award Shortlist for *The Outcast.*

Writings

FOR CHILDREN

We Are Tam, Ashton Scholastic (Sydney, Australia), 1983.
Aida's Ghost, Corgi Books (Neutral Bay, Australia), 1988.
Riddle of the Trumpalar, Scholastic (Gosford, Australia), 1990.
Challenge of the Trumpalar, Scholastic, 1990.
Monkey Hill Gold, Omnibus Books (Norwood, Australia), 1992.
The Outer Space Spy, illustrated by Mike Spoor, Jacaranda Press (Milton, Australia), 1992.
Dream Door of Shinar, illustrated by Garry Fleming, Harcourt (Sydney, Australia), 1992.
Kangaroo Kids, Bantam (Neutral Bay, Australia), 1992.
Jacaranda Shadow, Hodder & Stoughton (Sydney, Australia), 1993.
JB and the Worry Dolls, Hodder Headline (Rydalmere, Australia), 1994.
Outerspace Spy, Transworld, 1994.
Monster Builder, illustrated by Laurie McIntyre, Cool Dude Books (Paddington, Australia), 1996.
Duffy: Everyone's Dog Story (picture book), illustrated by Cathy Netherwood, Random House (Milsons Point, Australia), 1997.
Spook Bus, HarperCollins, 1997.
No Sooks on the Starship, Macmillan (Chippendale, Australia), 1998.

Wolf-Man, Pizza-Man, Bro-Man, Addison Wesley Longman (Melbourne, Australia), 1998.

"OUTCAST" TRILOGY

The Outcast, HarperCollins (Pymble, Australia), 1997.
The Punisher, HarperCollins, 1997.
The Rule Changer, HarperCollins, 1998.

FOR ADULTS

Sex is a Deadly Exercise, Transworld, 1987.
Sex is a Deadly Weapon, Transworld, 1990.
Deadly Sister Love, HarperCollins, 1998.

Work in Progress

Rage, a young adult novel; *My Sister's Keeper,* a murder mystery; *Rent a Head,* a science fiction novel; *Water Woman,* an erotic art novel; script-writing for *Sex is a Deadly Exercise;* a series on in-line skating.

Sidelights

Patricia Bernard left her native Australia at the age of eighteen to see the world, and has been traveling ever since. She spent a year working in various places in the United States, including New York, Washington, DC, Boston, Los Angeles, and New Orleans. She has visited seventy countries in Asia, Europe, and South America, has lived in twenty of them, and speaks five languages. Bernard was a painter of portraits and landscapes for fifteen years before she began her writing career at age thirty-two. She told *SATA:* "I started writing ... when a friend asked me to write down the stories I was telling at a kindergarten. Since then, every children's/teenage book I have written has been published.

"I hope to achieve racial and national harmony between children and parents in the linguistically diverse Australian schools, and to teach 'even the smallest thing' to the reader while they have a good time reading my books. I work from nine-to-nine, six days a week when writing, and longer when editing because I hate editing so much. My motto is 'if it is not fun, don't do it,' so when the sun shines I spend three hour lunches at the beach, editing and swimming, and I can be taken away from my computer by any simple excuse given by any friend who drops in and suggests a coffee, a champagne, or a swim. I also lecture in schools and to writers, librarians, and women's literary groups, mostly about myself, my books, and the benefits of turning off the television and reading.

"The purpose behind writing the *Outcast* trilogy was to invent an entire world with the same tensions as our own, and through a hero and a group of heroes, fix it up. I don't know who has influenced my work, but my favorite authors are Isabelle Allende, Margaret Atwood, and Charles Dickens. The advice I would give to aspiring writers in Australia is 'don't give up your day job. Our population is too small.'"

Patricia Bernard

For More Information See

PERIODICALS

Magpies, May, 1993, pp. 29-30.*

* * *

BERTRAND, Diane Gonzales 1956-

Personal

Born March 12, 1956, in San Antonio, TX; married Nick C. Bertrand (a self-employed businessman); children: two. *Education:* University of Texas-San Antonio, B.A., 1979; Our Lady of the Lake University, M.A., 1992. *Religion:* Catholic.

Addresses

Office—St. Mary's University, English Dept., One Camino Santa Maria, San Antonio, TX 78228.

Career

Visiting lecturer at St. Mary's University, San Antonio, TX, where she teaches creative writing and English composition and serves as faculty adviser for the university's literary magazine, the *Pecan Grove Review.* Named writer-in-residence, St. Mary's University, 1999. Presents workshops on creative writing for children, young adults, and adult audiences throughout Texas. *Member:* National Council of Teachers of English, Society of Children's Book Writers and Illustrators, Texas Council of Creative Writing Teachers, Austin Writers League, San Antonio Writers Guild, and Alamo Writers Unlimited.

Awards, Honors

National Hispanic Scholar, 1991.

Writings

Touchdown for Love, Avalon Books, 1990.
Close to the Heart, Avalon Books, 1991.
Carousel of Dreams, Avalon Books, 1992.
Sweet Fifteen, Arte Publico Press, 1995.
Alicia's Treasure, Arte Publico Press, 1996.
Sip, Slurp, Soup, Soup/Caldo, Caldo, Caldo (picture book), illustrated by Alex De Lange, Arte Publico Press, 1997.
Lessons of the Game, Arte Publico Press, 1998.
Trino's Choice, Arte Publico Press, 1999.
Family, Familia (picture book), illustrated by Pauline Rodriguez Howard, translated by Julia Mercedes Castilla, Arte Publico Press, 1999.

Poetry has been published in *Palo Alto Review, Concho River Review, English in Texas,* and *Chile Verde Review.*

Diane Gonzales Bertrand

Sidelights

Diane Gonzales Bertrand told *SATA:* "I always loved to create imaginary playmates as a child, and eventually transferred that creativity to the written page. My first 'novel' was written into a spiral notebook when I was in fifth grade. I kept adding to the story for the next fifteen years until I had filled almost seventy notebooks of two main characters, a host of minor characters, and a variety of plots and subplots. When I reviewed those notebooks about ten years ago, I was surprised that I had such a sense of dramatic action. I knew how to write with one viewpoint character, and I instinctively knew how to create a multidimensional story that could sustain the length of a novel.

"I came from a family of seven children, and the least expensive form of entertainment for us was a weekly trip to the library. I have many memories of my mother or father loading us into the family station wagon and heading for a library. To this day, all seven of us still love to read novels in our spare time.

"At Ursuline Academy, my junior English teacher allowed her students to turn in any kind of writing for extra points. So I wrote poetry and paragraphs about my teen life—whatever I was feeling at the time—and she would read it and encourage me to keep writing, no matter what. Her strong push for writing beyond the academic essays allowed me to explore new topics and

Family life and Mexican-American culture are celebrated in Bertrand's bilingual story of Mama's delicious soup.

find more creative ways to express myself. The other teacher who inspired me to take risks with my writing was Dr. Ann Semel at St. Mary's University. She encouraged me to write for children and young adults, something I hadn't considered before I enrolled in her fiction writing class.

"I enrolled in graduate school with a desire to become a better writing teacher. I wanted to learn new theories or modern teaching methods so that when I went back to teaching I'd be able to help students more. On the first day of class, I was told, 'A good writing teacher is a writer herself.' That philosophy completely changed my life.

"I never thought about being a role model until I began to create strong Mexican-American characters for my novels. I wanted women like myself—clever, funny, and educated—and men like my father and brothers—charismatic, sensitive, and loving—to be the essence of the world I created in my fiction. Those first three novels broke new grounds in romantic fiction since my editor had never published books with Mexican-American lead characters.

"I am very proud of the fact that my books give readers a sense of pride in their own customs and simple traditions. When I work with students in their classrooms, I like to remind them that their lives are wonderful sources for writing. I have learned to pay attention to the people and places around me and to capture those experiences in my own words, sometimes using the Spanish language that is part of who I am too."

Bertrand is noted for writing wholesome stories featuring Mexican-American characters and celebrating family life. In her picture book *Sip, Slurp, Soup, Soup/Caldo, Caldo, Caldo,* she tells the story of the delicious soup Mama makes while the whole family helps, making a rainy Sunday pass pleasantly. Featuring a bilingual text and the repeated refrain of *caldo, caldo, caldo* (the name of the traditional soup), *Sip, Slurp, Soup, Soup* relies on repetition to bring rhythm to the story of a homely family ritual. Ann Welton, reviewing the book for *School Library Journal,* maintained that Bertrand's repetitive text was both "brisk" and "rhythmic." In *Alicia's Treasure,* a novel for middle graders, ten-year-old Alicia's dreams come true when she is allowed to accompany her older brother to the seashore for a weekend visit to his girlfriend and her family. Alicia swims, surfs, picnics, disagrees with her brother, gets beach tar on her swimsuit, and generally has a great time while "Bertrand keeps the story moving as quickly as the weekend passes for Alicia," remarked Cheryl Cufari in *School Library Journal.*

Bertrand has also written a novel for teens, entitled *Sweet Fifteen,* in which the traditional Spanish coming-of-age ritual of *quinceanera* is depicted in its modern embodiment. The novel centers on a seamstress who has been hired to make the dress for Stefanie Bonillo's birthday celebration, but Stefanie is resisting her family's efforts to get her to participate in this traditional celebration because she is grieving the recent death of her father. "Ethnic values are honestly portrayed in this sincere novel," noted Jana R. Fine in *School Library Journal.* Chris Sherman, a reviewer for *Booklist,* praised Bertrand's focus on the evolving character of Rita, who finds love with Stefanie's uncle, friendship with Stefanie's mother, and a greater sense of her own identity through her involvement with the grieving family. "The story will engage readers ... from its beginning to its satisfying end," Sherman concluded.

Works Cited

Cufari, Cheryl, review of *Alicia's Treasure, School Library Journal,* July, 1996, p. 82.

Fine, Jana R., review of *Sweet Fifteen, School Library Journal,* September, 1995, p. 218.

Sherman, Chris, review of *Sweet Fifteen, Booklist,* June 1, 1995, p. 1750.

Welton, Ann, review of *Sip, Slurp, Soup, Soup/Caldo, Caldo, Caldo, School Library Journal,* August, 1997, p. 128.

For More Information See

PERIODICALS

Booklist, May 1, 1996, p. 1505.
Children's Books Review Service, Spring, 1995, p. 140.
Horn Book Guide, Fall, 1996, p. 289.
Journal of Adolescent and Adult Literacy, May, 1996, p. 693.

BLANCHET, M(uriel) Wylie 1891-1961

Personal

Born in 1891; died in 1961; married (widowed, 1926); children: five.

Career

Canadian nature writer and homemaker. Moved to Vancouver Island with family, 1922; explored Pacific Northwest by boat, with children, during summers.

Writings

The Curve of Time (memoir), William Blackwood & Sons (Edinburgh, Scotland), 1961, revised edition, Gray's Publishing (Sidney, British Columbia, Canada), 1977, reissued as *The Curve of Time: The Classic Memoir of a Woman and Her Children Who Explored the Coastal Waters of the Pacific Northwest,* Seal Press (Seattle, WA), 1993.

A Whale Named Henry, illustrated by Jacqueline McKay Mathews, Harbour Publishing, 1983.

Sidelights

In 1922 M. Wylie Blanchet moved to Vancouver Island with her husband and children. Four years later, following her husband's fatal sailing accident, she found herself a widow with five young mouths to feed. Friends and relatives advised her to leave the seacoast, but Blanchet bravely remained on the island and embraced the sea as a source of renewed life.

Beginning in the summer of 1928 she made annual excursions in her twenty-five-foot boat to show her children the natural wonders of the Northwest Coast. The dangers on such trips were real. Navigation could be problematic; hikes and climbs could be obscured by dense fog; animals such as bears and cougars sometimes watched the family; and once, one of the children broke a collarbone in a region where no professional help was available. Nevertheless, Blanchet and her brood survived and thrived.

Blanchet's book on the subject of those family sailing trips, *The Curve of Time,* was published in 1961, just a few months before the author's death. It received enthusiastic reviews and has become something of a cult classic among lovers of nature books. In *Aethlon: The Journal of Sports Literature,* Suzanne Schneidau praised the narrative, calling it "rich in artistic detail" for its figures of speech that made the landscape and seascape come alive. Schneidau also commented favorably on Blanchet's descriptions of visits to native villages and to the homes of individual trappers, and her attentive comparison of her own travels with the earlier explorations of Vancouver, Cook, and de Fuca. Praising the book for its suspense, she labeled it "a saga of courage and its intercourse with history and the beauty of

nature." *Kliatt* contributor Betty B. Page hailed the "warmth" of the book, asserting that Blanchet's "prose, like the waterfall she describes, sings." Page noted that physical descriptions, experiences, and feelings are all rendered in a "lyrical" fashion in *The Curve of Time.* A *Publishers Weekly* reviewer, while lamenting the absence of such details as dates, distances, and the ages of the children in the work, called Blanchet's memoir a "sweet volume." The book has been reprinted several times since its release in 1961. Unfortunately, Blanchet's death that same year deprived the reading public of the sequel volume that she was working on at the time.

Blanchet also wrote original stories for her young children. In the 1930s she penned *A Whale Named Henry* as bedtime material for the children; however, the book was not published until 1983, some fifty years after it was written. Through the eyes of principal character Henry, a killer whale, the narrative provides a realistic look at life in an inlet along British Columbia, with its tides and waves, fish and seaweed. Forty illustrations, along with assorted maps, add to the charm and informational quality of the book. *Canadian Children's Literature* contributor Bernard Schwartz, an art educator, gave high praise to the book's visual qualities, and predicted that it would be "most appealing" for an upper-elementary audience.

Works Cited

Review of *The Curve of Time, Publishers Weekly,* March 22, 1993, p. 77.

Page, Betty B., review of *The Curve of Time, Kliatt,* September, 1993, p. 41.

Schneidau, Suzanne, review of *The Curve of Time, Aethlon: The Journal of Sports Literature,* fall, 1993, pp. 199-200.

Schwartz, Bernard, review of *A Whale Named Henry, Canadian Children's Literature,* Nos. 39-40, 1985, pp. 106-07.*

*   *   *

BOYES, Vivien (Elizabeth) 1952-

Personal

Born July 9, 1952, in Colchester, England; daughter of Ivor Jardine Johnston (a company director) and Megan (a writer; maiden name, Lee) Boyes; married David Patrick Carter (a television lighting cameraman), September 3, 1977; children: Richard Carter. *Education:* University of London, B.Sc. (with honors), 1974. *Hobbies and other interests:* Gardening, photography, walking, reading.

Addresses

Home—107 Coldershaw Rd., West Ealing, London W13 9DU, England.

Career

British Broadcasting Corp., London, England, radio studio manager, 1974-79, technical instructor, 1979-82; freelance writer, broadcast training instructor, and sound operator, 1982—. St. John's Primary School, governor, 1989—. *Member:* Society of Authors.

Writings

The Druid's Head, Gomer Press (Llandysul, Wales), Beekman Publishers (Woodstock, NY), 1997.

Author of a script for the series *Science Scope,* broadcast by BBC-Radio. Contributor to periodicals, including *Camping and Walking, Good Housekeeping, The Lady, Mother and Baby, Parents,* and *Reader's Digest.* Poems have been broadcast on radio programs.

Work in Progress

The Raven's Son (tentative title), a story about one of the Iron Age characters who appears in *The Druid's Head.*

Sidelights

Author and radio broadcaster Vivien Boyes told *SATA:* "I have been writing in one way or another for most of

Vivien Boyes

my life. My mother, Megan Boyes, is a writer, too, so I was brought up to the sound of a typewriter. I started to scribble down stories as soon as I could hold a pencil. It was a lasting interest, and I went on to become a professional writer in my late teens."

Boyes's first published piece was a travel article for a magazine called *The Lady.* She went on to broadcast a number of her poems, short stories, and radio talks on BBC-Radio Derby, her local radio station at the time. Her interest in radio led to a full-time career on the technical side of radio with the British Broadcasting Corporation in London. She still wrote, but there was less time for it.

"It was only after my son was born," Boyes explained, "that I returned to serious professional writing. For awhile I wrote articles for women's magazines. I also wrote a number of pieces for BBC-Schools Radio. I was wondering about moving back into fiction writing when my son's primary school held a Book Week, where the children were encouraged to write a story, illustrate it, and make it into a small book. School staff members were also making books, and as I was a governor of the school, I decided to join in, producing a short story of around three thousand words. Upon reading it, I realized that the story was not complete. It was the beginning of a far larger tale, so I wrote more to see where the story would lead. The result was *The Druid's Head,* a time-slip adventure for children over ten, set partly in ancient Celtic times.

"Because I have to combine my writing with a part-time career in broadcasting, I find it hard to establish a routine for writing. I have some weeks where I am able to work solidly on a project for five days. Otherwise it is an eternal juggling act of days spent in radio studios, with writing sandwiched somewhere in between. Although this often feels frustrating, sometimes these enforced pauses in my work can stop me from becoming too stale. I am not sure that spending my entire life in front of a computer screen, immersed in the first century, would be good for my sanity.

"Once I am immersed in a book, I find it hard to remember where the initial idea came from—a thought, a character maybe. With *The Druid's Head* I had already made several visits over the years to Castell Henllys in Pembrokeshire, Wales, the Celtic hill-fort which provid-ed the rudiments of the setting for this book. Wandering around the reconstructed roundhuts, smelling the wood smoke from the fires and the scent of the damp, earth floors, it was easy to sense the presence of the original inhabitants. The people who had lived here could have been my distant ancestors, and I was curious about how life would have been for them. The more deeply I researched early Celtic history, the more I became fascinated by these colorful and surprisingly knowledge-able people. I was hooked. Soon I had the strong image of my Druid, Cigfran, and his young son, Uther, and I knew they had a story that they wanted to tell.

"I try to be disciplined when I am working on a book and to start with a plot summary, followed by a chapter-by-chapter breakdown of the story, anything to get me over the initial horror of having to put something down on paper. . . . Later the book starts to take on a life of its own as the story and characters begin to evolve from the writing. This is the exciting part. A book only begins to work for me when I can hear the characters talking inside my head as I write. In *The Raven's Son,* a boy I had intended to make into a warrior sat down beside his Druid cousin and asked to be trained as a Druid. It was not what I had planned at all. This is the stage when all my careful plot summaries go out the window.

"I do a lot of reading to research the Celtic background for my books, but I try to forget it when I am writing, so that the historical detail arrives by osmosis rather than a deliberate effort. I take lots of photographs of potential locations and refer to them as I write. Sometimes there have been spooky coincidences. In *The Druid's Head* I thought I had invented an appropriate grove for my Druid, all twisted oak trees and thick green moss. Some months later I found an identical grove when walking in Pembrokeshire. It was just as I had imagined it, and it even had the right mystic 'feel.' Then I discovered that there had been an Iron Age settlement of the right date on the site of this particular wood and, later, that there were rumors of a Druid school having been there. Gradually, as I wrote, I began to take such coincidences for granted and accept them as some form of synchronicity.

"Although I sometimes make rough drafts of odd pages using pen and paper, I rely heavily on my Apple Mac computer for the bulk of my writing. My work evolves, rather than springing fully-formed onto the page. I spend hours swapping paragraphs and even cutting and pasting chapters together and cannot imagine working in this kind of way without the computer. I also like to play favorite CDs on the computer as I work. My working environment is very much about establishing the right kind of mood, the right music, plenty of plants, a small tabletop fountain, and photographs and paintings of Pembrokeshire that I can gaze at while I am thinking.

"When it is sunny enough I take work out into the garden to correct. I have been more wary recently, since a friend told me that, one afternoon while I had been working, the police had been chasing a violent criminal through the land behind ours. I realized with horror that I had been out there all the time, only a hundred yards away. I must have been concentrating so hard on my writing that I had heard nothing. Sometimes it is not good to become too far removed from the real world!

"My books to date have had an early Celtic setting. Much of my time is spent researching this period and visiting Iron Age hill-forts in Britain. I am also interested in the true background to the Arthurian legends. These are from the Dark Ages, not medieval times, but so much has been written about Arthur that it would be hard to find a new angle. I am also learning Welsh—a reinforcement of my own Celtic roots. My grandmother was Welsh-speaking, but the language lapsed in my family when she moved to London. Despite all the Celtic research, I have a feeling that my next book may branch off in a totally different direction—urban London, maybe."

For More Information See

PERIODICALS

School Librarian, November, 1997, p. 190.

*　　*　　*

BRANFORD, Henrietta 1946-

Personal

Born January 12, 1946, in India; daughter of John (a soldier) and Sylvia (Longstaff) Branford; married Paul Carter (a photographer); children: Jack, Rose, Polly. *Education:* Goldsmiths' College, London, Certificate in Community and Youth Work, 1972. *Politics:* Labour party. *Hobbies and other interests:* Walking, landscape, countryside, food.

Addresses

Home—7 College Road, Southampton, SO19 9GD, England. *Agent*—David Higham Associates Ltd., 5-8

Henrietta Branford

Lower John St., Golden Square, London W1R 4HA, England.

Career

Writer, 1987—. Worked for a charity linking children and pensioners, 1967-70; worked as a volunteer school governor, 1988-98.

Awards, Honors

Smarties Book Prize, Book Trust, 1994, for *Dimanche Diller,* and 1998 (Bronze Award) for *Fire, Bed and Bone; The Guardian* Children's Fiction Award, shortlisted in 1995 for *Dimanche Diller* and in 1997 for *The Fated Sky,* winner in 1998 for *Fire, Bed and Bone;* Carnegie Medal Shortlist, Library Association (Britain), 1997, and Books in the Middle: Outstanding Titles, *Voice of Youth Advocates,* 1998, both for *Fire, Bed and Bone.*

Writings

NOVELS; FOR CHILDREN

Clare's Summer, illustrated by Elsie Lennox, HarperCollins (London), 1993.
Dimanche Diller, illustrated by Lesley Harker, HarperCollins, 1994, Chivers North America (Hampton, NH), 1995.
Dimanche Diller in Danger, illustrated by Lesley Harker, HarperCollins, 1994, Chivers North America, 1996.
Dimanche Diller at Sea, illustrated by Emma Chichester-Clark, HarperCollins, 1996.
The Fated Sky, Hodder Children's Books (London), 1996.
Spacebaby, illustrated by Ellis Nadler, HarperCollins, 1996.
Fire, Bed and Bone, Walker (London), 1997, Candlewick (Cambridge, MA), 1998.
A Chance of Safety, Hodder Children's Books, 1998.
White Wolf, Walker, 1998, Candlewick, 1999.

OTHER

Royal Blunder (short stories), illustrated by Nicki Bowers, Transworld (London), 1990.
Royal Blunder and the Haunted House (short stories), illustrated by James Mayhew, Transworld, 1994.
Birdo (picture book), illustrated by Wayne Anderson, Random House (London), 1995.
Someone Somewhere (picture book), illustrated by Lesley Harker, Random House, 1995.
Nightmare Neighbours (chapter book), illustrated by Tim Archbold, HarperCollins, 1995.
(Reteller) *The Theft of Thor's Hammer,* illustrated by Dave Bowyer, Heinemann (Jordan Hill, England), 1996.
Ruby Red: Tales from the Weedwater (short stories), illustrated by John Lupton, HarperCollins, 1998.
Hansel and Gretel, Scholastic (London), 1998.

Birdo was translated into Danish in 1995.

Work in Progress

Spacebaby and the Mega-Volt Monster, a sequel to *Spacebaby,* for HarperCollins, 1999; *Dipper Dockens* and *Dipper's Island,* both for Walker, 1999; *The Wonderful Secret,* a picture book (may be renamed *Prosper's Mountain*), for Hutchinson, 1999; *Little Pig Figwort,* a picture book illustrated by Claudio Munoz, for HarperCollins, 1999, and *Proud Pig Figwort,* a possible sequel; *Ice Pie,* a picture book, for HarperCollins; *Lonely Only and the Sunny Day,* a picture book; "Into the Dark," a short story to be included in a millennium anthology edited by Wendy Cooling, for Collins; *Beauty and the Beast,* a retelling illustrated by Quentin Blake, to form part of a commemorative anthology for Amnesty International; and "other projects at present too nebulous to mention!"

Foreign language editions are planned for *The Fated Sky, A Chance of Safety, Spacebaby, Fire, Bed and Bone, White Wolf,* and *The Wonderful Secret.* Negotiations have taken place for animation rights to *Spacebaby.*

Sidelights

English author Henrietta Branford is known internationally for her critically acclaimed works for children, which range from picture books to novels. She started her writing career at age forty, after pursuing a variety of other jobs and raising three children. She told *SATA:* "My training had been as a Youth and Community Worker, but when I felt ready to return to work—when my youngest child was settled into primary school—I wanted to try writing." Branford's first work, a picture book called *Royal Blunder,* chronicles the adventures of the title character, a magical cat. Royal Blunder can fly, change size, and give his owner rides on his back. Through the cat's escapades, children learn valuable lessons about such experiences as danger and loss. Julia Marriage praised the book's "skilful blend of humour, excitement and pathos" in a *School Librarian* review. Another successful picture book, *Birdo,* features the tale of young Jocasta, who is under the spell of a witch. With the help of her only friend, a wren named Birdo, Jocasta escapes from the witch and breaks the spell, bringing the story to a surprising ending. *School Librarian* contributor Prue Goodwin praised the book's magical, fairy-tale characteristics, noting the "ethereal quality about both the written and visual texts." Kevin Steinberger, writing for *Magpies,* said, "Stories like *Birdo* nourish the imagination, affirm worthy values, and invariably please with their exotic drama and mystery."

Branford is also the author of several novels for children, including the much-celebrated *Dimanche Diller.* In this work, the title character is rescued by a group of nuns after surviving a shipwreck that kills both her parents. However, Dimanche's troubles begin again when the nuns are tricked into giving her up to the evil Valburga Vilemile, who masquerades as Dimanche's aunt in order to steal the fortune left to the girl by her parents. The book chronicles the adventures of Dimanche and a special nanny, Polly Pugh, as they try to outwit Valburga. In a review for *The Junior Bookshelf,* D. A. Young called *Dimanche Diller* "an excellent light-hearted entertaining read with a captivating style of humour; a positive and enriching experience to be highly recommended." Dimanche's adventures continue in *Dimanche Diller in Danger* and *Dimanche Diller at Sea.* Branford's next novel, *The Fated Sky,* is set in Viking times. The main character, a young girl named Ran, lives with her mother and grandmother after the disappearance of her father and brother at sea. On the way to a neighboring farm for a winter celebration, Ran's mother is killed by wolves, and Ran is held to blame. Facing the threat of being sacrificed in recompense for the attack, Ran falls in love with a blind musician and escapes to Iceland to start a new life. Val Randall, writing in *Books for Keeps,* called *The Fated Sky* a "skillfully paced" and "beautifully written" novel.

The Fated Sky was followed by two novels with greatly differing settings. *Spacebaby* is the story of an unusually intelligent child named Moses. Moses can calculate the power of an electromagnetic wave and use the Internet to fix the earth's gravitational fault. As children read about Moses's adventures, they also get science lessons on topics such as photosynthesis and electricity in what Cherrie Warwick called an "unpredictable, clever and funny book" in a *School Librarian* review. Shortlisted for the Carnegie Medal and winner of the *Guardian* Award, *Fire, Bed and Bone* is set in fourteenth-century feudal England during the historic peasant revolt led by Wat Tyler. The story is told from the point of view of a hunting dog whose master and mistress are arrested for attending revolutionary rallies. The heroic hound rescues the couple's children and lets her owners know they are safe. Reviewers praised the way in which the novel entertains and, at the same time, educates children about an important historical period. A *Publishers Weekly* critic praised the novel, noting especially Branford's "subtle, poetic writing" and how the book "evokes both the splendor of nature and the turbulence of the times." Shelle Rosenfeld, writing for *Booklist,* commended Branford's "exceptionally drawn characters" and called the novel "both irresistible adventure and educational historical fiction." Writing in the *Riverbank Review,* Perry Nodelman called *Fire, Bed and Bone* "a model of what good historical fiction should be."

Branford told *SATA:* "My writing grew out of my childhood reading, which in turn grew out of an isolated rural upbringing—rich and fertile soil for a writer. My reading was demanding—the best of the classics. Books and pictures that have influenced my work are Shakespeare and the Bible—wonderful language in both of them. Also fairy tales retold by Andrew Land, George MacDonald's books, BB (Watkins-Pitchford), Rudyard Kipling, John Masefield, Tove Janson, Joan Aiken, and the illustrators BB, Quentin Blake, Maurice Sendak, Arthur Rackham, and Walter Crane.

"I don't tailor my work for any particular market—I write what I want to write and hope that someone will want to read it. My work for older readers tends to be

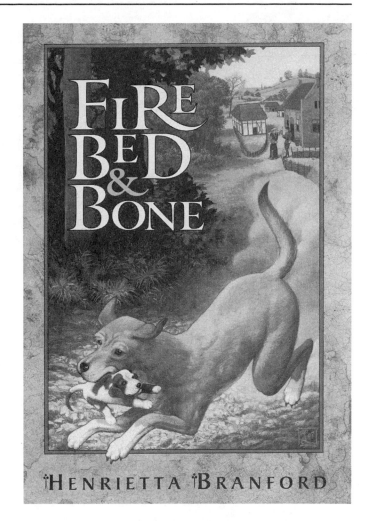

Set in fourteenth-century feudal England, Branford's story is narrated by a hunting dog who aids his master and mistress when they are arrested for attending rallies during the historic peasant revolt. (Cover illustration by Bryan Leister.)

tough and demanding, both emotionally and intellectually. I love language and refuse to dumb down. I hope my work for all ages expresses the value of love and courage. I want my books to say to children: 'take courage.' We can't always keep our children safe. But we can try to make them strong and brave.

"I don't illustrate my own work—if you could see my artwork you would understand why. On the whole I work a normal day, thinking, reading, daydreaming, pondering, writing, wondering, drafting, and redrafting over and over again. I read all my work several times aloud to check the rhythms.

"My advice to aspiring writers and illustrators is this: read and look at the best work you can find, and lots of it. Spend time with people of the age you wish to write for. Try hard to remember who you were back then. Don't compromise. Don't be market-led—write what you want to write. Good luck."

Works Cited

Review of *Fire, Bed and Bone, Publishers Weekly,* February 16, 1998, p. 212.

Goodwin, Prue, review of *Birdo, School Librarian,* August, 1995, p. 102.

Marriage, Julia, review of *Royal Blunder, School Librarian,* February, 1991, pp. 21-22.

Nodelman, Perry, review of *Fire, Bed and Bone, Riverbank Review,* fall, 1998, p. 31.

Randall, Val, review of *The Fated Sky, Books for Keeps,* November, 1996, p. 10.

Rosenfeld, Shelle, review of *Fire, Bed and Bone, Booklist,* March 15, 1998, p. 1240.

Steinberger, Kevin, review of *Birdo, Magpies,* July, 1995, pp. 21-22.

Warwick, Cherrie, review of *Spacebaby, School Librarian,* February, 1997, p. 23.

Young, D. A., review of *Dimanche Diller, Junior Bookshelf,* December, 1994, p. 211.

For More Information See

PERIODICALS

Junior Bookshelf, October, 1990, p. 227.
Kirkus Reviews, April 15, 1999, p. 627.
Magpies, March, 1995, p. 24.
Publishers Weekly, March 29, 1999, p. 105.
School Librarian, November, 1994, p. 150; February, 1997, p. 44.

*   *   *

BUELL, Janet 1952-

Personal

Born April 20, 1952; daughter of William F. (owner of an insurance agency) Buell, Sr. *Education:* Carthage College, B.A., 1974; Notre Dame College, M.Ed., 1993. *Politics:* Independent. *Hobbies and other interests:* Reading, anthropology, archaeology, indoor soccer, softball, hiking, health, and "possibilities."

Addresses

Home—251 Wallace Road, Goffstown, NH 03045. *E-mail*—jbuell@xtdl.com.

Career

Writer, educator. Round Lake School District, Round Lake, IL, grade school teacher, 1974-76; Timberlane Regional School District, Atkinson, NH, grade school teacher, 1976-86; Londonderry School District, NH, gifted program teacher and advanced math teacher, 1986—. Londonderry, New Hampshire cable television, creator, producer, and host of the children's show, *The Cosmic Learning Roadshow,* 1990-92. *Member:* Derry Regional Writers' Group.

Janet Buell

Awards, Honors

Anna Cross Giblin Nonfiction "Work in Progress" grant, Society of Children's Book Writers and Illustrators, for the "Time Travelers" series; Outstanding Children's Book, New Hampshire Writers' Project Literary Awards, for *Bog Bodies.*

Writings

NONFICTION; "TIME TRAVELERS" SERIES

Bog Bodies, Twenty-First Century Books, 1997.
Ice Maiden of the Andes, Twenty-First Century Books, 1997.
Ancient Horsemen of Siberia, Twenty-First Century Books, 1998.
Greenland Mummies, Twenty-First Century Books, 1998.

OTHER

Contributor to *The Guinness Book of Records* and numerous magazines, including *Cobblestone, Cricket, Special Reports, New Hampshire Editions, The Writer,* and *The Horse Digest.*

Work in Progress

A new nonfiction series; a novel. Current research interests include Leonardo da Vinci, natural history, creativity, memory, exploration, and the customs of other cultures.

Sidelights

Janet Buell told *SATA:* "Lots of kids dream about being authors when they grow up. I don't remember ever wanting that for myself. Mostly, when I bothered to think about growing up, I thought about being a veterinarian. I became a teacher instead—a stroke of luck, as it turns out, for my future as a writer.

"Back in the early 1980s, I was teaching third grade in Atkinson, New Hampshire. A man named Don Graves from the University of New Hampshire came to our school to study how children learn to write. I was really happy when he picked some students in my class as the subjects of his study.

"Don and his assistants spent lots of time watching these students. As they watched, the researchers saw how the children searched for ways through the writing process. For example, my kids always hoped their first drafts would be neat and clean so they wouldn't have to rewrite. They soon found out that neat and clean first drafts don't exist—at least not those that go on to be good pieces of writing.

"First drafts are ways to explore what you want to say. They can be very messy. All writers I know tug at their first words in some way or another. They change their minds. They rearrange. They cross out. They shuffle entire paragraphs from one place to another or annihilate them altogether. It's this tugging and rearranging—this hard work—that sets a writer apart from others who merely *want* to write.

"Don told me the only way I'd be able to teach my students to write well is to write. So I did. I wrote when my kids wrote—just like they wrote. I wrote drafts. I revised. I edited. I struggled to find words for the ideas buzzing about in my head. If you write, you know that struggle. I discovered that I *really* liked it.

"Then, as now, I was being open to possibilities. It's a philosophy that has stuck with me my whole life and has helped me to experience lots of different things. I've traveled different parts of the U.S., camping along the way. I've gone moth collecting at night with the Nature Conservancy. I've taught courses to adults. I've acted in a play and I started a show on a local cable network, with my students and me as hosts.

"Being open to possibilities launched me into a writing career. Around the time my students and I were learning to write, I went to a seminar for writers. Two women, who had recently started a history magazine for kids called *Cobblestone,* led one of the sessions. Later when I talked with them, they encouraged me to query the magazine. A query is a letter telling the editors about the article you'd like to write for them. It's the way a lot of magazine articles get written in this country.

"I figured I had nothing to lose by trying, so I sent the editors a query for an upcoming issue they were doing about cowboys and the old west. I had done a little research into the subject and discovered the interesting history of cattle branding. The editors thought it was interesting, too. They gave me a 'go-ahead' to write the article on speculation. When editors assign an article on speculation, it means they're not going to commit to buying it until they see if it's any good or not. Editors often give new writers assignments on speculation.

"As you can imagine, I was thrilled. Those feelings were dampened a bit by a few doubters. They warned me that my piece might not be accepted after all. I think they were trying to soften my disappointment if the article didn't get accepted. I didn't let that stop me. I knew that I could write a good article and I did. *Cobblestone* accepted it.

"I wrote more articles for *Cobblestone* and for other magazines. Then, one day I visited a local bog. After my visit, I wanted to learn more about this fascinating wetland. At the library I discovered the strange, grim secret buried in bogs. That secret is the bodies buried in some of them. These bodies are so old, yet so beautifully preserved, that they defy belief. It's very weird to see the face of a two thousand-year-old person, beard stubble and all. I also learned that technology has become so advanced that scientists can learn a lot about these ancient humans—even what they ate for their last meal!

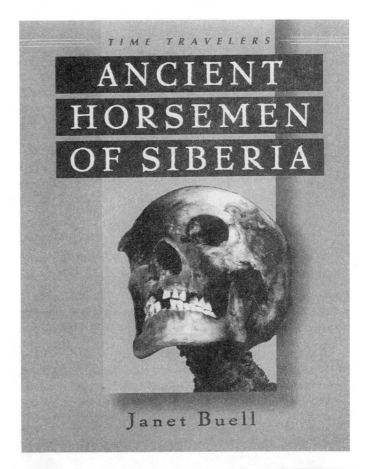

Buell describes the ancient burial site of a Pazyryk woman found preserved in an icy tomb with her horses and possessions, then explains to readers what the site reveals about the lives and culture of these people.

"Right away I knew I had to write a book about it. No one I knew had ever heard about bog bodies, and I wanted to tell everyone about them. Before I could start, though, I learned about other ancient human remains. Some of these remains were frozen on mountain tops or in arctic graves or on the high plateaus of Siberia. Instead of writing one book, I decided to write a series of books called *Time Travelers*.

"The next step was to write a proposal. A lot of people think you always write the book first and then look for a publisher. That's not the case with nonfiction. My proposal explained to publishers what I wanted to do. I sent it to five different publishers before Twenty-First Century Books accepted it.

"It took a little less than two years to write the four books in *Time Travelers*. Mostly I wrote during my summer break from teaching, but I also wrote during the school year—in the evenings or on weekends. For a long time it seemed like the books would *never* get done.

"Along the way I had help from my editor, of course, and from people in my writers' group. My writers' group meets twice a month to share with each other the things we've written. After we read, we critique each other's work. The writers in my group offer good criticism about what they think works in my writing and what doesn't. Having other writers critique in this way helps a lot. Instead of saying, 'I like this' or 'I don't like this,' they give reasons for liking or disliking something. They expect the same kind of careful reading for their work, too. It's also great to have friends who are writers. We talk about writing, books, movies, and other things related to something we all love—language.

"I hope to keep using language to make more books. I've really enjoyed getting awards for my work and recognition from book reviewers. Most of all, I like hearing from readers. Let me know what you think of my books!"

Commentators have responded favorably to Buell's *Greenland Mummies* and *Ancient Horsemen of Siberia*, books belonging to her *Time Travelers* series. *School Library Journal* contributor Cathryn A. Camper described *Greenland Mummies* as "useful to students studying Inuit life and sure to interest mummy enthusiasts." In the book, Buell explores evidence provided by the five hundred-year-old mummified remains of Inuit people discovered in Greenland by Hans and Jokum Gronvold. As she pieces together information from these rare scientific finds, Buell details the lives of the primitive Inuit people for her young readers. Camper praised the author's "fascinating details about how these people hunted with harpoons, constructed igloos and sod huts, battled frostbite, and gave themselves tattoos with needle and thread."

Ancient Horsemen of Siberia describes the ancient burial site of a Pazyryk woman found preserved in an icy tomb with her horses and possessions. As in *Greenland Mummies*, Buell examines in *Ancient Horsemen* what the site reveals about a people who lived long ago. In her review for *School Library Journal*, Elizabeth Talbot praised the author for going "beyond the [burial site] discovery to examine how the Russian archeologist Natalya Polosmak and her colleagues made educated guesses about the lives and culture of [these] individuals who rode horses and tended other animals." Talbot also applauded the author for clearly presenting a complex and interesting subject, and for further assisting the reader with the "valuable additions" of a glossary, a timeline, and suggestions for further reading.

Works Cited

Camper, Carolyn A., review of *Greenland Mummies*, *School Library Journal*, October, 1998, p. 152.

Talbot, Elizabeth, review of *Ancient Horsemen of Siberia*, *School Library Journal*, October, 1998, pp. 151-52.

*   *   *

BUTTERWORTH, Nick 1946-

Personal

Born in 1946, in Kingsbury, North London, England; married 1975; wife's name, Annette; children: Ben, Amanda.

Career

Author and illustrator of children's books. Graphics and typographic designer; TV AM (England), presenter for "Rub-a-Dub-Tub" children's program.

Awards, Honors

Runner-up, British Book Awards for Illustration, 1992, for *After the Storm*.

Writings

AUTHOR AND ILLUSTRATOR

B. B. Blacksheep and Company: A Collection of Favourite Nursery Rhymes, Macdonald, 1981.

My Mom Is Excellent, Walker (London), 1989, Candlewick, 1994.

My Dad Is Awesome, Walker, 1989, Candlewick, 1992.

(Editor) *Nick Butterworth's Book of Nursery Rhymes*, Aurum, 1990, Viking, 1991.

My Grandma Is Wonderful, Walker, 1991, Candlewick, 1991.

My Grandpa Is Amazing, Walker, 1991, Candlewick, 1992.

Amanda's Butterfly, Collins (London), 1991, Delacorte, 1991.

Jack the Carpenter and His Friends, Walker, 1991.

Jill the Farmer and Her Friends, Walker, 1991.

Busy People, Candlewick, 1992.

Making Faces, Walker, 1993, Candlewick, 1993.

When It's Time for Bed, HarperCollins (London), 1994, Little, Brown, 1994.

When There's Work to Do, HarperCollins, 1994, Little, Brown, 1994.

When We Go Shopping, HarperCollins, 1994, Little, Brown, 1994.
When We Play Together, HarperCollins, 1994, Little, Brown, 1994.
All Together Now!, HarperCollins, 1994, Little, Brown, 1995.
Thud!, Collins, 1997.
1-2-3—London, Collins, 1998.
A-B-C—London, Collins, 1998.
Jingle Bells, HarperCollins, 1998.

AUTHOR AND ILLUSTRATOR; "UPNEY JUNCTION" SERIES

Treasure Trove at Upney Junction, Macdonald, 1983.
A Windy Day at Upney Junction, Macdonald, 1983.
Invasion at Upney Junction, Macdonald, 1983.
A Monster at Upney Junction, Macdonald, 1983.

*AUTHOR AND ILLUSTRATOR; "PERCY THE PARK KEEPER"
SERIES*

One Snowy Night, Collins, 1989.
After the Storm, HarperCollins, 1992, published in the United States as *One Blowy Night,* Little, Brown, 1992.
The Rescue Party, Collins, 1993, Little, Brown, 1993.
The Secret Path, Collins, 1993, Little Brown, 1994.
A Year in Percy's Park (including *One Snowy Night, The Secret Path, The Rescue Party,* and *After the Storm*), Collins, 1995.
The Cross Rabbit, Collins, 1995.
Percy the Park Keeper Press-Out Book (including *The Fox's Hiccups* and *The Hedgehog's Balloon*), Collins, 1995.
The Fox's Hiccups, Collins, 1995.
The Treasure Hunt, Collins, 1996.
The Hedgehog's Balloon, Collins, 1996.
The Badger's Bath, Collins, 1996.

Nick Butterworth

Tales from Percy's Park (including *The Cross Rabbit, The Fox's Hiccups, The Hedgehog's Balloon,* and *The Badger's Bath*), Collins, 1996.
Percy the Park Keeper Activity Book, Collins, 1996.
Percy Helps Out: Sticker Book, Collins, 1996.
The Owl's Flying Lesson, Collins, 1997.
One Warm Fox, Collins, 1997.
Four Feathers in Percy's Park, Collins, 1998.
Percy the Park Keeper A-B-C, Collins, 1998.

Other works by Butterworth in the "Percy" series include *Percy in the Park 1-2-3, Percy in the Park Game's Book, Percy in the Park Coloring Book, Percy in the Park Sticker and Story Book,* and *A Year with Percy Coloring Book,* all published by Collins.

AUTHOR AND ILLUSTRATOR; WITH MICK INKPEN

The Nativity Play, Hodder and Stoughton (London, England), 1985, Little, Brown, 1985.
The House on the Rock, Marshall, Morgan & Scott (Basingstoke, England), 1986, Multnomah Press, 1986.
The Precious Pearl, Marshall, Morgan & Scott, 1986, Multnomah Press, 1986.
The Lost Sheep, Marshall, Morgan & Scott, 1986, Multnomah Press, 1986.
The Two Sons, Marshall, Morgan & Scott, 1986, Multnomah Press, 1986.
Nice and Nasty: A Book of Opposites, Hodder and Stoughton, 1987, published in the United States as *Nice or Nasty: A Book of Opposites,* Little, Brown, 1987.
I Wonder at the Zoo, Marshall Pickering (Basingstoke, England), 1987, Zondervan, 1987.
I Wonder in the Garden, Marshall Pickering, 1987, Zondervan, 1987.
I Wonder in the Country, Marshall Pickering, 1987, Zondervan, 1987.
I Wonder at the Farm, Marshall Pickering, 1987, published in the United States as *I Wonder on the Farm,* Zondervan, 1987.
Who Made . . . In the Country, HarperCollins, 1987.
Who Made . . . On the Farm, HarperCollins, 1987.
Who Made . . . At the Zoo, Marshall Pickering, 1987.
Who Made . . . In the Garden, Marshall Pickering, 1987.
Sports Day, Hodder and Stoughton, 1988.
The Magpie's Story: Jesus and Zacchaeus, Marshall Pickering, 1988.
The Mouse's Story: Jesus and the Storm, Marshall Pickering, 1988.
The Cat's Tale: Jesus at the Wedding, Marshall Pickering, 1988.
The Fox's Tale: Jesus Is Born, Marshall Pickering, 1988.
The Good Stranger, Marshall Pickering, 1989.
Just Like Jasper!, Hodder and Stoughton, 1989, Little, Brown, 1989.
The Little Gate, Marshall Pickering, 1989, HarperCollins, 1992.
The Rich Farmer, Marshall Pickering, 1989, HarperCollins, 1992.
The Ten Silver Coins, Marshall Pickering, 1989.
The School Trip, Hodder and Stoughton, 1990, Delacorte, 1990.

Wonderful Earth!, Hunt & Thorpe (Alton, England), 1990, Nelson, 1998.

Field Day, Delacorte, 1991.

Jasper's Beanstalk, Hodder and Stoughton, 1992, Bradbury Press, 1993.

Stories Jesus Told (including *The House on the Rock, The Lost Sheep, The Precious Pearl, The Two Sons, The Ten Silver Coins, The Rich Farmer, The Little Gate,* and *The Good Stranger*), Gold 'n' Honey (Sister, OR), 1994, Marshall Pickering, 1996.

Opposites, Hodder Children's, 1997.

ILLUSTRATOR; WITH MICK INKPEN; ALL WRITTEN BY ELIZABETH LAWRENCE IN CONSULTATION WITH NOREEN WETTON

Can You Do This?, Nelson, 1986.

Come Up and Play, Nelson, 1986.

Do You Like My Hat?, Nelson, 1986.

Do You Like My House?, Nelson, 1986.

I Am Going to Hide, Nelson, 1986.

It Is Too Big, Nelson, 1986.

Look What I Can Do, Nelson, 1986.

May I Come In?, Nelson, 1986.

May I Play with You?, Nelson, 1986.

Where Is the Monster?, Nelson, 1986.

Where Is the Mouse?, Nelson, 1986.

I Like Sausages, Nelson, 1986.

Mrs. Rabbit Gets Locked Out, Nelson, 1987.

Lolli and Pop in Trouble, Nelson, 1987.

ILLUSTRATOR; ALL WRITTEN BY ANNETTE BUTTERWORTH

Jake, Hodder & Stoughton, 1995.

Jake Again, Hodder Children's, 1996.

Jake in Trouble, Hodder Children's, 1997.

The Jake Collection (including *Jake Again* and *Jake in Trouble*), Hodder Children's, 1998.

OTHER

(Illustrator with Mick Inkpen) Malcolm and Meryl Doney, *Who Made Me?,* Marshall Pickering, 1987, Zondervan, 1992.

Also contributed illustrations to a series of Christian instructional booklets for children.

Adaptations

The "Percy the Park Keeper" series has been adapted as a cartoon for British television and several of the "Percy" books have been recorded on audio cassette.

Sidelights

Nick Butterworth is a British author-illustrator of children's books best known for his "Percy the Park Keeper" picture books, a series which started in 1989 with *One Snowy Night.* Published in fifteen languages, the series has sold more than two millions copies worldwide. Butterworth also worked in collaboration with author-illustrator Mick Inkpen for many years, and together they created the popular "Mice of Upney Junction" cartoon strip, as well as the picture books *Just Like Jasper* and *Jasper's Beanstalk.*

Born in a London suburb in 1946, Butterworth and his family moved to Romford, in the English county of Essex, when the author was three. There his parents took up the running of a sweet shop. From his father—who appeared in amateur reviews as a comedian before World War II—Butterworth inherited a sly sense of humor and an eye for comic situations. In Romford schools he was something of a passive student, but by the time he reached the Royal Liberty School, Butterworth fared much better academically. Sketching was one of his early passions. He and his brother would fill notebooks with comic-book style drawings; but whereas his brother later went into theology, Butterworth stuck with art. He intended to go to art school, but when his mother heard of a paid apprenticeship in the design department of a printing school, he was talked into that course instead of the study of studio art.

"I don't regret the way my life's gone," Butterworth told Stephanie Nettell in a *Books for Keeps* interview. "But I wish I'd worked harder. I would have liked to have been to art school, though they did send me one day a week to the printing department at Watford College." From an instructor at Watford, Butterworth learned of a London design firm looking for new talent. Joining the firm, Butterworth got his first taste of professional design. After some success freelancing, Butterworth decided to start his own design studio. In 1969, along with two colleagues he set up a design consultancy studio in Romford, working on "a lot of catalogue and packaging work," according to Butterworth. In 1970, his young friend Mick Inkpen joined the firm in his pre-Cambridge year off, and stayed on.

Butterworth's first book was the result of desultory doodling: he developed illustrations for four nursery rhymes which at the time he thought might make good greeting cards. When others saw these illustrations, they convinced Butterworth to make a book of the nursery rhymes and thus was born *B. B. Blacksheep and Company,* a book which a reviewer for *Growing Point* called a "refreshingly bizarre look at familiar jingles." Butterworth turned many of these nursery rhymes on their heads, looking at them from fresh and often humorous perspectives: Jack and Jill in this rendering are toothy rabbits; the mouse comes down the clock on a parachute; Humpty Dumpty is a chocolate Easter egg. Brian Alderson, reviewing the book in *Times Educational Supplement,* noted that Butterworth's collection of favorite nursery rhymes "are stylish and often unexpected."

Publication of this picture book brought an offer from the *Sunday Express* newspaper for a comic strip, and Butterworth and Inkpen subsequently developed the cheeky mice living in the deserted railway station at Upney Junction. The Butterworth-Inkpen collaboration extended to television, as well, with the two hosting a children's show for eighteen months. "I learned a lot from [Inkpen's] colouring," Butterworth told Nettell in his interview. "My work has always been line-oriented and it used to be more laboured . . . until I realised that reproducing reality isn't necessarily the best way of getting what you want across." Butterworth's draftsmanship rubbed off on Inkpen as much as Inkpen's spontaneity and appreciation for abstract line influenced Butterworth.

The Nativity Play, one of their earliest collaborations, was well received both in England and in the United States. A *Publishers Weekly* contributor commented that the duo "will delight readers of all ages ... with their Christmas book," and went on to note that the "sweet, funny story is illustrated perfectly by brightly colored scenes of feverish activity." In the story, children and their parents at a local school prepare for the Christmas pageant, with all the attendant confusion, missed cues, and last-minute stage fright. A reviewer for *Growing Point* noted of the British publication that "colour, exuberance and mood come over with heart-rending force in a descriptive picture book which encapsulates this infinitely varied once-a-year amateur enterprise." Denise M. Wilms, reviewing *The Nativity Play* for *Booklist,* concluded that "this is a droll diversion that will please children, who will recognize themselves, and amuse their parents, who will find chuckles between the lines."

Butterworth and Inkpen also worked together on *Nice or Nasty,* "a book about opposites with immediate appeal," according to a reviewer for *Publishers Weekly.* "Readers will find a memorable roller-coaster ride between up and down, first and last," continued this same reviewer. *Booklist* critic Ilene Cooper concluded that the "oversize

Lottie and Jack, two tiny mice who are antagonized by a menacing cat, devise a plan to repay him for ruining their Christmas.

illustrations are expertly executed, and the whole format has a clean, fresh look." However, the most popular collaborative effort of the two has remained the "Jasper" books, *Just Like Jasper* and *Jasper's Beanstalk.* "In another effort from this talented British team," noted a *Publishers Weekly* contributor in a review of the first title, "plump, likable Jasper the cat heads for the toy store with his birthday money." The problem once he gets there: what to buy? There are too many choices, but finally he decides on the purchase of a toy kitten, who is a ringer for himself. "Children will sympathize with Jasper's dilemma and appreciate his sound choice," concluded the reviewer. Janie Schomberg remarked in a *School Library Journal* review that the book was a "pleasant offering for toddler story hours," while a *Growing Point* critic concluded that "brilliant primary colours mark each scene and the book as a whole has a sense of excited movement to extend the simple joke of humanising a cat's thoughts but not its appearance." The two illustrator-writers returned to Jasper in 1992 with *Jasper's Beanstalk,* in which the amiable cat tries unsuccessfully to grow a bean plant. He plants it and lovingly tends to it, but when it fails to sprout he digs it up and throws it aside. Untended, however, the bean develops into a magnificent beanstalk. "Jasper is a delightful character," noted a reviewer for *The Junior Bookshelf,* "and many young children are likely to enjoy this story of his attempt at gardening." Stephanie Zvirin, writing in *Booklist,* called this second Jasper title a "delightful, bubbly book, ideal for group sharing," while Moira Small described it in a *Books for Keeps* review as

In **My Mom Is Excellent,** *written and illustrated by Butterworth, the young male narrator tells the reader about the incredible things his mother does.*

Amiable cat Jasper tries unsuccessfully to grow a bean plant, which thrives when he tosses it away in Butterworth's humorous picture book, written and illustrated with Mick Inkpen. (From Jasper's Beanstalk.*)*

a "delightful picture book with a simple story to help very young children understand how things grow."

Though Butterworth teamed up with Inkpen for a few more titles, mostly the two have concentrated on their individual work. For Butterworth, that has been primarily the "Percy the Park Keeper" books, a series still growing in number. Starting with *One Snowy Night,* the books highlight the trials and tribulations of a park keeper who looks remarkably like Butterworth himself. In this opening title, Percy finds his hospitality strained to the limit when one animal after the other comes to him seeking refuge from the snow. "The result—too many animals," commented Phyllis G. Sidorski in *School Library Journal.* The bedclothes become tangled, animals get lost in the shuffle. "The illustrations are lighthearted and the penultimate scene of the cluttered room is a wealth of eye-catching details," Sidorski added.

In *The Rescue Party,* Percy takes a day off and relaxes with his animal friends in the park. Things start out fine until a jumping game ends up with a rabbit tumbling down an abandoned well. Percy throws a rope down to rescue the frightened rabbit, who ties it to a log instead of herself. Not to worry; everything turns out happily in the end in this "cozy little story, distinguished by amiable illustrations," according to a critic for *Kirkus Reviews.* Jan Shephard, writing in *School Library Journal,* concluded that the "bright watercolor illustra-

tions depict the likable and humorous characters" and that the book was a "great read-aloud."

Further adventures of Percy include the aftermath of a storm, the park animals' housing problems, a fox with a serious case of the hiccups, and an angry bunny, among many others. In *The Secret Path,* Percy decides to get the park maze in order, and his furry friends decide to play a joke on him at the same time, finding their way to the center of the maze to surprise him when finally he gets there. Everyone receives a surprise when he arrives, however, for Percy has trimmed the maze into decorative shapes. Beverley Mathias, writing in *School Librarian,* called the book "great fun for everyone, including those under nine," while Carolyn Phelan dubbed it "simple and beguiling" in a *Booklist* review. "Butterworth's deft line-and-watercolor-wash artwork reflects the general tone of the text," Phelan commented, noting also that the "loving characters and the mild adventure will please young children."

Badger gets filthy digging all day in *The Badger's Bath,* and Percy decides it is time for him to take a bath. But Badger has other ideas about hygiene, so by the time Percy sets the soapy bath out under a tree, Badger has taken off. Instead of wasting the bath water, Percy dons swimming trunks and takes a soak himself. A reviewer for *The Junior Bookshelf* called the book a "charming story," remarking also that "Percy is such a realistically rotund and plain featured hero that the reader readily suspends disbelief." In *The Treasure Hunt,* Percy sets up a search for a treasure which he—without thinking—eats. Judith Sharman, writing in *Books for Keeps,* called this "another whimsical tale about Percy the Park Keeper and his friends." Trevor Dickinson commented in *School Librarian* that the illustrations in this book "are up to Nick Butterworth's usual very high standards—clear and quietly amusing."

Though best known for the Percy books, Butterworth does not rest on their laurels. He has dozens of books to his credit, among them the popular *Nick Butterworth's Book of Nursery Rhymes, Amanda's Butterfly,* and *When It's Time for Bed.* His 1995 work *All Together Now!* is a popular lift-the-flap book. "The flaps in this chuckly game of hide-and-seek themselves form part of the pictures," explained Nettell in her interview with Butterworth. The premise of this activity book is that a little boy's six animal friends are hiding from him at the outset of a picnic, and he must find them. A *Kirkus Reviews* contributor remarked that "not only do children have the satisfaction of finding the animals, but they have words to shout as they search." Mary Ann Bursk, writing in *School Library Journal,* noted that "toddlers will enjoy this interactive book one-to-one, while beginning readers will delight in sharing it with younger siblings." A Butterworth title dealing with Christmas is his 1998 book *Jingle Bells,* a story of Yuletide mice in a stable. "The simply told tale makes a good nonsectarian read-aloud," commented Anne Connor in *School Library Journal.* "Children will enjoy these plucky mice who work together to ensure a happier new year once their enemy is foiled," concluded Connor.

Plucky is an apposite term for many of Butterworth's picture-book protagonists. Whether it be the mice of Upney Junction, Jasper the cat, or Percy the Park Keeper, Butterworth imbues these characters with a sense of humor and quirky optimism. His texts and illustrations cover a wide spectrum of childhood concerns, from sharing to playing hide-and-seek. As Butterworth told Nettell, he has loads of ideas for new books and does not want to be simply pegged as Percy the Park Keeper's creator. "There's no next time—this is my go, and I must make the most of it."

Works Cited

Alderson, Brian, review of *B. B. Blacksheep and Company, Times Educational Supplement,* January 15, 1992, p. 33.

Review of *All Together Now!, Kirkus Reviews,* September 1, 1995, p. 1277.

Review of *B. B. Blacksheep and Company, Growing Point,* November, 1981, pp. 3980-81.

Review of *The Badger's Bath, The Junior Bookshelf,* August, 1996, pp. 140-41.

Bursk, Mary Ann, review of *All Together Now!, School Library Journal,* March, 1996, p. 167.

Connor, Anne, review of *Jingle Bells, School Library Journal,* October, 1998, p. 40.

Cooper, Ilene, review of *Nice or Nasty: A Book of Opposites, Booklist,* June 15, 1987, p. 1598.

Dickinson, Trevor, review of *The Treasure Hunt, School Librarian,* February, 1997, p. 17.

Review of *Jasper's Beanstalk, The Junior Bookshelf,* June, 1992, p. 100.

Review of *Just Like Jasper, Growing Point,* November, 1989, p. 5249.

Review of *Just Like Jasper, Publishers Weekly,* September 8, 1989, p. 66.

Mathias, Beverley, review of *The Secret Path, School Librarian,* February, 1995, p. 16.

Review of *The Nativity Play, Growing Point,* November, 1985, p. 4528.

Review of *The Nativity Play, Publishers Weekly,* December 6, 1985, p. 75.

Nettell, Stephanie, "Authorgraph No. 32: Nick Butterworth," *Books for Keeps,* May, 1995, pp. 16-17.

Review of *Nice or Nasty: A Book of Opposites, Publishers Weekly,* June 12, 1987, p. 83.

Phelan, Carolyn, review of *The Secret Path, Booklist,* April 15, 1995, p. 1505.

Review of *The Rescue Party, Kirkus Reviews,* October 1, 1993, p. 1270.

Schomberg, Janie, review of *Just Like Jasper, School Library Journal,* May, 1990, p. 81.

Sharman, Judith, review of *The Treasure Hunt, Books for Keeps,* March, 1997, p. 18.

Shephard, Jan, review of *The Rescue Party, School Library Journal,* February, 1994, p. 78.

Sidorski, Phyllis G., review of *One Snowy Night, School Library Journal,* December, 1990, p. 70.

Small, Moira, review of *Jasper's Beanstalk, Books for Keeps,* July, 1993, p. 10.

Wilms, Denise M., review of *The Nativity Play, Booklist,* March 1, 1986, p. 1014.

Zvirin, Stephanie, review of *Jasper's Beanstalk, Booklist,* June 15, 1993, p. 920.

For More Information See

PERIODICALS

Books for Keeps, July, 1991, p. 10; July, 1995, p. 7.

Bulletin of the Center for Children's Books, May, 1987, p. 163.

The Junior Bookshelf, February, 1990, p. 13; August, 1990, p. 166; December, 1990, p. 276; February, 1994, p. 13; December, 1996, p. 227.

Publishers Weekly, April 17, 1995, p. 56; September 25, 1995, p. 55; April 27, 1998, p. 61.

School Librarian, August, 1991, p. 99.

School Library Journal, March, 1991, p. 168; May, 1991, p. 76; December, 1991, p. 80; July, 1995, p. 55.

Times Educational Supplement, November 7, 1997, p. 13.

—*Sketch by J. Sydney Jones*

C

CHENG, Christopher 1959-

Personal

Born May 10, 1959, in Sydney, Australia; son of Winston and Margaret Cheng. *Education:* Kuring-Gai CAE, diploma of teaching, 1980; Macquarie University, graduate coursework in children's literature. *Religion:* Anglican. *Hobbies and other interests:* Collecting Australian children's books, listening to music, playing the

Christopher Cheng

piano and guitar, visiting zoos and the Australian bush, writing songs.

Addresses

Home—P.O. Box 279, Newtown, New South Wales 2042, Australia. *Agent*—Fiona Inglis, Curtis Brown (Australia), 27 Union Street, Paddington, New South Wales 2021, Australia. *Electronic mail*—chengc@ ozemail.com.au.

Career

Taronga Zoo, Sydney, Australia, public relations assistant, 1981-84; relief/substitute teacher, 1981-84; infants/ primary teacher at Bourke Public School, Bourke, Australia, 1984-86, North Sydney Demonstration School, Sydney, 1987, and Dulwich Hill Public School, Sydney, 1994; education officer, Taronga Zoo Education Centre, Sydney, 1987-93; Dymocks Booksellers, Sydney, national children's development manager, 1994-98. Purdue University, author-education consultant, 1998—. Has served as author-in-residence at several public schools. *Member:* Australian Society of Authors, Children's Book Council of Australia, (New South Wales branch; committee member, 1996-98), Australian Geographic Society, Australian Booksellers Association (children's booksellers special interest group; committee member, 1998), Zoo Friends Association.

Awards, Honors

Shortlist, Wilderness Society Environment Award for Children's Literature, 1994, for *The Eyespy Book of Rainforest Animals;* Notable Book, Children's Book Council of Australia, Picture Book of the Year, Wilderness Society Environment Award for Children's Literature, and Shortlist, Koala Awards, all 1998, all for *One Child.*

Writings

(With Libby Hathorn) *Stuntumble Monday,* illustrated by Melissa Webb, Collins Dove, 1990.

The Eyespy Book of Night Creatures, illustrated by Michael Davis, Ashton Scholastic, 1990.

The Eyespy Book of Endangered Animals, illustrated by Michael Davis, Ashton Scholastic, 1991.

Bancks' Ginger Meggs and Friends Pet Care Book, illustrated by James Kemsley, Ashton Scholastic, 1992.

The Eyespy Book of Rainforest Animals, illustrated by Stephen Michael King, Ashton Scholastic, 1994.

The Eyespy Book of Party Animals, illustrated by Debbie Coombs, Ashton Scholastic, 1995.

One Child, illustrated by Steven Woolman, ERA Publications, 1997.

Rainforests, Heinemann Library, 1998.

Alpine Regions, Heineman Library, 1998.

Also author of several educational series books; contributor of articles and reviews to journals, including *Classroom* and *Journal of the International Association of Zoo Educators.*

Work in Progress

Dragons, the Real and the Unreal (picture book), for ERA Publications; *Zoo-U-Later,* illustrated by Kerry Millard, for ABC Enterprises; *My Dad* (picture book); a novel.

Sidelights

Christopher Cheng told *SATA:* "Lots of people ask me, 'Did you love animals as a child?,' 'What pets did you keep?,' and often, 'You must have spent heaps of time in zoos as a child.' Well, that isn't so. I certainly had the usual household pets lots of children have. For a little while, when I was very young, I had a puppy dog—a silky terrier. At other times I have also had the goldfish in the bowl and the budgie in the cage. I also remember going to Taronga Zoo a few times—mostly for school excursions.

"I certainly didn't spend days in my school years hunting through the backyard, or turning over rock and wood piles trying to catch lizards and insects to study them like the future naturalist is often thought to do. In fact, I think that I would have gone nuts at the thought of studying bugs and bug life. But I do always remember loving the bush—the sounds of nature, the smells of nature, and the feeling of being surrounded by wild or natural life. I like being around and working with people, but I just love jumping into my car and escaping to my favorite place in the mountains when I really need to take a break for a day.

"As a kid I also spent oodles of time watching people, talking to people, and reading books, newspapers, magazines, comics, and the occasional shop window; in fact, anything that had words written on it. But I certainly didn't read heaps and heaps. I also read the animal books, lots of them, but to me it always seemed strange that the books were often about animals from other countries. I sometimes used to think that we didn't have any animals of our own—but we certainly do, and

Cheng's picture book champions the power of each individual to make a difference in the ecology of our planet. (Cover illustration by Steven Woolman.)

they are fantastic, and that is why I probably like talking so much about Australian animals.

"I certainly wasn't born loving animals, or the bush, or wanting to be a 'nature' person, but I was taught very early on to have respect for all living things. Once I started doing singalongs at the zoo, I just haven't stopped admiring the wonder and the awesomeness of *all* of nature—but especially the animals. And now, well, I just love being a *natural* person and writing books.

"For absolute ages I have been writing—not books, but letters. I wrote letters to my relatives overseas. I wrote letters to my friends who had moved away. I wrote letters in class at school when I should have been listening to the teacher. And when I had no one else to write to, I wrote letters to myself. When I started teaching all over New South Wales, I began letter writing in a really big way. I was a long way from home where all my friends were, and the only way to keep in touch was to write it all down. So I wrote letters and sent them back to my friends—wherever they were. These weren't ordinary two-page hand-written letters, though. They were computerised letters, four or five pages long, with graphics and titles and borders—just like a real book. Some of my friends still have those letters. They pull them out every now and again to remind me of my life in the country. And now that I am working overseas in America far away from my beautiful family (who really are so special) and my wonderful friends, the Christopher Cheng Chronicles are sent to fill them in on *most* of the things that I am doing.

"Writing books is a little different than writing letters, though. It's lots of fun, but it takes a lot more brain strain. I actually started writing books a few years ago when I was asked to put down on paper the stuff that kids would like to know about animals of the night. I had been working with animals for a few years by then, so I knew a few strange things about animals. So what better thing to do than put them down in a book. That began *Night Creatures,* then *Endangered Animals,* then more animal books—who knows what will come next! (I do.)

"I believe I have many stories to tell. I believe that kids like the stories I tell. I love telling stories to kids. And I think that I know what kids want to read—and hopefully my stories are part of that. And I love writing. I love to sit down and write to see the words flow onto the computer screen, words that were just scribbled notes in my *Ideas Book* that I carry with me just about everywhere. I am filling in number nine now! Or maybe the words were scribbled on the back of a shopping docket, on an unfilled page in my diary on a day yet to come, on anything that would take scribbling. I've even scribbled ideas on a table cloth—a paper table-cloth that I tore when I left the restaurant so that I could take my writings with me. And maybe those words matched with luscious pictures from a superbly talented illustrator will create a picture book—that's just magical.

"The ideas come to me from the child I see crying, from children calling to friends, playing games, pretending it wasn't them, from the child doing things. My ideas are the things that I see, I feel, I hear, I experience. My ideas are also memories—memories of what it was like for me as a child, happenings that I remember from teaching, things that I have heard people say. Some of my ideas have been transformed into stories in books, some of them are stories that I hope to be, and others will never be stories—at least not yet.

"And why do I write for kids? Because I love it. I love the kids I write for. I love their honesty, their openness and their 'realness.' They'll tell me if the story sucks, but they also tell me if the child in my story is them. I love sitting on the floor with a bunch of kids, listening to their stories and they in turn listening to me (and children today need and want to be listened to). Nothing is better than the adulation, the adoration, and the love that you receive from kids—for the highest of highs, that's it. I write for the children in me, for the child in you and the children all around us.

"*One Child* was based on many kids I taught, kids who were so cheesed off at hearing that the world was in a mess, who also felt that adults were more talk than

action. It was the kids who said *we can* make a difference ('we' as in the kids)—and they actually do something about it. It's a pity that it is the kids who show us the way. *One Child* is a celebration of our kids, of kids together, and our magical world. Which is my other great passion: the wonder, the beauty, the gloriousness of nature. It's amazing what eight years in a zoo can do in opening one's eyes. Let's take care of our wonderful world.

"And what do I love? My family, kids, and nature with all its wonder, beauty, and gloriousness."

For More Information See

PERIODICALS

Magpies, March 1998.

OTHER

Author's website at http://www.chrischeng.com.

* * *

COHEN, Miriam 1926-

Personal

Born October 14, 1926, in Brooklyn, NY; daughter of Jacob and Bessie Echelman; married Sid Grossman, 1949 (died, 1955); married Monroe D. Cohen (a professor), May 31, 1959; children: (first marriage) Adam; (second marriage) Gabriel, Jem. *Education:* Attended Newburgh Free Academy, 1943, and Antioch College, 1944-45. *Politics:* Independent progressive. *Religion:* Jewish.

Addresses

Home and office—3916 49th St., Sunnyside, NY 11104.

Career

Writer.

Awards, Honors

Parents' Choice award, 1984, for *Born to Dance Samba.*

Writings

"FIRST-GRADE FRIENDS" SERIES; ILLUSTRATED BY LILLIAN HOBAN

Will I Have a Friend?, Macmillan, 1967.
Best Friends, Macmillan, 1971.
The New Teacher, Macmillan, 1972.
Tough Jim, Macmillan, 1974.
When Will I Read?, Greenwillow, 1977.
"Bee My Valentine!," Greenwillow, 1978.
Lost in the Museum, Greenwillow, 1979.
First Grade Takes a Test, Greenwillow, 1980.
No Good in Art, Greenwillow, 1980.
Jim Meets the Thing, Greenwillow, 1981.
So What?, Greenwillow, 1982.

See You Tomorrow, Charles, Greenwillow, 1983.
Jim's Dog Muffins, Greenwillow, 1984.
Starring First Grade, Greenwillow, 1985.
Liar, Liar, Pants on Fire!, Greenwillow, 1985.
Don't Eat Too Much Turkey!, Greenwillow, 1987.
It's George!, Greenwillow, 1988.
See You in Second Grade!, Greenwillow, 1989.
The Real-Skin Rubber Monster Mask, Greenwillow, 1990.

OTHER

Born to Dance Samba, illustrated by Gioia Fiammenghi, Harper, 1984.
Marijuana, Its Effects on Mind and Body, Chelsea House, 1985.
Robert and Dawn Marie 4 Ever, Harper, 1986.
Laura Leonora's First Amendment, Lodestar, 1990.
Second-Grade Friends, illustrated by Diane Palmisciano, Scholastic, 1993.
Down in the Subway, illustrations by Melanie Hope Greenberg, DK Publishing, 1998.
Mimmy & Sophie Stories, illustrated by Thomas F. Yezerski, Farrar, Straus, 1999.

Author's works have been translated into Hebrew.

Adaptations

Will I Have a Friend? (filmstrip with cassette), Threshold Filmstrips, 1974.

Sidelights

Miriam Cohen is a writer with an agenda. An avid champion of the rights of children, she creates picture books and novels that showcase young people whose positive spirits turn adversity into something constructive. Frequently working as a team with illustrator Lillian Hoban, Cohen has written a series of popular picture books about a group of first graders that portrays the fears, joys, and curiosity of children beginning to forge their own path in the world. In addition to her picture books with Hoban, Cohen has also published several chapter books for older children, as well as several nonfiction titles.

Cohen was born in Brooklyn and grew up in Newburgh, New York, before enrolling at Antioch College. "School did not interest me very much," she recalled to *SATA*. "I only wanted to read. I read walking to school, at the dinner table, walking home from the library with the six books a week allowed me. I never thought of being a writer."

Her first book was written in the late 1960s, while Cohen was at home raising her infant son. "I've always been fascinated by the idea of bringing something into being that wasn't there before, like a painting or a play or a story," she explained to *SATA*. A meeting with an editor at Harper & Row encouraged the young mother to contemplate becoming an author. "I'd written a children's story (a very bad one) and I looked in the phone book for the nearest publisher," Cohen recalled. "Harper was closest to my apartment in Manhattan. So I just put

my first baby into his buggy with the story and pushed up the ten blocks. [The editor] looked at my work and said, 'This isn't it. But you *are* a writer. You must read everything that's been written for children, and then write something different, something that comes from you.'"

The editor's comments gave Cohen enough encouragement to keep trying. Eight years "and two babies" later her efforts paid off, and her first children's book was published in 1967. That story, *Will I Have a Friend?*, became the first in a long series of books written by Cohen and illustrated by Hoban. *Will I Have a Friend?* introduces young Jim and Paul, who are beginning their school career. Left with his dad's assurance that he would meet a new friend by the end of his first day of school, Jim worries as the hours go by and no friend emerges. Finally, during nap-time, he meets Paul, and the two find they have much in common. Praised as a "beguiling" and "meaningful picture book" by *Horn Book* contributor Virginia Haviland, *Will I Have a Friend?* proved popular with youngsters, parents, and reviewers alike, prompting Cohen and Hoban to continue the adventures of young Jim and his fellow classmates in the "First Grade Friends" series.

Cohen's and Hoban's work on their popular series of books would eventually span more than two decades. "First Grade Friends" includes many titles—from *Lost in the Museum* to *Liar, Liar, Pants on Fire!*—that reflect the antics of exuberant six- and seven-year-olds. "I loved watching nursery and kindergarten life as my boys went through," Cohen once related, explaining the inspiration for her "First Grade Friends" series. The third book in the series, *The New Teacher*, finds Jim, nervous at the arrival of a new instructor, telling jokes during morning recess about how terrible she is as a way of making himself feel more confident. "*The New Teacher* was written because I was angry and sad at the meanness of a few teachers (not those my boys had; they were wonderful)," Cohen explained. "But I didn't want my story to make little children anxious about school. So I made the new teacher's meanness only a fantasy rumor of how she *might* be. She isn't at all, as it turns out." Called a "little gem" by *School Librarian* critic Chris Brown, *The New Teacher* "has the same simplicity, the same humor, [and] the same appealing directness of text and illustrations" as its predecessors, in the opinion of a contributor to the *Bulletin of the Center for Children's Books.*

Other books in the "First Grade Friends" series include *Tough Jim,* in which Jim dresses as a muscle man for his class costume party; *When Will I Read?*, which reflects a child's frustration at being one of the last of his classmates to learn the secret of reading; and *"Bee My Valentine!,"* a mirror of many children's experiences as Valentine cards are handed around the classroom on that February day. In the entertaining *Lost in the Museum,* a field trip to New York City's Museum of Natural History turns into a search for missing students when the dinosaur bones become too much of a temptation for four boys. Academic-test anxiety is portrayed in *First*

The first title in a series of books about two young boys, Will I Have a Friend? *outlines Jim's worrisome first day of kindergarten and his emerging friendship with Paul. (Written by Miriam Cohen and illustrated by Lillian Hoban.)*

Grade Takes a Test, as Cohen "deals sensitively with the small insecurities of young children, including their problems with standardized tests," according to Ann A. Flowers of *Horn Book.* And in *Starring First Grade,* in the wake of the scramble for favorite roles in a performance of the *Three Billy Goats Gruff* to be acted out before the entire school, Jim finds himself cast as a silly old tree and feels a growing jealousy toward his friend Paul, who snagged the choice role: the troll. Each book features Hoban's illustrations of smiling, somewhat rumpled children from a variety of racial backgrounds.

In addition to her many books with illustrator Hoban, Cohen has authored several books for older readers that, like *Laura Leonora's First Amendment,* reflect the perceptions, thoughts, and apprehensions experienced by many middle graders and young teens. In her first teen novel, *Born to Dance Samba,* Cohen relates the story of eleven-year-old Maria Antonia, a young Brazilian girl

who hopes to qualify as the solo dancer at a public dance performance at Rio de Janeiro's annual carnival. Based on her own understanding of Brazilian culture gained during a two-year stay in that country, *Born to Dance Samba* shows the simple joys of even the poorest children, who make their home in the *barrio,* "and the fact that they make the best of their situation," according to a *Bulletin of the Center for Children's Books* contributor. "Cohen does much to encourage understanding," added *Booklist* reviewer Susan Roman, "not only by pointing up differences but also by showing the commonality of experiences felt by children in various parts of the world."

In *Robert and Dawn Marie 4 Ever,* Cohen introduces fourteen-year-old Robert, who narrates the story of his undying love for Dawn Marie. Living with a kindly elderly couple after his own mother decides that she can't handle raising children and so deposits him in a succession of foster homes, Robert meets and falls for a pretty Catholic school student who gives him the attention and affection that his mother never did. Praising the novel for being "sweet without being sugary," Zena Sutherland of the *Bulletin of the Center for Children's Books* noted that Cohen makes "the innocent rapture of a first love ... poignant and credible" by telling the story in Robert's own words. "Witty and compassionate, [*Robert and Dawn Marie 4 Ever*] is a testimony to the little acts of bravery and goodness that go unnoticed," added a *Kirkus Reviews* commentator.

Cohen's works are included in the Kerlan Collection at the University of Minnesota.

Works Cited

Review of *Born to Dance Samba, Bulletin of the Center for Children's Books,* September, 1984, p. 3.
Brown, Chris, review of *The New Teacher, School Librarian,* March, 1981, p. 21.
Flowers, Ann A., review of *First Grade Takes a Test, Horn Book,* December, 1980, p. 632.
Haviland, Virginia, review of *Will I Have a Friend?, Horn Book,* October, 1967, p. 581.
Review of *The New Teacher, Bulletin of the Center for Children's Books,* October, 1972, p. 24.
Review of *Robert and Dawn Marie 4 Ever, Kirkus Reviews,* November 1, 1986, p. 1651.
Roman, Susan, review of *Born to Dance Samba, Booklist,* May 1, 1984, p. 1236.
Sutherland, Zena, review of *Robert and Dawn Marie 4 Ever, Bulletin of the Center for Children's Books,* November, 1986, p. 45.

For More Information See

BOOKS

Something about the Author Autobiography Series, Vol. 11, Gale, 1991, pp. 69-84.

PERIODICALS

Kirkus Reviews, October 15, 1998, p. 1529.
Voice of Youth Advocates, December, 1990, p. 278.

*　　*　　*

CUETARA, Mittie 1957-

Personal

Born June 21, 1957, in Boston, MA; daughter of Edward A. (an architect) and Nancy (a consultant; present surname, Peters) Cuetara; married Sam Homans (a designer), September, 1991; children: Daniel, Stewart. *Education:* School of the Museum of Fine Art, Boston, B.F.A., 1985.

Addresses

Home—6530 Tremont St., Oakland, CA 94609. *Agent*—Julie Popkin, 15340 Albright St., Suite 204, Pacific Palisades, CA 90272.

Career

Freelance illustrator in Boston, MA, and San Francisco, CA, 1985-90; founder, art director, and principal illustrator at a greeting card company, San Francisco, 1990-93; writer and illustrator of children's books, 1993—. *Member:* Society of Children's Book Writers and Illustrators.

Writings

AUTHOR AND ILLUSTRATOR

Terrible Teresa and Other Very Short Stories, Dutton, 1997.
The Crazy Crawler Crane and Other Very Short Truck Stories, Dutton, 1998.

ILLUSTRATOR

Maria Lenhart, *Hidden Oregon,* Ulysses Press, 1996.

Illustrator of *Bay Area Green Pages.*

Sidelights

Mittie Cuetara told *SATA:* "I grew up in Cambridge, Massachusetts, and studied painting and animation at the Boston Museum School. For several years I worked as a freelance illustrator in San Francisco, then I started a small greeting card company. After three years of turning out cards and working as an art director, I sold my share of the company. I learned so much from that experience; it was better than four years of business college. Especially being art director, what an eye opener!

"People often said to me, 'Oh, you should write a children's book,' but it wasn't until my son Daniel was born that I ever really thought about it seriously. I remember nursing him on the couch and writing the beginning of *Terrible Teresa* in my head. Of course, when you have a kid you read so many kids' books, and you read each one so many times. I think every parent I know has at least one idea for a book in her head.

"I am critical of a lot of children's books, particularly those that 'talk down' to kids. I usually like books that aren't too sweet. When I was a kid, my brothers and I all loved Shel Silverstein and Tom Lehr. We probably only understood about one word in three, but we had all the poems and songs memorized, and we were so cool! *Doctor DeSoto* is the book I wish I had written myself. I liked *Martha Speaks* and *Eloise* and, when I was older, *Stuart Little* and then *Harriet the Spy.*

"My advice for aspiring writers is to figure out what you do best, and try to do that as well as you can. That will make you original and reflect your unique voice. I also recommend having a trust fund. As long as money is no object, you'll be fine."

Cuetara introduced a trademark style in her picture book debut, the well-received *Terrible Teresa and Other Very Short Stories.* This work features fourteen "short stories," each contained within a single two-page spread. The tales are "told in an abbreviated, comic-book style," noted a *Publishers Weekly* commentator, "with four vignette panels and a corresponding short line of (often nonsensical) verse." *School Library Journal* contributor Marlene Gawron called *Terrible Teresa* "an original, refreshing, and useful offering," noting that it will help young readers to develop their vocabulary because "the well-drawn illustrations are full of zany details" that help to clarify the meaning of unfamiliar words. Erin St. John Kelly, writing in the *New York Times Book Review,* cited examples of the witty text accompanying each panel of artwork, concluding: "Mittie Cuetara's drawings suggest what *New Yorker* cartoons for children might be like." *Booklist* reviewer Susan Dove Lempke asserted: "Young children will like hearing the stories read aloud, and the short, rhyming text makes the book a good choice for beginning readers."

Cuetara presents a book for young truck lovers in the same unique and successful format employed for *Terrible Teresa. The Crazy Crawler Crane and Other Very Short Truck Stories* uses rhyming text to describe the action in four cartoon panels, each set of four comprising a two-page spread that is devoted to one of fourteen different vehicles. "The poems are lighthearted and clever," acknowledged Christine A. Moesch in *School Library Journal,* "but it's the trucks that will capture the attention of the intended audience." A *Publishers Weekly* critic maintained: "Cuetara exploits her restrained format to full advantage, showcasing both her pithy wit and inventiveness." Heather Vogel Frederick, concluding a favorable assessment of *The Crazy Crawler Crane* in the *New York Times Book Review,* asserted: "Cuetara is a talented artist who clearly qualifies as the Dorothy Parker of picture book repartee."

Works Cited

Review of *The Crazy Crawler Crane and Other Very Short Truck Stories, Publishers Weekly,* July 13, 1998, p. 76.

Frederick, Heather Vogel, review of *The Crazy Crawler Crane and Other Very Short Truck Stories, New York Times Book Review,* April 11, 1999, p. 32.

Gawron, Marlene, review of *Terrible Teresa and Other Very Short Stories, School Library Journal,* November, 1997, pp. 78-79.

Kelly, Erin St. John, review of *Terrible Teresa and Other Very Short Stories, New York Times Book Review,* February 15, 1998, p. 26.

Lempke, Susan Dove, review of *Terrible Teresa and Other Very Short Stories, Booklist,* October 15, 1997, pp. 413-14.

Moesch, Christine A., review of *The Crazy Crawler Crane and Other Very Short Truck Stories, School Library Journal,* September, 1998, p. 165.

Review of *Terrible Teresa and Other Very Short Stories, Publishers Weekly,* August 18, 1997, p. 91.

D

D'ATH, Justin 1953-

Personal

Surname is pronounced "Darth"; born October 4, 1953, in Otaki, New Zealand; son of Ossian William (a farmer) and Noellie Claire (Caldwell) D'Ath; children: Fiona Piminni, Timothy Christopher. *Education:* Attended St. Columbans College, 1971-73. *Hobbies and other interests:* Mountain bike riding, movies, reading, watching TV sport, walking my dog.

Addresses

Home—23 Shakespeare St., Spring Gully, Victoria 3550, Australia. *Electronic mail*—jdath@britafe.vic.edu.au. *Agent*—Fiona Inglis, Curtis Brown, Ltd., Sydney, Australia.

Career

TAFE, Bendigo Regional Institute, teacher of professional writing. Teaches literacy and mathematics classes at a women's prison. Also managed a club at an Aborigine mission and worked as forklift driver, car builder, ranch worker, fruit picker, iron miner, sugar mill worker, store clerk, laboratory technician, and electrical worker. *Member:* Australian Society of Authors, Fellowship of Australian Writers, Children's Book Council.

Awards, Honors

More than fifty prizes for short stories; Alan Marshall Award from Fellowship of Australia Writers, Jessie Litchfield Award, and Caltex-Bendigo Advertiser Award, all for *The Initiate.*

Writings

FOR CHILDREN, EXCEPT AS NOTED

The Initiate (adult novel), Collins Australia (Sydney, Australia), 1989.
Infamous, Holy Angels (North Fitzroy, Australia), 1996.

Humungous, Holy Angels, 1997.
Fantabulous, Holy Angels, 1998.

Justin D'Ath

53

Why Did the Chykkan Cross the Galaxy?, illustrated by Geoff Kelly, Allen & Unwin (Sydney, Australia), 1998.

SNIWT, Allen & Unwin, 1999.

The Upside Down Girl, Allen & Unwin, in press.

OTHER

Contributor of adult stories and articles to magazines.

Work in Progress

The Secret of Rainbow Knob, for Allen & Unwin. Also, a novel, *Galahs;* a young adult novel, *Noddies.*

Sidelights

Justin D'Ath of Bendigo, Australia, told *SATA:* "I've always loved stories. When I was eight years old, I shared a room with two of my older brothers. The eldest, Billy, used to tell Philip and me a story every night after lights-out. Mostly they were stories he had read or the plots from movies, but when these ran out, we began inventing stories, each contributing characters and story lines. Ever since, I have been making up stories. I began my first novel when I was nine. My first published works were travel stories in magazines, but soon I was embellishing them so creatively that they became mostly fiction.

"For twenty years I wrote only for adults. It was only as my children grew up that I began thinking about children's stories. For several years I would tell bedtime stories almost every night, making them up as I went along. My daughter Fiona introduced me to contemporary children's writing, and I was hooked. Mind you, it took me another ten years to try my hand at it.

"I find writing for children is great fun. It's an escape. I laugh a lot at the unexpected things my characters say and do. I don't plan. I simply invent a character, usually ten or twelve years old, put her in an unusual situation, and start speaking in her voice. For me it's a natural process—part of me doesn't seem to have grown up.

"All my children's books have a boy and girl and dog in them, and they are all told in the first person and in very short chapters. My novel *SNIWT* (read that backwards) has the shortest chapter ever published. I like playing games with my readers. The books which have most influenced my work are the Coles Funny Picture Books. Published fifty or so years ago, they were marvelously interactive. Another influence was a series that included *The Squirrel Twins, The Beaver Twins,* et cetera.

"I've always been interested in nature and now, more than ever before, it is important to pass along a message [about nature]. Most of my books have a message, though it is buried way underneath the plot. Children pick it up, but mostly they have fun. My main message is: enjoy reading."

D'Ath's enjoyable, humorous tales, with their cleverly concealed environmental and various other social themes, have been well-received. Neville Barnard, writing in *Magpies,* said of *Why Did the Chykkan Cross the Galaxy,* "It is tempting to describe this text as a modern fable dealing with the importance of humour and enjoying life. But it probably isn't. It is just a funny story with masses of child appeal." As for *Humungous,* a reviewer for *Reading Time* predicted, "Younger readers may well enjoy this unusual and well-told tale, acquiring a concern for forestry issues along the way."

D'Ath continued to *SATA:* "Children are the most rewarding audience any writer can have. Read your work to an adult audience, and they will clap politely at the end. Read to children, and they will stick up their hands right in the middle of a passage and say, 'We've got a dog and his name is Robbie.' That's who I'm writing for when I sit down each morning at eight o'clock in front of my computer. All children should have books and dogs."

Works Cited

Barnard, Neville, review of *Why Did the Chykkan Cross the Galaxy?, Magpies,* July, 1998.

Review of *Humungous, Reading Time,* May, 1998.

For More Information See

PERIODICALS

Australian Book Review, August, 1997, p. 61.

* * *

DAVIS, David R. 1948-

Personal

Born October 29, 1948; son of A. D. Davis, Jr., and Margie Lacy Evjen; stepson of George P. Chiappini; married Leanne Terrell (a nurse), January 27, 1977; children: Christen, Caleb. *Education:* Attended Stephen F. Austin University and several other universities. *Hobbies and other interests:* Fishing, reading, "malingering."

Addresses

Home and office—704 Parker Dr., Clinton, MS 39056. *Electronic mail*—ddavis7@bellsouth.net.

Career

Writer and political cartoonist.

Awards, Honors

Award from Mississippi Press Association, 1996, for political cartoons.

Writings

A Redneck Night before Christmas, illustrated by James Rice, Pelican Publishing (Gretna, LA), 1997.

Former political cartoonist for *Madison County Journal.* Contributor of articles and cartoons to periodicals, including *Back Porch.*

Work in Progress

Another humor book for Pelican Publishing; writing and creating cartoon illustrations for *Travels with Grandpaw,* an oral history of the author's grandfather, Raymond Lacy (1905-1997) and the Lacy family of Texas.

Sidelights

David R. Davis told *SATA:* "I began my love affair with humor and cartooning in the first grade. That is the first time I remember getting the idea that I could do something that other kids did not do. I drew some dynamite comics about Flash Gordon. Unfortunately, they were on the page of schoolwork I was supposed to be doing at the time. I learned two things: one, I could draw; two, drawing did not always make you popular with the powers that be. That lesson has proved true all the rest of my life.

"I never gave cartooning and writing a serious shot until my late thirties. My wife came to me one day and told me that I would always wonder if I could have made it, if I didn't at least give it a try. I have been doing it ever since. It is a passion with me. It is almost beyond meaning whether the work is published or not. I will always do the stuff. Of course, the money makes it easier to get my three squares a day.

"The purpose of all my writing and drawing is to make people glad or mad. *A Redneck Night before Christmas* was a lark, written during the Christmas season late one night. I figured I could get away with it because I am from the South myself. Pelican Publishing rejected it the first time I sent it, but called me back after it was a hit in a magazine. I truly enjoy making folks laugh and see the good-natured humor in things. I reserve my more biting humor for politicians. After all, they deserve it.

"At present, I am working on a project that is close to my heart. *Travels with Grandpaw* is a comic-art-illustrated oral history based on the stories that my grandfather, Raymond Lacy, told me while I was growing up. They are about my relationship with him and about his family in East Texas in the early 1900s. They are funny, nostalgic, sad, and I hope, in some cases, moving. I guess you could say that this work is my love letter to Texas and my beloved grandfather.

"There are many writers and artists who have influenced me. Mark Twain has always been one of my patron saints. Another is Will Rogers. As far as cartooning goes, I revere Will Eisner and Herblock. I used to try to copy Herblock's political cartoons in the paper when I was a kid. Needless to say, I also loved Alex Raymond's rendition of Flash Gordon. One of my modern heroes is Art Spiegelman. *Maus* showed us all what can be done with comic art.

"My advice to aspiring writers and artists is: never give up. The world has too many lawyers and businessmen as it is. Don't listen to the common wisdom. If you were born to write or draw, you will be miserable doing anything else—no matter how much money you make. One more thing: 'twenty lines a day, genius or not.' I can't remember where I read that, but the author had the key to writing. Just do it.

"None of my work has been made into a movie yet ... but I keep hoping that Steven Spielberg will call soon."

*   *   *

de KAY, Ormonde (Jr.) 1923-1998

OBITUARY NOTICE—See index for *SATA* sketch: Born December 17, 1923, in New York, NY; died of lung cancer, October 2, 1998, in Manhattan, NY. Screenwriter, translator, poet, and author. De Kay graduated from Harvard University in 1947, where he had edited its literary journal, *The Advocate.* Between stints of active duty for the U.S. Naval Reserve during World War II and the Korean War, de Kay traveled throughout Europe, writing radio and film scripts. He co-wrote the award-winning 1949 film *Lost Boundaries* with M. J. Furland. During the 1960s, de Kay turned his attention to children's literature, penning biographies and other nonfiction for young people. Published by Random House, his juvenile literature included *Meet Theodore Roosevelt, Meet Andrew Jackson,* and *The Adventures of Lewis and Clark.* de Kay also translated Mother Goose nursery rhymes into French in his well-received 1971 publication *Rimes de la Mere Oie.* He contributed articles on historical topics to *American Heritage* magazine and to *Horizon,* where he was articles editor in the 1970s. De Kay's light verse was published in the *New Yorker, Harper's,* and the *Atlantic Monthly.* His last book publication, *From the Age That Is Past,* published in 1994, is a history of New York's Harvard Club, of which he was a member.

OBITUARIES AND OTHER SOURCES:

PERIODICALS

New York Times, October 23, 1998, p. C23.

*   *   *

DERVAUX, Isabelle 1961-

Personal

Born November 17, 1961, in Valenciennes, France; daughter of Pierre and Genevieve (Masson) Dervaux; married Jim Christie (an art director), 1994; children: Millie, Lucien. *Education:* Attended University of Lille, 1984.

Addresses

Home—73 Cumberland St., San Francisco, CA 94110. *Electronic mail*—idervaux@sirius.com. *Agent*—Riley Il-

Isabelle Dervaux

lustration, 155 West 15th St., Suite 4-C, New York, NY 10011.

Career

Illustrator for books, magazines, and advertising materials, 1984—. *Member:* Graphic Artists Guild.

Illustrator

Susan A. Couture, *Melanie Jane,* HarperCollins, 1996.
Karla Kuskin, *The Sky Is Always in the Sky,* HarperCollins, 1998.

Sidelights

France-born illustrator Isabelle Dervaux has illustrated two books for children: Susan A. Couture's *Melanie Jane,* and *The Sky Is Always in the Sky,* a collection primarily comprised of reprinted poems by the well-known poet Karla Kuskin. A reviewer for the *New York Times* described the latter work as "elegantly simple," while *School Library Journal* contributor Barbara Elleman wrote, "bright colored paper resembling the rainbow pads of yesterday (but with sharper hues) back simple, stylized paintings." Undoubtedly, Dervaux's artwork complementing Kuskin's poems led the critic to

conclude the volume "an appealing collection that children are likely to pick up on their own."

Works Cited

Elleman, Barbara, review of *The Sky Is Always in the Sky,* *School Library Journal,* July, 1998, p. 89.
New York Times, July 19, 1998.

*   *   *

DILLON, Diane 1933-

Personal

Born March 13, 1933, in Glendale, CA; daughter of Adelbert Paul (a teacher) and Phyllis (a pianist; maiden name, Worsley) Sorber; married Leo Dillon (an artist and illustrator), March 17, 1957; children: Lionel ("Lee"). *Education:* Attended Los Angeles City College, 1951-52, and Skidmore College, 1952-53; attended American Institute of Graphic Arts, 1955; graduated from Parsons School of Design, 1956; attended School of Visual Arts, 1957. *Hobbies and other interests:* Sculpture.

Addresses

c/o HarperCollins, 10 East 53rd St., New York, NY 10022.

Career

Artist and illustrator. Dave Fris Advertising Agency, Albany, NY, staff artist, 1956-57; freelance artist and illustrator, 1957—; instructor, School of Visual Arts, 1971-74. *Exhibitions:* Gallery on the Green, Boston, MA; Metropolitan Museum, New York City; Boulder Center for the Visual Arts, Boulder, CO; Butler Institute of American Art, Youngstown, OH; Delaware Art Museum, Wilmington, DE; Bratislava Book Show, Bratislava, Slovakia; American Institute of Graphic Arts, New York City; Art Directors Club of New York; Brooklyn Public Library, Brooklyn, NY; New York Historical Society; Earthlight Gallery, Boston; The Pentagon, Washington, DC; Delaware Museum, Washington, DC; Society of Illustrators, NY. *Member:* Society of Illustrators (president, 1987-89), Graphic Artists Guild (president, 1981-83).

Awards, Honors

(All received with husband, Leo Dillon) Honor book, Children's Spring Book Festival, *New York Herald Tribune,* 1963, for *Hakon of Rogen's Saga;* certificates of merit, Society of Illustrators, 1968-77; Children's Book of the Year, Child Study Association, 1968, for *Dark Venture,* 1971, for *The Untold Tale,* 1973, for *Behind the Back of the Mountain: Black Folktales from Southern Africa,* 1974, for *Burning Star* and *Songs and Stories from Uganda,* 1975, for *The Hundred Penny Box, Why Mosquitoes Buzz in People's Ears: A West African Tale,* and *Song of the Boat,* 1976, for *Ashanti to*

Zulu: African Traditions, and 1986, for *Brother to the Wind;* Hugo Award, International Science Fiction Association, 1971, for illustration of a series of science-fiction book jackets; Best Book, *School Library Journal,* 1971, for *The Untold Tale;* inclusion in Children's Book Show, American Institute of Graphic Arts, 1973-74, for *Behind the Back of the Mountain: Black Folktales from Southern Africa* and *The Third Gift,* and 1976, for *Ashanti to Zulu: African Traditions;* inclusion in Children's Book Showcase, Children's Book Council (CBC), 1974, for *Behind the Back of the Mountain: Black Folktales from Southern Africa,* 1975, for *Whirlwind Is a Ghost Dancing,* and 1976, for *Song of the Boat;* Outstanding Book of the Year, *New York Times,* 1975, for *Why Mosquitoes Buzz in People's Ears: A West African Tale* and *The Hundred Penny Box,* and 1990, for *The Tale of the Mandarin Ducks;* illustrator of Newbery Honor Book, *The Hundred Penny Box,* 1976.

Caldecott Medals, American Library Association (ALA), 1976, for *Why Mosquitoes Buzz in People's Ears: A West African Tale,* and 1977, for *Ashanti to Zulu: African Traditions;* Best Illustrated Children's Books, *New York Times,* 1976, for *Ashanti to Zulu: African Traditions,* and 1985, for *The People Could Fly: American Black Folktales;* Illustration Honor, *Boston Globe/Horn Book* Awards, 1976, for *Song of the Boat,* and 1977, for *Ashanti to Zulu: African Traditions;* Hamilton King Award, Society of Illustrators, 1977, for *Ashanti to Zulu: African Traditions;* Art Books for Children, Brooklyn Museum and Brooklyn Public Library, 1977 and 1978, for *Why Mosquitoes Buzz in People's Ears: A West African Tale;* highly commended, Hans Christian Andersen Medal, International Board on Books for Young People (IBBY), 1978; Lewis Carroll Shelf Award, 1978, for *Who's in Rabbit's House?: A Masai Tale;* Balrog Award, 1982, for lifetime contribution to sci-fi/fantasy art; honor list for illustration, IBBY, and honorable mention, Coretta Scott King Award, ALA, both 1986, both for *The People Could Fly;* Coretta Scott King Award for illustration, ALA, 1991, for *Aida: A Picture Book for All Ages,* and 1996, for *Her Stories: African American Folktales, Fairy Tales and True Tales; Boston Globe/Horn Book Award* for illustration, 1991, for *The Tale of the Mandarin Ducks;* Best Books, *Publishers Weekly* and *School Library Journal,* both 1998, both for *To Every Thing There Is a Season: Verses from Ecclesiastes.*

Illustrator

WITH HUSBAND, LEO DILLON

Erik C. Haugaard, *Hakon of Rogen's Saga,* Houghton, 1963.

Haugaard, *A Slave's Tale,* Houghton, 1965.

Basil Davidson and the editors of Time-Life, *African Kingdoms,* Time-Life, 1966.

Sorche Nic Leodhas (pseudonym of Leclair G. Alger), *Claymore and Kilt: Tales of Scottish Kings and Castles,* Holt, 1967.

F. M. Pilkington, *Shamrock and Spear: Tales and Legends from Ireland,* Holt, 1968.

Erik C. Haugaard, *The Rider and His Horse,* Houghton, 1968.

Audrey W. Beyer, *Dark Venture,* Knopf, 1968.

Frederick Laing, *Why Heimdall Blew His Horn: Tale of the Norse Gods,* Silver Burdett, 1969.

John Bierhorst and Henry R. Schoolcraft, editors, *The Ring in the Prairie: A Shawnee Legend,* Dial, 1970.

Alta Jablow, *Gassire's Lute: A West African Epic,* Dutton, 1971.

Alma Murray and Robert Thomas, editors, *The Search,* Scholastic, 1971.

Erik C. Haugaard, *The Untold Tale,* Houghton, 1971.

Verna Aardema, *Behind the Back of the Mountain: Black Folktales from Southern Africa,* Dial, 1973.

Eth Clifford (pseudonym of Ethel C. Rosenberg), *Burning Star,* Houghton, 1974.

W. Moses Serwadda, *Songs and Stories from Uganda,* Crowell, 1974.

Jan Carew, *The Third Gift,* Little, Brown, 1974.

Natalie Belting, *Whirlwind Is a Ghost Dancing,* Dutton, 1974.

Lorenz Graham, *Song of the Boat,* Crowell, 1975.

Harlan Ellison, editor, *Dangerous Visions,* New American Library, 1975.

Sharon Bell Mathis, *The Hundred Penny Box,* Viking, 1975.

Verna Aardema, reteller, *Why Mosquitoes Buzz in People's Ears: A West African Tale,* Dial, 1975.

Margaret W. Musgrove, *Ashanti to Zulu: African Traditions,* Dial, 1976.

Verna Aardema, reteller, *Who's in Rabbit's House?: A Masai Tale,* Dial, 1977.

Eloise Greenfield, *Honey, I Love: And Other Love Poems,* Crowell, 1978.

Frederick Laing, *Tales from Scandinavia,* Silver Burdett, 1979.

P. L. Travers, *Two Pairs of Shoes,* Viking, 1980.

J. Carew, *Children of the Sun,* Little, Brown, 1980.

Dorothy S. Strickland, editor, *Listen Children: An Anthology of Black Literature,* Bantam, 1982.

Mildred Pitts Walter, *Brother to the Wind,* Lothrop, 1985.

Virginia Hamilton, reteller, *The People Could Fly: American Black Folktales,* Knopf, 1985.

(Contributor) Mitsumasa Anno, compiler, *All in a Day,* Dowanya (Japan), 1986.

(Contributor) *Once Upon a Time: Celebrating the Magic of Children's Books in Honor of the Twentieth Anniversary of Reading Is Fundamental,* Putnam, 1986.

Michael Patrick Hearn, *The Porcelain Cat,* Little, Brown, 1987.

Barbara A. Brenner, *The Color Wizard: Level 1,* Bantam, 1989.

Alice Bach and J. Cheryl Exum, *Moses' Ark: Stories from the Bible,* Delacorte, 1989.

Leontyne Price, editor, *Aida: A Picture Book for All Ages,* Harcourt, 1990.

Katherine Paterson, *The Tale of the Mandarin Ducks,* Dutton, 1990.

Alice Bach and J. Cheryl Exum, *Miriam's Well: Stories about Women in the Bible,* Delacorte, 1991.

Claire Martin, *The Race of the Golden Apples,* Dial, 1991.

Nancy Willard, *Pish, Posh, Said Hieronymus Bosch,* Harcourt, 1991.

In their award-winning illustrations for Virginia Hamilton's collection of stories, Diane and Leo Dillon have created a vibrant backdrop for the unique tales centered on African-American females. (From Her Stories: African American Folktales, Fairy Tales, and True Tales.)

Nancy White Carlstrom, *Northern Lullaby,* Putnam, 1992.

Nancy Willard, *The Sorcerer's Apprentice,* Scholastic, 1993.

Virginia Hamilton, *Many Thousand Gone: African Americans from Slavery to Freedom,* Knopf, 1993.

Ray Bradbury, *Switch on the Night,* Knopf, 1993.

N. N. Charles, *What Am I?: Looking Through Shapes at Apples and Grapes,* Scholastic, 1994.

Virginia Hamilton, *Her Stories: African American Folktales, Fairy Tales and True Tales,* Scholastic, 1995.

(Contributor) *On the Wings of Peace: Writers and Illustrators Speak Out for Peace, in Memory of Hiroshima and Nagasaki,* Houghton Mifflin, 1995.

Howard Norman, *The Girl Who Dreamed Only Geese and Other Tales of the Far North,* Harcourt Brace, 1997.

To Every Thing There Is a Season: Verses from Ecclesiastes, Scholastic, 1998.

Illustrator of numerous book jackets; also illustrator of album covers. Contributor of illustrations to periodicals, including *Ladies' Home Journal, Saturday Evening Post,* and *Washington Post.* Artist of stained glass ceiling in Eagle Gallery, New York City.

Work included in the Kerlan Collection, University of Minnesota.

Adaptations

Why Mosquitoes Buzz in People's Ears was adapted as a filmstrip with audiocassette and as a motion picture, Weston Woods, 1977; *Ashanti to Zulu* was adapted as a filmstrip with audiocassette, Weston Woods, 1977; *Brother to the Wind* was adapted as a filmstrip with audiocassette, Weston Woods, 1988; *The People Could Fly* was released on audiocassette, Knopf, 1988; *The Tale of the Mandarin Ducks* was produced on video cassette by Weston Woods, 1998.

Work in Progress

Wind Child, by Shirley Rousseau Murphy, for HarperCollins; *Mansa Musa: The Lion of Mali,* by Khephra Burns, for Harcourt Brace.

Sidelights

Husband and wife Leo and Diane Dillon are a prolific and acclaimed team of American illustrators and artists. They are noted for producing imaginative, bold drawings and illustrations which range from the highly realistic to the abstract. Since the 1960s, they have gained renown for their collaborative book illustrations, which have stretched across a number of genres, including science fiction, medieval writings, literary classics, and folktales. They are perhaps best known, however, for their award-winning illustrations of children's picture books. The Dillons are the only illustrators to have received consecutive Caldecott Medals (1976 and 1977), annually bestowed by the American Library Association for the highest illustration achievement in children's literature. Unique in that they illustrate solely in collaboration, the Dillons describe their work as emanating from a "third artist." As they once related to *SATA:* "After a work is finished, not even we can be certain who did what. The third artist is a combination of the two of us and is different than either of us individually."

Though the Dillons work together as illustrators, they bring to their art very different personal backgrounds and experience. Leo Dillon was born March 2, 1933, in the East New York section of Brooklyn, New York City, the son of immigrant parents from Trinidad. Both of his parents—his father owned a small trucking business and his mother was a dressmaker—encouraged him in his drawing. One of his father's friends, a man named Ralph Volman, became his "mentor—a painter, a draftsman, a writer, a world traveler," Leo once described in *SATA.* "It was Ralph Volman who took me to Greenwich Village for the first time to see the annual sidewalk art show.... Volman gave me a drawing board. He came to our house every Sunday and would show me his pen-and-ink drawings, a very tight 'English style.' He also spent a good deal of time with my drawings, giving me criticism and encouragement." Another important early influence for Leo was illustrated books, which he would study for style. As he once told *SATA:* "I still have the one that changed my life—*The Arabian Nights.* I'd never before seen drawings of that quality, and still strive to equal that excellence. In our local library was a section of illustrated French classics, and although I couldn't read French, I was captivated by the drawings.... I couldn't get enough of the Old Masters."

As a youth, Leo showed much promise as an artist, and attended the High School of Industrial Design in New York City. He received training there for a commercial art career, and was particularly influenced by one teacher, Benjamin Clements, who "realized that I could do more than illustrate Coke bottles, and pushed me to expand my mind," Leo once told *SATA.* After graduation he enlisted in the U.S. Navy, in order to later be able to attend college on the GI Bill. "For the three years I spent in the service, I drew lots of portraits on 'commission' from guys who wanted pictures of their girlfriends," he related to *SATA.* "I painted in the ship's hold, and mixed

my pigments from nautical paint." After the Navy and on the advice of Clements, he enrolled in 1953 in New York's prestigious Parsons School of Design, where he would meet his future wife and working partner, Diane. "I had a scholarship to Pratt, a more commercial school, but I turned it down," he once told *SATA.* "I was intimidated at the prospect of being with 'artsy types,' but I so respected Clements that I swallowed my fear.... I worked like a demon at Parsons, and kept mostly to myself."

Diane (Sorber) Dillon was born March 13, 1933, in Glendale, California, and grew up in Los Angeles. Her father was a schoolteacher and inventor whose knowledge of drafting helped guide her early interest in drawing. She was also encouraged by her mother, a concert pianist and organist. "As a child I drew all the time," she once told *SATA,* "and my parents encouraged me, particularly my father, who had artistic talent. He would look carefully at what I'd done and then offer

Imitating artistic styles unique to a wide variety of cultures and time periods, the Dillons have illustrated verse from the biblical Book of Ecclesiastes. (From To Every Thing There Is a Season.*)*

corrections, telling me which side the shadow should fall on, for example. He was away for a year during the war from 1943 to 1944, and he sent me a set of pastels in a wood box, which meant a lot. It was not only permission to do what I wanted to do, but the *tools* I needed to do it with." As a young girl, Diane was also influenced by the fashion illustrations of the famous Dorothy Hood, whose drawings Diane would find in the newspapers. "Hood was way ahead of her time," Diane said. "Her drawing style was very modern. I loved the look of her line, so *different* from anything else being done then. The fact that those wonderful figures were drawn by a woman was an inspiration for me."

Although Diane demonstrated much artistic talent as a child and throughout high school, she did not receive serious art training until college. She attended Los Angeles City College from 1951 to 1952, where she majored in advertising art, but was forced to drop out after contracting tuberculosis. For a year she recuperated in a sanitarium, where she was to have no physical activity and spent most of her time reading, drawing, and knitting. After her recovery, she attended Skidmore College in Saratoga Springs, New York, during a time when, as she once commented in *SATA,* her "passions were life drawing and graphics." After two years of study at Skidmore, however, she was advised by a professor that she had taken all the art classes they offered there. Diane transferred in 1954 to Parsons School of Design, where Leo Dillon had already been studying for a year.

At Parsons, Diane and Leo discovered an immediate and mutual admiration for each other's work, yet they also became instant competitors. "I walked into a classroom and saw a student painting of various pieces of fabric and a sewing machine," Diane once related in *SATA.* "It was very realistic—the subtle shadows of the pins in the cloth and the way the folds were done gave it an extraordinary three-dimensional quality. I was immediately overcome by two feelings: 'I'm in over my head,' and 'Here is a challenge I *must* meet.' The painting was Leo's, and to this day, his work sets a standard for me." Leo similarly commented in *Horn Book* on first encountering Diane's work, and being instantly impressed. "One day I noticed a painting hanging on the wall at a student exhibition," he recalled. "It was a painting of a chair—an Eames chair—and I knew it had to be by a new student because nobody in our class at the time could paint like that.... This artist knew perspective, which is one of the most difficult things a beginner has to learn.... This artist was a whole lot better than I. I figured I'd better find out who he was. *He* was Diane."

"We spent a lot of time and energy trying to prove ourselves to each other," Leo recalled to *SATA.* "In the midst of all this, born of the mutual recognition of our respective strengths, we fell in love. We tried to keep our relationship a secret because in those days interracial couples were not easily accepted. We knew of couples like us who had been beaten up walking down the street." After graduation, Diane went to work for an advertising firm in Albany, New York, but returned the

following year to be with Leo. They were married in 1957, and Leo went to work as an art director for West Park Publications in New York. Diane stayed home, "determined to be the model 1950s housewife, and that didn't include drawing or painting," she wrote in *Horn Book.* The two, however, soon started collaborating professionally. Leo "casually began bringing work home, encouraging me to work with him on design problems, easing me back into art," Diane told *Horn Book.* "That was the beginning of our working together as one artist."

In the late 1950s and early 1960s, the Dillons worked as freelance artists under the name Studio 2. "Because we wanted to work in a variety of styles, we thought it better not to use our names," Diane once told *SATA.* "We figured, rightly, that we would have more variety if clients thought we were a studio full of artists." From the 1960s onward, they gained renown with a variety of drawings and illustrations—for textbooks, book jackets, album covers, and prints—and covered such wide-ranging subject matter as African folktales, Scandinavian mythology, science fiction and fantasy, medieval literature, and Shakespeare. They also, as Leo related to *SATA,* "did a lot of illustrations for articles and books on jazz musicians and what was then referred to as 'the black experience.' A big break for us was meeting Harlan Ellison, a Chicago magazine editor, who had us illustrate work by Nat Hentoff, Ben Hecht and other 'hip' writers. We also did the cover for *Gentleman Junkie and Other Stories of the Hung-Up Generation.* This cover was very important in terms of our development. We had the freedom to experiment with mixed media, hand-lettering and type. We used a strong black graphic style with vivid color, which was very bold for the times."

Throughout their collaborations, the Dillons have experimented with a variety of techniques to create effects complementing their broad range of illustrations. As they once related in *SATA,* their book-cover illustrations have employed such unusual elements as embroidery, plastic, and leading, to create a stained-glass effect. Many of their drawings have been noted for giving the appearance of woodcuts, which the Dillons achieve through an innovative use of the frisket—a type of cut stencil. They described in *SATA* the importance of technique to their collaboration. "Because we both work on every piece of art, we favor techniques that give us a lot of control. We don't leave ourselves open to 'accident.' We need a technique so sure that a line begun by one of us can be completed by the other with no visual hint of interruption. We are constantly experimenting with various types of media. This is exhilarating, but there are times when it's extremely frustrating, trying to overcome technical problems. That period of not knowing what is wrong can be excruciating. But over the years we've come to accept that trial and error is part of the process. Technique is to the graphic artist what words are to the writer."

In 1976 the Dillons illustrated a children's book, Verna Aardema's *Why Mosquitoes Buzz in People's Ears: A*

Nancy Willard's verse retelling of the story of a magician's assistant who catastrophically misuses the spell she learns is dramatically illustrated with paintings by Leo and Diane Dillon. (From The Sorcerer's Apprentice.*)*

West African Tale, and received the Caldecott Medal. "We were delighted that this book was perfect for reading aloud," they once commented to *SATA*. "It is an illustrator's job to go beyond the text, to illustrate what is between the lines, not just to repeat the words. *Mosquitoes* is a repetitive tale in which the events are interpreted by different animals, each with a distinct point of view. We found ourselves concentrating on the play between the animals." They expanded upon the original story by accenting several of the minor animal characters; in one case, they introduced a new character, a little red bird. "We began to think of her as the

observer or reader and added her to the other spreads," they described in their Caldecott Medal acceptance speech printed in *Horn Book.* "Thus on each page you will find her watching, witnessing the events as they unfold. On the last page, when the story is over, she flies away. For us she is like the storyteller, gathering information, then passing it on to the next generation." Commenting on the Dillons' achievement in *Mosquitoes, Horn Book* reviewer Phyllis J. Fogelman praised "their talent as artists who collaborate so completely," and cited "their amazing ability to capture so sensitively such warmth, humor, and feeling in art so stylized as that for *Why Mosquitoes Buzz in People's Ears.*"

Spurred on by the success of their first children's picture book, the Dillons embarked upon Margaret Musgrove's *Ashanti to Zulu: African Traditions,* which went on to garner them a second Caldecott Medal in 1977—the only time the honor has ever been consecutively bestowed. *Ashanti to Zulu* describes different traditions among the diverse cultures of Africa, focusing on such aspects as dwellings, clothing, hairstyles, and family life. "We wanted our illustrations for *Ashanti to Zulu* to be something other artists could look to as source material," the Dillons told *SATA.* "We strove for realism, for we wanted to be absolutely accurate with the details as well as have the elegance one normally associates with fairy tales." While the Dillons worked towards accurately depicting the differences among African cultures, they also imparted universal aspects. "We began to appreciate the grandeur in ordinary living, in what actually exists," they stated in their Caldecott Medal acceptance speech printed in *Horn Book.* "It is the intelligence in a person's eyes or the nuances of body language—things shared by all people—that make for real beauty. We strove to be accurate with the factual details but especially wanted to stress the things we all have in common—a smile, a touch, our humanity. We took artistic license with particular situations so that they reflected the tenderness that exists among all people."

Throughout the 1980s and 1990s, the Dillons collaborated with a variety of distinguished authors to produce a number of outstanding works for children. Among them is Michael Patrick Hearn's sorcerer's apprentice tale, *The Porcelain Cat.* Children's author Patricia MacLachlan noted in the *New York Times Book Review* that the "Dillon's extraordinary pictures add great depth and meaning" to the work. *School Library Journal* contributor Patricia Dooley called the collaboration between the Dillons and Hearn "a 'smashing' success."

In 1986 they combined their talent with eminent children's author Virginia Hamilton to create the first of three highly praised collections of African-American tales. *The People Could Fly: American Black Folktales* features the retelling of two dozen tales that originated from black slaves in America. Its 1993 companion volume, *Many Thousand Gone: African Americans from Slavery to Freedom,* relates the history of slavery in the United States and profiles the lives of familiar figures such as Frederick Douglass and Harriet Tubman as well as lesser-known figures remembered only by their first name. *School Library Journal* contributor Lyn Miller-Lachmann praised the Dillons' "refreshingly original" illustrations, noting that the "text and visuals combine to create a powerful and moving whole." The third compilation to date, 1995's *Her Stories: African American Folktales, Fairy Tales, and True Tales,* is a unique collection of tales centered around African-American females. "The Dillons' glowingly detailed acrylic illustrations extend the horror, comedy, rhythm, and spirit of the tales," wrote Hazel Rochman in *Booklist.* Hamilton

received the Coretta Scott King Award in 1996 for her text, as did the Dillons for their illustrations.

Other award-winning books illustrated by the Dillons include Katherine Paterson's picture book *The Tale of the Mandarin Ducks,* for which they received the *Boston Globe/Horn Book* Award in 1991. Two others are Nancy Willard's *Pish, Posh, Said Hieronymus Bosch,* published in 1991, and *The Sorcerer's Apprentice,* published in 1993. About the latter, Nancy Vasilakis wrote in *Horn Book,* "The whole enterprise is a masterful and creative meeting of the minds between author and illustrators." Finally, but certainly not the last from a long list, is Nancy White Carlstrom's *Northern Lullaby,* which features a young Native-American narrator saying goodnight to the world around her as she drifts off to sleep. Ilene Cooper, writing in *Booklist,* said that the "Dillon's art here is as fine as any work they've done before. A felicitous collaboration."

In 1998 the Dillons saw the publication of their work *To Every Thing There Is a Season: Verses from Ecclesiastes.* This forty-page picture book, which *Bulletin of the Center for Children's Books* reviewer Janice M. Del Negro called "a visual extravaganza," celebrates the familiar biblical verse. To create the work, the duo drew from a variety of cultures and artistic styles ranging from thousands of years ago to contemporary times. For example, the illustration paired with the line "A time to kill, and a time to heal," reflects a style inspired by seventh-century Mexican Mixtecs.

Reviewers were bowled over by the illustrations, although some critics, such as Del Negro, felt the book was "overproduced" in relation to the sophisticated illustrations paired with the simple verse. Similarly, *New York Times Book Review* contributor Valerie Sayers noted that while each picture "is lovely, apt, sometimes even dazzling ... the book's hurtling back and forth through times and artistic styles disrupts the rhythms of Ecclesiastes." Other critics, such as *School Library Journal* Patricia Pearl Dole, couldn't help but appreciate the book's "ecumenical, artistic, and cultural experience" and its "intrinsic plea for worldwide understanding."

Over the years these two talented artists have won acclaim and awards for their illustrations in a number of areas—picture books, book jackets, album covers, and prints. Yet, the Dillons still find children's literature an important and rewarding mode of expression. And as they approach the end of this century, the Dillons don't intend to slow down. Currently, they are working on two projects, *Wind Child* by Shirley R. Murphy, and *Mansa Musa: The Lion of Mali* by Khephra Burns. About writing for children, Leo and Diane once commented in *Fifth Book of Junior Authors and Illustrators,* "That children are our audience is at once a responsibility, an honor, and a profound joy."

Works Cited

Cooper, Ilene, review of *Northern Lullaby, Booklist,* June 15, 1992, p. 1834.

Del Negro, Janice M., review of *To Every Thing There Is a Season: Verses from Ecclesiastes, Bulletin of the Center for Children's Books,* November, 1998, p. 89.

Dillon, Diane, "Leo Dillon," *Horn Book,* August, 1977, pp. 423-25.

Dillon, Diane, and Leo Dillon, "Caldecott Award Acceptance," *Horn Book,* August, 1976.

Dillon, Diane, and Leo Dillon, "Caldecott Acceptance Speech," *Horn Book,* August, 1977.

Dillon, Diane, and Leo Dillon, *To Every Thing There Is a Season: Verses from Ecclesiastes,* Scholastic, 1998.

Dillon, Leo, "Diane Dillon," *Horn Book,* August, 1977, pp. 422-23.

Dole, Patricia Pearl, review of *To Every Thing There Is a Season: Verses from Ecclesiastes, School Library Journal,* September, 1998, p. 198.

Dooley, Patricia, review of *The Porcelain Cat, School Library Journal,* November, 1987, p. 90.

Entry on the Dillons in *Fifth Book of Junior Authors and Illustrators,* edited by Sally Holmes Holtze, H. W. Wilson, 1983, pp. 101-03.

Fogelman, Phyllis J., "Leo and Diane Dillon," *Horn Book,* August, 1976, pp. 378-83.

MacLachlan, Patricia, review of *The Porcelain Cat, New York Times Book Review,* November 8, 1987, p. 50.

Miller-Lachmann, Lyn, review of *Many Thousand Gone, School Library Journal,* May, 1993, p. 116.

Rochman, Hazel, review of *Her Stories: African American Folktales, Fairy Tales, and True Tales, Booklist,* November 1, 1995, p. 470.

Sayers, Valerie, review of *To Every Thing There Is a Season: Verses from Ecclesiastes, New York Times Book Review,* November 15, 1998, p. 55.

Vasilakis, Nancy, review of *The Sorcerer's Apprentice, Horn Book,* March-April, 1994, p. 193.

For More Information See

BOOKS

The Art of Leo and Diane Dillon, edited by Byron Preiss, Ballantine, 1981.

Children's Literature Review, Volume 44, Gale, 1997, pp. 17-49.

Newbery and Caldecott Medalists and Honor Book Winners, compiled by Jim Roginski, Libraries Unlimited, 1982.

PERIODICALS

Booklist, December 1, 1992, p. 665; November 1, 1993, p. 529; November 15, 1994, p. 605; September 15, 1997, p. 233.

Horn Book, September-October, 1993, p. 621; January, 1996, pp. 81-82; September-October, 1998, pp. 619-20.

Kirkus Reviews, September 15, 1998, p. 1383.

New York Times Book Review, November 16, 1997, p. 30.

Publishers Weekly, June 28, 1991, p. 101; August 8, 1994, p. 428; November 13, 1995, p. 60; July 27, 1998, p. 76.

School Library Journal, October, 1990, p. 111; January, 1992, p. 118; January, 1994, pp. 116-17.*

*   *   *

DILLON, Leo 1933-

Personal

Full name, Lionel John Dillon; born March 2, 1933, in Brooklyn, NY; son of Lionel J. (owner of a truck business) and Marie (a dressmaker; maiden name, Rodriques) Dillon; married Diane Sorber (an artist and illustrator), March 17, 1957; children: Lionel ("Lee"). *Education:* Attended Parsons School of Design, 1953, 1956; also attended School of Visual Arts, 1958.

Addresses

c/o HarperCollins, 10 East 53rd St., New York, NY 10022.

Career

Artist and illustrator. West Park Publishers, New York City, art editor, 1956-57; free-lance artist and illustrator, 1958—; School of Visual Arts, New York City, instructor, 1969-77. *Exhibitions:* Gallery on the Green, Boston, MA; Metropolitan Museum, New York City; Boulder Center for the Visual Arts, Boulder, CO; Butler Institute of American Art, Youngstown, OH; Delaware Art Museum, Wilmington, DE; Bratislava Book Show, Bratislava, Slovakia; American Institute of Graphic Arts, New York City; Art Directors Club of New York; Brooklyn Public Library, Brooklyn, NY; New York Historical Society; Earthlight Gallery, Boston; The Pentagon, Washington, DC; Delaware Museum, Washington, DC; Society of Illustrators, NY. *Military service:* U.S. Navy, 1950-53. *Member:* Society of Illustrators, Graphic Artists Guild.

Awards, Honors

(All received with wife, Diane Dillon) Honor book, Children's Spring Book Festival, *New York Herald Tribune,* 1963, for *Hakon of Rogen's Saga;* certificates of merit, Society of Illustrators, 1968-77; Children's Book of the Year, Child Study Association, 1968, for *Dark Venture,* 1971, for *The Untold Tale,* 1973, for *Behind the Back of the Mountain: Black Folktales from Southern Africa,* 1974, for *Burning Star* and *Songs and Stories from Uganda,* 1975, for *The Hundred Penny Box, Why Mosquitoes Buzz in People's Ears: A West African Tale,* and *Song of the Boat,* 1976, for *Ashanti to Zulu: African Traditions,* and 1986, for *Brother to the Wind;* Hugo Award, International Science Fiction Association, 1971, for illustration of a series of science-fiction book jackets; Best Book, *School Library Journal,* 1971, for *The Untold Tale;* inclusion in Children's Book Show, American Institute of Graphic Arts, 1973-74, for *Behind the Back of the Mountain: Black Folktales from Southern Africa* and *The Third Gift,* and 1976, for *Ashanti to Zulu: African Traditions;* inclusion in Chil-

In **The Color Wizard,** *an early reader and concept book, a resourceful sorcerer transforms his planet by magically coloring everything in it. (Illustrated by Leo and Diane Dillon.)*

dren's Book Showcase, Children's Book Council (CBC), 1974, for *Behind the Back of the Mountain: Black Folktales from Southern Africa,* 1975, for *Whirlwind Is a Ghost Dancing,* and 1976, for *Song of the Boat;* Outstanding Book of the Year, *New York Times,* 1975, for *Why Mosquitoes Buzz in People's Ears: A West Africn Tale* and *The Hundred Penny Box,* and 1990, for *The Tale of the Mandarin Ducks;* illustrator of Newbery Honor Book, *The Hundred Penny Box,* 1976.

Caldecott Medals, American Library Association (ALA), 1976, for *Why Mosquitoes Buzz in People's Ears: A West African Tale,* and 1977, for *Ashanti to Zulu: African Traditions;* Best Illustrated Children's Books, *New York Times,* 1976, for *Ashanti to Zulu: African Traditions,* and 1985, for *The People Could Fly: American Black Folktales;* Illustration Honor, *Boston Globe/Horn Book* Awards, 1976, for *Song of the Boat,* and 1977, for *Ashanti to Zulu: African Traditions;* Hamilton King Award, Society of Illustrators, 1977, for *Ashanti to Zulu: African Traditions;* Art Books for Children, Brooklyn Museum and Brooklyn Public Library, 1977 and 1978, for *Why Mosquitoes Buzz in People's Ears: A West African Tale;* highly commended, Hans Christian Andersen Medal, International Board on Books for Young People (IBBY), 1978; Lewis Carroll

Shelf Award, 1978, for *Who's in Rabbit's House?: A Masai Tale;* Balrog Award, 1982, for lifetime contribution to sci-fi/fantasy art; honor list for illustration, IBBY, and honorable mention, Coretta Scott King Award, ALA, both 1986, both for *The People Could Fly;* Coretta Scott King Award for illustration, ALA, 1991, for *Aida,* and 1996, for *Her Stories: African American Folktales, Fairy Tales and True Tales; Boston Globe/Horn Book Award* for illustration, 1991, for *The Tale of the Mandarin Ducks;* Best Books, *Publishers Weekly* and *School Library Journal,* both 1998, both for *To Every Thing There Is a Season: Verses from Ecclesiastes.*

Illustrator

WITH WIFE, DIANE DILLON

Erik C. Haugaard, *Hakon of Rogen's Saga,* Houghton, 1963.

Haugaard, *A Slave's Tale,* Houghton, 1965.

Basil Davidson and the editors of Time-Life, *African Kingdoms,* Time-Life, 1966.

Sorche Nic Leodhas (pseudonym of Leclair G. Alger), *Claymore and Kilt: Tales of Scottish Kings and Castles,* Holt, 1967.

F. M. Pilkington, *Shamrock and Spear: Tales and Legends from Ireland,* Holt, 1968.

Erik C. Haugaard, *The Rider and His Horse,* Houghton, 1968.

Audrey W. Beyer, *Dark Venture,* Knopf, 1968.

Frederick Laing, *Why Heimdall Blew His Horn: Tale of the Norse Gods,* Silver Burdett, 1969.

John Bierhorst and Henry R. Schoolcraft, editors, *The Ring in the Prairie: A Shawnee Legend,* Dial, 1970.

Alta Jablow, *Gassire's Lute: A West African Epic,* Dutton, 1971.

Alma Murray and Robert Thomas, editors, *The Search,* Scholastic, 1971.

Erik C. Haugaard, *The Untold Tale,* Houghton, 1971.

Verna Aardema, *Behind the Back of the Mountain: Black Folktales from Southern Africa,* Dial, 1973.

Eth Clifford (pseudonym of Ethel C. Rosenberg), *Burning Star,* Houghton, 1974.

W. Moses Serwadda, *Songs and Stories from Uganda,* Crowell, 1974.

Jan Carew, *The Third Gift,* Little, Brown, 1974.

Natalie Belting, *Whirlwind Is a Ghost Dancing,* Dutton, 1974.

Lorenz Graham, *Song of the Boat,* Crowell, 1975.

Harlan Ellison, editor, *Dangerous Visions,* New American Library, 1975.

Sharon Bell Mathis, *The Hundred Penny Box,* Viking, 1975.

Verna Aardema, reteller, *Why Mosquitoes Buzz in People's Ears: A West African Tale,* Dial, 1975.

Margaret W. Musgrove, *Ashanti to Zulu: African Traditions,* Dial, 1976.

Verna Aardema, reteller, *Who's in Rabbit's House?: A Masai Tale,* Dial, 1977.

Eloise Greenfield, *Honey, I Love: And Other Love Poems,* Crowell, 1978.

Frederick Laing, *Tales from Scandinavia,* Silver Burdett, 1979.

P. L. Travers, *Two Pairs of Shoes,* Viking, 1980.

J. Carew, *Children of the Sun,* Little, Brown, 1980.

Dorothy S. Strickland, editor, *Listen Children: An Anthology of Black Literature,* Bantam, 1982.

Mildred Pitts Walter, *Brother to the Wind,* Lothrop, 1985.

Virginia Hamilton, reteller, *The People Could Fly: American Black Folktales,* Knopf, 1985.

(Contributor) Mitsumasa Anno, compiler, *All in a Day,* Dowanya (Japan), 1986.

(Contributor) *Once Upon a Time: Celebrating the Magic of Children's Books in Honor of the Twentieth Anniversary of Reading Is Fundamental,* Putnam, 1986.

Michael P. Hearn, *The Porcelain Cat,* Little, Brown, 1987.

Barbara A. Brenner, *The Color Wizard: Level 1,* Bantam, 1989.

Alice Bach and J. Cheryl Exum, *Moses' Ark: Stories from the Bible,* Delacorte, 1989.

Leontyne Price, editor, *Aida: A Picture Book for All Ages,* Harcourt, 1990.

Katherine Paterson, *The Tale of the Mandarin Ducks,* Dutton, 1990.

Alice Bach and J. Cheryl Exum, *Miriam's Well: Stories about Women in the Bible,* Delacorte, 1991.

Claire Martin, *The Race of the Golden Apples,* Dial, 1991.

Nancy Willard, *Pish, Posh, Said Hieronymus Bosch,* Harcourt, 1991.

Nancy White Carlstrom, *Northern Lullaby,* Putnam, 1992.

Nancy Willard, *The Sorcerer's Apprentice,* Scholastic, 1993.

Virginia Hamilton, *Many Thousand Gone: African Americans from Slavery to Freedom,* Knopf, 1993.

Ray Bradbury, *Switch on the Night,* Knopf, 1993.

N. N. Charles, *What Am I?: Looking Through Shapes at Apples and Grapes,* Scholastic, 1994.

Virginia Hamilton, *Her Stories: African American Folktales, Fairy Tales and True Tales,* Scholastic, 1995.

(Contributor) *On the Wings of Peace: Writers and Illustrators Speak Out for Peace, in Memory of Hiroshima and Nagasaki,* Houghton Mifflin, 1995.

Howard Norman, *The Girl Who Dreamed Only Geese and Other Tales of the Far North,* Harcourt Brace, 1997.

To Every Thing There Is a Season: Verses from Ecclesiastes, Scholastic, 1998.

Illustrator of numerous book cover jackets; also illustrator of album covers. Contributor of illustrations to periodicals, including *Ladies' Home Journal, Saturday Evening Post,* and *Washington Post.* Artist of stained glass ceiling in Eagle Gallery, New York City.

Work included in the Kerlan Collection, University of Minnesota.

Adaptations

Why Mosquitoes Buzz in People's Ears was adapted as a filmstrip with audiocassette and as a motion picture, Weston Woods, 1977; *Ashanti to Zulu* was adapted as a filmstrip with audiocassette, Weston Woods, 1977; *Brother to the Wind* was adapted as a filmstrip with audiocassette, Weston Woods, 1988; *The People Could Fly* was released on audiocassette, Knopf, 1988; *The Tale of the Mandarin Ducks* was produced on video cassette by Weston Woods, 1998.

Work in Progress

Wind Child, by Shirley Rosseau Murphy, for HarperCollins; *Mansa Musa: The Lion of Mali,* by Khephra Burns, for Harcourt Brace.

Sidelights

See entry on Diane Dillon for joint "Sidelights" on Leo and Diane Dillon.

For More Information See

BOOKS

The Art of Leo and Diane Dillon, edited by Byron Preiss, Ballantine, 1981.

Children's Literature Review, Volume 44, Gale, 1997, pp. 17-49.

Newbery and Caldecott Medalists and Honor Book Winners, compiled by Jim Roginski, Libraries Unlimited, 1982.

PERIODICALS

Booklist, December 1, 1992, p. 665; November 1, 1993, p. 529; November 15, 1994, p. 605; September 15, 1997, p. 233.

Horn Book, September-October, 1993, p. 621; January, 1996, pp. 81-82; September-October, 1998, pp. 619-20.

Kirkus Reviews, September 15, 1998, p. 1383.

New York Times Book Review, November 16, 1997, p. 30.

Publishers Weekly, June 28, 1991, p. 101; August 8, 1994, p. 428; November 13, 1995, p. 60; July 27, 1998, p. 76.

School Library Journal, October, 1990, p. 111; January, 1992, p. 118; January, 1994, pp. 116-17.*

E

EGIELSKI, Richard 1952-

Personal

Born July 16, 1952, in New York, NY; son of Joseph Frank (a police lieutenant) and Caroline (an executive secretary; maiden name, Rzepny) Egielski; married Denise Saldutti (an illustrator), May 8, 1977. *Education:* Studied at Pratt Institute, 1970-71; graduated from Parsons School of Design, 1974. *Hobbies and other interests:* Playing the mandolin.

Addresses

Home—7 West Fourteenth St., New York, NY 10011.

Career

Illustrator, 1973—. *Exhibitions:* "Illustrators 16," 1974, and "Illustrators 18," 1976, Society of Illustrators, New York, NY.

Awards, Honors

The Porcelain Pagoda included in American Institute of Graphic Arts Book Show, 1976; Children's Book of the Year citation, Child Study Association of America, 1976, for *The Letter, the Witch, and the Ring;* certificates of merit, Society of Illustrators, 1978, 1981, 1984, and 1985; Best Books, *School Library Journal,* 1980, for *Louis the Fish;* plaque from Biennale of Illustrations Bratislava, 1985, for *It Happened in Pinsk;* Parents' Choice, 1985, for *Amy's Eyes;* Caldecott Medal, American Library Association (ALA), 1987, for *Hey, Al;* Parents' Choice Picture Book Award, 1989, for *The Tub People;* Best Illustrated Book, New York Times, 1998, for *Jazper.*

Writings

AUTHOR AND ILLUSTRATOR

Buz, HarperCollins, 1995.
The Gingerbread Boy, HarperCollins, 1997.

Jazper, HarperCollins, 1998.

ILLUSTRATOR

Moonguitars (reader), Houghton, 1974.
F. N. Monjo, *The Porcelain Pagoda,* Viking, 1976.
John Bellairs, *The Letter, the Witch, and the Ring,* Dial, 1976.
Miriam Chaikin, *I Should Worry, I Should Care,* Harper-Collins, 1979.
Chaikin, *Finders Weepers,* HarperCollins, 1980.
Isabel Langis Cusack, *Mr. Wheatfield's Loft,* Holt, 1981.
Miriam Chaikin, *Getting Even,* HarperCollins, 1982.
Jim Aylesworth, *Mary's Mirror,* Holt, 1982.
Miriam Chaikin, *Lower! Higher! You're a Liar!,* Harper-Collins, 1984.
Gelett Burgess, *The Little Father,* Farrar, Straus, 1985.
Richard Kennedy, *Amy's Eyes,* HarperCollins, 1985.
Miriam Chaikin, *Friends Forever,* HarperCollins, 1988.
Pam Conrad, *The Tub People,* HarperCollins, 1989.
William J. Brooke, *A Telling of the Tales: Five Stories,* HarperCollins, 1990.
Pam Conrad, *The Lost Sailor,* HarperCollins, 1992.
Conrad, *The Tub Grandfather,* HarperCollins, 1993.
Conrad, *Call Me Ahnighito,* HarperCollins, 1995.
Bill Martin, Jr., *Fire! Fire! Said Mrs. McGuire,* Harcourt, 1996.
William Wise, *Perfect Pancakes, If You Please,* Dial, 1997.
Alan Arkin, *One Present from Flekman's,* HarperCollins, 1999.
Pam Conrad, *The Tub People's Christmas,* HarperCollins, 1999.

ILLUSTRATOR; ALL WRITTEN BY ARTHUR YORINKS

Sid & Sol, Farrar, Straus, 1977.
Louis the Fish, Farrar, Straus, 1980.
It Happened in Pinsk, Farrar, Straus, 1983.
Hey, Al, Farrar, Straus, 1986.
Bravo, Minski, Farrar, Straus, 1988.
Oh, Brother, Farrar, Straus, 1989.
Ugh, Farrar, Straus, 1990.
Christmas in July, HarperCollins, 1991.

Adaptations

Louis the Fish, Reading Rainbow, PBS-TV, 1983; *The Tub People* has been adapted for audio cassette.

Sidelights

Richard Egielski is a master of "idiosyncratic and highly personal picture books," according to Anne Quirk in *Children's Books and Their Creators.* In collaboration with writers such as Arthur Yorinks and Pam Conrad, and in his own self-illustrated picture books, this American illustrator "has created some of the most quirky and original children's books of recent decades," Quirk noted. The winner of the 1987 Caldecott Medal, Egielski—though noted for the sometimes surreal nature of his content—presents illustrations with sharp lines and vivid colors; illustrations that enhance the text rather than simply amplify it. "I love to interpret text," Egielski once told *SATA.* "A good illustrator is never a slave to text. The text rarely tells him what to do, but, rather,

what his choices are. I only illustrate texts I truly believe in." In award-winning books such as *Hey, Al,* done in collaboration with Yorinks, and *The Tub People,* with Conrad, as well as in his own creations such as *Buz* and *Jazper,* Egielski has demonstrated, in the words of Quirk, the "singular vision, emotional urgency, and technical mastery of an artist at the top of his form."

Born in Queens, New York, in 1952, Egielski grew up in Maspeth, Queens, the son of a police lieutenant. "They called me 'the artist of the family,'" he once recalled for *SATA,* "but it seemed that there was one in every family. It didn't necessarily mean you were good at drawing, just that you enjoyed doing it." Egielski's earliest influences were comic books and movies. He retained his love for both and later looked back at his earliest cartoon sketches to realize that, as picture books had originally given rise to cartoons, the opposite happened for him: he started with cartoons and moved to picture books. As a youth he missed the influence of picture books. "I wasn't aware of picture books until I was old

The little wooden Tub People find Tub Grandfather lost and asleep under the radiator, and the family works together to revive him. (*From* The Tub Grandfather, *written by Pam Conrad and illustrated by Egielski.*)

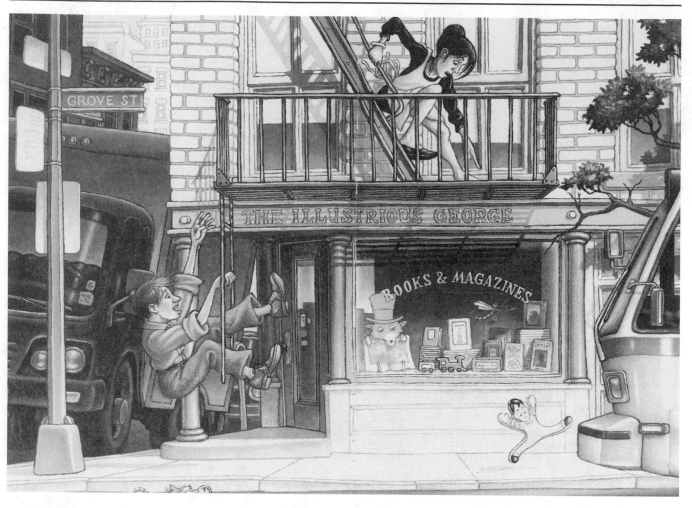

Egielski retells the popular tale of the Gingerbread Boy, giving the story a big-city twist. (From The Gingerbread Boy, *written and illustrated by Egielski.)*

enough to consider them 'baby books,'" he once told *SATA*. Books were not an essential ingredient of his childhood—a child of the 1950s, he grew up in a visual universe.

Catholic school was the bane of his early life, an institution that "felt like a concentration camp" to him. "All those things you hear about: nuns throwing eraser at students; rapping kids' knuckles with rulers, is all true," he told *SATA*. So when it came time for high school, Egielski did research, in the hopes of going to a public school. An interest in freedom, rather than art, led him to apply to New York's High School of Art and Design, but once accepted there his love for line and design became firmly established. "At the end of four years, I'd resolved to become a painter because I'd discovered such artists as Rembrandt and Goya, whose work made a deep impression on me," Egielski recalled. "They are the most illustrative of painters."

Upon graduation he attended the Pratt Institute for a year. The painting program there was heavily influenced by Abstract Expressionism and Egielski "felt like a dinosaur doing representational work," but that was where his heart was. He was attracted to narrative artists

such as N. C. Wyeth and ultimately determined that illustration was what he wanted, not fine art. The son of a middle-class family, he was practical about his career choices, opting for a field which produced a marketable product. In 1971 he transferred to Parsons School of Design, planning to become a commercial illustrator. His work as a student appeared in several magazines, but Egielski's direction changed after taking a class in picture books taught by Maurice Sendak. For Egielski, Sendak was that wonderful find, a real teacher. "An important teacher is one who exposes you to something new," Egielski told *SATA,* "and points out a direction you otherwise might have missed. In introducing me to the art of the picture books, Maurice Sendak became a crucial influence. The quality of his work is a continuing inspiration." Another important influence came about as a result of Egielski's years at Parsons: there he met the illustrator Denise Saldutti, whom he married in 1977.

Graduating from Parsons in 1974, Egielski was met with skeptical looks from editors to whom he took his portfolio. He was told his work was too strange and sophisticated for children's books, but once again Sendak came to his aid, introducing him to the young writer Arthur Yorinks, whose books were badly in need of a sympathetic illustrator. The two ultimately formed a collaborative bond, working together on eight titles, including the Caldecott Medal-winning *Hey, Al.* Unlike some authors and illustrators who work separately, these two worked closely on each project. Their first book together, *Sid & Sol,* was published in 1977. Over the next fourteen years the two worked on seven further titles.

Yorinks's texts often drew inspiration from such classic writers as Gogol and Kafka. His *Louis the Fish,* for example, was suggested by Kafka's *The Metamorphosis,* in which a man is turned into a large insect. The award-winning *Hey, Al* tells the story of a janitor and his dog who live in a cramped apartment and dream of a tropical island with plenty of room. When a tropical bird offers them the opportunity of living on such an island, they eagerly take it. Egielski's drawings for this book range from cramped and pinched illustrations of the apartment with legs going out of the frame, emphasizing the tiny space, to large and animated tropical animals that emphasize the exotic quality of the island. "Every aspect of the picture book as an art form is utilized to create an unforgettable partnership of pictures and words," noted Kay Vandergrift, chair of the Caldecott Medal committee, in *School Library Journal.* "Egielski takes us from the real world to a world of fantasy and back.... Shifts in framing techniques as well as in palette deftly mirror and expand the pattern of the text." Another Egielski-Yorinks title, *Oh, Brother,* tells the "uproarious misad-

ventures" of twin brothers, according to a *School Library Journal* commentator, as they travel from a home for lost boys to England, arguing all the while. The reviewer called the book a "playful look at brotherly love," and remarked especially on the "jolly good humor bursting from the illustrations."

Egielski has also teamed up with other authors to create books of distinction. Illustrating for Pam Conrad, he has published award winners such as *The Tub People* and its sequel, *The Tub Grandfather,* as well as *The Lost Sailor* and *Call Me Ahnighito.* Egielski created a cast of little wooden figures who inhabit the bathroom for *The Tub People;* in its sequel the Tub People move out to a cozier room where they discover the long-lost Tub Grandfather of the title. There is a sentimental reunion as the grandmother dances across the carpet with her newly refound husband; the Egielski-illustrated depiction of this is "almost heartachingly tender," according to Quirk in *Children's Books and Their Creators.* Carolyn Phelan remarked in *Booklist* that while this sequel may not have "the innate child appeal" of its predecessor, the reader should not "underestimate the charm or the power of Egielski's large-scale watercolor illustrations to bring the tub toys and this picture book to life." Joy Fleishhacker, reviewing the same title in *School Library Journal,* commented that "Egielski constructs a variety of moods through a clever use of perspective and the careful positioning of the figures in each scene."

Jazper the bug learns how to transform himself into various things with the help of some books of magic spells, and finds that his newfound knowledge protects him from some menacing moths. (From Jazper, *written and illustrated by Egielski.)*

In *The Lost Sailor,* Egielski joins Conrad to tell the story of a shipwrecked mariner. Ann A. Flowers, writing in *Horn Book,* found Egielski's work "clear, simple" and "almost stylized," while a *Publishers Weekly* contributor noted that "Egielski's watercolors pack more dramatic punch and, especially in his depictions of the solitary figure on the lush abandoned island, contain more food for the imagination." A further joint effort with Conrad is *Call Me Ahnighito,* the story of a meteorite that landed in the Arctic, told in the first person by the meteorite itself. "Egielski's interpretations of the Arctic are magnificent," noted Elizabeth S. Watson in *Horn Book,* who went on to praise the "provocative pictures of the frozen landscape, yellow northern light, and icy waters" which "depict the cold isolation that the voice describes." Carolyn Phelan, a reviewer for *Booklist,* concluded that "throughout the book, Egielski achieves subtle and exceptionally beautiful effects with color, texture, and light," while a critic for *Publishers Weekly* enthused that "Egielski's familiar art takes on a majestic quality" in this book.

Other collaborative efforts have been with Bill Martin, Jr., on his *Fire! Fire! Said Mrs. McGuire,* and with William Wise on *Perfect Pancakes, If You Please.* The former title provides "slapstick humor and fast-paced action" in a rhyming story, according to a *Publishers Weekly* contributor. Originally published in 1970, the new edition with Egielski's illustrations is "bigger, brighter, and more original in concept," according to Carolyn Phelan of *Booklist.* A critic for *Publishers Weekly* concluded that "Egielski's rumble-tumble stage business and inventive subplots combine with Martin's comic puns and rhythmic verve to make this picture book a five alarm delight." Wise's text about a king who offers his daughter's hand to the man who can make perfect pancakes was also adroitly accompanied by Egielski's "robust, richly colored illustrations" which "capture the comedy well," according to *Booklist* reviewer Stephanie Zvirin.

Egielski, who works primarily in watercolors and who once said that he would never try to write his own picture books, has also created three books that prove that one should never say "never." *Buz, The Gingerbread Boy,* and *Jazper* are all picture books written and illustrated by Egielski. In *Buz,* a boy eats a bug with his breakfast; the ensuing story follows the bug through the boy's system and the search for it by pills ordered by the doctor. Writing in *School Library Journal,* Wendy Lukehart commented that "Egielski makes effective use of double-page close-ups, interior and exterior perspectives, and page layout to build suspense and heightened dramatic impact." A *Publishers Weekly* reviewer called this debut solo book a "droll adventure," and concluded that "this book is ... great fun to read and to look at."

Egielski adapted the nursery rhyme *The Gingerbread Boy* for his next solo effort. In this story, he gives the tale a big-city twist, with the Gingerbread Boy getting loose in New York City and being chased by rats, construction workers, and even a mounted policeman. Judith Constantinides, in *School Library Journal,* felt that "Egielski's retelling is straightforward," and that his illustrations "adroitly evoke the city setting while giving a solid three-dimensionality and unique individuality to the Gingerbread Boy and his pursuers." Constantinides concluded that this "clever confection makes a fine addition to folklore collections." Ann A. Flowers, reviewing *The Gingerbread Boy* for *Horn Book,* dubbed Egielski's work "a smooth and sophisticated version of the famous tale," while Hazel Rochman noted in a *Booklist* review that "the combination of wild farce and luscious paintings make for great storytelling and a celebration of the city."

Returning to a bug motif for *Jazper,* Egielski created a Pinocchio-like boy insect in his eponymous hero. Jazper and his dad live in a rented eggshell while their more affluent neighbors inhabit full-size cans and cereal boxes. When Jazper's dad loses his job, the boy sets out to earn some money by house-sitting. And then the trouble begins, for Jazper runs afoul of five very strange moths. A *New York Times* Best Illustrated Book for 1998, *Jazper* is "sure to appeal to youngsters growing up on surreal dollops of Dr. Seuss, William Joyce, Daniel Kirk, William Steig, and earlier Egielski," maintained *School Library Journal* contributor John Sigwald.

Egielski has no regrets about the course his life has taken. His dreams of a fine arts career have actually come to fruition in his children's books. "I must say that I like the whole idea of creating picture books within the standard thirty-two page format," he once told *SATA.* "It's not unlike the sonnet form, in which the poet has so many lines in which to express himself. I don't feel at all constricted by this. On the contrary, the 'rules' of the form seem to set me free. I'm always discovering new things I can do. The picture book is an art form unto itself.... My illustration is my fine art. I have absolutely no reason to wish to liberate or wean myself from dependence upon text. It is through my illustrations that I express myself most deeply and fully."

Works Cited

Review of *Buz, Publishers Weekly,* July 17, 1995, p. 229.

Review of *Call Me Ahnighito, Publishers Weekly,* May 15, 1995, p. 73.

Constantinides, Judith, review of *The Gingerbread Boy, School Library Journal,* September, 1997, p. 180.

Review of *Fire! Fire! Said Mrs. McGuire, Publishers Weekly,* March 18, 1996, p. 68.

Fleishhacker, Joy, review of *The Tub Grandfather, School Library Journal,* March, 1994, p. 192.

Flowers, Ann A., review of *The Gingerbread Boy, Horn Book,* September-October, 1997, p. 587.

Flowers, Ann A., review of *The Lost Sailor, Horn Book,* March-April, 1993, p. 194.

Review of *The Lost Sailor, Publishers Weekly,* June 29, 1992, p. 63.

Lukehart, Wendy, review of *Buz, School Library Journal,* September, 1995, p. 175.

Review of *Oh, Brother, School Library Journal,* January, 1998, p. 43.

Phelan, Carolyn, review of *Call Me Ahnighito, Booklist,* May 1, 1995, p. 1579.

Phelan, Carolyn, review of *Fire! Fire! Said Mrs. McGuire, Booklist,* March 15, 1996, p. 1266.

Phelan, Carolyn, review of *The Tub Grandfather, Booklist,* October 15, 1993, p. 451.

Quirk, Anne, essay on Egielski in *Children's Books and Their Creators,* edited by Anita Silvey, Houghton Mifflin, 1995, pp. 219-20.

Rochman, Hazel, review of *The Gingerbread Boy, Booklist,* October 15, 1997, p. 409.

Sigwald, John, review of *Jazper, School Library Journal,* September, 1998, pp. 171-72.

Vandergrift, Kay, quoted in *School Library Journal,* March, 1987, pp. 78-80.

Watson, Elizabeth S., review of *Call Me Ahnighito, Horn Book,* July-August, 1995, p. 448.

Yorinks, Arthur, "Richard Egielski," *Horn Book,* July-August, 1987, pp. 436-38.

Zvirin, Stephanie, review of *Perfect Pancakes, If You Please, Booklist,* December 1, 1996, p. 670.

For More Information See

BOOKS

Sixth Book of Junior Authors and Illustrators, H. W. Wilson, 1989, pp. 85-86.

PERIODICALS

Booklist, August, 1995, p. 1955.
Bulletin of the Center for Children's Books, October, 1995, p. 51.
Kirkus Reviews, September 1, 1997, p. 1387.
Los Angeles Times Book Review, October 1, 1995, p. 7; December 3, 1995, p. 16.
New York Times Book Review, November 12, 1995, p. 30; January 4, 1998, p. 20.
Publishers Weekly, December 9, 1996, p. 67; August 3, 1998, p. 84.
School Library Journal, September, 1992, pp. 201-02; June, 1996, p. 117.

—*Sketch by J. Sydney Jones*

* * *

ELYA, Susan M(iddleton) 1955-

Personal

Born June 14, 1955, in Des Moines, IA; daughter of William Robert (a printing press operator) and B. Joanne (a bank teller; maiden name, McNeley) Middleton; married Robert A. Elya (a certified public accountant), December 28, 1985; children: Carolyn, Nicholas, Janine. *Education:* Iowa State University, B.A.; University of Nebraska at Omaha, M.A. *Politics:* Democrat. *Religion:* Methodist. *Hobbies and other interests:* Refinishing furniture, attending garage sales, gardening, reading, sewing.

Addresses

Home—1108 Merlin Ct., Alamo, CA 94507.

Career

Writer and educator. High school Spanish teacher in Ashland, NE, 1977-79; teacher of Spanish and English at Lewis Central Middle School in Council Bluffs, IA, 1979-85, and Spanish teacher at Lewis Central High School, Council Bluffs, 1983-85; Olive Peirce Junior High School, Ramona, CA, teacher of Spanish and English as a second language, 1986-87; Ramona High School, teacher of Spanish and English as a second language, 1986-87. *Member:* American Association of University Women, Society of Children's Book Writers and Illustrators, Authors Guild.

Writings

Say Hola to Spanish, illustrated by Loretta Lopez, Lee & Low, 1996.
Say Hola to Spanish, Otra Vez (Again!), illustrated by Lopez, Lee & Low, 1997.
Say Hola to Spanish at the Circus, Lee & Low, 1999.

Work in Progress

Eight Animales and *Eight Animales Bake a Cake,* for Putnam; twenty manuscripts for young readers, including one chapter book, three books in Spanish, three bilingual books, and picture books.

Sidelights

Susan M. Elya told *SATA:* "I have always wanted to make books. When I was eight, I wrote *The Enchanted Island.* I drew the pictures and stapled them into a construction paper book. Thirty-five years later, I still have it in the attic. One of my first poems was called 'If I Had a Penny.' It's up there, too. I kept diaries and journals for years but never tried to write for publication until I was thirty-two.

"I didn't sell a book for six-and-a-half years. In 1994, after submitting dozens of manuscripts and receiving hundreds of rejections, I finally sent the right thing to the right editor at the right time. *Say Hola to Spanish* was perfect for Lee and Low, the multicultural publisher looking for books about Spanish for English-speakers. My mother had told me all along that I should be using my Spanish in my manuscripts; after all, I had taught it for ten years in the public schools. I finally listened to her.

"I write whenever I can—at breakfast, during my children's naps, waiting for the car pool. I started *Eight Animales* while sitting in the car outside my daughter's piano lesson while my other two children played in the back seat. I keep all the tiny scraps of paper with story ideas on them. I never, ever write something in one sitting. The 'Say Hola' books were written one couplet at a time. I'd think of a rhyme on my way to somewhere and write it down at a stop light. Some of my best rhymes come to me while driving. I highly recommend keeping a pad of paper and pen in the car.

"Competition is fierce in children's book publishing, but I am proof that publishers still look at and buy unsolicited manuscripts. You have to figure out what you do well and use it in your writing. When in doubt about what that is, listen to your mother."

For More Information See

PERIODICALS

Booklist, May 1, 1996, p. 1509.
Publishers Weekly, October 27, 1997, p. 75.
School Library Journal, June, 1996, p. 100; January, 1998, p. 98.

F

FISHMAN, Cathy Goldberg 1951-

Personal

Born October 12, 1951, in Mesa, AZ; daughter of Joel H. and Peggy (maiden name, Fox) Goldberg; married M. Steven Fishman, September 6, 1981; children: Alexander Joshua, Brittany Paige. *Education:* Lesley College, B.Ed., 1973. *Religion:* Jewish.

Cathy Goldberg Fishman

Addresses

Home—1861 Central Ave., Augusta, GA 30904. *Electronic mail*—catfishG@groupZ.net.

Career

Elementary schoolteacher, 1973-75; day care director, 1976-78; children's bookstore owner, 1979-83; full-time mother and writer, 1983—. *Member:* Society of Children's Book Writers and Illustrators, Hadassah (past chapter president).

Awards, Honors

Parents Choice Award (Story Book Recommendation), 1998, for *On Hanukkah.*

Writings

PICTURE BOOKS, ILLUSTRATED BY MELANIE HALL

On Rosh Hashanah and Yom Kippur, Atheneum, 1997.
On Passover, Atheneum, 1997.
On Hanukkah, Atheneum, 1998.

Work in Progress

On Purim, for Atheneum; *On Shabbat; On Sukkot; Simchat Torah.*

Sidelights

Cathy Goldberg Fishman told *SATA:* "I grew up in Atlanta, Georgia, and was confirmed at The Temple on Peachtree Street in 1967. After graduating from Lesley College in Cambridge, Massachusetts, I moved to Augusta, Georgia, and taught elementary school for a few years, directed a day-care center and eventually opened a children's bookstore, Eeyore's Tale. The bookstore took up the downstairs part of an old house that was built in 1917 and I lived upstairs. I met my husband, Steven, at a Jewish Singles Party in Augusta and we married in 1981. When I became pregnant with my oldest child, I closed the store and became a full-time mom. We now have two children—Alexander and Brittany—two cats, a dog, a koi-goldfish pond and a compost heap with worms, but we still live in the same old house I had the bookstore in.

"My religious background was very 'Reform' and Steven grew up in an 'Orthodox' home. When we married, since all of Steven's family lived in Augusta, I became more involved in observant Judaism. As I learned more, and as my children grew and asked questions, I started putting thoughts on paper. I got the idea for my first book, *On Passover*, as I started thinking about the upcoming holiday when I was attending an Hadassah Regional Conference. It is now part of what I consider a series of Jewish holiday books.

"When I am not writing, or trying to be a 'full-time mom,' I am involved in volunteer activities in Hadassah and my synagogue, as well as working in the Fishman family business."

Cathy Goldberg Fishman has written a series of picture-book stories that explain the history and meaning of the Jewish holidays. Critics celebrated the warmth and vitality of the author's depiction of Passover in her first book, *On Passover*. Fishman's story centers on a young girl and her observations of the sights, sounds, and smells of this special day as she learns about the Jewish religion by questioning her mother about preparations for the holiday. "Fishman offers a clear, thorough presentation of the religious significance of this celebration that never sounds didactic," declared a reviewer for *Publishers Weekly*. Other critics emphasized the idyllic Jewish family life depicted in *On Passover* and in Fishman's next book, *On Rosh Hashanah and Yom Kippur*. In this picture book, as in Fishman's earlier work, a young girl narrates the story of how she and her family celebrate the High Holidays of the Jewish New Year and Day of Atonement, which are marked by particular rituals in the synagogue and special foods or fasting in the home. Fishman includes Hebrew words in italics in the text, and a one-page glossary with pronunciation and definitions concludes the volume. These two works contain "much the same vitality and sensitivity" as *On Passover*, according to *Booklist* contributor Stephanie Zvirin. *Bulletin of the Center for Children's Books* reviewer Betsy Hearne recommended *On Rosh Hashanah and Yom Kippur* as a teaching aid in both classroom and home settings.

Works Cited

Hearne, Betsy, review of *On Rosh Hashanah and Yom Kippur*, *Bulletin of the Center for Children's Books*, February, 1998, p. 199.
Review of *On Passover*, *Publishers Weekly*, February 24, 1997, p. 83.
Zvirin, Stephanie, review of *On Rosh Hashanah and Yom Kippur*, *Booklist*, October 1, 1997, p. 322.

For More Information See

PERIODICALS

Booklist, March 1, 1997, p. 1165.
Kirkus Reviews, April 1, 1997, pp. 553-54.
School Library Journal, April, 1997, p. 100; October, 1997, p. 117.

*   *   *

FOLEY, (Mary) Louise Munro 1933-

Personal

Born October 22, 1933, in Toronto, Ontario, Canada; daughter of William Angus (a pharmacist) and Mary (a homemaker; maiden name, Nicholls) Munro; married Donald J. Foley, August 9, 1957 (divorced, 1984); children: Donald, William. *Education:* Attended University of Western Ontario, 1951-52, and Ryerson Institute of Technology, 1952-53; California State University at Sacramento, B.A. (with honors), 1976. *Politics:* Republican. *Religion:* Presbyterian. *Hobbies and other interests:* Music, art.

Addresses

Home—Sacramento, CA.

Career

CHOK Radio, Sarnia, ON, copyeditor, 1953-54; CJSP Radio, Leamington, ON, copyeditor, 1954-56; KLIX-TV, Twin Falls, ID, copyeditor, 1956-58; KGMS Radio, Sacramento, CA, copyeditor, 1958-60; copy chief (retail) for Breuner's, Weinstock's, and Rhodes department stores, 1961-65; *New Argus*, Goldsboro, NC, columnist, 1966; author, 1967—; California State University at Sacramento, Institute for Human Management, editor, 1975-80; Fremont Presbyterian Church, Sacramento, executive secretary, 1984-94; Institute of Children's Literature, West Redding, CT, instructor, 1997—. *Member:* National League of American Penwomen, California Writer's Club, Society of Children's Book Writers and Illustrators, Novelists, Inc.

Awards, Honors

Advertising Club of Sacramento Award, 1971, "for excellence in creative, effective advertising in the field of brochures."

Writings

The Caper Club, illustrated by David K. Stone, Random House, 1969.
Somebody Stole Second, illustrated by John Heinly, Delacorte, 1972.
Sammy's Sister, Bobbs-Merrill, 1974.
A Job for Joey, Bobbs-Merrill, 1974.
No Talking, Bobbs-Merrill, 1974.
Tackle 22, illustrated by John Heinly, Delacorte, 1978.

Australia: Find the Flying Foxes!, illustrated by Barbara Carter, McGraw-Hill, 1988.
Blood! Said the Cat, Berkley, 1992.
Poison! Said the Cat, Berkley, 1992.
Thief! Said the Cat, Berkley, 1992.
In Search of the Hidden Statue ("Bepuzzled Junior" series), Bepuzzled, 1993.

"CHOOSE YOUR OWN ADVENTURE" SERIES, ALL PUBLISHED BY BANTAM

The Lost Tribe, 1984.
The Mystery of the Highland Crest, 1984.
The Mystery of Echo Lodge, 1985.
Danger at Anchor Mine, illustrated by Leslie Morrill, 1985.
Forest of Fear, 1985.
The Mardi Gras Mystery, 1987.
Mystery of the Sacred Stones, 1988.
The Cobra Connection, 1990.
Ghost Train, illustrated by Frank Bolle, 1991.

"TWISTAPLOT BOOKS" SERIES, ALL PUBLISHED BY SCHOLASTIC

The Train of Terror, illustrated by David Febland, 1982.
The Sinister Studios of KESP-TV, illustrated by David Febland, 1983.

"VAMPIRE CAT" SERIES

Vampire Cat, Tor, 1996.
My Substitute Teacher's Gone Batty!, Tor, 1996.

The Bird Brained Fiasco, Tor, 1996.
The Phoney-Baloney Professor, Tor, 1996.
The Catnip Cat-Astrophy!, Tor, 1996.

OTHER

(Editor) *Stand Close to the Door*, Institute for Human Service Management, 1976.
Women in Skilled Labor, Institute for Human Service Management, 1978.

Contributor of humorous daily column, in collaboration with husband, appearing in *Goldsboro (NC) News-Argus*.

Portions of Munro's work can be found at the De Grummond Collection at the University of Southern Mississippi.

Sidelights

Louise Munro Foley once told *SATA* that she enjoys writing "'fun' fiction for kids—rather than moralistic stories," asserting that "kids need escapist reading just as much as adults."

For More Information See

PERIODICALS

School Library Journal, March, 1989, p. 177.*

G

GOUGH, Sue 1940-

Personal

Born April 4, 1940, in London, England; daughter of Siegfried Charles Fairbairn (an aeronautical engineer) and Nancy Eileen Ellis (a teacher); married David Kenneth Gough (a forester), August 2, 1974; children: Ceinwen Anne, Anthony David. *Education:* Eton Hall Preparatory School (London) and South Hampstead High School (London), a suffragette founded school. *Religion:* Buddhist.

Addresses

Home—344 Savages Rd., Brookfield, Brisbane, Queensland 4069 Australia. *Electronic mail*—Goughs.DandS @uq.net.au. *Agent*—Anthony Williams Management, 1st fl., 50 Oxford St., Paddington, Sydney N8W 2021, Australia.

Career

Canberra Times, Canberra, ACT, arts writer, 1963-68; freelance writer and editor, 1968—; Jacaranda Press, editor, Brisbane, Queensland, Australia, 1970-74. National Theatre Critic, 1984-98. Queensland State Library (board member), and Literature Board of the Australia Council for the Arts.

Awards, Honors

Honour Book, Children's Book Council of Australia, 1993, for *A Long Way to Tipperary,* and 1994, for *Wyrd.*

Writings

YOUNG ADULT NOVELS

A Long Way to Tipperary, University of Queensland Press (St. Lucia, Queensland), 1992.
Wyrd, University of Queensland Press, 1993.
Here Comes the Night, University of Queensland Press, 1997.

OTHER

Queensland Colonial Years, Hodder Australia, 1984.
(With Dianne Weedon) *Tears in My Champagne* (biography), Champagne Publications (Brisbane, Queensland), 1984.
The Book of Brisbane, Oxford University Press, 1985.
Sugar, Hodder Australia, 1986.
Hard Times and High Hopes, Jacaranda, 1986.
Issues of Today: Conservation, Martin Educational, 1986.
Issues of Today: AIDS, Martin Educational, 1989.

Sue Gough

Unique Mammals of Australia, Jacaranda Young Inquirers, 1990.
Creatures of the Antarctic, Jacaranda, 1992.
Big Beasts, Fact or Fiction, Jacaranda, 1992.
Keeping in Touch through Time, Jacaranda, 1992.
Thommo Makes His Mark, Jacaranda, 1992.
From Raw to Ready, Jacaranda, 1992.
Tell It in Print, Jacaranda, 1992.
The Daggs Meet the Bad Beasts, Rigby Zapper Books, 1993.
Punk Rocker from Hell, Rigby Zapper Books, 1993.
The Monster Manual, Rigby Zapper Books, 1995.
(Editor) Jan Power, *Setting the Stage: Queensland Performing Arts Complex: The First Ten Years,* Boolarong Press (Brisbane, Queensland), 1995.

Also author of storylines for the television series *Barrier Reef:* "Coconut Ice" and "Scotch on the Rocks," both 1970.

Work in Progress

A first adult novel entitled *The Nether Regions,* and a fourth young adult novel entitled *The H.I.T.*

Sidelights

Sue Gough told *SATA:* "I spent a long time trudging along the trenches making a buck: ghostwriting, researching and creating school textbooks, rewriting legal studies texts and economic studies texts, even writing corporate annual reports. And then, in 1990 at the age of fifty, I learned how to fly. I starting writing fiction.

"It came as a surprise that my first novel, *A Long Way to Tipperary,* was such a success. It is a historical romp set in 1918. The book is still in print and still being studied in English classes all over Australia. On the back cover of that book it says that my aim was to 'entertain, by which I mean amuse, excite, sadden, surprise, instruct, mystify, satisfy and, in the nicest way, subvert.' I guess you could say this is the philosophy that fuels all my writing. Underneath the entertainment I deal with the big issues.

"My second novel, *Wyrd,* grew out of two major concerns: my interest in women's lost history and, in the present, the way in which young people give up their individual intelligence to 'group think' and so get sucked into cults.

"Novel number three, *Here Comes the Night,* is a sequel to *Tipperary* and set in 1939. It is my response to the neo-fascism rearing its head here in Australia and all over the world."

Gough's novels for young adults have been praised for their exuberant sense of humor, their wide casts of characters, and their concern with topical social issues. In her first novel, the award-winning *A Long Way to Tipperary,* the author creates a vigorous melange of characters who come together to form a travelling show under the direction of Mrs. Featherstonhaugh-Beau-

The sequel to **A Long Way to Tipperary,** *Gough's novel brings together a large cast of culturally diverse, displaced characters, who fight desperately against oppression in pre-World War II Calcutta.*

champ, a comic character who "could easily have stepped from the pages of *Pickwick Papers,*" a reviewer in *The Word* contended. The setting is 1918 Queensland, during the last days of the First World War, and Gough was credited with successfully incorporating a myriad of details that authentically reflect the period. Finally, "the broad tableau of characters introduces many diverse elements," observed Jane Connelly in *Magpies,* including "humour, romance, suspense, Aboriginal spirituality and the cultural diversity which is Australia." Connelly recommended the book for young adults and adults both as "not to be missed."

Gough's next novel for young adults, *Wyrd,* is a fantasy that interweaves the medieval world of Berengaria, the secret wife of Richard the Lionhearted, with the modern world of protagonist Trace in Sidney, Australia, through the discovery of Berengaria's journal. With her friends Ulla, Trixie and Veronica, Trace becomes involved in a plan to save Berengaria's journal from the misogynist Professor Horniman, who strives to block the dissemination of women's history. "The storyline is fascinating and original," asserted *Magpies* contributor Kim Caraher, who added: "Gough has a talent for revealing character and developing plot through vivacious and entertaining dialogue as part of short, meaningful scenes." Gough is also the author of *Here Comes the Night,* a sequel to her *Long Way to Tipperary* set in Calcutta, Bhutan, Prague, and Australia in 1939. The novel shares with its companion work a time frame that places it in the shadow of war, and a large cast of characters drawn from a wide range of cultures, each displaced in some way. "All these unlikely characters come together not just to fight against oppression but also to act out a prayer of peace and light, the drawing in the circus ring of a great and powerful mandala," commented Tess Brady in *Australian Book Review.*

"I am now working on my fourth novel," Gough continued to *SATA,* "which is set in Seattle in the near future. Tentatively titled *The H.I.T.,* it looks at the dilemma of boys hooked on that adrenalin hit and the ways in which virtual reality is misused by a top scientist to try to keep them out of trouble.

"The writers who have influenced me are the humanists: John Steinbeck, Emile Zola, Charles Dickens. And the zany writers such as Kurt Vonnegut, Jr., and Tom Robbins. And the English women writers who have a wicked sense of humour and style: Angela Carter, A.S. Byatt.

"Why do I write for children? Perhaps because that is where the magic is still possible. Perhaps because I am a case of arrested development. Perhaps because, being born into the world of war in London, books kept reality at bay.

"Children's writing is given a lot of affirmation in Australia at present but with a population of only 18 million it is still hard to make a living as a writer. Writers are dreamers. My current dream is to find an American agent or publisher who will give me a wider audience."

Works Cited

Brady, Tess, review of *Here Comes the Night, Australian Book Review,* November, 1997, p. 59.
Caraher, Kim, review of *Wyrd, Magpies,* July, 1994, p. 34.
Connelly, Jane, review of *A Long Way to Tipperary, Magpies,* July, 1992, p. 33.
Review of *A Long Way to Tipperary, The Word,* March, 1992.

For More Information See

PERIODICALS

Australian Book Review, November, 1997, p. 59.
Exposure, January, 1994, p. 17.
Horn Book, July-August, 1993, p. 498.
Magpies, September, 1997, p. 38.

GRAEBER, Charlotte Towner

Personal

Born in Peoria, IL; married Vance Graeber, 1963; children: two, and two stepchildren. *Education:* Attended University of Illinois.

Addresses

Home—Elgin, IL.

Career

Writer.

Awards, Honors

Friends of American Writers Juvenile Book Merit Award, older category, 1980, and Junior Literary Guild selection, both for *Grey Cloud;* Irma Simonton Black Award, Bank Street College of Education, 1982, and West Virginia Children's Book Award, Wise Library, West Virginia University, 1986, both for *Mustard;* Children's Book of the Year, Child Study Association of America, 1984, for *The Thing in Kat's Attic;* West Virginia Children's Award, 1989-90, Young Hoosier Award (grades 4-6), 1990, KC Three Award, 1989-90,

Charlotte Towner Graeber

Nene Award, 1990, Sequoyah Children's Award, 1990, Sunshine State Award (grades 3-5), 1992, and Iowa's Children's Choice Award, 1992, all for *Fudge.*

Writings

FOR CHILDREN

Grey Cloud, illustrated by Lloyd Bloom, Four Winds Press, 1979.

Mustard, illustrated by Donna Diamond, Macmillan, 1982.

The Thing in Kat's Attic, illustrated by Emily Arnold McCully, Dutton, 1984.

Fudge, illustrated by Cheryl Harness, Lothrop, 1987.

The Fluff Puff Farm, Worlds of Wonder, 1988.

Jake's Birthday Surprise, David C. Cook (Elgin, IL), 1990.

Olivia and the Real Life Pet, illustrated by DyAnne DiSalvo-Ryan, Simon & Schuster, 1995.

Nobody's Dog, illustrated by Barry Root, Hyperion, 1998.

"I LOVE TO READ" SERIES; ILLUSTRATED BY JACK STOCKMAN

Up, Down, and Around the Raintree, Chariot Books, 1984.

In, Out, and About the Catfish Pond, Chariot Books, 1984.

"MR. T AND ME" SERIES; ILLUSTRATED BY JOE BODDY

The Hand-Me-Down Cap, T. Nelson, 1985.

The Somebody Kid, T. Nelson, 1985.

The Silver Squawk Box, T. Nelson, 1985.

The Best Bike Ever, T. Nelson, 1985.

Phoney Baloney, the Counterfeit Kid, T. Nelson, 1985.

The Sidewalk Mockers, T. Nelson, 1985.

The Hard Luck Mutt, T. Nelson, 1985.

My Mr. T Doll, T. Nelson, 1985.

The Not-So-Great Place, T. Nelson, 1985.

Tackle Block Stop, T. Nelson, 1985.

I'm So-So, So What?, T. Nelson, 1985.

The Muscle Tussle, T. Nelson, 1985.

"SPEAK FOR ME" SERIES; ILLUSTRATED BY NEIL PINCHBECK

Jonah, Speak for God!, T. Nelson, 1986.

Moses, Speak for God!, T. Nelson, 1986.

Paul, Speak for God!, T. Nelson, 1986.

Peter, Speak for God!, T. Nelson, 1986.

OTHER

Contributor of articles and stories to periodicals.

Adaptations

"The Fluff Puff Farm" (cassette), Worlds of Wonder, 1988.

Work in Progress

Do You Read Me Papa Bravo, a novel.

Sidelights

Charlotte Towner Graeber told *SATA:* "As soon as I learned to print I began filling notebooks with sad and tearful poetry. By the time I reached fifth grade I was adding notebooks of short stories to the ones filled with poetry in my large closet. But it wasn't until high school that my writing came out of the closet when I realized I was *required* to write poems and essays for the English classes I was *required* to take. Soon I was not only writing my own assignments but was correcting and completing English assignments for a classmate who panicked at the sight of a compound sentence. In exchange I was patiently and painfully steered through high school algebra and geometry with passing grades.

"Shortly after high school my father relocated our family in the Chicago area, where I worked at a dime store, a bank, and an oil company before starting college. Then I began commuting on the Northwestern railroad into the city, riding the elevated train around the Chicago loop, then transferring onto a streetcar that eventually deposited me at the University of Illinois Chicago campus at Navy Pier on Lake Michigan. During the hours of travel to and from the campus I collected bits of dialogue, impressions, and background for my English composition assignments by observing my fellow commuters. To this day I find myself eavesdropping and making up stories about the strangers I observe.

"In 1963 I married Vance Graeber and we settled his two children and dog and my two children and cat in an old house on the Fox River in Elgin, Illinois, where I still live. Here wild geese, ducks, possums, muskrats, raccoons, and other wildlife share the river bank. Through the years we populated our home with a tame crow, a pet skunk, a flying squirrel, white mice, several canaries, a parrot, numerous cats, kittens, tropical fish, and a second dog.

"Still I always managed to find an unoccupied corner to write in—though often I worked with a cat on my lap, a bird on my shoulder, or a dog lying on my feet. During those years I sold my stories to various juvenile and denominational magazines. Eventually my husband converted an old shed on the edge of the river into a small workshop where I now write.

"A few years ago my husband introduced me to a man who breeds and races homing pigeons. At the time we had five cats, one dog, a parrot, a skunk, and a tankful of fish. My easy-going husband put his foot down. 'Enough is enough.' I had to agree. But my interest in homing pigeons continued and I began to write the story that grew into my first book, *Grey Cloud.*

"When my husband died in the crash of his experimental aircraft, I put aside work I had been doing on a novel with an aeronautical background. Ultimately I hope to complete *Do You Read Me Papa Bravo* as a tribute to my husband."

Graeber's novels for middle-grade readers often feature animals and young protagonists who learn something about themselves and the world around them through caring for their pets. In *Mustard,* the author is credited with handling the difficult topic of the death of a beloved pet with sensitivity. Mustard is Alex's cat, but at fourteen she is beginning to slow down, a fact Alex

Chad's plans to get a puppy are almost derailed when his mother finds out she is expecting twins in Graeber's story of a boy's heartfelt desire to have a pet. (From Fudge, *illustrated by Cheryl Harness.)*

refuses to accept until, chased by the neighbor's dog, Mustard suffers a heart attack. The narrative depicts Alex's sorrow and growing acceptance of what must be done as he and his parents take Mustard to the veterinarian for the last time and donate the cat's toys to a local shelter. Kate M. Flanagan, a reviewer for *Horn Book,* applauded the "understated manner" in which Graeber related this "poignant" tale.

There is sorrow at the heart of Graeber's next novel for middle readers too, for reviewers noted that in the background of *The Thing in Kat's Attic* is the realization that Kat, her sister Holly, and their mother, must learn how to care for themselves now that Kat's father has moved out of the house. Kat and Holly hear noises in the night coming from the ceiling, and their mother's mouse traps do not solve the problem. Kat's mother takes the dog up into the attic to chase unwanted squirrels back out the way they came in, and she then attempts to fix the loose shingle so that they won't come back. A reviewer for *School Library Journal* found merit in *The Thing in Kat's Attic* as a story about a single-parent family struggling to make it on its own. Denise M.

Wilms of *Booklist* called Graeber's "low-key story" suitable for younger readers, adding: "The dialogue is smooth and the exposition simple."

In *Fudge,* Graeber takes on a subject addressed frequently in children's literature: a child wants a pet, but his parents doubt that he can handle the responsibility. In this story, nine-year-old Chad is disappointed to learn that his parents have changed their mind after initially agreeing to allow him to have one of his baby-sitter's new puppies. Carol Kolb Phillips, a reviewer for *School Library Journal,* remarked that the "characters [in *Fudge*] are real, the action moves quickly, and the story line will interest children." Chad eventually proves to his parents that he can train and care for the animal himself, and "readers will be rooting for him to remember each of Fudge's meals and to clean up after every mess," remarked Betsy Hearne in *Bulletin of the Center for Children's Books.* Carolyn Phelan of *Booklist* called *Fudge* "a good, solid story for those venturing into short novels."

A child's strong desire for a pet is explored again in *Olivia and the Real Live Pet.* In the beginning of this novel for early readers, eight-year-old Olivia is excited about her upcoming birthday, not least because her aunt has promised to buy her a pet for a present. However, Olivia's excitement is dampened somewhat by the behavior of her friend Kevin, who has taken to mocking and teasing her, Olivia eventually learns, out of envy, for Kevin's beloved pet has recently died. "The emotion in this first chapter book is heartfelt," maintained Hazel Rochman in *Booklist.*

The life that is changed by a pet in *Nobody's Dog* is that of solitary Miss Pepper who, along with several of her neighbors, is initially certain that the abandoned dog sniffing at her garden gate isn't the right pet for her. "Graeber builds her tale as sturdily as a little house, using repetition to bolster the gentle cadences and colorful descriptions," a *Publishers Weekly* critic observed. *School Library Journal* contributor Lisa Dennis also found Graeber's tale "appealing," concluding: "Like the small pup, this book won't take up much room and will be quickly adopted by loving readers."

Works Cited

Dennis, Lisa, review of *Nobody's Dog, School Library Journal,* June, 1998, p. 106.

Flanagan, Kate M., review of *Mustard, Horn Book,* August, 1982, p. 402.

Hearne, Betsy, review of *Fudge, Bulletin of the Center for Children's Books,* July-August, 1987, p. 207.

Review of *Nobody's Dog, Publishers Weekly,* June 15, 1998, p. 59.

Phelan, Carolyn, review of *Fudge, Booklist,* August, 1987, pp. 1747-48.

Phillips, Carol Kolb, review of *Fudge, School Library Journal,* August, 1987, p. 83.

Rochman, Hazel, review of *Olivia and the Real Live Pet, Booklist,* June 1, 1995, p. 1770.

Review of *The Thing in Kat's Attic, School Library Journal,* December, 1984, p. 99.
Wilms, Denise M., review of *The Thing in Kat's Attic, Booklist,* January 1, 1985, p. 641.

For More Information See

PERIODICALS

Booklist, November 1, 1987, p. 489.
School Library Journal, July, 1995, pp. 61-62.

*   *   *

GREENBLAT, Rodney Alan 1960-

Personal

Born August 23, 1960, in San Francisco, CA; son of Arliegh and Josephine (Gandart) Greenblat; married Deena Lebow; children: Cleo, Kimberly. *Education:* School of Visual Arts, New York City, B.F.A., 1982.

Addresses

Agent—(fine arts) Gracie Mansion Fine Art, New York, NY; (commercial art) Tak Iwayoshi Interlink Planning

Rodney Alan Greenblat

Co., Tokyo, Japan. *Electronic mail*—rodney@whimsy load.com.

Career

Artist and illustrator. Center for Advanced Whimsy, New York City, founder and creative director. *Exhibitions:* Paintings and sculptures have been exhibited in galleries and museums around the world.

Writings

AUTHOR AND ILLUSTRATOR

Uncle Wizzmo's New Used Car, HarperCollins (New York City), 1990.
Aunt Ippy's Museum of Junk, HarperCollins, 1991.
Slombo the Gross, HarperCollins, 1993.
Thunder Bunny, HarperCollins, 1997.

OTHER

Creator of the character "Parappa" for the video game *Parappa the Rapper,* for Sony Playstation. Recordings include *Baby Sea Robot.*

Sidelights

Rodney Alan Greenblat fills his children's stories with energy, bright colors, movement, and a rich imagination. In Greenblat's picture book debut, *Uncle Wizzmo's New Used Car,* young narrators Jimi and Jodi accompany their uncle on his annual springtime trip to the big city of Fleeberville to purchase a "new" used car. The adventure takes them along a road filled with humorous side attractions, as the trio wind their way through the countryside and into smaller towns such as Snookersburg and Burgerworld. "In his first picture book for children, Greenblat displays a rich—and extremely colorful—imagination," asserted a *Publishers Weekly* commentator. Ilene Cooper of *Booklist* called *Uncle Wizzmo's New Used Car* a "rollicking story," praising the "free-form style of artwork" employed by Greenblat. "[The] pictures are a tumultuous blend of wild images . . . executed in childlike style," noted Cooper. *School Library Journal* contributor Leda Schubert maintained: "The jazzy, cartoonlike illustrations combine folk-art styles and perspectives with space-age colors and objects—a bit like Grandma Moses gone whacko."

Aunt Ippy's Museum of Junk introduces readers to another of Jimi and Jodi's eccentric relatives. In this story, the siblings are off on another excursion, helping their Aunt Ippy find a "Roto-Spinner" in her "Museum of Junk." Ippy, a dedicated pack-rat, never disposes of anything, housing in her museum everything for which she cannot find an immediate use. "Readers will be delighted to join the search party as it wanders through the Grand Parlor of Scraps, the Gallery of Absurd Bulk and the Chamber of Odds and Ends," noted a *Publishers Weekly* critic. *School Library Journal* contributor Shirley Wilton maintained that "Greenblat's exuberant, brightly colored, full-page pictures are done in a naive, cartoon style" that is "well suited to the comic mood and simple plot."

Works Cited

Review of *Aunt Ippy's Museum of Junk, Publishers Weekly,* May 24, 1991, p. 58.

Cooper, Ilene, review of *Uncle Wizzmo's New Used Car, Booklist,* April 1, 1990, p. 1548.

Schubert, Leda, review of *Uncle Wizzmo's New Used Car, School Library Journal,* June, 1990, p. 100.

Review of *Uncle Wizzmo's New Used Car, Publishers Weekly,* April 27, 1990, p. 60.

Wilton, Shirley, review of *Aunt Ippy's Museum of Junk, School Library Journal,* December, 1991, p. 92.

For More Information See

PERIODICALS

Children's Book Review Service, January, 1992, p. 51.

Publishers Weekly, July 12, 1993, p. 78; December 9, 1996, p. 67.

School Library Journal, February, 1994, p. 84; March, 1997, p. 159.

H

HALLIDAY, Brett
See JOHNSON, (Walter) Ryerson

*   *   *

HARRISON, Michael 1939-

Personal

Born June 7, 1939, in Oxford, England; married Anne Corben (a former teacher), December 30, 1970; children: Justin, Matthew. *Education:* University of Durham, B.A. (philosophy; with honors); University of Oxford, received advanced certificate of education. *Hobbies and other interests:* Walking, the cinema, artists' books.

Addresses

Home—65 Bainton Road, Oxford, England OX2 7A9.

Career

Freelance author and editor. Teacher in North Queensland, Australia, and London and Oxford, England, 1961-1994.

Awards, Honors

Books for the Teen Age citation, New York Public Library, 1999, for *It's My Life.*

Writings

POETRY ANTHOLOGIES; EDITOR WITH CHRISTOPHER
  STUART-CLARK

The New Dragon Book of Verse, Oxford University Press, 1977, published as *The Dragon Book of Verse,* Oxford University Press, 1997.
Poems 1 (includes teacher's book and cassette), Oxford University Press, 1979.
Poems 2 (includes teacher's book and cassette), Oxford University Press, 1980.
Narrative Poems, Oxford University Press, 1981.

Noah's Ark, Oxford University Press, 1983.
The Oxford Book of Christmas Poems, Oxford University Press, 1983.
Writing Poems, Oxford University Press, 1985.
The Oxford Treasury of Children's Poems, Oxford University Press, 1988.
The Young Dragon Book of Verse, Oxford University Press, 1989.
Peace and War: A Collection of Poems, Oxford University Press, 1989.
The Oxford Book of Story Poems, Oxford University Press, 1990.
A Year Full of Poems, Oxford University Press, 1991.
The Oxford Book of Animal Poems, Oxford University Press, 1992.
Writing Poems Plus, Oxford University Press, 1992.
Bright Star Shining: Poems for Christmas, Oxford University Press, 1993, Eerdmans, 1998.
The Oxford Treasury of Children's Poems, Oxford University Press, 1994.
The Oxford Treasury of Classic Poems, Oxford University Press, 1996.
The New Oxford Treasury of Children's Poems, Oxford University Press, 1997.
The Oxford Treasury of Time Poems, Oxford University Press, 1998.
One Hundred Years of Poetry, Oxford University Press, 1999.
The Oxford Treasury of Christmas Poems, Oxford University Press, 1999.

POETRY ANTHOLOGIES; EDITOR

Catch the Light, Oxford University Press, 1982.
Upright Downfall, Oxford University Press, 1983.
The Candy-Floss Tree, Oxford University Press, 1984.
The Crystal Zoo, Oxford University Press, 1985.
Bright Lights Blaze Out, Oxford University Press, 1986.
Splinters: A Book of Very Short Poems, illustrated by Sue Heap, Oxford University Press, 1988.

FICTION; FOR CHILDREN

(Reteller) *The Doom of the Gods* (mythology), illustrated by Tudor Humphries, Oxford University Press, 1985.

(Reteller) *The Curse of the Ring* (mythology), illustrated by Tudor Humphries, Oxford University Press, 1987.

Bags of Trouble (comedy), illustrated by David McKee, Anderson, 1988.

Trouble Abroad (comedy; sequel to *Bags of* Trouble), illustrated by David McKee, Anderson, 1990.

Trouble in Store (comedy; sequel to *Trouble Abroad* and *Bags of Trouble*), illustrated by David McKee, Anderson, 1991.

(Reteller) *Don Quixote* (based on Miguel de Cervantes's story), illustrated by Victor G. Ambrus, Oxford University Press, 1995.

It's My Life (thriller), Oxford University Press, 1997, Holiday House, 1998.

Facing the Dark (thriller), Oxford University Press, 1997.

Junk Mail (poems), Oxford University Press, 1998.

OTHER

Scolding Tongues: The Persecution of "Witches" (history for children), Stanley Thornes/Hulton, 1987.

(Compiler; with Christopher Stuart-Clark) *The Oxford Treasury of Children's Stories,* Oxford University Press, 1994.

(Reteller; with Christopher Stuart-Clark) *The Oxford Treasury of World Stories,* Oxford University Press, 1998.

Harrison's books have been translated into German and Italian.

Sidelights

Michael Harrison is a British editor and author who has become well known over the years for the children's poetry anthologies he has edited with Christopher Stuart-Clark for Oxford University Press. In addition to his editing efforts, Harrison has produced a number of adaptations and original fiction books for young readers. Harrison began his career as an English teacher, instructing children in Australia and England. As he told *SATA,* though, he left teaching for professional reasons: "I loved teaching children to write, but our National Curriculum made that more and more difficult, and I retired early and now do a lot of 'artists' books' workshops for children and adults in which I teach a variety of book forms and writing to fit them."

Harrison has a deep love for language, which explains his fascination with poetry, as well as with writing adaptations of old stories and myths. "I find plotting very difficult," he explained, "and so love retelling stories so that I can enjoy using words. It's the same impulse that makes me write poems: I think I find the words I'm using more interesting than what they're saying."

With collections such as *The Young Dragon Book of Verse* and *The New Oxford Treasury of Children's Poems,* Harrison and Stuart-Clark have gathered a broad representation of poems—from old and new, famous and less well-known poets—designed to delight a child's ears and stimulate the mind. The editors, stated I. Anne Rowe in a *School Librarian* review of *A Year Full of Poems,* "have long set standards in poetry books." And

while some reviewers have remarked that the team's anthologies are more likely to be collections that "a teacher or librarian would choose to use with children rather than [books] ... a child would choose spontaneously," as Richard Brown wrote in a *School Librarian* review of *The Young Dragon Book of Verse,* many critics consider these works to be standards any library should have. A *Junior Bookshelf* contributor, for example, called *The Oxford Book of Animal Poems* a "thoroughbred in the anthology stable and sure to be well-thumbed in the school library."

Of his own compositions, Harrison remarked, "I think the major influence on my writing has been Enid Blyton. I loved her books when I was a child, especially the 'Adventure' series, and would lose myself totally in them. When I became a teacher of English, I realised how badly written they were, how shallow, how formulaic. I looked for books of literary quality that gave the same intensity of grip, but found very few. I started to write one myself, but I found I couldn't do it." Instead, Harrison tried his hand at adapting old stories that he wanted to bring to the attention of a young audience. The works he has adapted have by no means been simple to retell. Harrison started with two books

Martin is abducted in an attempt to procure ransom from his father, but the kidnapper's daughter comes to Martin's assistance when he tries to escape.

based on the Norse Volsung Saga—*The Doom of the Gods* and *The Curse of the Ring*—and later tackled Cervantes's *Don Quixote*. Critics of Harrison's mythology adaptations have commented that while he manages to clarify the complicated plot for younger audiences, the violent story of gods, goddesses, heroes, and bloody revenge is too foreign to modern sensibilities for children to be able to sympathize with and understand the characters fully. "If I am less than totally enthusiastic in welcoming [*The Doom of the Gods*]," wrote a reviewer in *Junior Bookshelf*, " . . . it is purely on account of the subject." However, in a review of both of the Norse books, a *Kirkus Reviews* contributor asserted that "Harrison writes with wit and clarity" and "makes the complicated, sophisticated story . . . accessible and cohesive."

Critics similarly felt that Harrison's adaptation of *Don Quixote* could help bring this classic to the attention of a young audience. Here, Harrison shortens Cervantes's tale by removing a number of the original book's passages while keeping the more famous episodes. Some reviewers, such as *Magpies* critic Linnet Hunter, objected to these edits. Hunter believed that the cuts omit "any humor, character or energy in the narrative." On the other hand, Donna L. Scanlon, writing in *School Library Journal*, said that Harrison's "language captures the style of the original" and that the reteller "treats the original with respect." *School Librarian* critic Marcus Crouch also acknowledged that "Harrison remains faithful to the spirit" of Cervantes's story.

Before tackling Cervantes, Harrison had written a poetry anthology called *Junk Mail* and three works of fiction: *Bags of Trouble, Trouble Abroad,* and *Trouble in Store.* These latter three were originally to be adventure stories with young characters getting into perilous situations, but the author later changed his tactics. As he explained to *SATA,* "My own children were the same age as the heroes of the story, and I just couldn't put them into real danger. The [first] book turned into a comedy, *Bags of Trouble,* and had two sequels, the second of which, *Trouble in Store,* is very much a story about writing stories in school. When my children were grown up, I tried again, and managed to frighten myself—which is perhaps the real test—with *It's My Life.*"

It's My Life is a thriller about Martin, a teenager who is kidnapped by his mother's boyfriend. Martin's parents are divorced, and he lives with his mother. Mistakenly believing that her former husband has won a large sum of money in the lottery, Martin's mother gets her boyfriend to abduct Martin and take him to a houseboat. At first Martin doesn't realize who is behind the kidnapping, having never met the boyfriend, but when he does find out, he is horrified. Managing to sneak off the boat, he runs into a girl who turns out to be his abductor's daughter, Hannah. From this point, the novel turns into a cat-and-mouse chase. While finding some problems with the plotline and characterization, such as Hannah's unexplained motivation in helping Martin and the two-dimensional greediness of the adults, critics generally felt the story would appeal to teen readers.

"The fast pace and likable protagonists will keep the pages turning," averred Debbie Carton in *Booklist*. And *School Library Journal* contributor Janet Hilbun wrote that the "ingenuity and bravery of the two main characters and their ability to rebound from adversity results in a satisfying read."

Now living in Oxford, Harrison will likely continue his career as an editor of children's anthologies and occasional writer of fiction, including stories and poems. In addition to writing, he enjoys going to the theater and taking walks. As he told *SATA,* "I find walking is the best way of preparing to write—in France or Italy for choice—and then that the only way to write is to sit down and write."

Works Cited

Brown, Richard, review of *The Young Dragon Book of Verse, School Librarian,* August, 1990, pp. 115-16.

Carton, Debbie, review of *It's My Life, Booklist,* March 1, 1998, p. 1124.

Crouch, Marcus, review of *Don Quixote, School Librarian,* February, 1996, p. 18.

Review of *The Curse of the Ring* and *The Doom of the Gods, Kirkus Reviews,* September 15, 1987, pp. 1387-88.

Review of *The Doom of the Gods, Junior Bookshelf,* February, 1986, p. 34.

Hilbun, Janet, review of *It's My Life, School Library Journal,* April, 1998, p. 132.

Hunter, Linnet, review of *Don Quixote, Magpies,* March, 1996, p. 33.

Review of *The Oxford Book of Animal Poems, Junior Bookshelf,* February, 1993, pp. 31-32.

Rowe, I. Anne, review of *A Year Full of Poems, School Librarian,* February, 1992, p. 29.

Scanlon, Donna L., review of *Don Quixote, School Library Journal,* February, 1996, p. 105.

For More Information See

PERIODICALS

Booklist, December 15, 1992, p. 732; July, 1995, p. 1880; January 1, 1998, p. 804; September 1, 1998, p. 131.

Books for Keeps, March, 1993, p. 29.

Bulletin of the Center for Children's Books, March, 1998, p. 244.

Growing Point, July, 1990, pp. 5374-75; January, 1991, p. 5462.

Junior Bookshelf, April, 1990, p. 85; April, 1992, p. 72.

Kirkus Reviews, March 1, 1989, p. 377; April 1, 1998, p. 495.

Magpies, March, 1991, p. 36; September, 1993, p. 38; March, 1996, p. 45.

School Librarian, May, 1989, p. 70; February, 1996, p. 28.

School Library Journal, February, 1991, p. 94; April, 1991, p. 133; February, 1993, p. 28; September, 1995, p. 200; November, 1997, pp. 107-08.

Times Educational Supplement, July 3, 1987, p. 22.

HAUTZIG, Deborah 1956-

Personal

Born October 1, 1956, in New York, NY; daughter of Walter (a musician) and Esther (a writer; maiden name, Rudomin) Hautzig. *Education:* Attended Carnegie-Mellon University, 1974-75; Sarah Lawrence College, B.A., 1978. *Politics:* "Anything reasonable." *Religion:* Jewish.

Addresses

Office—c/o Random House, Inc., 201 East 50th St., New York, NY 10022.

Career

Random House, Inc., New York, NY, promotion assistant in library marketing for Random House, Knopf, and Pantheon Books, 1978-80; assistant editor and staff writer for Random House books, 1980—.

Awards, Honors

Best Books for Young Adults, American Library Association, 1978, for *Hey, Dollface.*

Writings

Hey, Dollface, Greenwillow, 1978.
The Handsomest Father, illustrated by Muriel Batherman, Greenwillow, 1979.
(Reteller) *Rumpelstiltskin,* Random House, 1979.
Second Star to the Right, Greenwillow, 1981.
(Editor) *The Christmas Story: Based on the Gospels According to St. Matthew and St. Luke,* illustrated by Sheilah Beckett, Random House, 1981, reissued with illustrations by Tony Chen, Happy House Books, 1987.
Little Witch's Big Night, illustrated by Alastair Graham, Random House, 1984.
(Adaptor) L. Frank Baum, *The Wizard of Oz,* illustrated by Joseph A. Smith, Random House, 1984.
Big Bird Visits the Dodos, illustrated by Joe Mathieu, Random House, 1985.
(Adaptor) *Follow That Bird,* Random House, 1985.
(With Marc T. Brown) *Happy Birthday, Little Witch,* Random House, 1985.
A Visit to the Sesame Street Hospital, illustrated by Joe Mathieu, Random House, 1985.
It's Not Fair!, illustrated by Tom Leigh, Random House, 1986.
The Story of the Nutcracker Ballet, illustrated by Diane Goode, Random House, 1986.
A Visit to the Sesame Street Library, illustrated by Joe Mathieu, Random House, 1986.
Why Are You So Mean to Me?, illustrated by Tom Cooke, Random House, 1986.
Sesame Street: Where Is My Skate?, Random House, 1987.
It's a Secret!, illustrated by Tom Leigh, Random House, 1988.
It's Easy!, illustrated by Joe Mathieu, Random House, 1988.

Get Well, Granny Bird, illustrated by Joe Mathieu, Random House, 1989.
Happy Mother's Day, illustrated by Normand Chartier, Random House, 1989.
(Reteller) *The Pied Piper of Hamelin: A Step 2 Book,* illustrated by S. D. Schindler, Random House, 1989.
Grover's Lucky Jacket, illustrated by Normand Chartier, Random House, 1989.
Big Bird at the Beach, illustrated by Carol Nicklaus, Random House, 1990.
(Adaptor) Hans Christian Andersen, *Thumbelina,* illustrated by Kaarina Kaila, Knopf, 1990.
Ernie and Bert's New Kitten, illustrated by Joe Mathieu, Random House, 1990.
Grover's Bad Dream, illustrated by Joe Mathieu, Random House, 1990.
Big Bird Plays the Violin, illustrated by Joe Mathieu, Random House, 1991.
(Adaptor) Hans Christian Andersen, *The Little Mermaid: A Step Three Book,* illustrated by Darcy May, Random House, 1991.
(Reteller) *The Nutcracker Ballet,* illustrated by Carolyn S. Ewing, Random House, 1992.
(Adaptor) Hans Christian Andersen, *The Wild Swans,* illustrated by Kaarina Kaila, Knopf, 1992.
(Reteller) *Aladdin and the Magic Lamp,* illustrated by Kathy Mitchell, Random House, 1993.
The Little Witch's Book of Magic Spells, illustrated by Marc T. Brown, Random House, 1993.
The Christmas Story, illustrated by Yoshi Miyake, Random House, 1994.
Night of Sentinels, Random House, 1994.
(Adaptor) *X-Men: Battle of the Sentinels,* illustrated by Aristides Ruiz and Josie Yee, Random House, 1994.
(Reteller) *Beauty and the Beast,* Random House, 1995.
(Adaptor) *Frances Hodgson Burnett's "The Secret Garden,"* illustrated by Natalie Carabetta, Putnam, 1995.
What's in a Doctor's Bag?, Random House, 1995.
(Adaptor) *A Little Princess,* illustrated by Natalie Carabetta, Putnam, 1996.
Walter the Warlock, illustrated by Sylvie Wickstrom, Random House, 1996.
Brain Quest Cars and Trucks, illustrated by Pierre Boutavant, Workman, 1997.
Brain Quest Farm Animals, Workman, 1997.
Little Witch, Random House, 1997.
Little Witch Goes to School, illustrated by Sylvie Wickstrom, Random House, 1998.
Devon, Greenwillow, in press.

Sidelights

Deborah Hautzig once told *SATA:* "I was born in New York City in 1956, and I was born to write. I love to write more than anything else in the world. I feel unified when I write—sort of like being married to myself. Technical ability means nothing without emotional validity, and emotional outpouring without craftsmanship and discipline is ultimately powerless—and usually pretty boring. So I try to make them work together, as best I can.

"I graduated from the Chapin School, spent one year as a Fine Arts major at Carnegie-Mellon University, then transferred to Sarah Lawrence College. In my free time, I love to write, read, paint, talk on the phone, and eavesdrop on buses. I love to travel and I love to laugh. I love honest people and I love kids—very compatible objects of affection.

"Books are kind of like children. You have a child and raise that child and think 'Oh! Now I know how to raise a child.' But then you have another child and you can't do it the same way because it's a *different child!* That's how it is with novels. The 'next book' is always a brand new challenge. Ulcer-inducing. But also thrilling.

"The one vital thing I tell myself about writing is: 'You're not out to teach; you're not out to preach. You're out to tell a story about real people, and anything else anyone derives from it is a fringe benefit.' I hope always to avoid didacticism. It's too easy to want to sound eloquent, wise, and witty, and use a book as a podium, rather than being true to its characters. You then dissipate and weaken your own book.

"When I write a book, I want to tell a good story, and tell it as well as I can. That's a given. If I can't grab a reader's attention and sustain interest, it doesn't matter a whit whether what I have to say is worth listening to! The other thing that's really important to me is honesty. Not factual honesty, or chronological honesty—but emotional honesty. Making things up is what fiction is all about. What matters is to tell the emotional truth. It's often painful but it's worth it."

Deborah Hautzig's first book, *Hey, Dollface,* is a novel for young adults that explores the inner life of a young girl as she reflects on a year in her life during which she becomes close friends with another girl at her private school. Val and Chloe share many of the experiences typical to childhood friendships, such as sleeping over at one another's house, sharing secrets, and playing hooky from school. But as adolescents, they are also beginning to experience sexual feelings, toward males, and toward each other. These feelings, and their repercussions, are "detailed with tender honesty," according to Ethel L. Heins in *Horn Book,* a judgment echoed by other reviewers. *Hey, Dollface* "explores in honest fashion the confused turbulence of the adolescent," wrote a reviewer for *Bulletin of the Center for Children's Books.* Awarded a Best Book for Young Adults citation by the American Library Association, Hautzig's narrative was praised for its insightful exploration of the birth of sexual feelings.

Hautzig treated the topic of anorexia nervosa with the same delicacy and insight in her next novel for young adults, *Second Star to the Right.* In this story, Leslie drifts from commonplace dieting into obsessive weight loss culminating in hospitalization before the roots of her drive to deny herself food are discovered in her misreading of the self-denying love of her mother. Hautzig's treatment of this topic was praised by reviewers who compared it to several other fictional treatments targeted at this age group. "What makes this the one I

"WAIT!" cried Cherry.

"You promised us a ride!"

"Oops! You're right," said Little Witch.

"But first, we need an extra-long broomstick."

In Little Witch Goes to School, *a story from Deborah Hautzig's popular series about the engaging eponymous heroine, Little Witch convinces her mother to let her go to school, but finds it difficult to follow her mother's orders to be very, very bad. (Illustrated by Sylvie Wickstrom.)*

wish I'd read first is the remarkable internal dialogue and character development," wrote Susan B. Madden in *Voice of Youth Advocates.* Pamela D. Pollack, reviewing *Second Star to the Right* for *School Library Journal,* contended that what makes Hautzig's narrative superior to other treatments of this popular topic is that she focuses on her character rather than on her character's disease: "Hautzig lays Leslie bare and makes her and her mother humanly understandable."

Hautzig has written several adaptations of classic fairy tales, and *The Christmas Story,* based on the story of the birth of Jesus found in the Bible. Reviewing *The Christmas Story,* a *Bulletin of the Center for Children's Books* commentator praised Hautzig's "simple, natural style," which closely approximates the original. Similarly, Hautzig's adaptation of Hans Christian Andersen's *Thumbelina* found favor with *Booklist* reviewer Carolyn Phelan because, although it is "slightly simplified, it remains true to the spirit of the classic story."

In addition to her novels for young adults and retellings of classic tales, Hautzig has also written numerous books featuring Jim Henson's muppet characters from the celebrated *Sesame Street* children's television program. She is also recognized for her popular "Little Witch" series of beginning readers for Random House.

Works Cited

Review of *The Christmas Story, Bulletin of the Center for Children's Books,* November, 1983, p. 43.

Heins, Ethel L., review of *Hey, Dollface, Horn Book,* December, 1978, pp. 644-45.

Review of *Hey, Dollface, Bulletin of the Center for Children's Books,* October, 1978, p. 30.

Madden, Susan B., review of *Second Star to the Right, Voice of Youth Advocates,* December, 1981, p. 30.

Phelan, Carolyn, review of *Thumbelina, Booklist,* December 1, 1990, p. 748.

Pollack, Pamela D., review of *Second Star to the Right, School Library Journal,* August, 1981, p. 75.

For More Information See

BOOKS

Fifth Book Junior Authors and Illustrators, Wilson, 1983, pp. 147-48.

PERIODICALS

Booklist, July, 1995, p. 1885.
School Library Journal, August, 1989, p. 122.*

*   *   *

HENDRY, Diana 1941-

Personal

Born October 2, 1941, in Wirral, Merseyside, England; daughter of Leslie Gordon (a hide and skin broker and songwriter) and Amelia (Kesler) McConomy; married George Hendry (a scientist), October 9, 1965 (divorced, April, 1981); children: Hamish, Kate. *Education:* University of Bristol, B.A. (with honors), 1984, M.Litt., 1987. *Politics:* "Variable, but never Tory." *Religion:* "A believer, but not a belonger." *Hobbies and other interests:* Playing the piano and yoga; "I love my children, dogs, piano, and a few friends. I'm not much good at traveling because I'm afraid of getting lost. I read and read and read."

Addresses

Agent—c/o Julia MacRae Books, Random House, 20 Vauxhall Bridge Rd., London SW1V 2SA, England.

Career

Sunday Times, London, assistant to literature editor, 1958-60; *Western Mail,* Cardiff, Wales, reporter and feature writer, 1960-65; freelance journalist for various newspapers in Liverpool and Bristol, England, 1965-80; Clifton College, Bristol, English instructor, 1987-90.

Diana Hendry

Tutor at Open University, 1991—, and University of Bristol, 1994—. Thornbury Arts Festival, arts director. Writer in Residence, Dumfries & Galloway Royal Infirmary. *Member:* Society of Authors, PEN.

Awards, Honors

Winner, Stroud Festival International Poetry Competition, 1976; shortlisted for Smarties Prize for Children's Books, England Book Trust, 1985; Peterloo Poetry Competition, third prize, 1991, second prize, 1993; Whitbread award, 1991, for *Harvey Angell;* first prize, Housman Poetry Society Competition, 1997; third prize, Bridport Short Story Competition, 1999.

Writings

Midnight Pirate, illustrated by Janet Duchesne, Julia MacRae, 1984.

Fiona Finds Her Tongue, illustrated by Victoria Cooper, Julia MacRae, 1985, expanded as *Fiona Says—,* illustrated by Dave McTaggart, Walker, 1998.

Hetty's First Fling, illustrated by Nicole Goodwin, Julia MacRae, 1985.

The Not-Anywhere House, illustrated by Mei-Yim Low, Julia MacRae, 1989, illustrated by Thor Wickstrom, Lothrop, 1991.

The Rainbow Watchers, illustrated by Low, Julia MacRae, 1989, illustrated by Wickstrom, Lothrop, 1991.

The Carey Street Cat, illustrated by Barbara Walker, Julia MacRae, 1989, illustrated by Wickstrom, Lothrop, 1991.

Christmas in Exeter Street, illustrated by John Lawrence, Julia MacRae, 1989, published in the U.S. as *Christmas on Exeter Street,* Knopf, 1989.

Sam Sticks and Delilah, illustrated by Janet Duchesne, Julia MacRae, 1990.

A Moment for Joe, illustrated by Duncan Birmingham, Julia MacRae, 1990.

A Camel Called April, illustrated by Elsie Lennox, Julia MacRae, 1990.

Double Vision (young adult novel), Julia MacRae, 1990, Candlewick Press, 1993.

Harvey Angell, Julia MacRae, 1991.

The Dream Camel and the Dazzling Cat, Walker (London), 1992.

Wonderful Robert and Sweetie-Pie Nell, illustrated by Andy Cooke, Walker, 1992.

Hannah and Darjeeling, Walker, 1992.

The Thing-in-a-Box, illustrated by Heap, A & C Black, 1992.

Kid Kibble, illustrated by Adriano Gon, Walker, 1992, Candlewick Press, 1994.

Back Soon, illustrated by Carol Thompson, Julia MacRae, 1993, BridgeWater, 1993.

Why Father Christmas Was Late for Hartlepool, illustrated by Sue Heap, Julia MacRae, 1993.

The Thing-on-Two-Legs, illustrated by Sue Heap, A & C Black, 1995.

Happy Old Birthday, Owl, illustrated by Sue Heap, Julia MacRae, 1995.

Flower Street Friends, illustrated by Julie Douglas, Walker, 1995.

Dog Dottington, illustrated by Margaret Chamberlain, Walker, 1995, published in the U.S. as *Dog Donovan,* Candlewick Press, 1995.

The Awesome Bird, Julia MacRae, 1995.

Strange Goings-On (poetry), Viking (London), 1995.

Making Blue, Peterloo Poets, 1995.

Harvey Angell and the Ghost Child, Julia MacRae, 1997.

Minders, Walker, 1998.

Contributor of poems, stories, and book reviews to anthologies and periodicals, including *Spectator* and *Encounter.*

Sidelights

Diana Hendry is the British-born author of several picture books and chapter books for young readers. Often drawing her plots from her own memories, Hendry has received critical praise and several awards for such titles as *Harvey Angell, Dog Donovan,* and *The Carey Street Cat.* Upbeat in theme, Hendry's books contain "lead characters [who] often seem to bring out the best in their supporting casts," according to *Books for Keeps* contributor Ted Percy. Even the most amusing tale has a kernel of knowledge waiting to be discovered by young readers. *The Carey Street Cat,* for example, Hendry's quiet story about a cat who catches a small piece of a star, contains a message: in the words of its

author: "Don't get too carried away by things. Keep your feet on the ground."

Born in 1941 and raised in England, Hendry had lofty ambitions as a child: first to be a novelist, second to be a concert pianist, and third, "to be Frank Sinatra.... The only books in the house when I was a child were a set of Charles Dickens books that my father bought from a traveling salesman and a leather bound book called *The Way to a Fortune,*" she once recalled to *SATA.* While growing up, Hendry visited many libraries, and her grandfather brought her books of her own to cheer her up when she was ill. "I wasn't encouraged to read—rather the opposite," Hendry concluded. "Perhaps that's why I did."

Despite her love of reading, Hendry didn't seriously begin writing for children until her days as a student at the University of Bristol, when she was looking for "a little relief from academic essays!" Many of the books Hendry has written since have been for younger readers. Her first book, *Midnight Pirate,* was a picture book. Her second, *Fiona Finds Her Tongue,* which was sparked by her own memories of being shy, was written for primary graders. In *Dog Dottington,* published in the U.S. as *Dog Donovan,* she reveals her love of dogs as she portrays a nervous family whose members are collectively afraid of EVERYTHING. After they overcome their initial nervousness and decide to get a dog, they pick the perfect pet—a canine companion named Hero who is more afraid than they are! Praising Hendry's comic touch as each of the Donovan family members overcome their own fears in comforting their new pet, Stephanie Zvirin

The fearful Donovan family members must overcome their own anxieties in order to comfort their apprehensive new pet dog in Hendry's comical picture book offering. (From Dog Donovan, *illustrated by Margaret Chamberlain.)*

noted in a *Booklist* appraisal that "this bubbly, comforting story shows how natural fears are and how they can be overcome."

Published in 1990, *Double Vision* is Hendry's first novel for older, teenage readers. Autobiographical in nature, the novel follows three siblings—fifteen-year-old middle sister Eliza Bishop and her two sisters. To be more like her glamorous older sister Rosa, Eliza is tempted to join the popular crowd until she recognizes that growing up and becoming an adult mean making your own choices . . . and having a heartbreak or two. Meanwhile, quirky younger sister Lily goes her own direction. Taking place in the same costal British town where its author was raised, *Double Vision* contains "family turmoil, sibling relations, romance, and blossoming self-awareness," according to *School Library Journal* contributor Gail Richmond, who praised Hendry's characterization of the three sisters. While noting that the novel takes place in the 1950s, *Booklist* reviewer Chris Sherman maintained that Hendry's novel possesses "a timeless quality . . . that will ensure a wide audience."

In a book for older elementary-aged readers, household turmoil is again the focus as a new attic tenant sparks curiosity in several family members. *Kid Kibble* takes its name from the nickname bestowed upon the newest boarder to rent out the attic in Jess and Ned's parents' house. In what *School Library Journal* contributor Christina Dorr called "an engaging story," Hendry paints Kid, a young biology teacher, as a fascinating character that gradually wins over the brother and sister with his collection of old bones, his impulsive trombone playing, and his mysterious suitcase that contains something alive. Despite their efforts to oust Kid from their home, his "enthusiasm, vulnerability, and cheerful nonconformity" endear him to both children, in the opinion of *Quill & Quire* contributor Joanne Schott.

Although she is a children's author, poetry has always been Hendry's first love. "My ideas seem to come in very different ways," she explained to *SATA*. "Sometimes it's two themes that rub together like sticks rubbed together to make a fire (not that I quite believe anyone has ever done this, although they say it's possible). Sometimes I get a title. Poems are different. I might plod at an idea, or something like a small electrical charge happens and I can't keep away from the poem until it's done."

"I seem to write a lot about houses and about children who are trying to make themselves feel at home in the world—maybe because I don't. I write because I love words. I write because I want to leave something behind that says 'I was here.' " Hendry believes that the writing process allows one to discover new meaning in things all around. "I suppose I also write to find out more about myself," she added.

Works Cited

Dorr, Christina, review of *Kid Kibble*, *School Library Journal*, November, 1994, p. 104.

Percy, Ted, review of *Dog Dottington*, *Books for Keeps*, May, 1995, p. 29.

Richmond, Gail, review of *Double Vision*, *School Library Journal*, April, 1993, p. 140.

Schott, Joanne, review of *Kid Kibble*, *Quill & Quire*, January, 1995, p. 43.

Sherman, Chris, review of *Double Vision*, *Booklist*, March 1, 1993, p. 1226.

Zvirin, Stephanie, review of *Dog Donovan*, *Booklist*, March 1, 1995, p. 1248.

For More Information See

PERIODICALS

Booklist, November 15, 1994, p. 601.
Books for Keeps, September, 1995, p. 25.
Bulletin of the Center for Children's Books, June, 1993, p. 317.
Junior Bookshelf, June, 1995, p. 94.
Magpies, March, 1996, p. 23.
Publishers Weekly, February 6, 1995, p. 85.
School Librarian, May, 1995, p. 59; May, 1996, pp. 62, 70.

*　　　*　　　*

HOLLAND, Julia 1954-

Personal

Born June 28, 1954, in Cuckfield, Sussex, England; daughter of Laurence Ernest (a sales manager) and Anne Susan Mary (maiden name, Brewer; present surname, Honour) Gates; children: Abi Lucy Stephenson. *Education:* Attended West Kent College of Further Education. *Politics:* Independent. *Religion:* Independent.

Addresses

Electronic mail—juliah@onthenet.com.au.

Career

Newton & Godin, Kent, England, copywriter, 1972-75; Wakefield Fortune Travel, London, England, marketing manager, 1977-81; freelance writer in England and Australia, 1981-93; *Greenweek*, Southport, Queensland, Australia, editor, 1993-94; freelance writer. Friends of Tamborine Mountain, vice-president.

Awards, Honors

Grant from Arts Queensland, 1998.

Writings

Through the Doorway, University of Queensland Press (St. Lucia, Australia), 1997.
Between the Shadows, Macmillan Education, 1997.
Nothing to Remember, University of Queensland Press, 1998.

Author of English-language textbooks for Taiwanese children.

Julia Holland

Work in Progress

A young adult novel.

Sidelights

Julia Holland told *SATA:* "Although I've always dabbled in creative writing (travel diaries, poetry, and a couple of novels abandoned after a few chapters), it was not until 1993 that I completed my first children's novel and found my niche. Having come relatively late to developing my own writing career, and having spent many years compromising with business writing, I am now passionately committed to writing about things which are significant to me. I particularly enjoy the freedom of writing for children and young adults. I can mix fantasy and reality in the proportions that appeal to me. My inclination is to combine a gripping narrative with more demanding themes than those usually found in 'fast fiction' (the readers' equivalent of fast food!).

"I believe that writing for young people demands a sense of responsibility which, while not evading more difficult or complex issues, should ultimately reflect an element of hope and the nobler aspects of the human spirit. I don't feel the reflection of an unrelentingly bleak reality is beneficial for the reader or society.

"An underlying preoccupation of mine is what makes life significant for people, and that includes both the mundane motivations and the bigger spiritual questions. My interests outside writing reflect this and include world myths and religions.

"I have always liked traveling and have enjoyed a couple of extended trips in Asia. I moved permanently to Australia in 1990 and find much to inspire me here, as well as the feeling that it offers an excellent environment in which to bring up my daughter."

For More Information See

PERIODICALS

Magpies, May, 1997, p. 34; November, 1998, p. 9.
Reading Time, November, 1998, p. 28.

*   *   *

HORNER, Jack
See HORNER, John R(obert)

*   *   *

HORNER, John R(obert) 1946-
(Jack Horner)

Personal

Born in 1946, in Shelby, MT; son of John (owner of a sand-and-gravel business) and Miriam Horner; married (third marriage), wife's name Celeste; children: (from first marriage) Jason. *Education:* Attended University of Montana.

Addresses

Office—Museum of the Rockies, Montana State University, Bozeman, MT, 59717.

Career

Managed sand-and-gravel business in Shelby, MT, 1973-75; Princeton University Museum of Natural History, Princeton, NJ, preparator, beginning 1975; Montana State University, Bozeman, MT, adjunct professor of paleontology and curator of paleontology at Museum of the Rockies, 1982—; writer. *Military service:* U.S. Marines, served in Vietnam, 1966-68.

Awards, Honors

Grants from National Science Foundation, 1983-91; honorary doctorate, University of Montana, and MacArthur fellowship, both 1986; Children's Science Book Award, New York Academy of Sciences, 1988, for *Digging Dinosaurs.*

Writings

FOR CHILDREN

(With James Gorman) *Maia: A Dinosaur Grows Up,* illustrated by Doug Henderson, Museum of the Rockies, Montana State University (Bozeman, MT), c. 1985.

John R. Horner, applying preservative to Tyrannosaurus Rex bones.

(With Don Lessem) *Digging Up Tyrannosaurus Rex,* Crown (New York City), 1992.

OTHER

(With James Gorman) *Digging Dinosaurs,* illustrated by Donna Braginetz and Kris Ellingsen, Workman (New York City), 1988, published as *Digging Dinosaurs: The Search That Unraveled the Mystery of Baby Dinosaurs,* HarperCollins, 1990.

Cranial Morphology of Prosaurolophus (Ornithischia: Hadrosauridae): With Descriptions of Two New Hadrosaurid Species and an Evolution of Hadrosaurid Phyolgenetic Relationships, illustrated by Kris Ellingsen, Museum of the Rockies, Montana State University (Bozeman, MT), 1992.

(With Don Lessem) *The Complete T. Rex: How Stunning New Discoveries Are Changing Our Understanding of the World's Most Famous Dinosaur,* Simon & Schuster (New York City), 1993.

(Editor, with Kenneth Carpenter and Karl F. Hirsch) *Dinosaur Eggs and Babies,* Cambridge University Press (Cambridge, England), 1994.

(With Edwin Dobb) *Dinosaur Lives: Unearthing an Evolutionary Saga,* HarperCollins (New York City), 1997.

Contributor to periodicals, including *Nature* and *Scientific American.*

Sidelights

John R. ("Jack") Horner is a celebrated paleontologist with considerable expertise on the subject of dinosaurs. He has published a number of books on dinosaurs aimed at both adult and juvenile audiences, including *Maia: A Dinosaur Grows Up, The Complete T. Rex,* and *Dinosaur Lives: Unearthing an Evolutionary Saga.* Although he never completed his college education due to difficulties resulting from dyslexia, Horner was able to enjoy and excel in paleontology classes. He continued to indulge in his interest in the field while managing, with his brother, the family's sand-and-gravel business in the mid 1970s. Hauling sand and gravel across Montana, Horner regularly searched landscapes for signs of Cretaceous rock, and if he found any, he would pull off the road and begin excavating for dinosaur bones.

Determined to devote himself to paleontology, Horner eventually found work at Princeton University, where he was hired to maintain the fossil findings of various field researchers. Under the encouragement of his supervisor, Don Baird, Horner commenced his own research into a curious fossil that he had found along Montana's Willow Creek anticline during the summer of 1977. After the fossil was identified as a dinosaur egg, Horner commenced an intensive study into baby dinosaurs and returned to Montana to conduct further excavations.

Once back in Montana, Horner experienced some unexpected good fortune while identifying various bones at a rock shop. Among the bones were parts of the remains of duck-billed hadrosaurs. The next day, while conducting field research, Horner uncovered an ancient dinosaur nest, including bones from more than a dozen baby dinosaurs. These newfound remains were later identified as parts of a previously unknown hadrosaur species. With funding from his supervisor back in Princeton, Horner was able to continue his research and make further discoveries, including the bones of approximately ten thousand hadrosaurs.

Upon detailed study of his findings at Willow Creek, Horner concluded that the baby hadrosaurs remained in their nests until they were approximately three months old and were nearly three feet in length. Horner also assessed the placement of various nests in the region and concluded that hadrosaurs conducted themselves in colonies similar to those established by penguins. In recognition of the apparent maternal instincts of these hadrosaurs, Horner named the species *Maiasaura peeblesorum,* which translates from Greek as "good mother lizard."

By the early 1980s Horner was leading teams of researchers along the Willow Creek anticline and was regularly receiving funding from federal foundations. In the next few years he entered into the debate about the possibility that dinosaurs might have been endotherms, warm-blooded creatures. Horner, assessing bone structure and likely growth rates of dinosaurs, interpreted his findings as indications that dinosaurs were endotherms. His contentions fueled further debate among paleontologists, some of whom questioned the likelihood that such conclusions could be determined from fossils. Horner also joined the faculty of Montana State University during these years, serving as both adjunct professor of geology and curator of the school's Museum of the Rockies. In 1986 he was honored with both a MacArthur Fellowship and an honorary doctorate from the University of Montana.

Horner has since published several works on dinosaurs. He teamed with James Gorman to create *Maia: A Dinosaur Grows Up,* a children's book detailing the life cycle of the Maiasaura species of hadrosaurs. Cathryn A. Camper, in a review for *School Library Journal,* commented that the book is important because of the authors' commitment to sharing the scientific process with children. She wrote, "Although the dinosaurs are personified, the fictionalization never becomes maudlin; while obviously directed at children, the story maintains a realistic viewpoint towards birth, life, and death." Peter Dodson, writing in *Science Books & Films,* called *Maia* "one of the most impressive juvenile dinosaur books ever written."

Horner also collaborated with Gorman on *Digging Dinosaurs,* which characterizes dinosaurs as social, even maternal, creatures. Horner worked with Don Lessem on *Digging Up Tyrannosaurus Rex* and *The Complete T. Rex,* two volumes devoted to one of the most imposing of dinosaurs. *Digging Up Tyrannosaurus Rex* recounts excavations that resulted in impressive findings, and *The Complete T. Rex* includes an examination of evidence indicating that the tyrannosaurus rex might have been endothermic. Cathryn A. Camper, in a review of *Digging Up Tyrannosaurus Rex* for *Five Owls,* commented that as with the earlier *Maia: A Dinosaur Grows Up,* Horner "continues to disseminate knowledge ... following the belief that current scientific discoveries should be made accessible to children as well as adults." A *Kirkus Reviews* commentator called *Digging Up Tyrannosaurus Rex* "an attractive and informative update on a popular subject," maintaining: "Horner's lucid text ... details the exacting task of excavating, preserving, and transporting the huge fossil remains."

Dinosaur Lives: Unearthing an Evolutionary Saga, which Horner wrote with Edwin Dobb, concerns various findings unearthed in Montana during excavations in the mid-1980s. Dale A. Russell, writing in the *Los Angeles Times Book Review,* described *Dinosaur Lives* as "clearly and entertainingly written," and he recommended it to readers "wishing to find out what it's like to be a superb itinerant bone hound."

Works Cited

Camper, Cathryn A., review of *Maia: A Dinosaur Grows Up, School Library Journal,* December, 1987, pp. 80-81.

Camper, Cathryn A., review of *Digging Up Tyrannosaurus Rex, Five Owls,* January-February, 1993, pp. 62-63.

Review of *Digging Up Tyrannosaurus Rex, Kirkus Reviews,* December 1, 1992, p. 1504.

Dodson, Peter, "The Perennial Joy of Dinosaurs," *Science Books & Films,* October, 1993, pp. 193-94.

Russell, Dale A., review of *Dinosaur Lives, Los Angeles Times Book Review,* July 20, 1997, p. 6.

For More Information See

BOOKS

Lessem, Don, *Jack Horner: Living with Dinosaurs,* Scientific American Books for Young Readers (New York City), 1994.

PERIODICALS

American Scientist, March-April, 1989, p. 208; July, 1989, p. 381.

Appraisal, autumn, 1989, p. 5; spring, 1993, p. 40.

BioScience, March, 1995, pp. 221-22.

Booklist, November 1, 1988, p. 439; April 15, 1992, p. 1518; January 15, 1993, p. 896; April 15, 1993, pp. 1480, 1501.

Children's Bookwatch, December, 1992, p. 7.

Instructor, March, 1989, p. 53.

Kirkus Reviews, September 15, 1987, p. 1394; March 15, 1993, p. 350.

Learning, September, 1993, p. 98.

Library Journal, December, 1987, pp. 80-81; January, 1989, p. 43; June 1, 1991, pp. 225-26; March 1, 1994, p. 55.

Library Talk, November, 1989, p. 30; May, 1993, p. 37.

Los Angeles Times Book Review, April 22, 1990, p. 8; July 3, 1994, p. 9.

New York Times Book Review, December 25, 1988, p. 11; October 12, 1997, p. 30.

People Weekly, June 21, 1993, p. 27.

Publishers Weekly, October 28, 1988, pp. 69-70; April 26, 1993, p. 67; May 12, 1997, p. 69.

Science Books & Films, January, 1989, p. 167; May, 1989, p. 289; April, 1993, p. 82; December, 1993, p. 269.

Scientific American, December, 1990, pp. 134-35; December, 1993, pp. 132-33.

Voice of Youth Advocates, April, 1991, p. 21.

*　　*　　*

HUNTER, Mollie 1922-
(Maureen Mollie Hunter McIlwraith)

Personal

Born Maureen Mollie Hunter McVeigh, June 30, 1922, in Longniddry, East Lothian, Scotland; daughter of William George (a motor mechanic) and Helen Eliza Smeaton (a confectioner; maiden name, Waitt) McVeigh; married Thomas "Mike" McIlwraith (a hospital catering manager), December 23, 1940; children: Quentin Wright, Brian George. *Education:* Attended Preston Lodge School, East Lothian, Scotland. *Politics:* Scottish Nationalist. *Religion:* Episcopalian. *Hobbies and other interests:* Theatre, music, physical exercise, travel.

Addresses

Home—"Rose Cottage," 7 Mary Ann Court, Inverness IV3 5B2, Scotland. *Agent*—A. M. Heath & Co. Ltd., 79 St. Martin's Lane, London WC2N 4AA, England; McIntosh & Otis, Inc., 457 Fifth Avenue, New York, NY 10017.

Career

Writer, 1953—. May Hill Arbuthnot Lecturer in the United States, 1975, and in 1976 toured New Zealand and Australia lecturing under the joint auspices of the British Council, the International Reading Association, and the education authorities for New Zealand and Australia; Dalhousie University, Halifax, Nova Scotia, writer-in-residence, 1980, 1981; 29th Anne Carroll Moore Spring Lecturer, 1986; Aberlour Summer School for Gifted Children, teacher of creative writing, 1987-88; organized and taught in writer's workshops for both adults and children. *Member:* Society of Authors.

Awards, Honors

Children's Books of the Year, Child Study Association of America (CSAA), 1968, for *The Ferlie,* 1970, for *The Walking Stones: A Story of Suspense,* 1971, for *The Thirteenth Member: A Story of Suspense,* 1972, for *A Sound of Chariots* and *The Haunted Mountain: A Story of Suspense,* 1974, for *The Stronghold,* 1975, for *A Stranger Came Ashore: A Story of Suspense,* 1976, for *Talent Is Not Enough: Mollie Hunter on Writing for Children,* 1977, for *A Furl of Fairy Wind,* and 1987, for *Cat, Herself;* Children's Spring Book Festival honor book, *Book World,* 1970, for *The Lothian Run;* Children's Book Award, CSAA, 1973, for *A Sound of Chariots;* Outstanding Book of the Year, *New York Times,* 1972, for *The Haunted Mountain: A Story of Suspense* and *A Sound of Chariots,* and 1975, for *A Stranger Came Ashore: A Story of Suspense;* Scottish Arts Council Award, 1973, for *The Haunted Mountain: A Story of Suspense,* and 1977, for *The Wicked One: A Story of Suspense;* Carnegie Medal, British Library Association, 1974, and Silver Pencil Award (Holland), 1975, both for *The Stronghold;* Best Books, *School Library Journal,* 1975, and Honor Book, *Boston Globe/ Horn Book* Award, 1976, both for *A Stranger Came Ashore: A Story of Suspense;* Books for the Teen Age, New York Public Library, and Notable Children's Trade Book in the Field of Social Studies, National Council for Social Studies-Children's Book Council (NCSS-CBC), both 1982, both for *You Never Knew Her as I Did!;* Best Books, *School Library Journal,* and Best Books for Young Adults, American Library Association (ALA), both 1986, both for *Cat, Herself;* Phoenix award, 1992, for *A Sound of Chariots;* Books for the Teen Age, New York Public Library, 1999, for *The King's Swift Rider: A Novel on Robert the Bruce.*

Writings

FOR CHILDREN; FANTASY NOVELS

Patrick Kentigern Keenan, illustrated by Charles Keeping, Blackie & Son, 1963, published in United States as *The Smartest Man in Ireland,* Funk, 1965.

The Kelpie's Pearls, illustrated by Keeping, Blackie & Son, 1964, illustrated by Joseph Cellini, Funk, 1966.

Thomas and the Warlock, illustrated by Keeping, Blackie & Son, 1967, illustrated by Cellini, Funk, 1967.

The Ferlie, illustrated by Michal Morse, Blackie & Son, 1968, illustrated by Cellini, Funk, 1968, published as *The Enchanted Whistle,* illustrated by Morse, Methuen, 1985.

The Walking Stones: A Story of Suspense, illustrated by Trina Schart Hyman, Harper, 1970, published in England as *The Bodach,* illustrated by Gareth Floyd, Blackie & Son, 1970.

The Haunted Mountain: A Story of Suspense, illustrated by Laszlo Kubinyi, Harper, 1972, illustrated by Trevor Ridley, Hamish Hamilton, 1972.

A Stranger Came Ashore: A Story of Suspense, Harper, 1975.

The Wicked One: A Story of Suspense, Harper, 1977.

A Furl of Fairy Wind: Four Stories (includes "A Furl of Fairy Wind," "The Enchanted Boy," "The Brownie," and "Hi Johnny", also see below), illustrated by Stephen Gammell, Harper, 1977.

Mollie Hunter

The Knight of the Golden Plain (also see below), illustrated by Marc Simont, Harper, 1983.

The Three-Day Enchantment (sequel to *The Knight of the Golden Plain,* also see below), illustrated by Simont, Harper, 1985.

The Brownie, illustrated by M. Christopherson, Byway Books, 1986.

The Enchanted Boy, illustrated by Christopherson, Byway Books, 1986.

A Furl of Fairy Wind, illustrated by Christopherson, Byway Books, 1986.

The Mermaid Summer, Harper, 1988.

(Reteller) *Gilly Martin the Fox* (picture book), illustrated by Dennis McDermott, Hyperion, 1994.

The Day of the Unicorn (sequel to *The Three-Day Enchantment*), Harper, 1994.

FOR YOUNG ADULTS; HISTORICAL NOVELS

Hi Johnny, illustrated by Drake Brookshaw, Evans, 1964, Funk, 1967, illustrated by M. Christopherson, Byway Books, 1986.

The Spanish Letters, illustrated by Elizabeth Grant, Evans, 1964, Funk, 1967.

A Pistol in Greenyards, illustrated by Grant, Evans, 1965, Funk, 1968.

The Ghosts of Glencoe, Evans, 1966, Funk, 1969.

The Lothian Run, Funk, 1970.

The Thirteenth Member: A Story of Suspense, Harper, 1971.

The Stronghold, Harper, 1974.

You Never Knew Her as I Did!, Harper, 1981, published as *Escape from Loch Leven,* Canongate (Edinburgh), 1987.

The King's Swift Rider: A Novel on Robert the Bruce, HarperCollins, 1998.

FOR YOUNG ADULTS; NOVELS

A Sound of Chariots (also see below), Harper, 1972.

The Third Eye, Harper, 1979.

The Dragonfly Years (sequel to *A Sound of Chariots*), Hamish Hamilton, 1983, published in United States as *Hold on to Love,* Harper, 1984.

Cat, Herself, Harper, 1985, published in England as *I'll Go My Own Way,* Hamish Hamilton, 1985.

NONFICTION

Talent Is Not Enough: Mollie Hunter on Writing for Children, Harper, 1976.

Flora MacDonald and Bonnie Prince Charles (for children), Methuen, 1987.

The Pied Piper Syndrome, and Other Essays, Harper, 1991.

PLAYS

A Love-Song for My Lady (one-act; produced at Empire Theatre, Inverness, Scotland, 1961), Evans, 1962.

Stay for an Answer (one-act; produced at Empire Theatre, 1962), French, 1962.

OTHER

Contributor of articles to numerous newspapers and magazines, including *Scotsman* and *Glasgow Herald;* contributor to anthologies.

Adaptations

A number of Hunter's books, including *The Kelpie's Pearls, The Lothian Run,* and *The Enchanted Whistle,* have been serialized on BBC-Radio programs; *A Stranger Came Ashore* has been read in serial form on Swedish radio and adapted for the stage in Sweden and Scotland; the four stories in *A Furl of Fairy Wind* are published on audio cassette in the United Kingdom; *The Walking Stones* and *The Wicked One* have been featured on Yorkshire TV's *Book Tower* program.

Sidelights

Scottish author Mollie Hunter has written numerous books for young readers that draw on her country's colorful past. The first of her many historical novels, *Hi Johnny,* was published a year after the author's 1963 debut fantasy novel *Patrick Kentigern Keenan,* signalling Hunter's pattern of alternating different types of books to draw upon her dual loves of history and folklore: fantasy for younger readers, historical novels for the early teens, and eventually more "realistic" novels for young adults. Throughout her long and prolific career as a writer, Hunter's declared aim has been two-fold: to entertain via fiction drawn from her native culture, but to do so in a way that expresses universal truths that apply to readers from any culture. The author is often praised for her skill as a literary stylist and a storyteller, for her ability to evoke place and atmosphere, and for her intimate knowledge of Scottish history, legend, and culture. In all of her books, Hunter profiles male and female protagonists who become involved in the struggle between good and evil. Often wreckless in their behavior, her passionate, quick-witted characters prove themselves through courageous acts in both the natural and supernatural worlds while dealing with difficult, often ambiguous political issues and philosophical questions. Although her works include suffering and death, Hunter stresses such values as loyalty, creativity, truth, and above all the redemptive power of love. She writes in a lyrical voice often laced with humor and invests her books with a deep affection for her native land as well as with sympathy for the poor and downtrodden. Highlighting Hunter's achievement, *Children's Literature in Education* contributor Peter Hollindale asserted: "Mollie Hunter is by general consent Scotland's most distinguished modern children's writer."

Hunter was born in 1922 in East Lothian, Scotland. The third of five children, she was raised amid a strong tradition of Scottish tales and their tellers. "I was three years old when my great-grandmother Hunter first talked and sang to me of the lawless forays carried out by the men that Scotland knew long ago as 'the Border reivers,'" Hunter once recalled to *SATA.* "She was ninety-three, her voice long since cracked and wasted, but there was still a wild, strange music in the very names I heard from her." To keep the name Hunter alive, the author later decided to use this part of her given name as her pen name.

Growing up in a small Scottish village enriched Hunter's imagination, and what began as a child's curiosity developed into a lifetime interest in Scottish history and folklore. The author enjoyed a cheerful early childhood, surrounded by a wealth of books and a strong sense of security, but tragedy struck in 1931 when Hunter's father died of an illness arising from wounds he sustained in World War I. Only nine years old at the time, Hunter later attempted to come to terms with her grief through her autobiographical novel *A Sound of Chariots*. In this work, Bridie McShane is also her father's special daughter and must deal with his death at the young age of nine. Through the loss of her father Bridie gains a sudden awareness of death and begins to see each passing minute as bringing her closer to her own end. Over the next four years, though, she comes to terms with the passing of time and begins writing as a means of expressing her emotions. By the end of the novel, Bridie has grown into an aware young woman on her way to maturity.

"*A Sound of Chariots* is a tough yet tender, humorous yet tragic, sometimes horrific yet always gentle and compassionate autobiographical (surely) novel," maintained a *Times Literary Supplement* contributor. Geraldine DeLuca, writing in the *Lion and the Unicorn*, contended that *A Sound of Chariots* is "absolutely uncontrived" and "captures the mind of a young adolescent the way few adolescent novels do." Eleanor Cameron concluded in the *New York Times Book Review:* "Whether it is a reliving or not, this is the most memorable of Miss Hunter's books, the distinguished account of a child's traumatic experiences and her struggle to gain the realization of selfhood."

Hunter's own loss and traumatic experience proved to be a turning point in her young life. "In all that I thought and did from then on," she recalled in an essay for *Something about the Author Autobiography Series* (*SAAS*), "I realised there was an even keener awareness of both myself and the world around me—so keen, sometimes, that I could hardly bear the experience. I began to take with me on my lonely expeditions a pencil and notebook—the notebook that held my previous attempts to express myself in some original form of words. And gradually, out of all this came one further realisation that embraced all the others. I was going to be a writer." Now that her goal was clear, Hunter had to face her first obstacle—getting a proper education. The Depression years, however, forced Hunter to leave school at the age of fourteen (the earliest age possible) and search for a job.

This too was not as simple as it appeared. When her daughter was unable to find a job locally, Hunter's mother eventually swallowed her pride and asked her Edinburgh family to take Hunter into their business. So began Hunter's routine that had her travelling to Edinburgh to work in one of her grandfather's flower shops six days a week. At the same time, she attended night school four nights a week and spent the other two studying and doing research at the National Library of Scotland. Night school eventually enabled Hunter to acquire a job in the Civil Service as a clerk, and her many hours at the library led to her first studies of magic, superstition, and folklore. And this course of study soon overlapped and flowed into the study of Hunter's own country—Scotland. "It was impossible for the library staff to guess, of course, that these two interests would remain with me lifelong," Hunter related in *SAAS*. "And I've no doubt that they found it peculiar to see me sitting there night after night—myself so young and all the books I drew from the stacks concerned with matters so ancient!"

Despite these interests, though, poetry remained Hunter's love. At the same time, romantic love began to overwhelm her emotions, and near the beginning of her eighteenth year Hunter met the young man who became the great and true love of her life. This blissful courtship was cut short, however, when Mike was drafted into the Navy for World War II. At the end of his year of training, with ten days leave before sailing, he and Hunter got married. These years of war and separation found Hunter returning to her library studies and doing volunteer work in a canteen. And of course there were the occasional visits from her husband that never lasted long enough. "Separated again, we wrote constantly to one another," Hunter recalled in *SAAS*. "Most of my writing during those years, in fact, was in my letters to him, most of the thoughts that would otherwise have been expressed in poetry went into those letters instead—although in the kind he wrote to me in return, I sometimes had the feeling that he was a better poet than I was!"

Once the war ended and her husband returned home, Hunter and he set about the business of building a family. After losing their first child, the couple was told that they would be unable to have more, and it took several years to prove the doctor wrong. In the time that passed before Hunter had her two sons, she occupied herself with helping her husband further his career. "He was so much in sympathy with my writing urge, however, that he took the first chance he could to buy me a typewriter—a battered old thing, but still the only one he could lay hands on during those post-war years of machine scarcity," recounted Hunter in *SAAS*. "And it was his encouragement, too, that was responsible for my writing my first book."

After moving around a bit, Hunter and her family settled in the north of Scotland in a mountainous region called the Highlands. She had resumed her historical research, was frequently publishing newspaper feature articles, and was experimenting with the short story when her husband suggested she use the results of her research to write a novel. Although she gasped at the idea at first, Hunter decided she had nothing to lose in at least having a try at it. "There had been so many marvellous stories in the stuff I had read!" she declared. "The one that had always intrigued me most, also, was one that centered around a mystery of identity—and it was the possible solution of this mystery that had been the subject of the research findings I had published! I had been a great fool, I thought, not to have realised that I had already given myself the bones of a book by doing so; and straight away I sat down to my typewriter."

Two years later Hunter had a very long novel which she spent a year revising before making a few attempts to publish it, all in vain. The manuscript was put away in a bureau, where it still lies to this day. The three years spent on the novel were not wasted, however, as Hunter realized with the help of her two sons. "Both out of doors and indoors, too, I entertained the boys as my mother had entertained me—with songs, poems, and stories, but especially with stories," she explained in *SAAS.* "And, of course, they had favourites among the stories I made up for them, particularly those I wove around a boastful Irishman I had invented, and whom I called Patrick Kentigern Keenan. He had flashed complete in my head, this Patrick, on a day when my elder son was only a tiny baby." When this same son was ten years old, he asked his mother why she didn't make a book out of the Patrick stories so he could read them for himself instead of waiting for her to tell them.

Once again, Hunter thought, why not? She had always been fascinated with the Celtic folktale and its poetic language. So, Hunter made a deal with her sons—she would write a part of the book every day if they would follow certain household rules. Both sides of the bargain were kept and Hunter sent the finished book off to a publisher. Attracting considerable notice in Great Britain, *Patrick Kentigern Keenan,* released in the United States as *The Smartest Man in Ireland,* showcases Hunter's talent for reproducing what she calls the "authentic voice" of folklore. The story, an original folktale reflecting the author's half-Irish heritage, describes how a group of malicious fairies are outwitted by a clever mortal. *Patrick Kentigern Keenan* was well-received, prompting the cry for an encore. "I was well away, by then, into the work of writing another kind of book for my children," Hunter recalled in *SAAS.* "And by then also, I was fully realising that *nothing* of either the study or the writing I had done up till that time, had been in any way a waste of effort."

Fantasy and history quickly became Hunter's specialties as she entered the most productive period of her writing career. "My feeling for poetry," she explained, "had been the spur to writing that first fantasy; and so what I had been doing, in effect, was to serve a long and thorough apprenticeship in two forms of writing—fantasy and the historical novel. For both forms, my research work had laid down a fertile seedbed of ideas."

Scottish legend and folklore invigorate such fantasies as *Thomas and the Warlock, The Ferlie, The Bodach,* and *A Stranger Came Ashore.* "In this group of stories," maintained Peter Hollindale in *Children's Literature in Education,* "which take as their theme the relationship between humankind and the many supernatural beings of Celtic myth, we find a narrative form under immaculate, almost flawless control." In all of these fantasies it is a child or adolescent who plays the crucial role and possesses insights not open to adults. This understanding of things, both natural and supernatural, requires the

young hero or heroine to have resolute courage. "Natural rhythms of youthful strength and aged weakness, of growth and decay, co-exist in the stories with the unearthly everlastingness of the nonhuman world," continued Hollindale.

In both *Thomas and the Warlock* and *The Ferlie,* humans cross the line between the real world and the fairy world, and it is the wisdom and courage of youth that save them. In the first book, Thomas Thomson, the local blacksmith and a well-known poacher, must face the wrath of the evil warlock Hugo Gifford after venturing too close to the Goblin Ha'. Thomas has allies to help fight the warlock, however—the most important being his young son, Alexander, who is the only one who knows the fairy rhyme that will tell his father what to do. Margery Fisher, writing in *Growing Point,* observed that *Thomas and the Warlock* is "a very open, active and lively tale; its magic is brisk rather than mysterious." *The Ferlie* similarly pits the young orphan Hob Hazeldene against a ferlie, or fairy. Hob is obsessed with a sweet music he hears in his dreams, and is delighted when he is able to make a whistle upon which he can play the tune. The music, however, is that of a ferlie, and Hob must resist its efforts to lure him into the fairy world. In her *Growing Point* review of the book, Fisher described *The Ferlie* as "a brilliant, clear-cut, robust story." Polly Goodwin concluded in the *Washington Post* that Hunter "puts a dramatic climax on a well-told tale touched with magic."

The Bodach and *A Stranger Came Ashore* are also filled with otherworldly magic. Set in the Scottish Highlands, *The Bodach* (known in the United States as *The Walking Stones*) is the tale of an old man's fight to stop the electric company from flooding his valley. Skilled in ancient Druidic rites, the Bodach and his young pupil Donald use their magic to stop the water from coming for as long as they can. "Unreal? Not in Mollie Hunter's crisply told tale," stated Jane Yolen in the *Washington Post Book World.* Yolen added: "Readers, fantasy and fact lovers alike, will be caught up in the reality of unreality." A *Kirkus Reviews* contributor concluded that *The Bodach* is "as graceful an unhurried talespin as ever you please or a silver-tongued Bodach could match." In *A Stranger Came Ashore,* Hunter explores the legend of the Selkie Folk, seals that live in the water around the Shetland islands off northern Scotland. The narrative, recounted by Robbie, the brother of bride-to-be Elspeth, focuses on who will be the bridegroom—Elspeth's love Nicol Anderson, or Finn Learson, who appears mysteriously from the sea one night. Robert Bell, writing in the *School Librarian,* found Hunter's style effective in conveying the tension of the story, noting that "the language is direct, commanding and evocative." Ann Thwaite concluded in the *Times Literary Supplement* that *A Stranger Came Ashore* contains plenty "to attract and hold a young reader, and Mollie Hunter's love of the Shetlands and their selkie-legends is pervasive."

In Hunter's fantasies, the supernatural world is so close to the real world that the two often overlap. "The matter of these stories accords completely with the manner of their telling," maintained Hollindale. "The narrative comes essentially from a *speaking* voice of distinctive quality. It is matter-of-fact and brisk, daring the reader (or listener) to find anything implausible in its strange tales; it is confidential and intimate; but it is also spare and economical, almost bardic in its adroit and dignified simplicity; and it is full of humour and full of music, not least the music of Gaelic idiom and sentence-forms. These diverse qualities merge, with remarkable consistency and control, to express a wide span of moods and emotions within a taut narrative structure."

In an interview published in *Top of the News,* Hunter explained that she gets a different kind of satisfaction from each of the various genres in which she writes: "partly because each calls for a technique that's specific to itself and partly because each indulges some aspect of my own nature. In the fantasies, for instance, I'm indulging the dreamy, mystical side of my nature, the side that has always relied on intuition rather than on any reasoning process and that has, consequently, always been attracted to the supernatural . . . . I also have a very practical side to my nature, and this comes out in the plot structuring required for my historical novels."

In such historical novels as *The Spanish Letters, A Pistol in Greenyards, The Ghosts of Glencoe,* and *The Stronghold,* Hunter brings to life past events through young characters who have conflicting loyalties and who must show bravery and courage in the face of powers stronger than themselves. Taking place in sixteenth-century Edinburgh, *The Spanish Letters* centers on Jamie Morton, a fifteen-year-old as tough, proud, dirty, and honest as the city which had bred him. Jamie is one of the Edinburgh "Caddies," a group of men and boys organized to perform as guides and message-runners. In the year following the defeat of the Spanish Armada, Jamie is hired to guide an English agent who is working to derail the covert activities of Spanish plotters. "As a story of derring-do, romance, intrigue, swash and buckle," asserted Zena Sutherland in the *Saturday Review,* "*The Spanish Letters* has everything; it is saved from being just another dramatic adventure story by the smooth integration of historical details and by Mollie Hunter's deft writing."

For her next historical novel, Hunter chose an obscure event from Scottish history. *A Pistol in Greenyards* takes place in the Scottish Highlands during the nineteenth century, at a time when thousands of poor Scots families were evicted from their homes on ancestral clan lands so that the land could be taken over and used for sheep-farming. Hunter's novel was inspired by an actual incident wherein a young boy armed with a pistol succeeded in making a drunken sheriff's officer back down from his threats of violence. "I read letters, diaries, newspapers on the period," Hunter commented in her *Talent Is Not Enough.* "I talked to old people with intimate experience of crofting life, and got from them old tales and childhood memories. In Gaelic-speaking company I sat apart, letting the music of the old tongue fill my ears. Summer day after summer day I left my own comfortable home in the Highlands to wander among the poor little ruins of stone houses which mark the sites of the clearances, and the pain of the parting which had happened there was keen again." Shortly after publishing *A Pistol in Greenyards* Hunter happened to meet a man whose grandfather, as a boy, had been among those standing constant guard to warn of the coming of the land-grabbers. "Many and many a time, this man told me, he had heard his grandfather telling of how it was in the clearance of Greenyards," Hunter recalled. "And, he added, when he read my book: 'It could have been my grandfather himself talking.' I have never been paid a greater compliment on any of my writing."

Hunter followed *A Pistol in Greenyards* with *The Ghosts of Glencoe,* based on yet another incident in Scottish history—the fearsome Massacre of Glencoe, which took place in 1692. In this story, a sixteen-year-old junior officer in the regiment responsible for the massacre, rebels, at the risk of his own life, against the orders to kill. A *Times Literary Supplement* contributor contended that Hunter's "portraits of the principals on both sides are brilliantly done." A *Junior Bookshelf* reviewer observed that Hunter succeeds in "presenting a piece of history as a novel that is convincing as a novel without distorting the facts."

Hunter's Carnegie Medal-winning novel, *The Stronghold,* contains themes that are similar to those found in her other historical works; there are opposing loyalties, the realities of power and weakness, and courageous young characters. Set in the first century A.D. in a primitive community on an island in the Orkneys, off the coast of Scotland, the novel provides a hypothesis for the origins of the wondrous circular stone defense towers known as the "brochs." Because the tribe is constantly threatened by neighbors, the young, physically handicapped Coll designs the towers and stands firm against the resistance of the dominating Druid priests. It is only after a sacrifice is made to appease the gods that Coll is able to persuade the tribe to build an experimental broch. The broch saves the community from an attack and also repairs the tension-filled relationship between the island's leading Druid-priest and the warrior-chief. *The Stronghold* is "a tumultuous yet clearly conceived and tautly constructed novel, narrated in one evoking scene after another," asserted Eleanor Cameron in the *New York Times Book Review.* Fisher, in her *Growing Point* review of the novel, maintained: "A close, detailed reconstruction of the past in practical terms . . . helps to establish a brilliantly imagined picture of an ancient society which we can only know now through conjecture."

After the publication of *The Stronghold,* Hunter's writing progressed to a different level; she found another voice for her novels, a voice she discovered through the character of Bridie McShane in *A Sound of Chariots.* "I was still writing the historical and the fantasies, of course, but I was also beginning to find an altered perspective for my imagination," explained Hunter in *SAAS.* "I realised that there were other and different types of books to be gleaned out of the experiences of my own life rather than from the material of my study," From these experiences Hunter wrote a number of young-adult novels, including *The Third Eye, The Dragonfly Years,* and *Cat, Herself.* "All the female characters I had created both before and after [Bridie's] time had been as strongly drawn as I could make them; yet ... none of them had been the protagonist of a book," Hunter continued. "But now, in these young-adult novels, I *was* speaking through female protagonists. And by doing so, it seemed to me, I was finding a furtherance of the release that Bridie had given me—and so also confirming in myself a specific *kind* of voice through which to tell each of these stories."

In *The Third Eye,* Hunter's voice is expressed in the character of Jinty Morrison. The youngest of three girls, Jinty resides with her family in Ballinford, Scotland, during the Depression. Having a psychic sensitivity makes Jinty more aware of the problems and troubles of people around her. The pasts and secrets of other characters are revealed through a series of flashbacks and through Jinty's observations of local gossip and community activities. "Mollie Hunter works out her plot so expertly and directs her narrative so firmly that we are drawn completely into the book, getting to know the characters in the slow, partial manner of real life," asserted Fisher in *Growing Point. The Third Eye,* concluded Marcus Crouch in the *Junior Bookshelf,* is "a book to savour, to read slowly and then to read again, noting how beautifully every episode is dovetailed into the main structure."

Hunter returned to her first female protagonist, Bridie McShane, in *The Dragonfly Years* (also known as *Hold on to Love*). Bridie is still residing in Edinburgh, where she takes evening classes and works as a florist's apprentice in the time just before World War II. As she develops a friendship with a classmate, Peter McKinley, Bridie also develops her political awareness and her writing. The relationship between Bridie and Peter grows closer to love, but is nearly destroyed because of an argument. Peter stubbornly joins the Navy just before war breaks out, and it is only after this that Birdie realizes her love for him. Writing in the *Times Educational Supplement,* Mary Hoffman stated: "Despite the mushy ending, the book makes a powerful point: it is only with the victory of independence that you recognize your necessary involvement with the rest of humankind."

Although Bridie gave Hunter the voice to tell her young-adult tales, it was the story of Catriona McPhie that gave this voice its full strength. "It was when I wrote the present-day story of *Cat, Herself* ... that I found this voice speaking out on the loudest and clearest note I could summon for it; and speaking, too, in a way that enabled me to use aspects of my own life more fully than ever before," recalled Hunter in *SAAS.* Cat McPhie is a member of one of Scotland's many travelling families, also known as tinkers, and she and Hunter share many characteristics. "Through this girl, I could recreate all the halcyon days of my own childhood, making her as physically hardy as myself, giving to her

all my own love of freedom, all my own sensuous pleasure in the colours, the shapes, the smells, the very *feel* of the countryside I have always so passionately loved," Hunter explained. Cat is also very independent, which enables her to break free of the tinker's traditional role and eventually find a husband who allows her to be herself. Hunter "depicts the caravan life of tinkers with authority and captures the flavor of their folklore and customs during their travels through the Scottish countryside," observed Ethel R. Twichell in *Horn Book. Cat, Herself* "is as finely crafted as we have come to expect from Mollie Hunter," concluded *School Librarian* contributor Christine Walker.

"So, also, the wheel on which my life had been turning came full circle at last," continued Hunter in *SAAS.* "Or in a manner of speaking, at least, that was so; because there have been other books since that girl's story was written, other books that have taken me back to the medium of fantasy that started it all. And why? Because now I have grandchildren, along with whom has come a renewal of the childhood demand for the story. And that, it seems to me, is the most delightful of all renewals for one who, at heart, has never really been other than just a storyteller!"

Also included as part of the turning wheel of Hunter's life and writing career are essays in which she discusses and examines the craft to which she is most dedicated—storytelling. "Passing on stories is the endeavor to which Mollie Hunter is most deeply committed," declared Janet Hickman in *Language Arts.* This commitment and Hunter's sense of responsibility to her child readers are evident in her book of essays, *Talent Is Not Enough.* Based on a series of Hunter's lectures, the five essays collected in *Talent Is Not Enough* reveal the author's theories on good writing and storytelling. "The whole collection of essays is an extraordinary combination of various patterns of thought and expression," Paul Heins remarked in the book's introduction. *Talent Is Not Enough,* concluded Mary M. Burns of *Horn Book,* is "enhanced by the wit and felicitous style which is characteristic of [Hunter's] novels" and "should be required reading for all who would write or evaluate books for children—and for adults." Hunter continueed her examination of the meeting point between writers and readers in her collection *The Pied Piper Syndrome, and Other Essays.* "In these essays, one of Hunter's most important recurring themes is the invaluable gift of imagination," maintained Susan A. Burgess in *School Library Journal.* Burgess added: "By revealing her own thoughts so generously and articulately, Hunter demonstrates how all of us who work with children and books can understand each other better."

More recent books by Hunter have included the picture book *Gilly Martin the Fox* and *The King's Swift Rider: A Novel on Robert the Bruce. Gilly Martin* retells an old Gaelic folk tale about a clever fox who helps a young prince win the hand of a beautiful young lady. Filled with giants, witches, shape-shifting, and other staples of fantasy literature, the story "flows smoothly and carries readers along as easily as Gilly Martin changes from fox to sturdy row boat to sailing ship," maintained *School Library Journal* contributor Judith Gloyer. Hunter was praised by *Quill & Quire* reviewer Joanne Schott for "her sure touch, combining fidelity to the oral tradition with phrasing and structure that flow easily for contemporary readers."

In *The King's Swift Rider*, sixteen-year-old Martin Crawford serves Robert the Bruce, the thirteenth-century king of Scotland, in Robert's fight for independence from England. "This is the mesmerizing story of that struggle and final victory, told with the panache and passion characteristic of Mollie Hunter's historical fiction," enthused Mary M. Burns of *Horn Book*. "Readers will devour this powerful, stirring novel in one sitting," maintained a *Kirkus Reviews* critic, who added that Hunter depicts the book's many battle scenes in a way that portrays war as both "brutal" and "captivating." Hunter tempers the savagery of ancient warfare with Martin's pacifist nature and explores his dilemma of wishing to support his king and yet honor his personal desire to become a man of the cloth.

Hunter takes a more fanciful look at warfare in *The Knight of the Golden Plain* and *The Day of the Unicorn*, her books about Sir Dauntless, who seeks adventure until it is time to break for tea. In these picture books for younger readers, Hunter "navigates between classic derring-do and a child's imaginative simulation of it with wit and skill," according to a *Kirkus Reviews* commentator.

To become a successful author, Hunter once noted in *Horn Book*, one must cultivate "the capacity to endure loneliness—not that loneliness itself is peculiar to the creative mind.... To say ... that the writer's lot is a lonely one is not to complain of this, but simply to make the point that to be creative is to be different from those who are not; and so, to that extent also, to be cut off from those others.... A writer, indeed, could be likened to a person locked for life in a cell—someone to whom the mere fact of imprisonment has taught things he wants desperately to convey. He compiles a code, spends the rest of his life using this to tap out messages on the wall of his cell, and all the time he taps he is asking himself, *'Is there anyone out there listening? Can they hear me? Do they understand?'*" Hunter's critical acclaim and popularity among children suggest that she both understands and connects with her primary audience. "At its lowest ... what I am trying to achieve with my writing is just to entertain," Hunter related in her *Top of the News* interview, adding: "At it's highest, my writing is an attempt to create form and beauty and maybe a grain or so of truth out of my personal chaos. Usually I fall between two stools and succeed only in producing a readable story. That's not much to achieve, it's true; but if it gives some lasting pleasure to any reader, anywhere, I'll not quarrel with it."

Works Cited

Bell, Robert, review of *A Stranger Came Ashore, School Librarian,* March, 1976, p. 50.

Burgess, Susan A., "Connecting with Readers," *School Library Journal,* March, 1993, p. 136.

Burns, Mary M., review of *The King's Swift Rider, Horn Book,* January-February, 1999, p. 64.

Burns, "Of Interest to Adults: *Talent is Not Enough: Mollie Hunter on Writing for Children,*" *Horn Book,* December, 1976, pp. 637-38.

Cameron, Eleanor, "At Her Back She Always Heard," *New York Times Book Review,* November 5, 1972, p. 6.

Cameron, review of *The Stronghold, New York Times Book Review,* July 21, 1974, pp. 8, 10.

"Casualties of Change," *Times Literary Supplement,* May 25, 1967, p. 447.

Crouch, Marcus, review of *The Third Eye, Junior Bookshelf,* August, 1979, p. 221.

Review of *The Day of the Unicorn, Kirkus Reviews,* June 15, 1994, p. 846.

DeLuca, Geraldine, review of *A Sound of Chariots, Lion and the Unicorn,* fall, 1978, pp. 92-96.

Fisher, Margery, review of *The Ferlie, Growing Point,* December, 1968, p. 1239.

Fisher, review of *The Stronghold, Growing Point,* September, 1974, p. 2455.

Fisher, review of *The Third Eye, Growing Point,* November, 1979, p. 3595.

Fisher, review of *Thomas and the Warlock, Growing Point,* May, 1967, p. 920.

Review of *The Ghosts of Glencoe, Junior Bookshelf,* April, 1967, p. 123.

"The Gift of the Gab," *Times Literary Supplement,* September 28, 1973, p. 1113.

Gloyer, Judith, review of *Gilly Martin the Fox, School Library Journal,* June, 1994, p. 119.

Goodwin, Polly, review of *The Ferlie, Washington Post,* November 3, 1968, p. 16.

Heins, Paul, introduction to *Talent Is Not Enough,* by Mollie Hunter, Harper, 1976, pp. ix-xiii.

Hickman, Janet, "The Person behind the Book—Mollie Hunter," *Language Arts,* March, 1979, pp. 302-06.

Hoffman, Mary, "No Longer an Island," *Times Educational Supplement,* June 17, 1983, p. 28.

Hollindale, Peter, "World Enough and Time: The Work of Mollie Hunter," *Children's Literature in Education,* autumn, 1977, pp. 109-19.

Hunter, Mollie, "If You Can Read," *Horn Book,* August, 1978.

Hunter, in an interview with M. K. for *Top of the News,* winter, 1985, pp. 141-46.

Hunter, in an essay for *Something about the Author Autobiography Series,* Volume 7, Gale, 1989, pp. 139-54.

Hunter, *Talent Is Not Enough: Mollie Hunter on Writing for Children,* Harper, 1976.

Review of *The King's Swift Rider, Kirkus Reviews,* October 15, 1998, p. 1532.

Schott, Joanne, review of *Gilly Martin the Fox, Quill & Quire,* April, 1994, p. 42.

Sutherland, Zena, review of *The Spanish Letters, Saturday Review,* May 13, 1967, p. 57.

Thwaite, Ann, "Fey, Fi, Fo, Fum," *Times Literary Supplement,* September 19, 1975, p. 1053.

Twichell, Ethel R., review of *Cat, Herself, Horn Book,* July-August, 1986, p. 455.

Walker, Christine, review of *I'll Go My Own Way, School Librarian,* March, 1986, p. 73.

Review of *The Walking Stones, Kirkus Reviews,* August 1, 1970, p. 800.

Yolen, Jane, review of *The Walking Stones, Washington Post Book World,* November 8, 1970, p. 8.

For More Information See

BOOKS

Children's Literature Review, Volume 25, Gale, 1991, pp. 62-91.

Greenway, Betty, *A Stranger Shore: A Critical Introduction to the Works of Mollie Hunter,* Scarecrow Press, 1988.

The Thorny Paradise: Writers on Writing for Children, edited by Edward Blishen, Kestrel Books, 1975, pp. 128-39.

PERIODICALS

Booklist, April 1, 1994, p. 1460.

Horn Book, May-June, 1993, pp. 346-47.

School Library Journal, December, 1998, p. 126.

I–J

IRWIN, Ann(abelle Bowen) 1915-1998
(Hadley Irwin, a joint pseudonym)

OBITUARY NOTICE—See index for SATA sketch: Born October 8, 1915, in Peterson, IA; died of complications from hepatitis C, September 13, 1998, in Des Moines, IA. Educator and author. Irwin was best known as one half of the writing team recognized by the joint pseudonym Hadley Irwin. Together with friend and collaborator Lee Hadley, Irwin wrote thirteen novels for young adults that have been praised for addressing with honesty and compassion a variety of serious and sensitive issues—from parental divorce to drug use to prejudice and sexual abuse—facing many adolescents. Often set in the rural Midwest where both writers grew up, Hadley and Irwin's books offer young readers inspiration through the depiction of undaunted protagonists who face adversity with fortitude. Irwin's ideas for these books were inspired by the many teenagers she came to know during years of high school teaching. The author majored in music at Morningside College in Sioux City, Iowa. She taught music and English at the high school level for some three decades beginning in 1937. Irwin later returned to school and earned a master's degree from the University of Iowa, enabling her to teach at the college level. Working at Iowa State University, she began collaborating with Lee Hadley, another instructor at the school. Their first co-written novel, published under the pseudonym Hadley Irwin, was released in 1979. The pair teamed to write several further young adult works, enjoying success with readers both in the U.S. and overseas. Works that Irwin co-authored under the pseudonym Hadley Irwin include: What about Grandma? (1982), Abby, My Love (1985), Can't Hear You Listening (1990), The Original Freddie Ackerman (1992), Jim-Dandy (1994), and Sarah with an H (1995). Abby, My Love was adapted for television as a "CBS Schoolbreak Special" in 1988.

OBITUARIES AND OTHER SOURCES:

PERIODICALS

Detroit Free Press, September 18, 1998, p. 4B.

New York Times, September 20, 1998, p. 51.
Publishers Weekly, October 5, 1998, p. 37.
Washington Post, September 18, 1998, p. B6.

* * *

IRWIN, Hadley
See IRWIN, Ann(abelle Bowen)

* * *

JOHNSON, JOHNNY
See JOHNSON, (Walter) Ryerson

* * *

JOHNSON, (Walter) Ryerson 1901-1995
(Johnny Johnson; Kenneth Robeson, Brett Halliday, house pseudonyms)

OBITUARY NOTICE—See index for SATA sketch: Born October 19, 1901, in Divernon, IL; died May 24, 1995, in FL. Western, mystery, science fiction, and children's writer. Johnson received his B.S. degree in 1926 from the University of Illinois. He worked as a coal miner while attending school, then held various jobs on the East Coast, including warehouse manager for U.S. Gypsum Company in Boston. He worked his way to Europe and back as a seaman, traveling through Europe playing the musical saw. He was the editor of Popular Publications (1945), and editor and staff writer of Adult Leadership for the Adult Education Association of the U.S.A. from 1952 to 1954. His first book, Barb Wire, appeared in 1947. Johnson published at least twenty-five books over his career, mostly in the western and mystery genres, and a number of children's books including four titles in the "Bob and Bee Blake" series (1963). His last books included Monsters That Move Earth (1978), Sticky Icky Movement Activities (1985), Why Is Baby

Crying? (1989), *The Best Western Stories of Ryerson Johnson* (1990) edited by Bill Pronzini and Martin H. Greenberg, *Kenji and the Magic Geese* (1992), and *Torture Trek and Eleven Other Action-Packed Stories of the Wild West* (1995), edited by Pronzini and Greenberg. He was also the ghost writer, under the pseudonym Brett Halliday, of several novels in the "Mike Shayne" mystery series, and, under the pseudonym Kenneth Robeson, of three novels in the "Doc Savage" series, including *The Fantastic Island* (1966), *Land of Always-Night* (1966), and *The Motion Menace* (1971). These were the first book appearances of novels originally published in the pulp magazine *Doc Savage,* in the 1930s. Johnson was author and editor of *Two Hundred Years of Lubec History,* chief copy editor and writer for *Young Children's Encyclopedia* (1967-70), and author of most of the fiction sections for *Westward the Nation,* a fifth-grade reader. He was a member of Mystery Writers of America, Writers Guild of America West, and Authors League of America. He received the Jane Addams Award from the Women's International League for Peace and Freedom for *The Monkey and the Wild Wild Wind* (1963). Johnson noted in an interview that "in an age of specialization I have liked to remain something of a jack-of-all-trades. If you specialize you box yourself in—[and] rule out too much of the rest of life."

OBITUARIES AND OTHER SOURCES:

BOOKS

Xenograffiti: Essays on Fantastic Literature, by Robert Reginald, Borgo Press, 1996, p. 172.

PERIODICALS

Locus, July, 1995, p. 62.

—Robert Reginald and Mary A. Burgess

*   *   *

JUSTUS, May 1898-1989

OBITUARY NOTICE—See index for *SATA* sketch: Born May 12, 1898, in Del Rio, TN; died November 7, 1989, in Monteagle, TN. Children's book writer. Justus studied at the University of Tennessee and became a writer of children's books dealing with the ways and lore of the Smoky Mountain region. She also taught handicapped and retarded children in her home. Her first book, *Peter Pocket: A Little Boy of the Cumberland Mountains,* appeared in 1927, and she eventually produced more than three dozen books over her career. Her last published works included *You're Sure Silly, Billy!* (1972), *Jumping Jack* (1974), *Fun for Hunkydory* (1976), *Broccoli and Bubble Gum* (1985), and a book of poems, *My Lord and I.* Two collections, *All Through the Year* and *Some One Is Knocking,* include her poems which had been published in juvenile magazines from 1925 to 1970. She received Julia Ellsworth Ford Prizes for *Gabby Gaffer's New Shoes* (1935) and *Near-Side-and-Far* (1936), and a Boys' Club Award for *Luck for Little Lihu* (1950). *New Boy in School* was on the New York Times Best Books List in 1963, and *The Tale of a Pig* was used by the Canadian Broadcasting Corporation in the television series *The Friendly Giant* in 1970. Justus's books, correspondence, and manuscripts are gathered in the May Justus Collection at the University of Tennessee.

—Robert Reginald and Mary A. Burgess

K

KEANEY, Brian 1954-

Personal

Born January 10, 1954, in London, England; son of John (a boiler operator) and Kathleen (a homemaker) Keaney; married Rosemary Brownhill (a teacher), August 21, 1976; children: Emily Jane, Kathleen Maeve. *Education:* Attended St. Ignatius College, London, 1965-72; University of Liverpool, B.A. (with honors), 1975; Liverpool Institute of Education, Postgraduate Certificate in Education, 1976. *Politics:* "Left of center, not affiliated to any party." *Religion:* "Cultural Catholic."

Brian Keaney

Addresses

Home and office—111 Drakefell Rd., London SE4 2DT, England. *Agent*—A. M. Heath and Co., 79 St. Martin's Lane, London WC2N 4AA, England.

Career

Teacher in London, England, 1976-86; writer-in-residence in Redbridge, England, 1988-90, and London, 1990-91; freelance writer, 1991—. *Member:* Society of Authors, National Association of Writers in Education.

Writings

FOR YOUNG PEOPLE

Don't Hang About, Oxford University Press, 1985.
Some People Never Learn, Oxford University Press, 1987.
No Need for Heroes, Oxford University Press, 1989.
If This Is the Real World, Oxford University Press, 1991.
Boys Don't Write Love Stories, Oxford University Press, 1993.
Family Secrets, Orchard Books (London, England), 1997.
The Private Life of Georgia Brown, Orchard Books, 1998.
Bitter Fruit, Orchard Books, 1999.

Sidelights

Brian Keaney told *SATA:* "My parents were Irish immigrants. When they came to London in the 1940s there were signs in lodging houses that said 'No Irish Need Apply.' There was nothing for them but hard work and the support of their own community. As a consequence, I was brought up in a cultural bubble in the heart of London, and I grew up feeling slightly at odds with my surroundings. This was one of the factors that made me a writer.

"The respect my parents had for books and learning, though they themselves were largely uneducated, was another important element. Equally influential was the spoken language I heard all around me every day. My mother was and is a great natural talker and storyteller, and hearing the priest's thundering sermons each Sunday in church also had its effect.

"Mine was an intense childhood, and not entirely carefree. My father held very strong opinions on most subjects, and there were often dreadful clashes of will between us. I sometimes think that I write for children because I am trying to return in my imagination to my own childhood in order to work out those conflicts.

"My books are about young people who face problems that seem to them insoluble and the ways they find to deal with those difficulties. I believe the strategies we devise as children for our own survival create our identities, and it is identity above all that interests me."

The first of Keaney's books for young people, *Don't Hang About,* is a collection of stories centering on the author's experiences growing up in East London during the 1960s. In this work, Keaney shares with young readers his own teenage problems, including conflicts with peers, parents, and teachers, as well as the prejudice he encountered as the son of Irish-Catholic immigrants. "The author speaks with a direct voice to his teenage audience and avoids any hint of patronising his readers," maintained *School Librarian* contributor Julia C. Marriage, who added: "The strength of the book lies in the fact that the author writes from his own experience ... in an imaginative manner." A critic for *Junior Bookshelf* characterized *Don't Hang About* as "social history," asserting: "If you want to know how it felt to be a minority in the 'Sixties, here it is."

If This Is the Real World is another of Keaney's books for adolescents that offers "a mirror of contemporary life," according to a *Junior Bookshelf* reviewer. The story details the plight of teenage protagonist Danny, who searches for the father who abandoned him and his family some eight years earlier. "Brian Keaney is excellent with colloquial conversation," maintained the *Junior Bookshelf* commentator, "skilled at detailing the domestic/school/urban community life-style, and good at communicating a young person's emotions/hopes/fears." The reviewer also had high praise for what he described as the "expertly envisaged" school settings and the "similarly genuine" scenes of home life in the book. "The most attractive element of the book," contended *School Librarian* contributor Robert Dunbar, "is in watching Danny grow .... He comes to appreciate the essential differences between the easy escape offered by dream worlds and the increasingly tough realities to be faced in having to accept some of life's harsher aspects."

Keaney again takes up the issue of a father's absence in *Family Secrets.* In this novel, Kate and her single mother Anne travel to Ireland, where Kate's grandmother has suffered a stroke. There, Kate finds her father, experiences her first love, and gains an understanding of her grandmother, who for years would have nothing to do with Kate and her mother. Val Randall, writing in *Books for Keeps,* maintained that "the story strenuously avoids the glibness of tying all ends neatly together but gives positive indications of a brighter future for all the protagonists." *School Librarian* contributor Audrey Baker, who called *Family Secrets* "an enjoyable novel," also cited a tone of optimism pervading the work, noting that "there is no complete resolution but there is a note of hope and Kate has decided that whatever happens openness is best."

Thirteen-year-old Matthew writes to an imaginary female confidante in *Boys Don't Write Love Stories,* another of Keaney's well received novels for young adults. In this book, narrator Matthew writes of tensions at home and at school: his parents are confined to a loveless marriage and seem to prefer being away from home, his school-skipping older sister is an animal-rights fanatic who threatens to do something criminal to advance her cause, and Matthew himself is struggling with a bully at school. *School Librarian* contributor Robert Dunbar claimed: "The novel's central concern, a young teenager's awareness of an adult world which is hurtfully unfair and frequently absurd, is presented with some sharpness, not least in the pared dialogue which dominates the text." A reviewer for *Junior Bookshelf* offered a commendation frequently voiced in assessments of Keaney's books, noting that "the school bits are well done."

Works Cited

Baker, Audrey, review of *Family Secrets, School Librarian,* November, 1997, p. 213.

Review of *Boys Don't Write Love Stories, Junior Bookshelf,* June, 1993, p. 105.

Review of *Don't Hang About, Junior Bookshelf,* April, 1986, p. 77.

Dunbar, Robert, review of *Boys Don't Write Love Stories, School Librarian,* August, 1993, p. 122.

Dunbar, Robert, *If This Is the Real World, School Librarian,* February, 1992, p. 31.

Review of *If This Is the Real World, Junior Bookshelf,* December, 1991, p. 264.

Marriage, Julia C., review of *Don't Hang About, School Librarian,* September, 1986, pp. 269-70.

Randall, Val, review of *Family Secrets, Books for Keeps,* November, 1997, p. 27.

For More Information See

PERIODICALS

School Library Journal, November, 1997, p. 213.

*   *   *

KLIROS, Thea 1935-

Personal

Born in 1935 in New York, NY; children: Adrian, Hilary. *Education:* Attended Bennington College and Yale University.

Thea Kliros

Addresses

Home and office—313 East 18th St., New York, NY 10003. *Agent*—(art) Wanda Nowak, 231 E. 76th St., New York, NY 10021.

Career

Painter, 1960-70, with exhibits in Washington, DC and Spain; freelance fashion illustrator, 1970-89; children's book illustrator, 1989—. *Exhibitions:* Society of Illustrators; American Illustration Today; Millbrook Gallery, Millbrook, NY. *Member:* Graphic Artists Guild.

Awards, Honors

Award of Merit from Society of Illustrators.

Illustrator

James M. Barrie, *The Story of Peter Pan,* text adapted by Daniel O'Connor, original illustrations by Alice B. Woodward, Dover, 1992.

Rudyard Kipling, *How the Leopard Got His Spots and Other Just So Stories,* Dover, 1992.

Robert Louis Stevenson, *A Child's Garden of Verses,* Dover, 1992.

Philip Smith, editor, *Irish Fairy Tales,* Dover, 1993.

Anna Sewell, *Black Beauty,* Dover, 1993.

Rudyard Kipling, *The Elephant's Child and Other Just So Stories,* Dover, 1993.

Philip Smith, editor, *Aladdin and Other Favorite Arabian Nights Stories,* Dover, 1993.

Hans Christian Andersen, *The Little Mermaid and Other Fairy Tales,* Dover, 1993.

L. M. Montgomery, *Anne of Green Gables: A Big Imagination,* retelling by Rebecca Anne Krafft, Anytime Books, 1993.

Montgomery, *Anne of Green Gables: Adventures at School,* retelling by Krafft, Anytime Books, 1993.

Rudyard Kipling, *Mowgli Stories from "The Jungle Book,"* Dover, 1994.

Robert Blaisdell, reteller, *Robin Hood,* Dover, 1994.

Frances Hodgson Burnett, *The Secret Garden,* Dover, 1994.

Philip Smith, editor, *Favorite North American Indian Legends,* Dover, 1994.

Brian Doherty, *The Story of Pocahontas,* Dover, 1994.

Jacob Grimm and Wilhelm K. Grimm, *Show White and Other Fairy Tales,* Dover, 1994.

Joseph Jacobs, *Favorite Celtic Fairy Tales,* Dover, 1994.

Selma O. Lagerlof, *The Wonderful Adventures of Nils,* translated from Swedish and edited by Velma Swanson Howard, Dover, 1995.

Washington Irving, *The Legend of Sleepy Hollow and Rip Van Winkle,* Dover, 1995.

Carlo Collodi, *The Adventures of Pinocchio,* adapted by Robert Blaisdell, Dover, 1995.

Victor Hugo, *The Hunchback of Notre Dame,* abridged by Blaisdell, Dover, 1995.

E. T. A. Hoffmann, *The Story of the Nutcracker,* adapted by Blaisdell, Dover, 1996.

Frances Hodgson Burnett, *A Little Princess,* adapted by Blaisdell, Dover, 1996.

Robert Louis Stevenson, *Kidnapped,* adapted by Blaisdell, Dover, 1996.

Howard R. Garis, *Uncle Wiggily Bedtime Stories,* Dover, 1996.

Bram Stoker, *Dracula,* adapted by Robert Blaisdell, Dover, 1997.

Velveteen Rabbit Sticker Storybook, Dover, 1997.

Mark Twain, *The Prince and the Pauper,* adapted by Robert Blaisdell, Dover, 1997.

Louisa May Alcott, *Little Women,* adapted by Blaisdell, Dover, 1997.

Three Little Pigs Sticker Storybook, Dover, 1997.

Louisa May Alcott, *Little Men,* adapted by Robert Blaisdell, Dover, 1997.

Mary Wollstonecraft Shelley, *Frankenstein,* adapted by Blaisdell, Dover, 1997.

Beauty and the Beast Sticker Storybook, Dover, 1997.

Kenneth Grahame, *The Wind in the Willows,* adapted by Blaisdell, Dover, 1998.

Howard R. Garis, *Favorite Uncle Wiggily Animal Bedtime Stories,* Dover, 1998.

Johanna Spyri, *Heidi,* adapted by Robert Blaisdell, Dover, 1998.

James M. Barrie, *The Study of Peter Pan,* Dover, 1998.

Victoria Fremont, editor, *Favorite Animal Poems,* Dover, 1998.

Pinocchio: Full-Color Sturdy Book, Dover, 1998.

Anna Grossnickle Hines, *What Can You Do in the Rain?,* Greenwillow, 1999.

Hines, *What Can You Do in the Sun?,* Greenwillow, 1999.

Hines, *What Can You Do in the Wind?,* Greenwillow, 1999.

Hines, *What Can You Do in the Snow?*, Greenwillow, 1999.

Brenda Shannon Yee, *Sand Castle*, Greenwillow, 1999.

ADAPTER OF ORIGINAL ILLUSTRATIONS BY HARRISON CADY; TEXT BY THORNTON W. BURGESS

The Adventures of Peter Cottontail, Dover, 1991.
... *Reddy Fox*, Dover, 1991.
... *Grandfather Frog*, Dover, 1992.
... *Chatterer the Red Squirrel*, Dover, 1992.
... *Buster Bear*, Dover, 1993.
... *Danny Meadow Mouse*, Dover, 1993.
... *Jerry Muskrat*, Dover, 1993.
... *Poor Mrs. Quack*, Dover, 1993.
... *Jimmy Skunk*, Dover, 1994.
... *Johnny Chuck*, Dover, 1994.
... *Bobby Raccoon*, Dover, 1995.
Old Mother West Wind, Dover, 1995.

Mrs. Peter Rabbit, Dover, 1998.

Work in Progress

Writing and illustrating two picture books.

Sidelights

Thea Kliros told *SATA:* "As a child I was read to every night. My earliest memory of a story, from when I was under five years old, was *Alice in Wonderland.* I remember being terrified, yet loving the pictures. Reading became an obsession and a joy, as was drawing. When I recall the illustrations in the books that meant so much to me, I hope to be able to create images for children to enjoy, images that will enhance their love of books."

Autobiography Feature

Kathleen Krull

1952-

I am not famous. Mine is not a "household name," even in my own house.

But each of us has our own little claim to fame, and currently mine is as the author of the "Lives of" series. With witty caricatures by Kathryn Hewitt (whose paintings actually inspired the series), these are six books about the really famous people—and what the neighbors thought of them. Through the eyes of the neighbors, we have looked at musicians, writers, artists, athletes, presidents, and (to come) great women. "Neighbors" is just an excuse for me to talk about the most personal information I find in my research—the gossip we all like to know, the odd bits that make these icons of history a bit more human. As do most writers, I like to ask nosy questions—what did these extremely famous people do in the middle of the night, how did they affect their neighbors, who were their girlfriends and boyfriends (and why), how much money did they have and how did they spend it, what did they eat and drink, how did they dress, what about their hair, and so on.

In school presentations I blab on about these rude questions and talk about neighbors so much that sometimes students ask *me:* "Well, what do your neighbors think of *you?*"

And now, in the style of my own "Lives of" books, I will tell you.

Early Neighbors

Kathleen Krull (rhymes with "lull") had serious neighbors to start with—United States Army personnel at Fort Leonard Wood in Missouri. Her father, Kenneth Krull, was stationed at this army base, though he went AWOL (Absent With Out Leave) at one point to marry nineteen-year-old Helen Folliard. Their goal was to create children who were on one side 100 percent Irish and on the other side a blend of German, Russian, possibly Bohemian (Czech), maybe a bit of American Indian.

Neighbors considered Kathleen a basic baby, perhaps more spoiled than most (she was an only child for her first nineteen months). Actually, they hardly got to know her because Mr. Krull soon finished his army duty, started work in Chicago as an artists' representative, and moved the family to Illinois. Krull grew up in Wilmette, a leafy suburb on the shores of Lake Michigan, and considers it her hometown.

New neighbors mostly noticed the well-traveled two miles between the Krull house and the outstanding Wilmette Public Library. Inspired by her parents (both kept books by their bedside for reading each night), Krull started trying to learn to read at age five. Little Golden Books and inexpensive editions of classics littered her room. (Today she believes there's no such thing as owning too many

Kathleen Krull

books and having them around the house.) She succeeded about a year later. By then she was sharing her books with three younger brothers—Kenneth, Carleton, and Kevin. (Kenny learned to read before she did, which she found very annoying.)

What does a mom do with four kids under six? This one took them to the library a lot. Krull became a book addict of the type she hopes librarians still see, checking out six or more books at a time. Quickly growing near-sighted, she sported hideous glasses with sparkly blue frames, usually askew. But these weekly visits were mind-altering escapes into a parallel universe that seemed to her better in many ways than the real one. So it was a pleasant childhood of total book immersion. (TV exposure was minimal, as Mrs. Krull considered TV unhealthy.)

Graduating from picture books, Krull devoured all the fairy tales, myths, and legends she could find, then moved right along to Beverly Cleary and Lois Lenski. Over the years, neighbors saw her carting around historical fiction (Laura Ingalls Wilder, Elizabeth Speare's *Calico Captive* and *The Witch of Blackbird Pond*), biography (the Land-mark Books series on people like Helen Keller, Elizabeth Blackwell, Susan B. Anthony, anything on queens), intelli-gent romance (Mary Stolz, Betty Cavanna), adventure (Scott O'Dell's *Island of the Blue Dolphins*, Gertrude Chandler Warner's "Box Children" series), fun books (like Louise Fitzhugh's *Harriet the Spy* and Astrid Lindgren's *Pippi Longstocking),* anything on Indians, and lots of British and American history.

Her absolute favorites were fantasy (Edward Eager's magical books, those by Carol Kendall) and mystery. The "Famous Five" series by English author Enid Blyton was addictive, and she raced Kenny to see who could read the

most and report on them in the library's summer reading club. All this reading seemed to lead her naturally to start wanting to express herself on paper. (Today she believes that reading a lot is the main job requirement for being a writer.)

Neighbors disagree on whether Krull was a leader or simply bossy. One summer, for example, she organized her brothers into the Secret Garage Club. She wrote a manual for the SGC (unfortunately now lost) with all its rules in different colored inks. The SGC met in the garage every morning until noon for age-appropriate activities she devised to keep everyone busy (or out of her hair). These included locking baby Kevin up in a tool shed. He didn't seem to mind, because she had dubbed the shed a "Mummy Closet" and him the "Keeper of the Mummy Closet." But neighbors pondered whether this was wildly creative on her part, or simply brother abuse.

Every day during the school year, neighbors could see Krull in her dark blue uniform walking or riding her bike a mile away to St. Joseph's School. There she was taught by tough nuns of the Franciscan order (they wore scary black habits). Several had a lasting and positive effect on her. Her third-grade teacher, Sister de Maria, took a kind interest in her writing, and Krull penned (penciled, actually) her earliest works just for her. These were sappy poems in imitation of Edward Lear and Robert Louis Stevenson, with a hint of Dr. Seuss influence. Many of the verses featured nuns (a good word for rhyming).

In fifth grade Krull began piano lessons with stern-but-fair Sister Mary Jane, who had a major impact and became in some ways a role model.

For Sister Della, her eighth-grade teacher, she wrote short horror stories a la Edgar Allan Poe. This high-energy nun (who left the convent the following year and is now known as Marie Tollstrup) praised Krull's writing with frothy enthusiasm—indeed, she was the first person to suggest that Krull could be a writer when she grew up. (Up until then, she had assumed she'd become a nun.)

Otherwise, Krull struck most people as an average student. Her strengths in English, spelling, and music were balanced by weaknesses in gym (very uncoordinated), math, science (at one point she believed there were seven suns), geography, being on time, and many other areas. She almost never contributed to class discussions, but instead was constantly in trouble for exchanging gossip and giggles with friends during class. She recalls spending most of second grade standing in the corner, the punishment for talking in class.

Her mother saved nearly every scrap she scribbled on, which could have given Krull subconscious encouragement that she was writing for posterity. Fortunately, her earliest efforts have never been published. They include *A Garden Book* (second grade), *The History of Queersville* (sixth), and *Death Waits until after Dark* (eighth), about a teacher who jumps out the window.

In fifth grade, obsessed with hair, she brought forth *Hair-Do's and People I Know.* This was an illustrated collection of bizarre girls, boys, nuns, trees, and lots of hair, complete with a copyright notice and cover blurbs from the *New York Times* (which she made up). Still irritated with a fourth-grade teacher who was always punishing her for talking, she gave this poor woman extra hair—a beard and mustache. It was Krull's first realization that one motive for writing could be revenge.

Around age ten, her mother or grandmother gave her a pink, leather-bound diary with its own lock and key. Putting her very own thoughts and experiences on blank paper seemed so perverse, so intoxicating, such a delicious secret. (Today she believes that everyone should keep a diary and that it's the single most important thing a would-be writer or artist can do.) She was enchanted, though it wasn't until sixth grade that she got the hang of diary-writing.

Sixth grade was a big year, as it turned out, and neighbors raised eyebrows at some of her antics. She had a notorious crush on Mr. Banks, her teacher (who was not only not a nun, but a man!). She also liked Raymond, a boy in her class (he had nice hair). Into the pink diary went weighty observations about fights with her moody girl-friends, arguments with brothers, getting in lots of trouble for being too giddy, lectures from both parents on being a lady. Trivia received equal space—she included nauseating details about various illnesses, her laughable bowling scores, what she ate for dinner, which songs were playing on the radio, even the description of a bug crawling across a diary page. She did neglect to mention John F. Kennedy's assassination that year or indeed any other event beyond her own tiny, but slowly expanding world.

It took years to develop the knack of writing every day, but for now she would just pop in once in a while and bring the "reader" up to date. Neighbors, of course, never viewed the pink diary, though Krull was to find out that she *did* in fact have readers. A few samples of what they would have read:

> *January 3. A peaceful day with no brothers around:* "We went to the library, my mom and I, and I got some real good books." *January 8. The teacher unknowingly moves her desk closer to her friends:* "Oh, joyful day! Today Mr. Banks changed the seating arrangement around." *This arrangement ends within days. January 10. She makes a short story out of the way she shows off at school:* "As luck would have it Mr. Banks came in then and said, 'Miss Krull, you will sit and keep silent today.' And that's a pretty bad punishment." *April 20. Her first "date" with Raymond:* "I had a cherry Coke! He paid! HILARIOUS!" *April 28. Forbidden romance with Raymond faltering already:* "I'm beginning to like him a whole lot but it's getting harder to give excuses to my parents! Cruel parents! Nipping in the bud a spring romance!"

Unfortunately, Krull's brothers were out of control with curiosity about this little pink book. She went to great lengths to hide or disguise it, but to no avail. One brother would snoop through her private stuff, pick the locks, do whatever he had to do. Adding insult to injury, he'd write snide commentary in the diary itself. This was an appalling case of sister abuse. Krull's fury was visible even to the neighbors. She was bitter, not just at the invasion of privacy, but also at how powerless she felt. Her parents didn't take the crime as seriously as she thought they should. In fact, she could tell they thought her plight was kind of funny. The injustice!

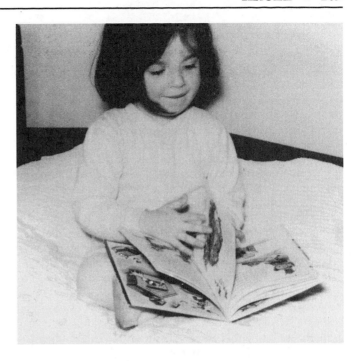

A reader since five.

She once even attempted to run away from home, after a fight with her parents about something trivial. While they thought she was doing homework up in her bedroom, she took the screen off her second-story window, perched on the ledge, and hurled herself into the bushes below.

Neighbors reached for phones to call an ambulance, but she was OK. Then she took off on foot for the house of one of her best friends (which, probably coincidentally, was near the library).

But Krull was not a true rebel at heart. When she got to her friend's house, she thoughtfully (but oddly) called her parents to let them know where she was. They demanded her immediate return. The total time of the caper was about one hour, not including the subsequent stern lectures.

She never ran away again. She did, however, spend many long hours at that window, her "window to the world" (actually, just the cul-de-sac of Highcrest Drive). Neighbors couldn't fail to notice her spectral presence, and sometimes she overheard local boys asking her brothers what on earth she was doing up there all the time. Playing with dolls was the usual theory. But no—she was reading, and thinking. Listening to music. And starting to write more and more. By this time, the library really was becoming a home away from home. One summer day, after parking her bike, she stubbed her toe on the library door. She ignored it—immersed in the "new book" section— until several queasy librarians pointed to the trail of blood her sandals were tracking everywhere.

They kindly provided first aid, and Krull fell more in love with the place than ever. She didn't know any writers in person, but already she was starting to have a filmy, alluring dream of being one of them—someone whose books got checked out, one of those names on the spines of those library books.

Middle Neighbors

During her high school years, neighbors viewed Krull walking every day—rain, shine, or blizzard—across a long park to Regina Dominican. Nuns of the Dominican order (they wore glowing white habits) ruled over this all-girls school. The girls had to wear uniforms of ugly brown blazers and tweed skirts but competed to assert their individuality in whatever ways they could.

Krull stood out more than most. She clomped through hallways in black-and-white saddle shoes, above which were knee socks or tights in neon colors or electric patterns. She glued colorful beads to her ears with clear nail polish, in imitation of forbidden pierced ears (Removing them at night was agony.) She wore pink and purple make-up and elaborate nail decor. Above all she experimented with hair and was famous among classmates for showing up on class picture day with outlandish hairdos.

When outside of uniform, Krull made all of her own clothes. Neighbors couldn't help noticing their . . . uniqueness. Her father worked with artists in the advertising business, and he often brought her bolts of unusual fabrics that had been used in photographing an ad. She would take the brocades, velvets, gauzes, corduroys, and paisleys, and adapt them into eye-popping outfits with the help of Simplicity patterns. The time was the 1960s, when many dressed in a psychedelic mode, but Krull ended up looking like no one else.

By now she *never* spoke up in class, and teachers frequently lowered her grades for not participating. She was more of a listener, an observer. She was a patient listener with friends and gossiped compulsively in the hallways, on the phone, at slumber parties, at the beach, and along the streets of Wilmette. If e-mail had been invented then, she would have been firing off twenty posts a night.

Meanwhile there was the low-tech but trusty diary. During her freshman year, she filled four diaries covered in fake leopard skin. Sophomore year burst the seams of a fat green diary. That's how much her world was enlarging. Her most over-used word was "embarrassment"—nearly everything seemed a source of it.

Discovering the manual typewriter when she was sixteen felt like the *Star Wars* shift into hyperspeed. She stopped writing by hand and began a sophisticated adventure called a journal. The only disadvantage was that now her family and neighbors always knew *exactly* what she was up to—there's nothing like manual typewriter keys to echo through a quiet neighborhood like gunfire shots. Regina girls were equally intrigued, because she often typed her journal on the other side of a wall from the room where the school's choral group practiced. (That's where she spent her study hall time, as well as gym class—still uncoordinated, she was exempted from gym because of scoliosis, or curvature of the spine.)

Ambitiously, pompously, she called the new journal "Reveries: A Journal of Incidents, Insight, Impressions, and Illusions with Illustrations by the Author." An essay by George Orwell gave her the idea to begin each entry by recording her dreams. It seemed a challenge, a useful writing exercise, to take the elastic, nonverbal threads of dreams and weave them into words. She noticed recurring

Krull (far left) reacting to having three brothers by age six.

themes, insights into waking life, psychic premonitions, things that frightened her into nightmares.

She also kept track of books she was reading and analyzed them. Continuing to scour the "new books" section at the library each week, she pirated away contemporary novels, historical fiction, and really just about anything—books on how the brain works, art books, religion, history.

She had love affairs with certain authors, dead and alive—in freshman year J. D. Salinger, and later Ernest Hemingway, F. Scott Fitzgerald, Francoise Sagan, Gore Vidal, Katherine Anne Porter, and numerous others. She checked out every book ever written by Daphne du Maurier. Her very favorite writers were Tom Wolfe and Vladimir Nabokov.

Neighbors got nervous when Mr. Krull started letting his daughter drive his car whenever he wasn't using it. It was a blue-green, very sporty Firebird convertible, and her friends were envious. But Krull, showing perhaps unusual responsibility for her age, was already holding down several jobs. Besides a heavy baby-sitting schedule, she also played the intimidating organ at St. Joseph's Church every Sunday (thanks to the efforts of Sister Mary Jane) and was paid well for it even though she often made mistakes (neighbors would twitch).

Also, librarians had forgiven her for dripping blood all over their nice library and ultimately hired her to work there! Shelving books each afternoon after school was her dream job—the salary might have been one dollar an hour, but she was in book heaven. She lasted several years there, but, alas, was eventually fired for various infractions of the rules. These included reading too much while she was supposed to be working. A career as a librarian was not to be.

Yet some parents around the neighborhood trusted her so much that they allowed their children to come to her house for piano lessons, and this was a lucrative business one summer. Neighbors even bought doughnuts and cupcakes from her during the few years she worked at a bakery chain in Wilmette and Evanston.

Outside of work and school, Krull's most visible (and audible) activities were musical. She kept up with her piano studies and frequently accompanied soloists in their recitals, appeared in her own recitals, and performed for local theater productions. When she practiced at school, girls would gather outside the door of the practice room to listen to Bach Inventions, thundering Chopin preludes, and a rendition of Simon and Garfunkle's "Bridge over Troubled Waters" that never failed to drop jaws. From her bedroom window blared the sounds of the Beatles, Rolling Stones, other rock groups, and much classical music. Neighbors winced while she taught herself violin and viola so she could join the Regina orchestra.

One summer she attended music camp at Northwestern University in Evanston (writing furiously in her journal each night about all the new people and new music she was encountering). She also took folk guitar classes with her mother and studied composition at the North Shore Center of Music in Winnetka.

Internally, though, she was more serious about writing than anything else. At age seventeen, she stated her mission: "My optimistic dream is to support myself by writing novels, but I doubt whether this will prove realistic. I am not sure exactly why I like to write, but I know that I find all aspects of it (yes, even revision) exciting. There are about a dozen writers whose style impresses me tremendously, but I am intent on developing my own. I would like to find my own combination of others' styles and ideas."

Literary ferment included exchanging droll verses with her best friend on a nearly daily basis for over a year. Her private notebooks percolated with doodles, odd ramblings, quotes from favorite books, false starts to several novels, and lists of ideas and "Instant Electric Plots." She had an especially bizarre habit of writing letters and not mailing them, instead collecting them into a melodramatic notebook

Krull, age thirteen, in family portrait: "I was trying to smile like the others, but I can tell my eyes were bothering me. This was the summer I was adjusting from glasses (with geeky blue frames that sparkled) to sophisticated contact lenses."

House in Wilmette, Illinois, where Krull lived from age ten until she left for college. "My window to the world was the center one on the second story."

called "Dear John: A Collection of Letters I Will Never Send."

Dare she try to get her words into print? Her mother helped her submit an essay to the *Chicago Tribune*. Called "The Art of Swimming," it was full of irony about her continued athletic incompetence, and it was rejected. (Some twenty years later, though, the *Tribune* saw the light with a humorous piece called "Serious Earrings," about Krull's fiascoes with the colored beads and clear nail polish.)

Her aunt, Therese Folliard, fostered her fiction attempts and encouraged her to submit short stories to *Seventeen* magazine's annual contest. Krull failed to win with one called "A Night in the Life of Cornelia Doonkle-hoffer." However, her constant doodling was noticed by her father, who arranged for it to appear in an advertisement for a feminine hygiene product—which did make it into the pages of *Seventeen*.

She succeeded in publishing a few enigmatic short stories in her school's literary magazine—"Incident in the Cafeteria," for example, in which just about nothing happens. She also took a journalism class and found bliss in working on the newspaper her senior year.

One English teacher, Sister Jean Bernard, made a point of showing personal interest in her writing. Alas, she disapproved of the plays Krull experimented with (which made fun of certain other teachers—she was still exploring the idea of revenge). Krull also found her Russian history teacher particularly stimulating.

History and music were two majors that tempted her once she reached Lawrence University, a small liberal arts college in Appleton, Wisconsin. But there was never genuine wavering from her first choice, English. Narrowly escaping taking a single science class, she took every course she could in British and American literature and foreign literature in translation. With her courses perpetually demanding lengthy term papers, Krull did little writing outside of assignments. On several occasions, professors read her papers aloud in class to show the other students what they should be doing (while she turned pink).

After reading *A Room of One's Own,* she became obsessed with the works of Virginia Woolf and wrote her senior thesis on several of Woolf's novels. A few of Krull's on-campus neighbors associated her so closely with Woolf that they assumed the two were somehow related or at least looked alike, which was not the case.

Meanwhile, the career decision had been made—Krull wanted to be a writer. But how to do it? And how to pay bills in the meantime? How on earth could you generate income with your own words? While trying to solve the mystery, she hung out at the college's career-planning office and inhaled *Publishers Weekly,* the trade magazine for the book publishing industry. (It is still her favorite magazine.) A solution finally solidified: What about taking a detour into publishing? It would be a way to work with real writers, learn from them, participate in a highly creative world, and get a paycheck all at the same time.

On the day after graduating from Lawrence *magna cum laude,* with an English major and a music minor, Krull began her first job in children's book publishing. She was a secretary, a typical entry-level job. Working with bookish, like-minded people proved to be a rewarding career initiation after all. She was working as an editor at Western Publishing/Golden Books, in Racine, Wisconsin, when she got her first two books published there: *The Bugs Bunny Book,* an urbane debut, to be sure, and a Little Golden Book called *What Will I Be? A Wish Book.* She was about twenty-two.

Her last publishing job, as senior editor, ended ten years and two thousand miles later.

In between, she learned more about writing while editing hundreds of books, working with Tomie dePaola, Eve Bunting, Patricia Hermes, Anne Lindbergh, Jane Yolen, Charles Mikolaycak, Arnold Adoff, Amy Schwartz, Judy Delton, Lael Littke, and other notable authors and artists. Particular peaks occurred when she met or worked with heroes from her childhood—Mary Stolz, Alice and Martin Provensen, Theodor Geisel (Dr. Seuss), Maurice Sendak, Carol Kendall. She also learned about the business of publishing from her bosses (like the illustrious mystery writer Betty Ren Wright) and her often scintillating coworkers.

Working in publishing was an apprenticeship. While on the job, she crafted more books of her own—mysteries in the "Trixie Belden" series, the music for a collection of Christmas carols, and a twenty-four-book concept series. In this sneaky way, she subverted the usually interminable and excruciating process of getting those all-important first publishing credentials. Not that she didn't endure plenty of rejections later, but her first credits came from companies that were employing her, and, my, it was like a narcotic to see her name on a book.

Neighbors in the apartment buildings where she lived found her nondescript for the most part, though sometimes landlords received complaints when she played her invigorating Scott Joplin rags too loud on her piano.

By the time she left the corporate publishing world and eased into writing her own books full-time, she was living in sunny San Diego, California. "I always have to live near water," she once insisted, and an apartment within a mile of the Pacific Ocean was paradise. Even the neighbors were congenial, like the one next door—Paul Brewer, a divorced artist and picture framer with two amusing daughters.

Demonstrating once again her fascination with neighbors, Krull married him in 1989 at the Algonquin Hotel in New York City, on Halloween.

A few years later, getting completely carried away, they bought a house from their next-door neighbors because they liked its pool.

Recent Neighbors

How Krull wishes she could write her own blurbs from the *New York Times* now! But reviewers and award committees mostly have been generous with her books, and she has been able to support herself as a writer for over a decade so far.

Krull does not think she is as eccentric as the people she writes about. Neighbors might disagree. They know her as someone who blasts her radio and CDs too loud (weird rock music, classical, and music from around the world), inflicts their ears with mistakes when she is playing the piano, asks nosy questions, goes in and out of her house with huge armloads of books, and splashes noisily in her pool. They see her out working in her garden and notice her eavesdropping on others at the neighborhood coffee shop. She usually seems in need of a haircut and obviously dresses strictly for comfort.

Neighbors are most likely to bump into her at the library. Some of her most sublime times are while raiding the "new books" section for eclectic stimulation, still in search of books that will change her life. (Bookstores are

Senior picture.

Krull, age sixteen, behind the wheel of her father's Firebird convertible. "Uh,oh."

addictive as well, but there is something special about a library—it's free, democratic, with material preselected by librarians who know what they're doing.)

Mainly she seems to stay in her house: "I take my writing very seriously," she says. She writes every day, including weekends, starting in the morning and winding down when she is brain-dead. She follows Hemingway's advice and tries to end each session while the writing is going well, which makes it easier to get jump-started the next day. Writing a book can seem daunting, but it's like exploring a tunnel: each day she polishes and refines what she wrote the day before and takes it a few steps forward—this is a never-ending process that results in all of her manuscripts being revised over and over. She is constantly searching for ways to make her writing fresher and clearer, using combinations of words and phrases that only she would use. She usually stumbles out of her office at four or five in the afternoon.

Her husband thinks what she does is so cool that he has changed his career to join her in the children's book field, illustrating his own and other writers' books. Most recently he illustrated *Oh No, It's Robert*, by Barbara Seuling. (Sometimes Krull models for his drawings—once she had to pose with underwear on her head.)

Her stepdaughters, Melanie and Jacqui, have at times expressed interest in being writers and have given her book ideas. "I try to cultivate my own experience of childhood," Krull says, "and it has been extremely helpful to me to refresh that by knowing my stepdaughters." They are now in college, still amusing and fascinating human beings.

Krull continues to keep a journal, now on computer, and long since minus her illustrations. She finds it a valuable, indeed indispensable, tool in her writing. This is where she tries to sort the mysteries of life, to observe the world around her and comment—actually, gossip. (Neighbors appear in it constantly.) She tries not to be boring,

even though she is positive she no longer has snoopy readers around.

Getting ideas for books is the least of her problems. Krull thinks that once you start tuning your brain to a writerly frequency—in other words, paying attention—ideas are everywhere. Some ideas jump out of her journal. Others arise from reading the newspaper, observing the children she knows (including those in her neighborhood), keeping up with what other people are publishing, her own reading. Miraculously enough, sometimes people even *give* her ideas, for free.

In choosing which ones to work on, she focuses on what most intrigues her, or in areas where there seems to be something new to say. She asks herself, "Am I passionate enough about this idea to spend a year or two of my life on it?" (Some of her books have taken a lot longer than a year before getting published.)

Because she is a self-supporting writer—how sad that no one has died and left her a trust fund!—she gets most delirious when she thinks she is about to fill a gap in the marketplace. Most of her books—about the Mexican Days of the Dead, great folk songs for kids, musicians and other eccentrics, inspiring heroines like Wilma Rudolph, traveling around the fifty states—result from her perception that the idea has no competition, or that what is already there is outdated.

Whenever she gets an idea for a book, she jots it on the nearest scrap of paper. Something about restaurants must be particularly conducive to ideas, because she often finds herself resorting to a restaurant napkin.

For example, one day she was eating a fish lunch with artist Kathryn Hewitt at Anthony's Star of the Sea, an airy seafood restaurant right on the ocean. She had long esteemed Hewitt's high-spirited way with caricatures—those funny humans with the big heads—and she was eager to do a book with her. Full of adrenaline, Krull scrawled

In California with husband, Paul Brewer, and the Pacific Ocean in background, about 1989.

Krull (right) has a part-time job as a model for children's book illustrations by her husband. (Illustration from Paul Brewer's The Grossest Joke Book Ever, *1997.)*

away on an Anthony's Star of the Sea napkin, all about a proposed book bursting with all the people whose music meant so much to her at different times in her life. The book turned out to be *Lives of the Musicians,* published almost ten years after this lunch.

While researching Beethoven, Krull found out one day that the Great One's favorite meal was macaroni and cheese. This humble, appealing tidbit helped her focus on other concrete details to look for, and soon she hit upon neighbors as a way to make these ultra-famous but dead musicians come alive. Everyone can relate to the idea—we *all* have interesting neighbor stories (and Krull is positive she's not the only eavesdropper around). The neighborly point of view produced a "warts and all" attitude that seemed lively and humanizing. And it was particularly relevant to the musicians because their work is not quiet. As Krull knew from her own clashes with neighbors over the years, they always hear what you're up to. And they always have opinions.

The approach turned out to work for other groups of people as well, although Krull and Hewitt had no idea at the time that *Lives of the Musicians* would be the start of a whole series. But now, as creators of biographies, they hope they are helping to establish a context for our cultural heritage—a noble mission.

Krull also likes the more frivolous idea of paying attention to chatty talk about other people, otherwise known as gossip. She thinks of gossip as the answers to what enquiring minds *really* want to know—"and kids are born with enquiring minds. It's one of their most endearing, most identifying characteristics." Gossip is underrated as a motive for studying history.

As JFK once said about or to J. Edgar Hoover, "All history is gossip."

What does it take to have a career as a biographer? Being nosy (which comes naturally to Krull and, as it happens, to most kids), not being afraid to ask questions, being a good listener (she believes musical training can really help here), having good research skills (having nuns for teachers is an advantage). Being empathetic is a plus— choosing a point of view, cultivating honesty and integrity. Certain knacks are valuable—the ability to organize, to make up your own mind, to see connections—especially ironies.

"Biographies," says Krull, "are really a way of learning about ourselves—and I learn so much from the 'Lives of' books. For example, what is it like to live a creative life? What are the secrets of success—well, I can tell you two: perseverance and single-mindedness."

She likes to see all the disadvantages other people had to overcome: Clara Schumann started her musical career with speech and hearing handicaps, while Beethoven had an abusive father and was supporting his whole family at age twelve (as was Charles Dickens). Bach kept ending up in jail because of his temper, Mark Twain was in trouble all during childhood, Tchaikovsky felt worthless his whole life. Woody Guthrie was made fun of for his small size and his family's mental illness, while the Bronte sisters lived in isolation with a father who hated children. Picasso was dyslexic and had trouble reading and writing, Jack London grew up poor and uneducated, Jane Austen's education ended at eleven. With a father who didn't believe in work, Louisa May Alcott supported the family; and Mary Cassatt's father said he'd rather see her dead than painting. Vincent van Gogh's paintings were considered so deranged that he sold only one during his lifetime. Edgar Allan Poe's mother died when he was two, and his life went downhill from there.

"Kids who live in the real world and have all kinds of their own obstacles to overcome can take inspiration and comfort from many of these true life stories," Krull believes. One of her theories is that overcoming hardship and weakness can be the very thing that makes a person strong and get a lot accomplished: "These were people who never gave up, no matter what cards they were dealt. They had talent, yes, but they were different from a lot of other talented people. Their traumas help to put our own difficulties—brothers snooping in your diary, for example—in perspective."

By far the most frequent question Krull gets asked is "Where do you *get* this stuff?" Are there secrets to learning the intimate details of other people's lives?

She plays detective in her own way, using mostly secondary sources and scouring them for tasty details that make straightforward facts come alive: "I'm taking the

Scary stepmother trick-or-treating with scary step-daughters, Melanie (left) and Jacqui, 1995.

fruits of other people's labors, the most scholarly biographies I can find, and looking for the juicy parts. Then I try to distill what I learn in a fresh way." A latecomer to the Internet, she didn't use it with the first five "Lives of" books. But she thinks it's the coolest thing that's been invented during her lifetime, a rapturous enhancement to curiosity, and she can't wait to see how it will change the world.

She researches tons of material, gleaning a mountain of gossip she thinks is most tantalizing, and then revises, tinkers, revises, edits, whittles, tweaks, and then does some more revising to get what she hopes is the very tiptop of the mountain. If there is a magic key to what she does, it's this: after she soaks up all the information, she doesn't use it all. Lots of fascinating stuff gets jettisoned at this point. She uses only the most savory cream of the crop—plus the facts that move the narrative along. She seeks out the arc, or shape, of the person's life. For example, athlete Wilma Rudolph's life had the starkest arc possible, from her childhood with every possible disadvantage, to her golden moments of Olympic triumph. Krull took her story from *Lives of the Athletes* and made a whole separate book out of it in *Wilma Unlimited: How Wilma Rudolph Became the World's Fastest Woman.* But every life story has a beginning, middle, and end—Krull aims for the most dramatic part and tries to propel momentum toward that. What traits enabled our icons to overcome what obstacles?

Lives of the Musicians was inspired by Krull's love of music (and, of nearly equal importance—love of gossip). *Songs of Praise* came straight out of her unusual experiences as a teen organist. But an element of passion is in all of her books. *Lives of the Writers* was play, not work, getting to research Robert Louis Stevenson (author of the first book she remembers ever reading—*A Child's Garden of Verses*), E. B. White, Emily Dickinson, Shakespeare, and others whose works meant much to her.

Wish You Were Here was sparked, believe it or not, by her admiration for Jack Kerouac's *On the Road,* which created a desire to make her own guide to America. Her heroine, Emily, derives from her own niece, Emily Krull, who was perplexed about the difference between Illinois and California.

With *Wilma Unlimited,* Krull was fascinated by powerful women (because she knows many) and polio (because she might have had it). *V Is for Victory* started with an interest in her own family's wartime history and the idea that World War II affected virtually every family in the world. With *Gonna Sing My Head Off,* she wanted to help preserve the folk songs she and her brothers had grown up on. Anyone who got married on Halloween would naturally be drawn to the Mexican version of the celebration, the Days of the Dead, which inspired *Maria Molina and the Days of the Dead.* (Krull and her husband collect the skeleton dolls—especially brides and grooms—sold in the marketplace at this time of year.) *They Saw the Future,* all about famous psychics in history, came about because as a teen she was obsessed with Alvin Toffler's *Future Shock* (and obnoxiously quoted from it to her mother nonstop). As an adult, Krull has been rumored to visit psychics.

With *Lives of the Presidents,* Krull observed the way people get so passionate about which presidents they love and hate. She does too, and has been paying attention to the

Krull at play: "I always have to live near water," about 1991.

presidents since JFK. She can still recall throwing up all night during the Nixon-Kennedy debates in 1959. (She had stomach flu.) One day she lost a game of "King of the Mountain" to a girl in her largely Republican neighborhood, and as a penalty the other girl made her swear she would make her parents vote for Nixon (as if she could do this). Of course—even though she failed to note it in her diary—she also remembers what she was doing in sixth grade when the announcement came over the school loudspeaker that Kennedy had been shot.

Alex Fitzgerald's Cure for Nightmares and *Alex Fitzgerald, TV Star,* two chapter books, are dear to her heart. They are autobiographical in various ways, like fictionalizing the disorientation of moving from Chicago to San Diego. *Nightmare* came about after trying to help her stepdaughter Jacqui conquer recurring bad dreams, and *TV Star* is based on some of the feelings of Krull's early piano successes.

Krull doesn't label herself an "informational books author" and rarely even uses the term "nonfiction"—one of the world's great ugly words. She seems to write several different kinds of books, and she hopes to continue the pattern. Many of her books blend fiction with nonfiction. In any case, her favorite definition of literature is Ezra Pound's—"news that stays news"—and this doesn't seem to her to exclude nonfiction. She adores the open minds

that kids have—there's so much to tell them, so much that hasn't been said or can be put in a new way, and she'll use any format that seems most likely to succeed. "The 'hidden agenda' to all my work is to create books that will mean as much to readers as books have meant to me," she says.

A writer's life is not perfect, or at least Krull's isn't. Loneliness can be a problem—even after many years away from the corporate world, she still misses the camaraderie of office coworkers, the gales of laughter enlivening the halls. "You have to like being alone to be a writer," she comments. Pets would probably help, but she is allergic to all of them. She belongs to two writers' groups and a quilt group. Having nine nieces and nephews (so far) is stimulating. E-mail is vital, and she uses it mostly for gossip.

The notorious "writer's block" is not generally a difficulty. All Krull has to do to cure it is to walk over to the desk where household business gets done and look over the mortgage and other bills. Life as a writer or artist is financially precarious, and she can think of only one remedy: "Work hard."

One sore spot is rejection, which can hurt like a wind-sucking blow to the stomach. She tries to see it in terms of her work, not herself as a person, and it does help that rejections are usually in writing, not to her face. "Belief in yourself and persistence are the keys," she says. "Courage and stamina, simply the competitive desire to stick it out, to last longer than others." The "Lives of" books have taught her that sometimes these qualities can outweigh talent.

A common nuisance for all writers involves physical stagnation, leading to sleepiness, or worse, a brain deprived of blood flow. Eight or ten hours can pass—and Krull has barely moved. (Neighbors spying in her second-story window now would die of boredom.) She often wishes she had the discipline of Charles Dickens, who made a point of spending one hour walking for every hour he spent writing.

Dickens probably never used a mud mask, Krull's favorite technique to keep things moving. (When you wash off the dried mud, it makes your face tingle and perks you up.) She also visits an acupuncturist (she *does* live in California) and takes breaks for trips to the library, dancing and jumping around (luckily the neighbors can't see), swimming (she finally learned how), and walking in the nearby canyon or along the ocean.

Nuns from her early life would have a hearty laugh if they knew Krull was now speaking in schools about her books. After all, she never said a word in any classes *they* taught. To overcome her fear of public speaking, she had to take singing lessons and speech therapy.

Fear of the unknown can be a headache. Getting up in the morning with the prospect of a long blank day ahead, with no rules and no one to tell you what to do next, can be scary. That and most other challenges can often be put in their place via a sense of humor.

On the plus side, Krull finds something or someone to be grateful for nearly every day. She feels genuinely privileged to be in the children's book field. For one thing, she can't be fired—especially for reading too much. But mainly her life seems literally a dream come true—to have thought as a child about seeing "Kathleen Krull" on a book and then to walk into libraries today and find it there.

She even gets to hand out her own books to her own neighbors. (Whether they want them or not.)

Writings

FOR CHILDREN; FICTION

(Under pseudonym Kathleen Cowles) *The Bugs Bunny Book,* Western, 1975.

(Under pseudonym Kathleen Cowles) *The Seven Wishes,* Western, 1976.

(Under pseudonym Kathleen Cowles) *Golden Everything Workbook Series,* Western, 1979.

(Under pseudonym Kathleen Cowles) *What Will I Be? A Wish Book,* Western, 1979.

(Under pseudonym Kevin Kenny, with mother, Helen Krull) *Sometimes My Mom Drinks Too Much,* illustrated by Helen Cogancherry, Raintree, 1980.

Maria Molina and the Days of the Dead (picture book), illustrated by Enrique Sanchez, Macmillan, 1994.

NONFICTION; "BEGINNING TO LEARN ABOUT" SERIES, WITH RICHARD L. ALLINGTON; ALL PUBLISHED BY RAINTREE

Colors, illustrated by Noel Spangler, 1979.
Shapes, illustrated by Lois Ehlert, 1979.
Numbers, illustrated by Tom Garcia, 1979.
Opposites, illustrated by Eulala Conner, 1979.
Hearing, illustrated by Wayne Dober, 1980.
Looking, illustrated by Bill Bober, 1980.
Tasting, illustrated by Noel Spangler, 1980.
Smelling, illustrated by Lee Gatzke, 1980.
Feelings, illustrated by Brian Cody, 1980.
Touching, illustrated by Yoshi Miyake, 1980.
Thinking, illustrated by Tom Garcia, 1980.
Writing, illustrated by Yoshi Miyake, 1980.
Reading, illustrated by Joel Naprstek, 1980.
Talking, illustrated by Rick Thrun, 1980.
Spring, illustrated by Lynn Uhde, 1981.
Summer, illustrated by Dennis Hockerman, 1981.
Winter, illustrated by John Wallner, 1981.
Autumn, illustrated by Bruce Bond, 1981.
Letters, illustrated by Tom Garcia, 1983.
Words, illustrated by Ray Cruz, 1983.
Stories, illustrated by Helen Cogancherry, 1983.
Science, illustrated by James Teason, 1983.
Time, illustrated by Yoshi Miyake, 1983.
Measuring, illustrated by Noel Spangler, 1983.

OTHER NONFICTION

It's My Earth Too: How I Can Help the Earth Stay Alive (picture book), illustrated by Melanie Hope Greenberg, Doubleday, 1992.

Wilma Unlimited: How Wilma Rudolph Became the World's Fastest Woman (picture book), illustrated by David Diaz, Harcourt, 1996.

SONG BOOKS

(Piano arranger) *The Christmas Carol Sampler,* illustrated by Margaret Cusack, Harcourt, 1983.

(Piano arranger and editor) *Songs of Praise,* illustrated by Kathryn Hewitt, Harcourt, 1989.

Gonna Sing My Head Off: American Folk Songs for Children, illustrated by Allen Garns, Knopf, 1992.

FOR MIDDLE-GRADERS; FICTION

(Under house pseudonym Kathryn Kenny) *Trixie Belden and the Hudson River Mystery,* Western, 1979.

Alex Fitzgerald's Cure for Nightmares, illustrated by Irene Trivas, Little, Brown, 1990; revised edition, illustrated by Wendy Edelson, Troll, 1998.

Alex Fitzgerald, TV Star, illustrated by Irene Trivas, Little, Brown, 1991; revised edition, illustrated by Wendy Edelson, Troll, 1998.

NONFICTION

V Is for Victory: America Remembers World War II, Knopf, 1995.

Wish You Were Here: Emily's Guide to the 50 States, illustrated by Amy Schwartz, Doubleday, 1997.

They Saw the Future: Psychics, Oracles, Scientists, Inventors, and Pretty Good Guessers, illustrated by Kyrsten Brooker, Atheneum, 1999.

A Kid's Guide to America's Bill of Rights: Curfews, Censorship, and the 100-pound Giant, illustrated by Anna Divito, Avon, 1999.

"LIVES OF" SERIES; ALL ILLUSTRATED BY KATHRYN HEWITT

Lives of the Musicians: Good Times, Bad Times (and What the Neighbors Thought), Harcourt, 1993.

Lives of the Writers: Comedies, Tragedies (and What the Neighbors Thought), Harcourt, 1994.

Lives of the Artists: Masterpieces, Messes (and What the Neighbors Thought), Harcourt, 1995.

Lives of the Athletes: Thrills, Spills (and What the Neighbors Thought), Harcourt, 1997.

Lives of the Presidents: Fame, Shame (and What the Neighbors Thought), Harcourt, 1998.

Lives of Great Women: The Famous, The Infamous (and What the Neighbors Thought), Harcourt, in press.

"WORLD OF MY OWN" SERIES; PHOTOS BY DAVID HAUTZIG

City within a City: How Kids Live in New York City's Chinatown, Lodestar, 1994.

The Other Side: How Kids Live in a California Latino Neighborhood, Lodestar, 1994.

Bridges to Change: How Kids Live on a South Carolina Sea Island, Lodestar, 1995.

One Nation, Many Tribes: How Kids Live in Milwaukee's Indian Community, Lodestar, 1995.

FOR ADULTS

12 Keys to Writing Books That Sell, Writer's Digest, 1989.
Presenting Paula Danziger, Twayne, 1995.

Also contributor of articles and book reviews to *Book Links, Chicago Tribune, Horn Book, Kirkus Reviews, Los Angeles Times Book Review, New York Times Book Review,* and *Publishers Weekly,* and of monthly children's book reviews to *L.A. Parent Magazine* and *San Diego Parent Magazine.*

L

LITTLE, (Flora) Jean 1932-

Personal

Born January 2, 1932, in T'ai-nan, Formosa (now Taiwan); daughter of John Llewellyn (a physician and surgeon) and Flora (a physician; maiden name, Gauld) Little. *Education:* University of Toronto, B.A., 1955; attended Institute of Special Education; received teaching certificate from University of Utah. *Religion:* Christian. *Hobbies and other interests:* Designing and hooking rugs.

Addresses

c/o Viking Canada, 10 Alcorn Ave., Ste. 300, Toronto, ON M4V 3B2, Canada.

Career

Teacher of children with motor handicaps, Canada; specialist teacher at Beechwood School for Crippled Children, Guelph, Ontario; children's writer. Visiting instructor at Institute of Special Education and Florida University; summer camp director and leader of church youth groups. *Member:* Canadian Authors Association, Writers' Union of Canada, Authors League of America, Council for Exceptional Children, United Church Women.

Awards, Honors

Canadian Children's Book Award, joint award of American and Canadian branches of Little, Brown, 1961, for *Mine for Keeps;* Vicky Metcalf Award, Canadian Authors Association, 1974, for body of work inspirational to Canadian boys and girls; Governor General's Literary Award for Children's Literature, Canada Council, 1977, for *Listen for the Singing;* Children's Book Award, Canada Council, 1979; Children's Book of the Year Award, Canadian Library Association, and Ruth Schwartz Award, Ontario Arts Council, both 1985, for *Mama's Going to Buy You a Mockingbird; Boston Globe-Horn Book* Nonfiction Honor Award, 1988, for *Little by Little: A Writer's Education;* Reading Magic Award, *Parenting Magazine,* 1991, for *Stars Come Out Within;* Violet Downey Book Award, Imperial Order of Daughters of the Empire, 1996, for *His Banner over Me;* Mr. Christie's Book Award, Christie Brown & Co., 1997, for *Gruntle Piggle Takes Off.*

Writings

It's a Wonderful World (poems), privately printed, 1947.
Mine for Keeps, illustrated by Lewis Parker, Little, Brown, 1962.
Home from Far, illustrated by Jerry Lazare, Little, Brown, 1965.
Spring Begins in March, illustrated by Lewis Parker, Little, Brown, 1966.
When the Pie Was Opened: Poems, Little, Brown, 1968.
Take Wing, illustrated by Jerry Lazare, Little, Brown, 1968.
One to Grow On, illustrated by Jerry Lazare, Little, Brown, 1969.
Look through My Window, illustrated by Joan Sandin, Harper, 1970.
Kate, Harper, 1971.
From Anna, illustrated by Joan Sandin, Harper, 1972.
Stand in the Wind, illustrated by Emily Arnold McCully, Harper, 1975.
Listen for the Singing, Dutton, 1977.
Zephyr, J. Little (Winnipeg, MB), 1983.
Mama's Going to Buy You a Mockingbird, Viking, 1984.
Lost and Found, illustrated by Leoung O'Young, Viking, 1985; Puffin, 1987.
Different Dragons, Viking, 1986.
Hey World, Here I Am!, illustrated by Barbara DiLella, Kids Can Press, 1986, published in the United States with illustrations by Sue Truesdell, Harper, 1989.
Little by Little: A Writer's Education (autobiography), Penguin, 1987.
Invitations to Joy: A Celebration of Canada's Young Readers and the Books They Love ("Canadian Children's Book Centre Annual Lecture" series), Canadian Children's Book Centre, 1989.

Stars Come Out Within, Viking, 1990.

(With Maggie de Vries) *Once upon a Golden Apple,* illustrated by Phoebe Gilman, Viking, 1991.

Revenge of the Small Small, illustrated by Janet Wilson, Viking, 1991.

Jess Was the Brave One, illustrated by Janet Wilson, Viking, 1991.

Jenny and the Hanukkah Queen, illustrated by Suzanne Mogensen, Viking, 1995.

His Banner over Me, Viking, 1995.

(With Claire Mackay) *Bats about Baseball,* illustrated by Kim LaFave, Viking, 1995.

Gruntle Piggle Takes Off, illustrated by Johnny Wales, Viking, 1996.

The Belonging Place, Viking, 1997.

Emma's Magic Winter, pictures by Jennifer Plecas, Harper-Collins, 1998.

What Will the Robin Do Then?: Winter Tales, Viking, 1998.

Also author of novel *Let Me Be Gentle.* Contributor to periodicals, including *Horn Book, Canadian Library Journal,* and *Canadian Author and Bookman.*

Little's works have been translated into Dutch, German, Danish, Japanese, and Russian; published in braille; and recorded on audio cassette.

Jean Little

Adaptations

Home from Far was adapted to film and released by Beacon Films, 1984. *Mama's Going to Buy You a Mockingbird* and *Different Dragons* were adapted as television movies by PBS Video, 1987 and 1988, respectively.

Sidelights

Jean Little is recognized throughout Canada and the United States for her candid and unsentimental portrayals of adolescent life. A teacher of handicapped children, Little herself is only partially sighted, and she uses much of her real-life experience as the basis for her books. Her characters often deal with physical disabilities, including cerebral palsy or blindness, or confront psychological difficulties involving fear or grief. However, none of her characters find magical cures for their problems. Instead they learn to cope with and survive the challenges they face, and thus they are led to greater self-understanding. "Ultimately," explained Meguido Zola in *Language Arts,* "that is the real thrust of Jean Little's novels—recognizing and mastering the enemy within rather than tilting at the one without." For her writings, Little has won numerous awards, including a Canadian Children's Book Award, a Governor General's Literary Award, and a Vicky Metcalf Award.

Little was born in 1932 in Formosa, now known as Taiwan. Soon afterward, doctors detected scars over both her corneas, the "windows" that cover the eyes. Though she could see—she responded to light as an infant—her eyesight was significantly impaired, and she was diagnosed as legally blind. Her pupils were also off-center, so she had trouble focusing on one object for more than a brief moment. Later, schoolchildren would taunt her by calling her "cross-eyed."

Fortunately, Little's family was very supportive. Her parents read to her frequently, and as she gained limited vision, they taught her to read on her own. "Reading became my greatest joy," she wrote in her autobiography *Little by Little: A Writer's Education.* By 1939, Little's family had moved to Toronto, Canada. There, she first attended a class for students with vision problems. By fourth grade, however, she transferred into a regular class and no longer received specialized treatment—large-print books, for example, or oversized lettering on the chalkboard. As a result, she struggled with many everyday tasks. "If I wanted to read what was written on the board," she recalled in *Little by Little,* "I would have to stand up so that my face was only inches away from the writing. Then I would have to walk back and forth, following the words not only with my eyes but with my entire body."

As Little progressed through school, she discovered that she enjoyed writing. Noticing her obvious talent, her father encouraged her and often edited her work. "From the first my Dad was my greatest critic and supporter," she once told *SATA.* "He plagued me to rewrite." When Little was fifteen, her father collected and printed her

In the mid-1800s, orphaned Elspet Mary frets about being uprooted from her home in Scotland to immigrate to Canada, regretting all that she must leave behind. (Cover illustration by Janet Wilson.)

first booklet of poems, *It's a Wonderful World*. A few years later, when the magazine *Saturday Night* published two of her verses, her father proudly read them aloud. "I listened," she remembered in *Little by Little*, "and [when] his voice broke, I knew why I wanted to be a writer."

Deciding to pursue a degree in English, Little entered Victoria College's English language and literature program. Just before classes began, though, her father suffered a severe heart attack. Throughout the following weeks and months his health improved just slightly, yet his enthusiasm for his daughter's schoolwork never diminished. "When I got to college [my father] did research on every essay topic I had," she once recalled in *SATA*, "and insisted on tearing apart everything I wrote. He drove me crazy. Not until he died did I come to appreciate his unflagging zeal on my behalf."

Following her freshman year, Little completed her first novel, *Let Me Be Gentle*, about a large family with a mentally retarded six-year-old girl. "When I carefully typed 'The End,'" she wrote in *Little by Little*, "I gazed

at that stack of typed pages with intense satisfaction.... I was convinced that the entire world would be as fond of my characters as I was. After all, I had written a practically perfect book." Nevertheless, her manuscript was soon returned by publisher Jack McClelland, who pointed out its choppiness and lack of focus. Little was hardly discouraged, though—McClelland also told her she had talent.

In 1955, Little graduated with her bachelor's degree in English, and although she primarily wanted to write, she applied for a position teaching handicapped children. With her experience—she had spent three summers working with children with motor handicaps—and additional training, she was hired. For the next six years she worked with handicapped children in camps, at special schools, and in their homes. She also taught at the Institute of Special Education in Salt Lake City, Utah, and at Florida University. These years helped inspire her to write for children. "Remembering how I had never found a cross-eyed heroine in a book," she remarked in *Little by Little*, "I decided to search for books about children with motor handicaps. I did not for one moment intend to limit my students to reading about crippled kids. I knew that ... they actually became [fictional animal characters] Bambi, Piglet and Wilbur. I did not think they needed a book to help them adjust. I did believe, however, that crippled children had a right to find themselves represented in fiction."

As Little explained to Zola in *Language Arts*, the few books of the late 1950s and early 1960s that did portray handicapped children presented inaccurate views of them. Full of self-pity, the children were usually shown brooding over their limitations while dreaming of becoming more like their "normal" friends. And typically, by each story's end, they would undergo miraculous recoveries. "How my [students] laughed at all this silliness," Little told Zola. "And yet how cheated they felt. And so my first book—was for them."

Mine for Keeps revolves around Sally Copeland, a young girl with cerebral palsy, a disability frequently resulting from a lack of oxygen during birth. In the novel, Sally returns home after years of seclusion in a residential treatment center, learning to adjust to classes at a regular school. Her family and friends, too, must adapt to her special needs. *Mine for Keeps* "was different from *Let Me Be Gentle*," Little recalled in *Little by Little*, "because I had intended the first for my family and friends and only afterwards wondered if it were publishable. This one I had written purposely for strangers to read. I had worked much harder and longer on it." Not knowing exactly how to proceed after her manuscript was finished, Little took the advice of a librarian and submitted the story to the Little, Brown Canadian Children's Book Award committee. And in May of 1961—in a letter signed by the same Jack McClelland who had rejected *Let Me Be Gentle* years earlier—she found out her book had won.

Little dedicated *Mine for Keeps* to her father, and since its publication in 1962 she has gone on to write more than twenty-five additional books for children. Among these are *Look through My Window* and *Kate,* a pair of stories that center on both Emily, a withdrawn, only child, and Kate, a young girl of both Jewish and Protestant descent. In *Look through My Window* Emily deals with her family's sudden move to the country and with the prolonged visit of her four boisterous cousins. She also begins to recognize the value of her newfound friendship with Kate. In *Kate,* the title character struggles to understand not only her religion but also herself and her family's roots. She learns, too, to treasure her friendship with Emily. "*Kate* is a beautiful tribute to the power of love," concluded John W. Conner in *English Journal.*

Little addresses the subject of blindness in *From Anna* and *Listen for the Singing,* the latter a winner of the Governor General's Literary Award for Children's Literature in 1977. In the first story, Anna, a shy and awkward young girl, moves with her family from Germany to Canada just before the start of World War II. The move is painful for her since she not only dreads living in a strange land, she also fears her new teachers—who will undoubtedly criticize her inability to read. However, when Anna is found to have impaired vision, she is placed in a special class, and there she begins to overcome her insecurities. *Listen for the Singing,* which opens the day England declared war on Germany, follows Anna as she begins her first year in a public high school. Because of her nationality, she faces hostility and prejudice, yet she also finds friends who are willing to defend her. In addition she comes to accept her disability and is then able to help her brother survive the shock of a tragic accident. "This is a story of courage ... in one of its more unspectacular guises," declared Susan Jackel in *World of Children's Books:* "the courage of a young person who anticipates almost certain humiliation and nonetheless wins through to a number of small victories."

In 1985, Little won the Canadian Children's Book of the Year Award for *Mama's Going to Buy You a Mockingbird.* As the narrative unfolds, twelve-year-old Jeremy learns that his father, Adrian, is dying of cancer. To ease Jeremy's sorrow, Adrian introduces him to Tess, a strong, compassionate young girl who has withstood several tragedies of her own. Through Tess, Jeremy discovers the strength to survive his father's death, while also finding the courage to comfort his grieving mother and sister. "The story has depth and insight," noted a reviewer for *Bulletin of the Center for Children's Books,* "and it ends on a convincingly positive note."

As a writer who enjoys sharing her life's stories, Little has also novelized works based on the lives of others, such as *His Banner over Me* and *The Belonging Place.* In *His Banner over Me,* published in 1995, Little writes about her mother's childhood. Flora (Gorrie) Gauld, the daughter of missionary parents, was born in Taiwan. At age four, Gorrie's family, except for her father, returns home to Canada and stays with maternal relatives. Within a few years, though, Gorrie's mother rejoins her husband, leaving the children with their Aunt Jen. "Little's fictionalized, but well-researched, account of what it is like for children to be separated from parents ... will enlighten many, as well as provide an example of a life ... [dedicated] to the missionary ideal," observed *School Library Journal* contributor Tana Elias. Calling the book "finely crafted," *Canadian Children's Literature* contributor Ruth Compton Brouwer described *His Banner over Me* as a "gentle story that acknowledges complexity and pain in intercultural and family

Nana must be making jokes on purpose.
Ryder decided to throw her a curve.

"Nana, I think I might like to be a deep sea diver
like your friend Marlin."

Nana had a comeback ready.
"What a great sinker!" she said.

Ryder must come up with creative ways to communicate when he attempts to discuss his future with his baseball-loving grandmother, who is intently involved with the game she is watching on TV. (From Bats about Baseball, *written by Little with Claire Mackay and illustrated by Kim LaFave.)*

Emma and her new friend Sally use their imaginary magic boots to help them overcome their shyness. (From Emma's Magic Winter, *written by Little and illustrated by Jennifer Plecas.)*

relationships but that celebrates connectedness rather than conflict." In 1997's *The Belonging Place,* Little digs deeper into her family's history, writing about a young orphaned girl trying to find a sense of belonging.

Another common thread Little displays in her work is the importance of a child's imagination. In some cases, it's a child coming up with an imaginative solution to a problem, such as Patsy Small in *Revenge of the Small Small.* When Patsy, the youngest member of her family, is fed up with her siblings' teasing, she comes up with an imaginative way to make them stop. Using her new art supplies, she builds a little town, complete with a cemetery and grave markers bearing the names of her mean sister and brothers. Her siblings quickly repent. "Patsy is a loveable and imaginative heroine who finds creative ways to deal with her insensitive siblings," wrote *Quill & Quire* contributor Joanne Findon. Little dedicated this book to her younger sister Pat who pretended to bury the Little family years before.

In *Bats about Baseball,* written with Claire Mackay, Ryder must come up with creative ways to win his baseball-loving grandmother's attention. Once baseball season hits, Nana is glued to the television. Or so he thinks. One day when Ryder tries to start a conversation about his future career, he thinks Nana isn't listening. Readers, however, realize that Nana *is* listening; she just responds in baseball lingo. When Ryder figures out Nana's way of communicating, he has much fun with Nana. *Quill & Quire* contributor Sarah Ellis called the work "an immensely deft and good-humoured book."

In *Emma's Magic Winter,* published in 1998, Emma and Sally use their imagination by pretending their winter boots are magic. Doing so helps each girl overcome her own shyness and helps Emma to read aloud in front of her class. "A magical selection in any season," deemed Dina Sherman, writing in *School Library Journal.* Praising Little's first book for young readers, *Horn Book* contributor Martha V. Parravano declares that *Emma's Magic Winter* "is about believable contemporary kids, with not a whiff of babyishness about it."

When not writing, Little keeps abreast of her audience by working with young people in the church, schools, and community. She also closely monitors the field of children's literature. "Children's books are chiefly what she reads," observed Zola in *Language Arts.* "She reads them because, for the most part, they are among the few books that still rejoice in life, still pulse with awe and wonder at its miracle, and still communicate a sense of growth and hope and love. It is in this spirit that she writes, to celebrate life."

Works Cited

Brouwer, Ruth Compton, review of *His Banner over Me, Canadian Children's Literature,* Number 79, 1995, pp. 71-73.

Conner, John W., review of *Kate, English Journal,* March, 1972, pp. 434-35.

Elias, Tana, review of *His Banner over Me, School Library Journal,* December, 1995, p. 120.

Ellis, Sarah, review of *Bats about Baseball, Quill & Quire,* March, 1995, p. 78.

Findon, Joanne, review of *Revenge of the Small Small, Quill & Quire,* October, 1992, p. 31.

Jackel, Susan, Review of *Listen for the Singing, World of Children's Books,* spring, 1978, pp. 81-83.

Little, Jean, *Little by Little: A Writer's Education,* Viking, 1987.

Review of *Mama's Going to Buy You a Mockingbird, Bulletin of the Center for Children's Books,* June, 1985, p. 189.

Parravano, Martha V., review of *Emma's Magic Winter, Horn Book,* September-October, 1998, pp. 110-11.

Sherman, Dina, review of *Emma's Magic Winter, School Library Journal,* October, 1998, p. 106.

Zola, Meguido, "Profile: Jean Little," *Language Arts,* January, 1981, pp. 86-92.

For More Information See

BOOKS

Children's Literature Review, Volume 4, Gale, 1982.

Egoff, Sheila, "And All the Rest: Stories," *The Republic of Childhood: A Critical Guide to Canadian Children's Literature in English,* Oxford University Press, 1975.

PERIODICALS

Books in Canada, June, 1997, pp. 33-34.
Booklist, February 1, 1993, p. 989; June 1, 1995, p. 1786.
Bulletin of the Center for Children's Books, May, 1997, p. 328.
Horn Book, March, 1996, p. 231.
Publishers Weekly, March 8, 1993, p. 76.
Quill and Quire, November, 1990; September, 1996, p. 72; May, 1997, p. 40.
School Library Journal, August, 1995, p. 125.*

*　　*　　*

LUCKETT, Dave 1951-

Personal

Born February 9, 1951, in Sydney, Australia; son of Terence (a minister) and Gwyneth Elizabeth (a secretary; maiden name, Williams) Luckett; married Sally Barbara Beasley (a psychologist), January 7, 1984; children: Evan John. *Education:* Teachers College of Western Australia (now Edith Cowan University), diploma in education, 1974; University of Western Australia, B.A., 1983. *Politics:* "Unaligned; generally vote Labour." *Religion:* "None (agnostic)."

Addresses

Home and office—69 Federal St., Tuart Hill 6060, Western Australia.

Career

Teacher at secondary schools in Western Australia, 1974-75; federal public servant, Perth, Australia, 1977-97.

Awards, Honors

Aurealis Award, Best Australian Fantasy Novel, 1998, and shortlist, Premier's Book Award, 1998, both for *A Dark Winter.*

Writings

The Adventures of Addam, illustrated by Timothy Ide, Omnibus Books (Norwood, Australia), 1995.
Night Hunters, Omnibus Books, 1995.
The Best Batsman in the World, illustrated by David Kennett, Omnibus Books, 1996.
The Wizard and Me, Omnibus Books, 1996.
The Last Eleven, illustrated by David Kennett, Omnibus Books, 1997.
A Dark Winter, Omnibus Books, 1998.
A Dark Journey, Omnibus Books, 1999.

Work in Progress

The third volume of the "Tenabran trilogy" that began with *A Dark Winter* and *A Dark Journey.*

Sidelights

Dave Luckett told *SATA:* "The main blame [for my writing career] can be fixed on science fiction fandom, science fiction conventions, and Barbara Hambly, who first told me I could write. I write science fiction and fantasy because I love it. It has its dark moments, but generally it assumes a future (or at least a heroic past) that means more to me than all the kitchen-sink realism of the mainstream—a realism that is no more real than any fiction, when you come right down to it. My great regret is that I won't be around to see the ships leave for the stars. My great hope is that they will go anyway."

For More Information See

PERIODICALS

Australian Book Review, August, 1995, p. 62; December, 1996, p. 86.
Magpies, May, 1996, p. 43.

M–N

MAESTRO, Betsy C(rippen) 1944-

Personal

Surname is pronounced "Ma-*es*-troh"; born January 5, 1944, in New York, NY; daughter of Harlan R. (a design consultant) and Norma (in education; maiden name, Sherman) Crippen; first marriage was dissolved; married second husband, Giulio Maestro (an author and illustrator), December 16, 1972; children: (second marriage) Daniela Marisa, Marco Claudio. *Education:* Southern Connecticut State College, B.S., 1964, M.S., 1970. *Hobbies and other interests:* Reading, cooking, photography, travel, art, antiques.

Addresses

Home and office—74 Mile Creek Rd., Old Lyme, CT 06371.

Career

Deer Run School, East Haven, CT, kindergarten and first grade teacher, 1964-75; writer, 1975—. *Member:* National Education Association, Connecticut Education Association.

Awards, Honors

Junior Library Guild selection, 1975, for *A Wise Monkey Tale,* 1978, for *Busy Day,* 1979, for *On the Go,* 1981, for *Harriet Reads Signs and More Signs,* and 1986, for *Ferryboat;* Children's Book of the Year, Child Study Association of America, 1976, for *Fat Polka-Dot Cat and Other Haiku,* 1987, for *The Story of the Statue of Liberty,* and 1996, for *The Voice of the People: American Democracy in Action;* Children's Choice selection, International Reading Association and Children's Book Council, 1978, for *Harriet Goes to the Circus,* and 1979, for *Lambs for Dinner;* Notable Book citation, American Library Association, 1981, for *Traffic,* 1987, for *A More Perfect Union,* and 1991, for *The Discovery of the Americas;* Notable Children's Trade

Book in the Field of Social Studies, National Council for Social Studies and Children's Book Council, 1986, for *Ferryboat,* and 1991, for *The Discovery of the Americas;* Pick of the Lists, American Booksellers Association, 1986, for *The Story of the Statue of Liberty,* 1987, for *A More Perfect Union: The Story of Our Constitution,* 1991, for *The Discovery of the Americas,* 1994, for *Exploration and Conquest: The Americas After Columbus, 1500-1620,* 1996, for *The Voice of the People: American Democracy in Action,* and 1998, for *The New Americans: Colonial Times, 1620-1689.*

Writings

PICTURE BOOKS; ALL ILLUSTRATED BY GIULIO MAESTRO, EXCEPT AS NOTED

A Wise Monkey Tale (retelling), Crown, 1975.
Fat Polka-Dot Cat and Other Haiku (poetry), Dutton, 1976.
In My Boat, Crowell, 1976.
Lambs for Dinner (retelling), Crown, 1978.
Traffic: A Book of Opposites, Crown, 1981.
The Key to the Kingdom, Harcourt, 1982.
The Guessing Game, Grosset, 1983.
(With Ellen DelVecchio) *Big City Port,* Four Winds, 1983.
Ferryboat, Crowell, 1986.
The Story of the Statue of Liberty, Lothrop, 1986.
The Grab-Bag Party, Golden Press, 1986.
The Pandas Take a Vacation, Golden Press, 1986.
The Perfect Picnic, Golden Press, 1987.
The Travels of Freddie and Frannie Frog, Golden Press, 1987.
Taxi: A Book of City Words, Clarion, 1989.
Temperature and You, Lodestar, 1989.
Snow Day, Scholastic, 1989.
Delivery Van: Words for Town and Country, Clarion Books, 1990.
A Sea Full of Sharks, Scholastic, 1990.
All Aboard Overnight: A Book of Compound Words, Clarion, 1992.
How Do Apples Grow?, HarperCollins, 1992.
Bike Trip, HarperCollins, 1992.
Take a Look at Snakes, Scholastic, 1992.

The Story of Money, Mulberry Books, 1993.

Bats: Night Fliers, Scholastic, 1994.

Why Do Leaves Change Color?, illustrated by Loretta Krupinski, HarperCollins, 1994.

The Story of Religion, Clarion Books, 1996.

Coming to America: The Story of Immigration, illustrated by Susannah Ryan, Scholastic, 1996.

The Story of Clocks and Calendars: Marking a Millennium, Lothrop, 1999.

"HARRIET" SERIES; ALL ILLUSTRATED BY GIULIO MAESTRO

Where Is My Friend? A Word Concept Book, Crown, 1976.

Harriet Goes to the Circus, Crown, 1977.

Harriet Reads Signs and More Signs, Crown, 1981.

Around the Clock with Harriet: A Book about Telling Time, Crown, 1984.

Harriet the Elephant, Crown, 1984.

Harriet at Play, Crown, 1984.

Harriet at School, Crown, 1984.

Harriet at Home, Crown, 1984.

Harriet at Work, Crown, 1984.

Through the Year with Harriet: A Time Concept Book, Crown, 1985.

Dollars and Cents for Harriet: A Money Concept Book, Crown, 1988.

"MAN AND ELEPHANT" SERIES; CONCEPT BOOKS, ALL ILLUSTRATED BY GIULIO MAESTRO

Busy Day: A Book of Action Words, Crown, 1978.

On the Go: A Book of Adjectives, Crown, 1979.

On the Town: A Book of Clothing Words, Crown, 1983.

Camping Out: A Book of Action Words, Crown, 1984.

"THE AMERICAN STORY" SERIES; INFORMATIONAL PICTURE BOOKS; ALL ILLUSTRATED BY GIULIO MAESTRO

A More Perfect Union: The Story of Our Constitution, Lothrop, 1987.

The Discovery of the Americas, Lothrop, 1991.

The Discovery of the Americas Activity Book, Lothrop, 1992.

Exploration and Conquest: The Americas after Columbus, 1500-1620, Lothrop, 1994.

The Voice of the People: American Democracy in Action, Lothrop, 1996.

The New Americans: European Settlement in North America, 1620-1689, Lothrop, 1996.

The New Americans: Colonial Times, 1620-1689, Lothrop, 1998.

OTHER

Several of Maestro's works have been translated into Spanish.

Betsy C. Maestro and Giulio Maestro

Adaptations

The Discovery of the Americas was released on audio cassette by Spoken Arts, Incorporated, in 1993 and as a video cassette by Live Oak Media. Spoken Arts also released *A More Perfect Union* and *The Story of the Statue of Liberty* as audio cassettes in 1993.

Work in Progress

The New Nation, Struggle for a Continent, Westward Movement, and *Liberty or Death: The American Revolution,* all for Lothrop.

Sidelights

The popular author of concept books and informational picture books as well as fiction and retellings in picture book form, Betsy C. Maestro (who also writes as Betsy Maestro) is well known for the books on which she has collaborated with her husband, illustrator Giulio Maestro. Many of Betsy Maestro's early works are picture books featuring child and animal characters and are directed to preschoolers and readers in the early primary grades. She is also recognized for creating a series of more sophisticated books for older children on American history and government, several of which have been recognized as exceptional. In her works for primary graders, Maestro characteristically uses a story format to introduce concepts such as language, numbers, space, time, money, nature, and everyday activities. Her books for a more mature audience that explore the history of America give background on subjects such as the Constitution, the Statue of Liberty, and immigration into the United States, and outline the histories of religion and democracy.

Maestro is also the creator of Harriet, a white elephant on roller skates whose adventures at home, at school, at the circus, in the city, and in the country introduce children to concepts such as learning to read signs and to tell time. As a literary stylist, Maestro uses lively, caption-like sentences in her books for young children and smooth, straightforward prose when writing for an older audience. The author is praised for her range, understanding of children, clear writing style, and ability to explain complicated subjects in an understandable manner. In addition, she is highly regarded for the lucid, balanced approach that she brings to her nonfiction for older readers. As a collaborator with her husband, Maestro is lauded for the intelligence of her concepts, the deftness of their execution, and the harmony of her texts with Giulio's illustrations. The couple's works are generally regarded as informative, attractive, and accessible books that appeal to children, parents, and teachers alike. Writing in *Horn Book,* Anita Silvey commented, "Books that seek to entertain the young while teaching them concepts are generally quite dreary, but Betsy and Giulio Maestro are masters at combining these two factors to create delightful and enjoyable books."

Born in Brooklyn, New York, Maestro is the daughter of a design consultant and an educator. Her mother, who taught nursery school and later became a guidance counselor and school administrator, filled their home with books. "My early favorites," Maestro once told *Something about the Author* (*SATA*), "were the Margaret Wise Brown books and the 'Madeline' books. As I got older I turned to Elizabeth Enright, and the 'Nancy Drew' and 'Hardy Boys' series. My nose was always in a book." When she wasn't reading, Maestro explored New York City and studied ballet and piano. The author recalled that her earliest ambition was to be a teacher; in high school, she began to work with children during her summer vacations. "In fact," she told *SATA*, "all my jobs involved kids: baby-sitting, tutoring, playground supervisor."

Maestro majored in early childhood education at Southern Connecticut State College, and after graduation she taught kindergarten and first grade for eleven years at Deer Run School in East Haven, Connecticut. In her interview in *SATA*, the author noted, "I was often dismayed by the lack of imaginative nonfiction material available for children." While a teacher, she got married and divorced, received her master's degree in elementary guidance in 1970, and met Giulio Maestro, a freelance artist and writer. The couple, who married in 1972, have two children, Daniela and Marco. Marco has collaborated on several riddle books with his father. After her marriage, Maestro realized, as she told *SATA*, "that I had access to a number of editors. So I got up my courage and tried my hand at writing books."

Maestro's first book, *A Wise Monkey Tale,* is a variant of an old folktale in which little Monkey fools four large jungle animals into helping her out of a hole. The tale demonstrates how the main character uses her wits to save herself. Writing in *School Library Journal,* Carol Chatfield noted, "The age old problem of landing in a jam is treated inventively here with a minimum of description and plenty of colorful pictures," while Zena Sutherland of *Bulletin of the Center for Children's Books* commented, "The humor of the situation is just right for the read-aloud audience . . . ." In 1978, Maestro published *Lambs for Dinner,* a retelling of the folktale "The Wolf and the Seven Little Kids" by the Brothers Grimm. In this book, a wolf tries to trick four lamb siblings into coming with him so that—in a true double-entendre—he can have them for dinner. After the wolf disguises himself as Mama Sheep, he succeeds in getting the lambs to open the door. When their real mother rushes to the wolf's house, she finds her children sitting at his table and waiting for him to serve them bread and soup. Caroline S. Parr of *School Library Journal* wrote: "The play on words is just right for beginning readers," while Zena Sutherland of *Bulletin of the Center for Children's Books* commented favorably on the story's construction and stated, "the tale's operative phrase opens up opportunities for discussion of the alternative meanings words may have." In an interview in *Junior Library Guild,* Maestro commented, "Since story hour is part of every day in the kindergarten, I noticed particular favorites with the children, not just individual books, but often types of stories that seem to appeal to them more than others. Certain themes that are recurrent in folk

Now Owl was FIRST, Turtle was SECOND,
Dog was THIRD, Lizard was FOURTH,
Cat was FIFTH, Snake was SIXTH,
Monkey was SEVENTH, Duck was EIGHTH,
Mouse was NINTH, and Harriet was TENTH.

White elephant Harriet, protagonist of several Maestro concept books, joins the members of a circus troupe in a picture book written to introduce young readers to numbers. (From Harriet Goes to the Circus, *written by Betsy C. Maestro and illustrated by Giulio Maestro.)*

literature, such as the idea of a clever animal outsmarting others, or an animal or person in a serious predicament finding an ingenious solution, always seem to produce fascination and delight in young children."

In 1976, the Maestros introduced their popular character Harriet the elephant in *Where Is My Friend?* In this word concept book, the protagonist searches for her mouse companion up, down, between, and around trees and through a gate, under a rock, over a hill, and into a cave before finding the mouse in front of her nose. A reviewer in *Publishers Weekly* noted, "The book is a joyful combination of a story and an introduction to word usage." Barbara Elleman of *Booklist* commented that *Where Is My Friend?* is "a visual delight as well as a useful word-concept book." In *Harriet Goes to the Circus,* a book that teaches children about ordinal numbers, the elephant goes from first to last in line to get into the circus. When she gets inside the tent, she finds that the chairs have been arranged so that everyone—no matter what their place in the queue—gets a clear view. Writing in *Horn Book,* Mary M. Burns called Harriet "a pachyderm with persistence" and concluded that the "combination of a simple story line with large, uncluttered poster-like illustrations ... provides an effective and joyous introduction to ordinal

numbers for preschoolers." The Maestros have also published a series of board books for the very young featuring what *New York Times Book Review* contributor Carrie Carmichael called their "Babar-reminiscent elephant." These works, which depict the industrious young elephant at home, at school, at work, and at play, introduce youngsters to common words associated with familiar childhood activities. In a review of *Harriet at Home* in *School Library Journal,* Tom S. Hurlburt concluded, "These books will catch the eye and hold the interest of most young children as well as beginning readers." With *Dollars and Cents for Harriet,* the Maestros show how Harriet learns to manage money. By undertaking five jobs that pay her a dollar apiece, the little elephant earns enough money to buy herself a colorful kite. Writing in *School Library Journal,* Martha Rosen predicted, "Harriet is one 'white elephant' who will not end up just sitting on a shelf." Maestro told *SATA,* "I don't really remember how we decided to make Harriet an elephant. Giulio loves to do animals and we knew we needed an especially winning character. We also wanted the character to be very graphic. Because Giulio was thinking in terms of bold, bright illustrations, it seemed white would be the best color, so she would really stand out in every spread. Harriet as an elephant

Through the observations of passengers, Betsy C. Maestro informs young readers about the operation of ferryboats. (Illustrated by Giulio Maestro.)

rather than a child doesn't pose a problem for kids. They know it's pretend and meant for fun."

In addition to their "Harriet" books, the Maestros have featured an elephant in another of their popular series. In these works, which introduce children to action words, adjectives, and words about clothes, the collaborators use the humorous adventures of an urbane mustachioed man—who is first introduced as a circus clown—and his good-natured elephant friend to provide backgrounds for language concepts. The first volume in the series, *Busy Day: A Book of Action Words,* takes the pair from waking and washing through a hard-working day in their traveling circus. A reviewer in *Publishers Weekly* noted, "The Maestros' new book is uncommonly imaginative and a source of fun for toddlers as well as an artful introduction to verbs." R. J. DeSanti of *School Library Journal* observed that Betsy Maestro's text "will serve admirably for the development of sight reading vocabulary skills." In the next book in the series, *On the Go: A*

Book of Adjectives, the two friends use a vacation day to go to the beach. As the pair travels to and from the beach and during their activities there, young readers are exposed to the meanings of such words as full, lost, noisy, hot, cold, dirty, brave, and happy. A reviewer for *Publishers Weekly* commented, "The Maestros score once again," calling the book a treat for beginners who laughed and learned about verbs in the pages of *Busy Day. School Library Journal* contributor Daisy Kouzel called *On the Go* a "must-have complement." In their subsequent adventures, the man and elephant team engage in leisure activities such as playing tennis, going camping, and attending a concert while introducing children to clothing words and verb usage. Writing in *School Library Journal* about *On the Town: A Book of Clothing Words,* Liza Bliss noted, "Readers familiar with the Maestro style will recognize the fresh, good-natured approach and the resourcefulness which make *On the Town* click." Bliss also commented that words such as T-shirts, bathing suits, and sandals "are introduced with never an intrusion into the readers' enjoyment or a shadow of didacticism." Assessing *Camping Out: A Book of Action Words*, Anita Silvey of *Horn Book* maintained that the book "not only celebrates the joy of camping, it also celebrates the joy of verbs."

In 1986, the Maestros published the first of their picture books on American history, *The Story of the Statue of Liberty*. Outlining how the famous icon was created over a fifteen-year period by French sculptor Frederic Bartholdi, the book is acknowledged for Betsy Maestro's fascinating, accurate text and for its distinctiveness in using Giulio Maestro's pictures rather than photographs to illustrate the story. Writing in *Bulletin of the Center for Children's Books*, Zena Sutherland called *The Story of the Statue of Liberty* "far and away the most attractive of the spate of books celebrating the centennial of the Statue of Liberty." In her review in *School Library Journal*, Deborah Vose exclaimed, "At last, an outstanding picture book on the Statue of Liberty." On the heels of the success of *The Story of the Statue of Liberty*, the Maestros published *A More Perfect Union: The Story of Our Constitution*, a work written to celebrate the bicentennial of the Constitution. In what is regarded as a straightforward account filled with lavish illustrations, the Maestros explain the creation and ratification of the seminal document that led to the adoption of the Bill of Rights. Writing in *School Library Journal*, Christine Behrmann called *A More Perfect Union* "the simplest and most accessible history of the Constitution to date." A critic in *Kirkus Reviews* predicted, "This should be invaluable as explanation to younger children of the year's bicentennial celebrations of the Constitution," while a reviewer in *Publishers Weekly* asserted that among the many books spawned by the bicentennial of the Constitution, perhaps no others were "so perfectly designed to explore with younger readers the serious message behind the celebration."

The Maestros published their first book for older children, *The Discovery of the Americas*, in 1991. In this work, the first volume of the couple's informational series "The American Story," Betsy Maestro describes the many expeditions before Columbus as well as Columbus's voyage to the New World. The author presents information on hunting and agrarian societies while outlining the diverse histories of the Asian and European explorers who discovered—and rediscovered—this new land. In addition, Maestro explains how European discovery brought about the demise of the native cultures. Giulio Maestro provides watercolor paintings and maps to illustrate the facts. Like the other books in the series, this volume is praised for its depth and scope. Ruth Semrau of *School Library Journal* commented, "The dazzlingly clean and accurate prose and the exhilarating beauty of the pictures combine for an extraordinary achievement in both history and art." Calling *The Discovery of the Americas* "[a]n outstanding book," a critic in *Kirkus Reviews* noted that the information "is lucid, well balanced, and scrupulous in distinguishing conjectures from documented facts." A reviewer in *Publishers Weekly* added, "As the 500th anniversary of Columbus's famed discovery approaches,

this attractive work is an essential resource." The Maestros also produced an activities book as a companion to *The Discovery of the Americas*.

In the second volume of "The American Story" series, *Exploration and Conquest: The Americas after Columbus, 1500-1620*, Betsy Maestro outlines the history of European exploration and colonization in North, Central, and South America. In her discussion, Maestro pointedly addresses the negative effects of this colonization on native peoples as well as the beginnings of the African slave trade. Cyrisse Jaffe of *School Library Journal* called the book "a good introduction to a complex topic from a multicultural perspective." Carolyn Phelan of *Booklist* declared *Exploration and Conquest* "a useful overview of the period in a format accessible to a wide age range."

In yet another volume of the series, *The New Americans: Colonial Times, 1620-1689*, Betsy Maestro provides an overview of European immigration in North America during the Colonial period while detailing the development of religious, social, and economic institutions. Giulio Maestro contributes watercolors and sketches in color pencil in both spot illustrations and double-page spreads. A reviewer in *Publishers Weekly* noted that Betsy Maestro "provides abundant detail about colonial life, putting her information in a perspective that lets a

A volume from "The American Story Series," **The New Americans: Colonial Times 1620-1689** *provides an overview of European immigration to North America and details the development of religious, social, and economic institutions. (Written by Betsy C. Maestro and illustrated by Giulio Maestro.)*

child of today easily appreciate the differences between then and now." Anne Chapman Callaghan of *School Library Journal* stated that the volume is an "excellent, evenhanded account" and "a fine work that will be well used and create a lot of interest."

Betsy Maestro once told *SATA,* "I concentrate on what a given concept means in the life of a young child. Our concept books are not intended solely to impart information. Of course they accomplish this aim, but always in a way that is closely allied with children's experiences and emotional life." Maestro also once commented, "When you work on picture books for young children, it is impossible to think of the story or concept separately from the illustration. The two are one. I have been very lucky in that, since Giulio and I work together most of the time, we both have a lot of input in each area and give each other suggestions and advice. I loved books as a child (and still do!) and enjoy sharing the ones I write with all the children we know." In an interview in *SATA,* Giulio Maestro described some of his wife's contributions to their working relationship: "Betsy is very sensitive to the visual requirements of a good children's book—the balance between type and illustrations, how many lines a given page can comfortably accommodate, and rhythm, which is so important for a book intended to be read aloud. She has come to know what kind of language poses problems in terms of illustration (overly descriptive writing, for example) and what kind of writing is especially conducive to being illustrated. She visualizes the whole book as she writes and even includes page breaks."

In evaluating her career, Betsy Maestro told *SATA,* "Writing for children is much more difficult than most people realize. Picture book authors are often asked, 'Do you plan to write for grown-ups?' as though that would signify 'graduation' for us. In my opinion, most people who ask the question have a low regard for children. I have no interest in writing for adults. A good children's book is like poetry—you have comparatively few words to work with, and your text must sing. It must work equally well read silently or read aloud. I love the challenge of taking something complicated and expressing it simply. I hope that my books help give children an early love of reading and learning."

[For more information on Betsy Maestro, please see the entry on Giulio Maestro in this volume.]

Works Cited

Behrmann, Christine, review of *A More Perfect Union, School Library Journal,* September, 1987, pp. 175-76.

Bliss, Liza, review of *On the Town, School Library Journal,* November, 1983, p. 66.

Burns, Mary M., review of *Harriet Goes to the Circus, Horn Book,* August, 1977, pp. 430-31.

Review of *Busy Day, Publishers Weekly,* March 6, 1978, p. 101.

Callaghan, Anne Chapman, review of *The New Americans, School Library Journal,* March, 1998, p. 198.

Carmichael, Carrie, "Designed for the Smallest," *New York Times Book Review,* November 11, 1984, p. 57.

Chatfield, Carol, review of *A Wise Monkey Tale, School Library Journal,* January, 1976, pp. 38-39.

DeSanti, R. J., review of *Busy Day, School Library Journal,* September, 1978, p. 120.

Review of *The Discovery of the Americas, Kirkus Reviews,* May 15, 1991, pp. 673-74.

Review of *The Discovery of the Americas, Publishers Weekly,* May 24, 1991, p. 59.

Elleman, Barbara, review of *Where Is My Friend?, Booklist,* February 15, 1976, p. 856.

Hurlburt, Tom S., review of *Harriet at Home, School Library Journal,* December, 1984, pp. 73-74.

Jaffee, Cyrisse, review of *Exploration and Conquest, School Library Journal,* September, 1994, pp. 232-33.

Kouzel, Daisy, review of *On the Go, School Library Journal,* September, 1979, p. 117.

Maestro, Betsy, "A Wise Monkey Tale," *Junior Library Guild,* September, 1975.

Review of *A More Perfect Union, Kirkus Reviews,* July 1, 1987, p. 996.

Review of *A More Perfect Union, Publishers Weekly,* June 26, 1987, p. 74.

Review of *The New Americans, Publishers Weekly,* March 16, 1998, p. 66.

Review of *On the Go, Publishers Weekly,* May 7, 1979, p. 83.

Parr, Caroline S., review of *Lambs for Dinner, School Library Journal,* January, 1979, p. 44.

Phelan, Carolyn, review of *Exploration and Conquest, Booklist,* November 1, 1994, pp. 503-04.

Rosen, Martha, review of *Dollars and Cents for Harriet, School Library Journal,* January, 1989, p. 65.

Semrau, Ruth, review of *The Discovery of the Americas, School Library Journal,* April, 1991, p. 114.

Silvey, Anita, review of *Camping Out: A Book of Action Words, Horn Book,* May-June, 1985, p. 328.

Sutherland, Zena, review of *A Wise Monkey Tale, Bulletin of the Center for Children's Books,* February, 1976, p. 100.

Sutherland, Zena, review of *Lambs for Dinner, Bulletin of the Center for Children's Books,* March, 1979, p. 122.

Sutherland, Zena, review of *The Story of the Statue of Liberty, Bulletin of the Center for Children's Books,* April, 1986, p. 153.

Vose, Deborah, review of *The Story of the Statue of Liberty, School Library Journal,* April, 1986, p. 76.

Review of *Where Is My Friend?, Publishers Weekly,* January 19, 1976, p. 102.

For More Information See

BOOKS

Children's Literature Review, Volume 45, Gale, 1997, pp. 62-92.

Sixth Book of Junior Authors and Illustrators, Wilson, 1989, pp. 184-85.

PERIODICALS

Booklist, November 15, 1994, p. 608; February 1, 1996, p. 935.

Bulletin of the Center for Children's Books, November, 1994, p. 95; February, 1996, pp. 195-96; May, 1996, p. 307; May, 1999, p. 322.
Kirkus Reviews, March 1, 1998, p. 341.
School Library Journal, July, 1993, p. 73; May, 1996, p. 106.

—*Sketch by Gerard J. Senick*

*　　*　　*

MAESTRO, Giulio 1942-

Personal

Given name is pronounced "*Jool*-yoh," and surname, "Ma-*es*-troh"; born May 6, 1942, in New York, NY; son of Marcello (a writer) and Edna (Ten Eyck) Maestro; married Betsy Crippen (a writer and teacher), December 16, 1972; children: Daniela Marisa, Marco Claudio. *Education:* Cooper Union, New York City, B.F.A., 1964; further study in printmaking at Pratt Graphics Center, New York City, 1965-68. *Hobbies and other interests:* Painting, woodworking, reading, gardening, travel, making jam.

Addresses

Home and office—74 Mile Creek Rd., Old Lyme, CT 06371.

Career

Design Organization, Inc. (advertising design), New York City, assistant to art director, 1965-66; Warren A. Kass Graphics, Inc. (advertising design), New York City, assistant art director, 1966-69; freelance writer and illustrator, 1969—. *Exhibitions:* Exhibitor at the Society of Illustrators Show, New York City, 1968, 1974; American Institute of Graphic Arts, New York City, 1974; Art Director's Club, New York City, 1978, 1982; Fourteenth Exhibition of Original Pictures of International Children's Books, Japan, 1979.

Awards, Honors

Children's Book of the Year, Child Study Association of America, 1969, for *From Petals to Pinecones,* 1974, for *Two Good Friends, Number Ideas through Pictures, Gray Duck Catches a Friend,* and *Milk, Butter and Cheese,* 1975, for *Oil: The Buried Treasure, A Pack of Riddles, The Great Ghost Rescue,* and *Who Said Meow?,* 1976, for *Fat Polka-Dot Cat and Other Haiku,* 1986, for *Train Whistles, Razzle-Dazzle Riddles, Space Telescope,* and *Hurricane Watch,* 1987, for both *Sunshine Makes the Seasons* and *The Story of the Statue of Liberty,* 1995, for *Our Patchwork Planet,* and 1996, for *The Voice of the People: American Democracy in Action;* Junior Library Guild selection, 1973, for *Three Kittens,* 1974, for *Two Good Friends, One More and One Less,* and *Egg-Ventures,* 1975, for *Who Said Now?* and *A Wise Monkey Tale,* 1976, for *Where Is My Friend?,* 1977, for *Three Friends Find Spring,* 1978, for *Busy Day* and

Fiddle with a Riddle, 1979, for *On the Go,* 1981, for *Harriet Reads Signs and More Signs,* and 1986, for *Ferryboat; The Tortoise's Tug of War* was included in the American Institute of Graphic Arts Children's Book Show, 1971-72, as was *Three Kittens,* 1973-74; Notable Book, American Library Association, 1974, for *Two Good Friends,* 1981, for *Traffic,* 1987, for *A More Perfect Union,* and 1991, for *The Discovery of the Americas;* Merit Award, Art Directors Club of New York, 1978, for *Harriet Goes to the Circus;* Children's Choice selection, International Reading Association-Children's Book Council, 1978, for *Harriet Goes to the Circus,* 1979, for *Lambs for Dinner,* 1980, for *Fiddle with a Riddle,* 1982, for *Moonkey,* and 1984, for *Halloween Howls;* Outstanding Science Trade Book for Children, National Science Teachers Association, 1985, for *Fish Facts and Bird Brains;* Notable Children's Trade Book in the Field of Social Studies, National Council for Social Studies and Children's Book Council, 1986, for *Ferryboat,* and 1991, for *The Discovery of the Americas;* Pick of the Lists, American Booksellers Association, 1986, for *The Story of the Statue of Liberty,* 1987, for *A More Perfect Union: The Story of Our Constitution,* 1991, for *The Discovery of the Americas,* 1994, for *Exploration and Conquest: The Americas After Columbus, 1500-1620,* 1996, for *The Voice of the People: American Democracy in Action,* and 1998, for *The New Americans: Colonial Times, 1620-1699;* Books for the Teen Age and 100 Titles for Reading and Sharing, New York Public Library, and Outstanding Science Trade Book for Children, National Science Teachers Association-Children's Book Council, all for *Our Patchwork Planet.*

Writings

FOR CHILDREN; AUTHOR AND ILLUSTRATOR

(Reteller) *The Tortoise's Tug of War,* Bradbury, 1971.
The Remarkable Plant in Apartment 4, Bradbury, 1973, British edition as *The Remarkable Plant in Flat No. 4,* Macmillan, 1974.
One More and One Less, Crown, 1974.
Leopard Is Sick, Greenwillow, 1978.
Leopard and the Noisy Monkeys, Greenwillow, 1979.
A Raft of Riddles, Dutton, 1982.
Halloween Howls: Riddles That Are a Scream, Dutton, 1983.
Riddle Romp, Clarion, 1983.
Just Enough Rosie, Grosset, 1983.
What's a Frank Frank?: Tasty Homograph Riddles, Clarion, 1984.
Razzle-Dazzle Riddles, Clarion, 1985.
What's Mite Might?: Homophone Riddles to Boost Your Word Power!, Clarion, 1986.
Riddle Roundup: A Wild Bunch to Beef Up Your Word Power, Clarion, 1989.
More Halloween Howls: Riddles That Come Back to Haunt You, Dutton, 1992.
Macho Nacho and Other Rhyming Riddles, Dutton, 1994.

AUTHOR AND ILLUSTRATOR; NONFICTION; ALL WRITTEN WITH SON, MARCO MAESTRO

Riddle City U.S.A.: A Book of Geography Riddles, Harper-Collins, 1994.
What Do You Hear When Cows Sing? And Other Silly Riddles, HarperCollins, 1996.
Geese Find the Missing Piece: School Time Riddle Rhymes, HarperCollins, 1999.

ILLUSTRATOR

Joseph J. McCoy, *Swans,* Lothrop, 1967.
Millie McWhirter, *A Magic Morning with Uncle Al,* Collins & World, 1969.
Katherine Cutler, *From Petals to Pinecones: A Nature Art and Craft Book,* Lothrop, 1969.
Rudyard Kipling, *The Beginning of the Armadillos,* St. Martin's, 1970.
Katherine Cutler, *Creative Shellcraft,* Lothrop, 1971.
Jo Phillips, *Right Angles: Paper-Folding Geometry,* Crowell, 1972.
Vicki Kimmel Artis, *Gray Duck Catches a Friend,* Putnam, 1974.
Tony Johnston, *Fig Tale,* Putnam, 1974.
Harry Milgrom, *Egg-Ventures,* Dutton, 1974.
Mannis Charosh, *Number Ideas through Pictures,* Crowell, 1974.
Carolyn Meyer, *Milk, Butter and Cheese: The Story of Dairy Products,* Morrow, 1974.
Sarah Riedman, *Trees Alive,* Lothrop, 1974.
Melvin Berger, *The New Air Book,* Crowell, 1974.
Eva Ibbotson, *The Great Ghost Rescue,* Walck, 1975.
Maria Polushkin, *Who Said Meow?,* Crown, 1975.
William R. Gerler, compiler, *A Pack of Riddles,* Dutton, 1975.
John Trivett, *Building Tables on Tables: A Book about Multiplication,* Crowell, 1975.
Sigmund Kalina, *How to Make a Dinosaur,* Lothrop, 1976.
Melvin Berger, *Energy from the Sun,* Crowell, 1976.
Isaac Asimov, *Mars, the Red Planet,* Lothrop, 1977.
Eva Barwell, *Make Your Pet a Present,* Lothrop, 1977.
Caroline Anne Levine, *Knockout Knock Knocks,* Dutton, 1978.
Gaile Kay Haines, *Natural and Synthetic Poisons,* Morrow, 1978.
John Trivett and Daphne Trivett, *Time for Clocks,* Crowell, 1979.
Vicki Cobb, *More Science Experiments You Can Eat,* Lippincott, 1979.
Joanne E. Bernstein, *Fiddle with a Riddle: Write Your Own Riddles,* Dutton, 1979.
Isaac Asimov, *Saturn and Beyond,* Lothrop, 1979.
Boris Arnov, *Water: Experiments to Understand It,* Lothrop, 1980.
Andrea Griffing Zimmerman, *The Riddle Zoo,* Dutton, 1981.
Mike Thaler, *Moonkey,* Harper, 1981.
Caroline Anne Levine, *The Silly Kid Joke Book,* Dutton, 1983.
Seymour Simon, *The Dinosaur Is the Biggest Animal That Ever Lived, and Other Wrong Ideas You Thought Were True,* Lippincott, 1984.

ILLUSTRATOR; NONFICTION; EDITED BY RICHARD SHAW

(Illustrated with others) *The Fox Book,* Warner, 1971.
(Illustrated with others) *The Bird Book,* Warner, 1974.
(Illustrated with others) *The Cat Book,* Warner, 1973.
(Illustrated with others) *The Mouse Book,* Warner, 1975.

ILLUSTRATOR; NONFICTION; ALL WRITTEN BY ELYSE SOMMER

The Bread Dough Craft Book, Lothrop, 1972.
Designing with Cutouts: The Art of Decoupage, Lothrop, 1973.
Make It with Burlap, Lothrop, 1973.
(With Joellen Sommer) *A Patchwork, Applique, and Quilting Primer,* Lothrop, 1975.

ILLUSTRATOR; NONFICTION; ALL WRITTEN BY FRANKLYN M. BRANLEY

The Beginning of the Earth, Crowell, 1972, revised edition, 1987, published as *The Beginning of Our Earth,* Harper, 1988.
Comets, Crowell, 1984.
Space Telescope: A Voyage into Space Book, Crowell, 1985.
Sunshine Makes the Seasons, revised edition, Crowell, 1985.
Hurricane Watch, Crowell, 1986.
Rockets and Satellites, revised edition, Crowell, 1987 (Maestro was not associated with the earlier edition).
Tornado Alert!, Crowell, 1988.

ILLUSTRATOR; PICTURE BOOKS; ALL WRITTEN BY MIRRA GINSBURG

What Kind of Bird Is That?, adapted from the Russian tale by Vladimir Suteyev, Crown, 1973.
Three Kittens, translated from the Russian tale by Vladimir Suteyev, Crown, 1973.
Kitten from One to Ten, Crown, 1980.

ILLUSTRATOR; NONFICTION; ALL WRITTEN BY ROMA GANS

Millions and Millions of Crystals, Crowell, 1973.
Oil: The Buried Treasure, Crowell, 1975.
Caves, Crowell, 1976.

ILLUSTRATOR; FICTION; ALL WRITTEN BY JUDY DELTON

Two Good Friends, Crown, 1974.
Two Is Company, Crown, 1976.
Three Friends Find Spring, Crown, 1977.
Penny-Wise, Fun-Foolish, Crown, 1977.
Groundhog's Day at the Doctor, Parents Magazine Press, 1980.

ILLUSTRATOR; "HARRIET" SERIES; ALL WRITTEN BY BETSY C. MAESTRO

Where Is My Friend? A Word Concept Book, Crown, 1976.
Harriet Goes to the Circus, Crown, 1977.
Harriet Reads Signs and More Signs, Crown, 1981.
Around the Clock with Harriet: A Book about Telling Time, Crown, 1984.
Harriet the Elephant, Crown, 1984.
Harriet at Play, Crown, 1984.
Harriet at School, Crown, 1984.
Harriet at Home, Crown, 1984.

Harriet at Work, Crown, 1984.

Through the Year with Harriet: A Time Concept Book, Crown, 1985.

Dollars and Cents for Harriet: A Money Concept Book, Crown, 1988.

ILLUSTRATOR; "MAN AND ELEPHANT" SERIES; ALL WRITTEN BY BETSY C. MAESTRO

Busy Day: A Book of Action Words, Crown, 1978.

On the Go: A Book of Adjectives, Crown, 1979.

On the Town: A Book of Clothing Words, Crown, 1983.

Camping Out: A Book of Action Words, Crown, 1984.

ILLUSTRATOR; "THE AMERICAN STORY" SERIES; ALL WRITTEN BY BETSY C. MAESTRO

A More Perfect Union: The Story of Our Constitution, Lothrop, 1987.

The Discovery of the Americas, Lothrop, 1991.

The Discovery of the Americas Activity Book, Lothrop, 1992.

Exploration and Conquest: The Americas after Columbus, 1500-1620, Lothrop, 1994.

The Voice of the People: American Democracy in Action, Lothrop, 1996.

The New Americans: European Settlement in North America, 1620-1689, Lothrop, 1996.

The New Americans: Colonial Times, 1620-1689, Lothrop, 1998.

ILLUSTRATOR; OTHER PICTURE BOOKS; ALL WRITTEN BY BETSY C. MAESTRO

A Wise Monkey Tale (retelling), Crown, 1975.

Fat Polka-Dot Cat and Other Haiku (poetry), Dutton, 1976.

In My Boat, Crowell, 1976.

Lambs for Dinner (retelling), Crown, 1978.

Traffic: A Book of Opposites, Crown, 1981.

The Key to the Kingdom, Harcourt, 1982.

The Guessing Game, Grosset, 1983.

(With Ellen DelVecchio) *Big City Port,* Four Winds, 1983.

Ferryboat, Crowell, 1986.

The Story of the Statue of Liberty, Lothrop, 1986.

The Grab-Bag Party, Golden Press, 1986.

The Pandas Take a Vacation, Golden Press, 1986.

The Perfect Picnic, Golden Press, 1987.

The Travels of Freddie and Frannie Frog, Golden Press, 1987.

Taxi: A Book of City Words, Clarion, 1989.

Temperature and You, Lodestar, 1989.

Snow Day, Scholastic, 1989.

Delivery Van: Words for Town and Country, Clarion Books, 1990.

A Sea Full of Sharks, Scholastic, 1990.

All Aboard Overnight: A Book of Compound Words, Clarion, 1992.

How Do Apples Grow?, HarperCollins, 1992.

Bike Trip, HarperCollins, 1992.

Take a Look at Snakes, Scholastic, 1992.

The Story of Money, Clarion, 1993.

Bats: Night Fliers, Scholastic, 1994.

The Story of Religion, Clarion Books, 1996.

The Story of Clocks and Calendars: Marking a Millennium, Lothrop, 1999.

ILLUSTRATOR; RETELLINGS; ALL WRITTEN BY RUTH LERNER PERLE

(With Susan Horwitz) *Little Red Riding Hood with Benjy and Bubbles,* Holt, 1979.

(With Susan Horwitz) *The Fisherman and His Wife with Benjy and Bubbles,* Holt, 1979.

(With Susan Horwitz) *Rumpelstiltskin with Benjy and Bubbles,* Holt, 1979.

Sleeping Beauty with Benjy and Bubbles, Holt, 1979.

ILLUSTRATOR; NONFICTION; ALL WRITTEN BY MARVIN TERBAN

Eight Ate: A Feast of Homonym Riddles, Clarion Books, 1982.

In a Pickle, and Other Funny Idioms, Clarion, 1983.

I Think I Thought, and Other Tricky Verbs, Clarion, 1984.

Too Hot to Hoot: Funny Palindrome Riddles, Clarion, 1985.

Your Foot's on My Feet!: And Other Tricky Nouns, Clarion, 1986.

Mad as a Wet Hen!: And Other Funny Idioms, Clarion, 1987.

Guppies in Tuxedos: Funny Eponyms, Clarion, 1988.

Superdupers: Really Funny Real Words, Clarion, 1989.

It Figures!: Fun Figures of Speech, Clarion, 1993.

ILLUSTRATOR; NONFICTION; ALL WRITTEN BY HELEN RONEY SATTLER

Fish Facts and Bird Brains: Animal Intelligence, Dutton, 1984.

Train Whistles: A Language in Code, revised edition, Lothrop, 1985.

Our Patchwork Planet: The Story of Plate Tectonics, Lothrop, 1995.

OTHER

Maestro's books have been published in England, France, Germany, Spain, Japan, and the Netherlands. His papers are housed in permanent collections at the De Grummond Collection, University of Southern Mississippi, and the Kerlan Collection, University of Minnesota.

Adaptations

Sunshine Makes the Seasons was released on audio cassette by HarperCollins in 1988. *The Discovery of the Americas* was released on audio cassette by Spoken Word, Incorporated, in 1993 and as a video cassette by Live Oak Media. Spoken Arts also released *A More Perfect Union* and *The Story of the Statue of Liberty* as audio cassettes in 1993.

Work in Progress

The New Nation, Struggle for a Continent, Westward Movement, and *Liberty or Death: The American Revolution,* all for Lothrop.

Sidelights

A popular, prolific, and highly respected illustrator who is also an author and reteller, Maestro is best known for his volumes of riddles and the books on which he has collaborated as artist with his wife, Betsy C. Maestro (who also writes as Betsy Maestro). As an author, Maestro has created several volumes of riddles designed to build the vocabularies of young readers through humor. Centering on such themes as Halloween, place names, homophones, and the game of Hinky Pinky, which incorporates rhyming punch lines, these books feature a variety of puns, phrases, slang expressions, and other forms of wordplay. Maestro has also written two books about the character Leopard as well as a humorous fantasy about a plant run amok in an apartment house and a retelling of an African trickster tale.

Maestro has provided pictures for works by his wife that include concept books for preschoolers and primary graders, retellings, and informational picture books for older children on American history and government as well as on such subjects as sharks, bats, money, and religion. In addition, the pair have collaborated on storybooks in picture book form that feature child and animal characters. Maestro has also illustrated concept books written by his wife that explore city words, temperature, and the route of a delivery van. The artist has also provided pictures for series of books by such authors as Franklyn M. Branley, Judy Delton, Marvin Terban, Mirra Ginsburg, Helen Roney Sattler, and his son, Marco Maestro, as well as for individual works by Rudyard Kipling, Melvin Berger, Vicki Cobb, and Seymour Simon, among others. As an illustrator, Mae-

Giulio Maestro's watercolor paintings and maps grace the first volume of "The American Story Series," written by Betsy C. Maestro. (From The Discovery of the Americas.*)*

stro is praised for his versatility, technique, and attention to detail as well as for the clarity, color, humor, and effectiveness of his pictures. Maestro's illustrations, which are characteristically done as watercolors and line art with washes, range from small cartoonlike drawings to rich, opulent double-page spreads that include panoramic views and unusual perspectives. In his use of color, Maestro favors subdued pastels and earth tones as well as vibrant colors such as pink, purple, orange, turquoise, scarlet, and yellow, depending on the style of each book. The artist is also noted for the nonsexist, multicultural orientation of his pictures. Although he is sometimes criticized for creating texts that are secondary to his art and for what some commentators have regarded as an awkward drawing of people, Maestro is most often regarded as an artist whose paintings and pictures are instructive, visually delightful, and well balanced with the ideas that they illustrate.

Born in Brooklyn, New York, Maestro is the son of a writer and a homemaker. He once commented: "I was born in New York City and lived in Greenwich Village most of my life. My family owned a house on Charlton Street, and I attended the Little Red School House from kindergarten through grade six. I started drawing and painting before I even went to school." He once told *Something about the Author* (SATA), "From the time I was a child, I always held a pencil, crayon, or paintbrush in my hand." As a boy, Maestro's idols were animator Walt Disney and cartoonist Walt Kelly, the creator of the "Pogo" comic strips. Maestro recalled in *SATA*, "I even wrote to the Disney studio and to Kelly personally. The Disney studio sent me illustrative material, and Walt Kelly wrote me a letter personally, saying, 'If you really want to do this, you have to draw every day. You really have to keep at it.' Enclosed was an original drawing as well. A letter from Walt Kelly—it's hard to put into words what a thrill that was for me. It lent weight to all the drawing I was doing. I always assumed that I would grow up to become an artist as well. Thinking back to Kelly's kindness to me, I make it a point to answer every letter I receive from kids, and to enclose a drawing or a poster." While attending high school, Maestro realized that his talent extended beyond cartooning when he discovered that he could draw realistically or abstractly in a number of mediums. This discovery, he told *SATA*, "felt great, but it certainly didn't help me to figure out what I 'would do in life.' If anything, it confused the issue somewhat because my options had increased."

After graduating from high school, Maestro attended Cooper Union, an art school in New York City that was, he noted in *SATA*, "renowned for its studio school and faculty members who were all working artists. The one drawback was that the faculty members had narrow viewpoints about art—you did it their way, or they didn't bother with you. When I think back on it, I remember how angry I was. Students would be praised by one teacher and criticized by the next for the same work. It was confusing at the time. Now I realize that all the personal opinions and 'visions' of the various teachers were useful, though at the time it seemed impossible to reconcile them. I can remember endless

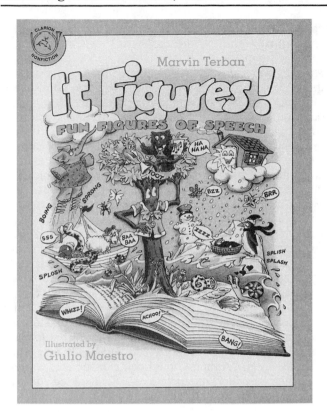

Marvin Terban

It Figures!
FUN FIGURES OF SPEECH

Illustrated by
Giulio Maestro

Six figures of speech are illuminated for aspiring young writers through quotes and examples, and further elucidated by Giulio Maestro's comical illustrations. (Cover illustration by Giulio Maestro.)

discussions on the subject of 'what is art.' ... These discussions would have been much more fruitful if one of our teachers had had a sense of humor and admitted that there were no hard answers."

During his senior year, Maestro took a course in commercial art. The presence of this course at Cooper Union led to discussions about the merits of fine art versus commercial art. Maestro told *SATA,* "People would sometimes draw a distinction between 'fine art' and illustration. The assumption was that so-called fine artists have more talent. I feel that all artists are illustrators. The only really valid distinction has to do with money. Commercial artists get paid for their work, which is not necessarily the case with artists who make art for themselves. The idea that when you are getting paid you are compromising your principles isn't necessarily true. After all, Michelangelo was compensated for painting the Sistine Chapel."

During his senior year at Cooper Union, Maestro prepared a portfolio of his work and, immediately after graduation, was hired as an assistant to the art director of the Manhattan art department of *Reader's Digest* Magazine. After one year, he held a similar position at the advertising firm Design Organization, Inc. A year later, he became the assistant art director at another advertising design firm, Warren A. Kass Graphics, Inc., where he stayed for two more years. During his career in advertising, Maestro did layout and design work. He

found this experience useful, but, as he told *SATA,* "I was doing virtually no drawing on the job and I was expending an awful lot of energy on projects I didn't care very much about." Maestro decided to embark on a career as an illustrator. As he recalled in *SATA,* "I hoped that the book field would offer me what I most wanted." Gradually, he began to make the acquaintance of people in the publishing industry and started to get assignments designing book jackets. When he received an assignment to illustrate *The Beginning of the Armadillos* by Rudyard Kipling, Maestro was able to become a full-time illustrator. "I was extremely fortunate," he told *SATA.*

Soon after illustrating *The Beginning of the Armadillos,* Maestro wrote and illustrated his first book, *The Tortoise's Tug of War.* A picture-book retelling of a South American variation of an African tale, the story describes how a tortoise challenges a whale and a tapir to a tug of war, sets them to pulling against each other until exhaustion sets in, then claims victory. A critic in *Kirkus Reviews* noted, "[It's] the lush pictures that predominate, and in fact the backgrounds—especially a spectacular deep blue sea—quite subordinate Tortoise's cleverness to the artist's performance." Writing in *Horn Book,* Virginia Haviland stated, "The author's version is acceptable, but his retelling is less significant than his full-color paintings, which are lively and distinctive in composition and color." In 1973, Maestro produced his first original picture book, *The Remarkable Plant in Apartment 4.* In this work, the author-illustrator describes how a small plant, grown overnight in young Michael's room, spreads throughout the apartment building in which he lives. The presence of the plant—which has become a tree—inspires the tenants to do creative things with its roots and branches and to enjoy the tropical birds, insects, and flowers that it brings forth. Writing in *Growing Point,* Margery Fisher commented, "In watercolour and ink the details of the strange event are brilliantly shown." A critic in *Kirkus Reviews* averred, "We have the feeling that Maestro's plant is rooted in precariously shallow ground, but his freewheeling foliage makes the greening of a city block an enticingly euphoric occasion."

In 1975, Giulio illustrated Betsy Maestro's picture-book retelling of *A Wise Monkey Tale.* The story, which outlines how little Monkey fools several large animals into helping her out of a deep hole, is illustrated by lively, colorful jungle scenes. Writing in *Booklist,* Denise M. Wilms noted the story's folktale influence, taking into account "its simple, patterned plot and repetitious jingle, both of which make it admirably suited to preschoolers, who can enjoy listening while they gaze at the artist's splashy display." Zena Sutherland of the *Bulletin of the Center for Children's Books* stated, "Monkey's clever triumph ... is stressed by the bright, bold illustrations of a grinning monkey and her worried companions." The next year, the Maestros produced *Where Is My Friend? A Word Concept Book,* the first of their popular series of books featuring Harriet the roller-skating elephant. In this work, which is designed to introduce young children to word concepts, Harriet demonstrates the meaning of words such as up, down, between, around, over, and into as she searches for her friend, a mouse, whom Harriet finally discovers right in front of her nose. A reviewer in *Publishers Weekly* exclaimed, "What a pleasure it is to gaze at Giulio Maestro's huge, blazingly colored pictures of all the doings." Writing in *Booklist,* Barbara Elleman enthused, "Large black letters and simple, bright objects positioned against multicolored backgrounds make this a visual delight as well as a useful word-concept book." In subsequent books featuring Harriet, the Maestros show their heroine, described by Carrie Carmichael in the *New York Times Book Review* as a "Babar-reminiscent elephant," at home, at school, at work, at play, and at the circus. In the process, young readers learn words associated with familiar childhood activities as well as how to recognize signs, tell time, and count money. The "Harriet" books are often praised for their illustrations, rendered with large, stylized poster-like pictures in bright colors surrounded by heavy black lines. In a review of *Harriet Goes to the Circus* in *Children's Book Review Service,* Madge M. Dhus noted, "The large print and superb illustrations make the book irresistible for 'picture readers,'" while a reviewer in *Publishers Weekly,* assessing *Around the Clock with Harriet,* maintained: "Gala pictures in poster-bold hues are a cinch to captivate the toddler set." Writing in *School Library Journal* about *Dollars and Cents for Harriet,* Martha Rosen predicted, "Harriet is one 'white elephant' who will not end up just sitting on a shelf." Noting the team's "usual flair for color and clarity," Rosen concluded that the Maestros created an "attractive and appealing

concept book that should be popular with the preschool and primary grade audience."

Another popular set of books created by the Maestros is the "Man and Elephant" series. Picture books that introduce children to verbs, adjectives, and words that describe clothes, the volumes feature the humorous adventures of a debonair mustachioed man, who is first introduced as a circus clown, and his good-natured elephant companion. The series, which is illustrated in cartoonlike drawings filled with bright colors, profiles the friends as they work in their traveling circus, play tennis, attend a concert, go camping, and go to the beach, among other activities. In assessing *Busy Day: A Book of Action Words,* a reviewer in *Publishers Weekly* commented, "The Maestros' new book is uncommonly imaginative and a source of fun for toddlers as well as an artful introduction to verbs." *School Library Journal* contributor Daisy Kouzel noted that the brightly colored illustrations help to make *On the Go: A Book of Adjectives* "useful to parents and teachers of slow or recalcitrant learners." Writing in *School Library Journal* about *On the Town: A Book of Clothing Words,* Liza Bliss asserted, "Although the book can serve as a great vocabulary builder, its uncluttered, lighthearted illustrations are a joy in themselves."

While illustrating books for his wife and other authors, Maestro continued to create books of his own. For example, his book of Halloween riddles, *Halloween Howls: Riddles That Are a Scream,* features nearly sixty pun-filled riddles about witches, ghosts, vampires, monsters, and other supernatural beings and is illustrated with funny, bright pictures. A reviewer in *Publishers Weekly* asserted that "since kids dearly love this brand of humor, the book should be very popular among boys and girls planning Halloween festivities." Writing in *Booklist,* Karen Stang Hanley expressed that Maestro's pictures "accentuate the silliness and make this an eye-catching Halloween item." In 1992, Maestro published a companion volume, *More Halloween Howls: Riddles That Come Back to Haunt You.* With *Macho Nacho and Other Rhyming Riddles,* Maestro invites readers to guess the answers to more than fifty riddles with rhyming punch lines. Writing in *School Library Journal,* Amy Adler asserted, "[T]his slim volume, with its whimsical watercolor illustrations, has enough charm to entice children to open it and discover the fun inside."

In addition to his own works, Maestro has also collaborated as a writer with his son Marco on three books of riddles: *Riddle City, U.S.A.: A Book of Geography Riddles, What Do You Hear When Cows Sing? And Other Silly Riddles,* and *Geese Find the Missing Piece: School Time Riddle Rhymes.* In a review of *Riddle City, U.S.A.,* a book that fashions its riddles around American place names, Linda Greengrass of *School Library Journal* commented, "[M]ost collections can always use a new riddle book, and one that throws in a little geography can't hurt." Reviewing *What Do You Hear When Cows Sing?,* a book of playful riddles featuring animals, trains, and other topics with child appeal, *School Library Journal* contributor Mary Ann

Giulio Maestro provided the humorous illustrations for **What Do You Hear When Cows Sing?,** *a book of playful riddles written with his son Marco.*

Bursk predicted, "Children will love the silly pictures, laugh at the riddles, enjoy sharing them with others, and expand their vocabularies all at the same time," while Hazel Rochman of *Booklist* concluded that the jokes "need sharing, and they are sure to make reading a social experience."

As illustrator and writer respectively, both Giulio and Betsy Maestro have been lauded for the picture books they have created on American history for primary and middle graders. The first of these works, *The Story of the Statue of Liberty,* depicts the fifteen-year creation of Lady Liberty by French sculptor Frederic Bartholdi. The volume is considered distinctive for providing the youngest children with an interesting, appropriate introduction to its subject, and for using Giulio Maestro's breathtaking paintings to tell the statue's story rather than the photographs or line drawings used in similar studies. Writing in *Bulletin of the Center for Children's Books,* Zena Sutherland commented, "From one flag-centered endpaper to another, this is a well-designed book," while Deborah Vose of *School Library Journal* exclaimed, "At last, an outstanding picture book on the Statue of Liberty." Elizabeth S. Watson of *Horn Book* said that Maestro's watercolors "show amazing detail and are extremely rich." *A More Perfect Union: The Story of Our Constitution* is generally considered another straightforward account of a milestone in U.S. history. Christine Behrmann, writing in *School Library Journal,* called the volume "the simplest and most accessible history of the Constitution to date," while Betsy Hearne of the *Bulletin of the Center for Children's Books* noted, "the Maestros have succeeded in producing a smooth, informationally balanced text and some impressive double-page spreads...." For the "American Story" series of illustrated informational books for older children about the early development of the Americas, Maestro created illustrations in pencil and watercolors that incorporate both detailed maps and sweeping landscapes and seascapes. Writing in *School Library Journal* about the first book in the series, *The Discovery of the Americas,* Ruth Semrau noted that Maestro has achieved "a happy mingling of artistic maps that include clear, descriptive diagrams of voyages and land routes, balanced with beautiful interpretations of broad landscapes in luscious colors of sky, cloud, sea, mountain, and forest." Semrau called *The Discovery of the Americas* "an extraordinary achievement in both history and art," while a reviewer in *Publishers Weekly* concluded that "this attractive work is an essential resource." Subsequent volumes, which outline the history of America through the seventeenth century, also feature Maestro's detailed watercolor and pencil art as well as maps, spot illustrations, and double-page spreads. Together, concluded a reviewer in *Publishers Weekly* of *The New Americans: Colonial Times, 1620-1689,* these works "provide a vivid picture of the century's pivotal events."

Maestro told SATA, "First and foremost, I'm an illustrator. I don't put myself in the same category with Arnold Lobel, whose writing and drawing were equally brilliant. I don't fancy myself a great storyteller, but I love words and wordplay. My first-grade stories are fine, but haven't been terribly successful in the marketplace. The riddle and word concept books fare much better. The riddle books are full of homonyms, puns, and plays-on-words, often fairly sophisticated. They're intended not only to be brain-teasers to the reader, but also good ammunition for stumping friends. I'm happy that my publishers didn't attempt to lower the difficulty level of these books. One of my pet peeves is that too often educators and publishers expect too little of kids. The ability to use language effectively has to be nurtured. Young minds should be encouraged to think more complex thoughts and be exposed to rich language in reading materials. I hope my word-play books, through humour in text and pictures, help children to take joy in the subtleties of language and word meanings."

Regarding his collaboration with his wife, Maestro commented, "Betsy and I have evolved a very good way of working together. We talk at the conceptual stage of a book, but I don't interfere with her writing if I can help it. Neither does she interfere with my drawings. But from the outset we agree on an overall visual style for the book." In discussing the concept books he has created with his wife, Maestro mused, "Of course, every book for kids could be called a concept book. When Betsy and I describe one as such, it simply means that we have set out to present a given concept in a coherent and concentrated way.... These books aim to marry education and entertainment. However, the story line or entertainment aspect never overshadows the concept being presented." He added, "My guiding principle for the 'Harriet' illustrations (as well as all our concept books) is: 'Keep it simple.' Don't introduce anything that will confuse, clutter, or distract from the text." In evaluating his career, Maestro concluded, "I think back to the advice Walt Kelly gave me. After decades as an artist, his words ring truer today and bear repeating. 'Draw anything and everything you like. The important thing is to draw every day.' It's the same advice I now give children who ask me how they can learn to draw well. I tell them 'practice, practice, practice.'"

[For more information on Giulio Maestro, please see the entry on Betsy C. Maestro in this volume.]

Works Cited

Adler, Amy, review of *Macho Nacho and Other Rhyming Riddles, School Library Journal,* November, 1994, p. 100.

Review of *Around the Clock with Harriet, Publishers Weekly,* April 13, 1984, p. 72.

Behrmann, Christine, review of *A More Perfect Union, School Library Journal,* September, 1987, pp. 175-76.

Bliss, Liza, review of *On the Town, School Library Journal,* November, 1983, p. 66.

Bursk, Mary Ann, review of *What Do You Hear When Cows Sing?, School Library Journal,* March, 1996, p. 190.

Review of *Busy Day, Publishers Weekly,* March 6, 1978, p. 101.

Carmichael, Carrie, "Designed for the Smallest," *New York Times Book Review,* November 11, 1984, p. 57.

Dhus, Madge M., review of *Harriet Goes to the Circus, Children's Book Review Service,* April, 1977, pp. 84-85.

Review of *The Discovery of the Americas, Publishers Weekly,* May 24, 1991, p. 59.

Elleman, Barbara, review of *Where Is My Friend, Booklist,* February 15, 1976, p. 856.

Fisher, Margery, review of *The Remarkable Plant in Flat No. 4, Growing Point,* September, 1974, p. 2461.

Greengrass, Linda, review of *Riddle City U.S.A., School Library Journal,* July, 1994, pp. 111-12.

Review of *Halloween Howls, Publishers Weekly,* August 19, 1983, p. 78.

Hanley, Karen Stang, review of *Halloween Howls, Booklist,* October 1, 1983, p. 299.

Haviland, Virginia, review of *The Tortoise's Tug of War, Horn Book,* April, 1972, p. 137.

Hearne, Betsy, review of *A More Perfect Union, Bulletin of the Center for Children's Books,* October, 1987, p. 34.

Kouzel, Daisy, review of *On the Go, School Library Journal,* September, 1979, p. 117.

Maestro, interview with Marguerite Feitlowitz for *Something about the Author,* Volume 59, Gale, 1990, pp. 119-128.

Review of *The New Americans, Publishers Weekly,* March 16, 1998, p. 66.

Review of *The Remarkable Plant in Apartment 4, Kirkus Reviews,* April 15, 1973, p. 453.

Rochman, Hazel, review of *What Do You Hear When Cows Sing?, Booklist,* January 1, 1996, p. 850.

Rosen, Martha, review of *Dollars and Cents for Harriet, School Library Journal,* January, 1989, p. 65.

Semrau, Ruth, review of *The Discovery of the Americas, School Library Journal,* April, 1991, p. 114.

Sutherland, Zena, review of *The Story of the Statue of Liberty, Bulletin of the Center for Children's Books,* April, 1986, p. 153.

Sutherland, Zena, review of *A Wise Monkey Tale, Bulletin of the Center for Children's Books,* February, 1976, p. 100.

Review of *Taxi, Kirkus Reviews,* February 15, 1989, p. 296.

Review of *The Tortoise's Tug of War, Kirkus Reviews,* January 1, 1972, p. 2.

Vose, Deborah, review of *The Story of the Statue of Liberty, School Library Journal,* April, 1986, p. 76.

Watson, Elizabeth S., review of *The Story of the Statue of Liberty, Horn Book,* May-June, 1986, pp. 339-40.

Review of *Where Is My Friend?, Publishers Weekly,* January 19, 1976, p. 102.

Wilms, Denise, review of *Temperature and You, Booklist,* May 1, 1990, p. 1708.

Wilms, Denise M., review of *A Wise Monkey Tale, Booklist,* November 15, 1975, p. 456.

For More Information See

BOOKS

Children's Literature Review, Volume 45, Gale, 1997, pp. 62-92.

Sixth Book of Junior Authors and Illustrators, Wilson, 1989.

PERIODICALS

Kirkus Reviews, June 15, 1996, p. 902; March 1, 1998, p. 341.

Publishers Weekly, July 29, 1996, p. 86.

School Library Journal, June, 1996, p. 144; September, 1996, p. 218.

—*Sketch by Gerard J. Senick*

*   *   *

McGUIGAN, Mary Ann 1949-

Personal

Surname is pronounced Mick-GWIG-in; born August 3, 1949, in Bronx, NY; daughter of Jame and Mary (maiden name, Kearney; present surname, Detko) McGuigan; children: Matthew Pritchard, Douglas Pritchard. *Education:* St. Peter's College, A.B., 1972; Trenton State College, graduate study. *Politics:* "Left of Venus." *Religion:* Roman Catholic.

Addresses

Home—8 Falcon Ct., Old Bridge, NJ 08857. *Office*—Bloomberg Financial Markets, 100 Business Park Dr., P.O. Box 888, Princeton, NJ 08542-0888. *Electronic mail*—heddagab@aol.com. *Agent*—Charlotte Sheedy, 65 Bleecker St., 12th Floor, New York, NY 10012.

Career

Teacher of English and reading at elementary, junior high, and high schools in Jersey City, NJ, 1972-75, Old Bridge, NJ, 1975-79, Trenton, NJ, 1979-80, and Middletown, NJ, 1980-81; Moody's Investors Service, New York City, editor of financial publications, 1981-84; A. Foster Higgins, Inc., Princeton, NJ, communications consultant, 1984-93; Bloomberg Financial Markets, Princeton, managing editor of *Wealth Manager,* 1993—. Vantage Press, Inc., New York City, worked as editor of fiction and nonfiction, between 1981 and 1984.

Awards, Honors

Books for the Teen Age, New York Public Library, 1995, for *Cloud Dancer,* and 1998, for *Where You Belong;* finalist, National Book Award, 1997, for *Where You Belong;* finalist, National Magazine Award, American Society of Magazine Editors, 1995, editorial excellence award, *Folio,* 1996, and Business Award, New York Press Club, 1996, all for *Bloomberg* Magazine; finalist, Excellence in Video Award, Michigan Advertising Group, for a Kellogg Company videotape; first place award, *Business Insurance,* for a *Reader's Digest* communication project; two recognition awards, New York chapter of International Association of Business Communicators.

Mary Ann McGuigan

Writings

Cloud Dancer (young adult novel), Scribner (New York City), 1994.
Where You Belong (young adult novel), Atheneum (New York City), 1997.

Contributor of essays and stories for adults to magazines and newspapers, including *New York Times, Image, Dawn, New York Sunday Newsday,* and *Bloomberg.*

Work in Progress

A young adult novel, *Crossing into Brooklyn.*

Sidelights

Mary Ann McGuigan told *SATA:* "The creator must have been on a bender the day he was supposed to hand me the blueprints for my earth plane debut, because it looks as if central casting took over instead and gave me the starring role in a 'B' movie—a corny one. In real life, the shy, skinny kid from a poor whacko Irish family in the Bronx doesn't get to have her dreams come true. All I ever wanted to be was a writer. By age fourteen—having attended thirteen different grammar schools in a free-fall flight from landlords who wanted their rent—I knew I wasn't Ivy League material. I thought writers

were well educated, well traveled, knew which fork to use, and had parents who spent the majority of their time sober. I thought I'd try anyway.

"I had the good sense to keep the first stories I wrote to myself. They were awful. I didn't have a clue what good writing was until college, when the Jesuits introduced me to all the dead white men who had already said everything there was to say better than anyone else could hope to say it. Nowhere in the required reading, however, could I find anything that quite captured what it was like to grow up the way I did. So I respectfully concluded the Jesuits were wrong.

"Still, it took me another twenty years to find the courage and the voice to get some stories told. That came together as soon as I knew who my audience would be: it would be me—and all the kids like me who grew up looking for a way out. I wanted *Where You Belong* to be a story about courage, not the kind that soldiers draw on or the kind that astronauts and adventurers need, but the kind that ordinary people must summon when they believe they are alone and without hope.

"Fiona and Yolanda are growing up in the Bronx, where circumstances can easily conspire to make life seem hopeless. Fiona has much to contend with: poverty, violence, a family whose center cannot hold. But these desperate conditions are not what threaten Fiona most. It is instead the knowledge that it has become pointless to seek comfort—or even safety—from those she loves. She has been set adrift. What finally anchors her is a friend. In Yolanda's strength, Fiona witnesses the courage needed to see the joys that wait beyond the day, and in her friendship, she finds the right to believe that she deserves them. As they find their place in the world, young people—and the not so young—may often feel lost. I offer Fiona's journey to all those struggling to find their way home."

For More Information See

PERIODICALS

Booklist, June 1, 1997, p. 1695.
Bulletin of the Center for Children's Books, May, 1997, pp. 328-29.
Kirkus Reviews, March 1, 1997, p. 385.
School Library Journal, July, 1997, p. 96.
Voice of Youth Advocates, October, 1994, p. 212; August, 1997, pp. 187-88.

*   *   *

McILWRAITH, Maureen Mollie Hunter
See HUNTER, Mollie

METZENTHEN, David 1958-

Personal

Born December 27, 1958; son of Ron Arthur (a sharebroker) and Joan (Grey) Metzenthen; married, wife's name Fiona Miriam (a business manager); children: Ella, Liam. *Education:* Attended Anglican grammar school in Yarra Valley, Australia. *Politics:* "Green." *Religion:* Agnostic.

Addresses

Office—c/o Penguin Books, 487 Maroondah Hwy, Ringwood, Victoria 3134, Australia.

Career

Writer.

Awards, Honors

Honour Book, Book of the Year-Older Readers, Children's Book Council of Australia, 1998, for *Gilbert's Ghost Train.*

Writings

Danger Wave, Scholastic (Australia), 1990.
Lee Spain, Scholastic, 1991.
Brocky's Bananagram, Scholastic, 1994.
Roadie, Omnibus Books (Norwood, South Australia), 1995.
Johnny Hart's Heroes, Puffin (Ringwood, Australia), 1996.
Animal Instinct, Omnibus Books, 1996.
Gilbert's Ghost Train, Ashton Scholastic (Gosford, Australia), 1997.
Cody and Zero, Addison Wesley Longman (Melbourne, Australia), 1997.
Lefty Lemon Kicks Goals, Addison Wesley Longman, 1997.
Finn and the Big Guy, Penguin (Ringwood, Victoria), 1997.
The Diary of Fat Robby Pile, Addison Wesley Longman, 1997.
Rodney the Surfing Duck, illustrated by Steve Axelson, Addison Wesley Longman, 1997.
Falling Forward, Omnibus Books, 1998.
Fort Island, illustrated by Peter Gouldthorpe, Penguin, 1998.
Mick the Mimic, illustrated by Matt Golding, Addison Wesley Longman, 1998.
The Red Hot Footy Fiasco, illustrated by Matt Golding, Addison Wesley Longman, 1998.
Stony Heart Country, Penguin, 1999.
The Hand-Knitted Hero, illustrated by David Cox, Penguin, 1999.

Work in Progress

Tiff and the Trout, for Penguin.

Sidelights

David Metzenthen told *SATA:* "I write to give to my reader what I feel to be the most important things that I know or think about. I am interested in what we all seek in life, how we pursue happiness and fulfillment. I am a realist Australian writer who believes that place and landscape influence character and, because I care deeply about my country, I spend a lot of my writing time trying to show the 'soul' of the land of this place. I try to write simply, but I also try to present complex issues that face us all as we go about our lives. I love words and the way that good prose can be almost magical in its ability to convey deeply felt and complex meaning.

"I also believe I owe my readers the best, most entertaining work I can possible create."

Metzenthen's prose has been lauded in reviews of his works for young people. *Magpies* contributor Anne Briggs commended Metzenthen's delightful language in *Falling Forward,* the poignant story of the relationship between two "damaged" young men. Briggs maintained that "the book is studded with memorable scenes expressed with delicacy and tenderness." Describing the author's text in *Johnny Hart's Heroes,* where two drifters leave a sideshow to become drovers for a sheep farmer, critic Kerry Neary observed: "Metzenthen uses a laconic prose ... that mirrors the heat-burdened laziness of an outback summer. It is sparked with an imagery that is sometimes breathtaking in its originality."

Works Cited

Briggs, Anne, review of *Falling Forward, Magpies,* September, 1998, p. 39.
Neary, Kerry, review of *Johnny Hart's Heroes, Magpies,* May, 1996, p. 50.

For More Information See

PERIODICALS

Australian Book Review, July, 1996, p. 60; December, 1996, p. 86; May, 1997, p. 60.
Magpies, March, 1992, p. 33; July, 1995, p. 26; May, 1997, p. 36.
Reading Time, August, 1998, p. 10; February, 1999, p. 31.

*   *   *

MOSS, Jeff(rey) 1942-1998

OBITUARY NOTICE—See index for *SATA* sketch: Born June 19, 1942, in New York, NY; died of colon cancer, September 25, 1998, in Manhattan, NY. Scriptwriter, poet, composer, and lyricist. One of the original writers for the groundbreaking children's program *Sesame Street,* Moss helped create the characters Cookie Monster and Oscar the Grouch. Born and raised in Manhattan, Moss graduated from Princeton University, and took a job as a production assistant on the children's show *Captain Kangaroo.* From that show he was recruited by the Children's Television Workshop to help create a new kind of children's program that would appeal to adults as well as children, with the intention of educating as well as entertaining them. The result, *Sesame Street,* is considered a watershed in children's television, setting a standard for quality as well as enjoyability that has influenced a generation of children worldwide. Since 1969, the show has been aired in 130 countries to more than 120 million viewers. Some of his most memorable contributions to the program have been in the form of songs; Moss wrote the music and lyrics for "Rubber Ducky" and "The People in Your Neighborhood," among many others. His songs appear on four Grammy Award-winning recordings, and he was nominated for an Academy Award for his original song score for the film *The Muppets Take Manhattan* in 1984. Moss wrote a number of Sesame Street books, including *The Sesame Street Book of Poetry* and *The Sesame Street Songbook,* as well as several other collections of poems and stories in verse, most notably his well-received *The Butterfly Jar.* For his work as a scriptwriter, composer, and lyricist for *Sesame Street,* Moss earned fifteen Emmy awards and two gold records.

OBITUARIES AND OTHER SOURCES:

PERIODICALS

Los Angeles Times, October 1, 1998, p. A22.
New York Times, September 26, 1998, p. A13.
Publishers Weekly, October 19, 1998, p. 33.
Washington Post, September 27, 1998, p. B8.

*   *   *

NORTHEAST, Brenda V(ictoria) 1948-

Personal

Born February 3, 1948, in Bristol, England; daughter of Clifford James and Joyce Edna (maiden name, Newberry; present surname, Cornwell) Sanders; married Brian Haddon Williams (divorced, 1975); married Laurence Trevor Northeast (a postal services officer); children: Angelique Wilson, Steven Williams, Robert Williams, Jason Williams, Tyson Northeast, Felicity Northeast, David Northeast, Michael Northeast. *Education:* Attended art school as an adult. *Politics:* "Democratic." *Religion:* Christian.

Addresses

Home—36 Maltarra Rd., Munno Para, South Australia 5115. *Office*—P.O. Box 888, Gawler, South Australia 5118.

Career

Writer and illustrator. School visitor, lecturing on art and art history. *Member:* Australian Society of Authors, Society of Book Illustrators, Royal Art Society of Adelaide, Adelaide Writers Centre, Arts Law Centre.

Writings

For the Love of Vincent, self-illustrated, Reed Books Australia (Port Melbourne, Australia), 1995.
For the Love of Auguste, self-illustrated, Reed Books, 1997.

Work in Progress

A book on Monet.

Sidelights

Born in Bristol, England, author and illustrator Brenda V. Northeast was two when her parents migrated to Australia. There they spent two years touring the outback while her father did handyman carpentry at different sheep and cattle stations along the way. Northeast remembers many a night sleeping "under the blanket of a star-filled sky, surrounded by the sounds of the outback." At that early age, she recalls imitating those sounds of dingoes, crows, and kangaroos. Later, after her parents separated, she and her brothers moved to New Zealand with their grandparents, where she spent most of her growing-up years. At the age of nineteen, married and with two children, she returned to Australia.

Northeast began her career in illustrating and writing in 1993. To date she has produced two picture books introducing children to "Art Appreciation." One of

Brenda V. Northeast

these, *For the Love of Vincent,* is about Vincent Van Gogh, represented in Northeast's story by a delightful bear named Vincent van Bear. The second book, *For the Love of Auguste,* is personalized by Bearre Auguste as he introduces us to the life and art of Renoir. These books are selling in New Zealand and France as well as Australia. Northeast is presently researching the life of Monet for a similar effort.

Northeast concluded: "I would like very much to see my books in animation, and the characters as soft toys. I particularly would love to see my books sold throughout the United States of America.

"I have thoroughly enjoyed creating the first two books and the joy, excitement and enthusiasm that they have brought to so many 'children' of all ages.

"There will be more creations as I delve into the hidden treasures I am unlocking from within my inner self!"

For More Information See

PERIODICALS

Magpies, September, 1997, p. 6.

P

POTOK, Chaim 1929-

Personal

Born Herman Harold Potok, Hebrew given name, Chaim (pronounced "Hah-yim") Tzvi, February 17, 1929; son of Benjamin Max (a businessman) and Mollie (Friedman) Potok; married Adena Sara Mosevitzky (a psychiatric social worker), June 8, 1958; children: Rena, Naama, Akiva. *Education:* Yeshiva University, B.A., (summa cum laude), 1950; Jewish Theological Seminary, ordination, M.H.L., 1954; University of Pennsylvania, Ph.D., 1965. *Religion:* Conservative Judaism. *Hobbies and other interests:* Painting and photography.

Addresses

Home—20 Berwick Street, Merion, PA 19066.

Career

Writer. Leaders Training Fellowship, Jewish Theological Seminary, national director, 1954-55; Camp Ramah, Los Angeles, CA, director, 1957-59; Har Zion Temple, Philadelphia, PA, scholar-in-residence, 1959-63; Jewish Theological Seminary, member of faculty of Teachers' Institute, 1963-64; *Conservative Judaism,* New York City, managing editor, 1964-65; Jewish Publication Society, Philadelphia, associate editor, 1965-66, editor-in-chief, 1966-74, special projects editor, 1974—. Instructor, University of Judaism, Los Angeles, 1957-59; visiting professor of philosophy, Bryn Mawr College, 1985, University of Pennsylvania, 1983, 1991—, and Johns Hopkins University, 1995—. Occasional commentator for National Public Radio. *Military service:* U. S. Army, chaplain in Korea, 1956-57; became first lieutenant. *Member:* Rabbinical Assembly, PEN, Authors Guild, Artists Equity.

Awards, Honors

National Book Award nomination for *The Chosen,* and Edward Lewis Wallant Prize, both 1967; Athenaeum Award, 1969, for *The Promise;* Professional and Scholarly Publishing Division special citation, AAP, 1984, for participating in the completion of the new translation of the Hebrew Bible; National Jewish Book Award, 1990, for *The Gift of Asher Lev;* National Foundation for Jewish Culture Achievement Award, 1997; O. Henry Short Story Prize, 1998; Books in the Middle: Outstanding Titles of 1998, *Voice of Youth Advocates,* 1999, and Best Books for Young Adults, American Library Association, 1999, both for *Zebra and Other Stories.*

Chaim Potok

Writings

FICTION

The Chosen, Simon & Schuster, 1967, Knopf, 1992.
The Promise (sequel to *The Chosen*), Knopf, 1969.
My Name Is Asher Lev, Knopf, 1972.
In the Beginning, Knopf, 1975.
The Book of Lights, Knopf, 1981.
Davita's Harp, Knopf, 1985.
The Gift of Asher Lev (sequel to *My Name Is Asher Lev*), Knopf, 1990.
I Am the Clay, Knopf, 1992.
Hanukkah Lights: Stories from the Festival of Lights, Dove, 1997.
Zebra and Other Stories (short stories), Knopf, 1998.

Hanukkah Lights was also produced on audiocassette by Dove Audio, 1996 and 1997.

NONFICTION

The Jew Confronts Himself in American Literature, Sacred Heart School of Theology, 1975.
Wanderings: Chaim Potok's History of the Jews, Knopf, 1978.
Ethical Living for a Modern World, Jewish Theological Seminary of America, 1985.
Tobiasse: Artist in Exile, Rizzoli, 1986.
The Gates of November: Chronicles of the Slepak Family, Knopf, 1996.

PLAYS

The Chosen (musical), first produced on Broadway at the Second Avenue Theatre, July 7, 1988, first produced as a drama in Philadelphia, PA, by the Arden Company, March 16, 1999.

Also author of *Sins of the Fathers* (two one-act plays), and *The Play of Lights*, both produced in Philadelphia at the Annenberg Theatre.

OTHER

The Tree of Here (picture book), illustrated by Tony Auth, Knopf, 1993.
The Sky of Now (picture book), illustrated by Auth, Knopf, 1995.
(Editor with Nahum M. Sarna) *JPS Torah Commentary*, Jewish Publication Society, 1996.

Contributor to *Jewish Ethics* (pamphlet series), Leaders Training Fellowship, 1964-69. Also contributor to *May My Words Feed Others*, edited by Chayym Zeldis, Barnes, 1974; *Literature and the Urban Experience*, edited by Michael C. Jaye and Ann C. Watts, Rutgers University Press, 1981; *From the Corners of the Earth*, by Bill Aron, Jewish Publication Society, 1985; *The Jews in America*, edited by David C. Cohen, Collins, 1989; *Tales of the Hasidim*, by Martin Buber, Pantheon, 1991; *A Worthy Use of Summer*, edited by Jenna Weissman Joselitt with Karen S. Mittelman, National Museum of American Jewish History, 1993; *Graven Images*, by Arnold Schwartzman, Abrams, 1993; and *I Never Saw Another Butterfly*, edited by Hana Volavkova, Pantheon, 1993. Contributor to periodicals, including *Ladies Home Journal, Commentary, American Judaism, Saturday Review, Kenyon Review, New York Times Book Review*, and *New York Times Sunday Magazine*.

Adaptations

The Chosen, a movie based on Potok's novel starring Maximilian Schell, Robby Benson, Rod Steiger, and Barry Miller, was produced by Twentieth Century-Fox, 1982.

Sidelights

Ordained rabbi Chaim Potok never saw himself in a traditional religious role. He has worked as a writer, rabbi, and professor, often concerning himself with Orthodox and Hasidic Jews and how they merge their beliefs with twentieth-century life. Robert J. Milch wrote in the *Saturday Review*: "Judaism [is] at the center of all [Potok's] works.... [It motivates] his characters and provid[es] the basis for their way of looking at themselves, each other, and the world." Potok has used his rabbinical training to invent a believable world often populated by highly educated Jewish leaders and students. Above all, the writer's "primary concern is the spiritual and intellectual growth of his characters—how and what they come to believe," observed Hugh Nissenson in the *New York Times Book Review*.

Some critics compare Potok to Sholom Aleichem, the turn-of-the-century Russian-Yiddish author of short stories and novels. The conflicts contained in Potok's books are cultural, religious, and scholarly. "That his novels have been best-sellers requires some explanation given the rather esoteric nature of his subject matter," commented Edward Abramson in *Chaim Potok*. "Many non-Jews think that the Jewish community is a homogeneous one with each member having substantially the same beliefs as the other." The critic further explained that "there is a wide divergence in the interpretation of law and ritual among Liberal, Reform, Conservative, Orthodox and Hasidic Jews."

Potok's father, Benjamin Max Potok, was born a Hasidic Jew in Poland when tensions were rising between Jewish and Gentile residents. (Hasidism, a sect originating in Poland in the eighteenth century, arose in reaction to growing Jewish formalism and heavy emphasis on scholarship. The Hasids formed tight communities that did not merge with the rest of society.) The elder Potok served in World War I, fighting in a Polish unit of the Austrian army despite the fact that most of the other soldiers were Gentiles. When his service was over, Benjamin came home to find a pogrom—an organized massacre of Jewish residents—decimating his community. Fortunately, Potok was able to leave Poland for the United States, eventually marrying and settling in New York City.

Chaim Potok grew up in a close-knit Jewish community in the Bronx. Life in the city was frequently hard and sometimes violent, notably toward the immigrant Jews. In addition, the Potok family also had to deal with the economic difficulties brought on by the Depression. Young Potok found happiness, however, in a variety of things. "There were books and classes and teachers; there were friends with whom I invented street games limited only by the boundaries of the imagination," Potok once wrote.

Art appealed to Potok from childhood. One summer, Potok's parochial school hired an artist to teach a painting class. Potok's father and teachers dissuaded the boy from the idea of pursuing art as a career (in large part because Hasids see art as a frivolous pursuit, or a rebellion against God). Potok commented: "Scholarship—especially Talmudic scholarship—is the measure of an individual. Fiction, even serious fiction—as far as the religious Jewish tradition is concerned—is at best a frivolity, at worst a menace." While Potok's parents generally disregarded their son's writing impulses, they nevertheless allowed him to write short pieces.

Potok attended an Orthodox Jewish day school, or yeshiva, where the studies included traditional Jewish writings. As Potok's biographer, Edward Abramson, explained, "This learning was largely restricted to discussion and study of the Talmud [which consists of civil, religious, and ethical laws based upon Jewish teaching and biblical interpretation, originally passed down orally over the ages from Israel's earliest history], a collection of sixty-three books usually set out in eighteen folio volumes."

Potok's high-school teachers assigned such traditional reading matter as *Ivanhoe* and *Treasure Island.* In 1945, however, Potok read with great enthusiasm *Brideshead Revisited,* Evelyn Waugh's popular story of early twentieth-century British upper-class life. After completing *Brideshead,* Potok decided to become a writer. "I remember finishing the book and marveling at the power of this kind of creativity," the author once wrote. As Potok told Abramson: "Somehow Evelyn Waugh reached across the chasm that separated my tight New York Jewish world from that of the upper-class British Catholics in his book.... From that time on, I not only read works of literature for enjoyment but also studied them with Talmudic intensity in order to teach myself how to create worlds out of words on paper.... In time I discovered that I had entered a tradition—modern literature."

Another important influence on Potok was James Joyce's *Portrait of the Artist as a Young Man.* The novel truly affected the young man's opinion of his place in the world. "Basic to [the novel] was ... the iconoclast, the individual who grows up inside inherited systems of value and [will not tolerate] ... the games, masks, arid hypocrisies he sees all around," Potok remarked.

As he grew older, Potok saw that his close religious community clashed with modern society in many areas. Potok wrote in *Literature and the Urban Experience* that he was "deep inside [the Jewish world], with a child's slowly increasing awareness of his own culture's richness and shortcomings.... [However] there was an echoing world that I longed to embrace.... It seemed to hold out at the same time the promise of worldly wisdom ... and ... the creations of the great minds of man."

Potok combined his interests in the religious and secular worlds by pursuing both Conservative Jewish and Gentile studies, receiving his bachelor's degree in English Literature from Orthodox Yeshiva University. Soon after, the author left Fundamentalist Judaism to adopt Conservatism—a decision he made with great difficulty. Nevertheless, Potok needed to find new fields of knowledge that could intertwine with his religious beliefs, and such knowledge turned up in the commentaries and methods of Gentile critics. "It was just this ... that made it possible for him to achieve a reconciliation with Judaism," Edward Abramson noted. Potok remarked in *Chaim Potok:* "The problems that troubled me [were] resolved by ... the scientific approach to the sacred texts of Judaism.... They give the sources a form, a vitality which is impossible within a fundamentalist stance."

Potok eventually attended the Jewish Theological Seminary in New York City. His seminary work led to Potok's ordination as a Conservative rabbi in 1954. As a young rabbi, Potok traveled to the Far East immediately after the Korean War. Once there, he served in the United States Army with first a medical, then a combat engineers, battalion. Potok's experiences in the Orient upset all his former convictions concerning civilization and religion. "In the shattered villages of Korea ... in the teeming Chinese hovels of Hong Kong, in the vile back streets of Macao, all the neat antique coherence of my past came undone," he once explained. "It was not the anguish of my own people that sundered me ... but the loveliness and the suffering I saw in the lives of pagans." Soon after, the author drew on his Korean experiences for his first novel.

In 1958, Potok married Adena Mosevitzky; he also finished and submitted his Korean novel, but publishers rejected it (most claimed the work lacked commercial value). Potok began a second novel despite the failure of the first. Soon after his daughter Rena was born, the author and his family moved to Israel where Potok wrote his doctoral dissertation; he also worked on the first draft of his second novel. Upon returning to the States, the Potok family settled in Brooklyn, and Potok went back to the Jewish Theological Seminary, now as a member of the Teachers' Institute. At about the same time, he took a position at *Conservative Judaism,* work which ultimately led to his position as managing editor. In 1965, Potok's daughter Naama was born, and the author received his doctorate in philosophy from the University of Pennsylvania; he also wrote a series of pamphlets under the umbrella title *Jewish Ethics* for the Leaders Training Fellowship and became editor at the Jewish Publication Society. (Much of Potok's long-term work with the Society involved the translation of the Hebrew Bible into English.)

It wasn't until 1965 that Potok completed his best-selling second novel, *The Chosen.* The book explores the conflict between the world of the Hasidim and that of Orthodox Jews. In the *Dictionary of Literary Biography,* S. Lillian Kremer explained that "The Crown Heights-Williamsburg section of Brooklyn, an area heavily populated by Jews, is the setting for a drama of religious commitment.... Potok's descriptive and dramatic portrayal of scholarly endeavor brings new depth and breadth to American-Jewish fiction." Kremer also commented that the novel "captures the joy and intensity of Talmudic learning."

The two main characters in *The Chosen* are Reuven Malter, son of a progressive Talmudic scholar, and Danny Saunders, heir-apparent to the position of Zaddik, or spiritual leader, of the Hasidic community. A *Commentary* reviewer explained further: "Hasidism is hardly intelligible without ... the Zaddik, the spiritual superman whose holy living not only provides ... [i]nspiration for [his followers] lives' but who raises them aloft with him through [his] spiritual powers.... The Zaddik's prayer on behalf of his followers can achieve results far beyond the scope of their own puny efforts at prayer." Two forces run at odds in Danny's life: the encouragement of his Conservative tutor—Reuven's father, who guides the boy's intellectual growth—and Reb Saunders's tightly proscribed rules for his heir. Saunders has brought Danny up in a world of silence, where the only conversations occur during discussions of Scripture.

One of Potok's strong points in fashioning *The Chosen* is his explanation of Talmudic scholarship. "The elder Malter, patterned after the novelist's beloved father-in-law ... is the idealized Jewish teacher," wrote Kremer. "Just as he fuses the best in Judaic scholarship with the best in secular culture, Reuven combines intellectual excellence in sacred and secular studies."

In 1969, the author completed *The Promise,* a sequel to *The Chosen.* Reuven prepares to become a rabbi, but clashes with apostate scholar Abraham Gordon. Simultaneously Danny—now a student of clinical psychology—treats young Michael Gordon, the scholar's disturbed son. The family achieves unity, however, through Danny Saunders's betrothal and marriage to Rachel Gordon, his young patient's sister. The book's theme, said Kremer, focuses on how "each character defines himself, understands himself, and celebrates himself as a twentieth-century Jew." In the *New York Times Book Review,* Nissenson wrote that "despite an occasional technical lapse, Potok has demonstrated his ability to deal with a more complex conception and to suffuse it with pertinence and vitality."

My Name Is Asher Lev concerns a Hasidic artist. As in his earlier books, Potok relates Asher's experiences in the first person. Asher's story is "the mature artist's retrospective portrait of his childhood [and] a reexamination of his attitudes," wrote Kremer. Asher's parents dislike his interest in art, often scolding him for his apathy towards Biblical scholarship. Asher often dreams of his deceased grandfather, a noted scholar. In the dreams, his grandfather condemns Asher for his devotion to art. Some members of the Hasidic community even consider Asher's gifts demonic, but the Rebbe—who leads the community and also employs Asher's father—unexpectedly champions the boy.

Asher's goal is "to develop his aesthetic sense through painting," observed Abramson in *Chaim Potok.* Like Danny Saunders, Asher is born into the role of heir-apparent. In the latter case, Asher's future position entails working as an international emissary for the Rebbe. The tumult over Asher's studies increases when he begins to paint nudes and crucifixions. Although Asher sees the cross as a non-religious symbol, his father sees it as a figure for anti-Semitism. The crisis comes to a head over Asher's painting, the "Brooklyn Crucifixion." Eventually, Asher must choose between his community and his painting.

In 1973, Potok and his family left the United States to live in Jerusalem. Two years later, he published his next work entitled *In the Beginning.* As with many of his other novels, *In the Beginning* deals with anti-Semitism. "Rarely has the rage of the Jew been so honestly portrayed," remarked Nissenson, who added that "by the power of his own intellect [Potok comes] to grips with the theme implicit in all of his previous work: the problem of sustaining religious faith in a meaningless world.... It successfully recreates a time and a place and the journey of a soul." The author goes beyond America's treatment of Jews and looks at its historical precedence.

In the Beginning focuses on the relationship between David Lurie, a Jewish boy, and Eddie Kulanski, a Gentile. Other main themes in the work revolve around Biblical scholarship and the State of Israel. "The narrator here is a brilliantly gifted Orthodox Jewish boy who eventually accommodates himself to modern life," explained Nissenson. Through David, Potok uses stream-of-consciousness writing to depict the tragedies endured by the Jews in Europe. When David hears of the losses sustained by Jews during World War II, he enters a dreamland where an imaginary hero fights Nazi oppressors. David deeply loves the Torah, and sees it as a symbol of hope for all Jews. He alienates his family, however, when he adopts the shocking belief that using Gentile scholarship will bridge the gulf separating Jew and Gentile.

A *Time* reviewer writes that *In the Beginning* makes the reader "wholly aware of what it must have been like to belong to such a family and such a religion at such a time. Conveying vividly the exact feel of unfamiliar territory is a job almost exclusively performed by journalists.... That novels can accomplish that task superlatively is one of the reasons why they are still written—and read." Michael Irwin, writing in the *Times Literary Supplement,* noted that Potok "catches beautifully the atmosphere of a family party or a school quarrel. Rarer than this is the skill with which he shows how what a child learns and what it experiences are fused and transformed by the imagination." Daphne Merkin stated in *Commentary* that while Potok tends to stick to "fertile Jewish territory," he has hit "a formula for success ... in which the only limits to artistic achievement are the limits of his own imagination." She also noted, however, that "Potok's rendition of Orthodox life is entertaining and informative, but his work does not expand to the dimensions it reaches for."

In 1978, the author saw publication of the nonfiction work *Wanderings: Chaim Potok's History of the Jews.* In *The Christian Science Monitor,* Michael J. Bandler described the book: "Using hundreds of eminent sources and texts in several languages ... [Potok] has fashioned an intelligent, thorough and credible one-volume chronicle that breathes with a passion that is more common to fiction than history.... It should be savored, scene by provocative scene, mulled over and retained." A *Maclean's* contributor mentioned a different consideration: "Behind Potok's account of the Jewish struggle to stay alive ... is [his] own moral search: to understand how a people managed to survive both the seduction of comfort ... [and] diabolical tortures ... to remain Jews."

Three years later, Potok finished *The Book of Lights.* Steeped in the Jewish mysticism of the Kabbalah and full of moral decisions fraught with anguish, the work marked a new departure for the author. Johanna Kaplan, writing in the *New York Times Book Review,* called the novel "The story of [a] dark and baffling inner journey." *The Book of Lights* tackles the subject of moral responsibility and the atom bomb, a dilemma epitomized by the characters Gershon Loran and Arthur Leiden. In the novel, Potok's characters work to incorporate their faith with a secular society. The book culminates in Jerusalem, where Gershon works to resolve his spiritual dilemmas.

Much of the impetus for Potok's sixth work of fiction, *Davita's Harp,* was an experience of sexism his wife suffered while in her teens. The novel takes place in Depression-era New York. Both of Davita's parents— her Protestant newspaperman father and Jewish mother—have abandoned religious beliefs for communism. Seeking security, the girl explores Judaism and attends a yeshiva. Once there, Davita discovers a prejudice against female scholars; when she makes top marks, the young girl is denied a highly coveted school award because she is female. "Davita's commitment to patriarchal Judaism is deeply shaken at her graduation," explained Patty Campbell in *Wilson Library Bulletin.* The school gives the Akiva award "to a boy to save the school the public shame of a girl as best student," Campbell noted. Critics praised the book's use of commonplace items to establish the setting. "The idealistic underworld of American communism in the thirties leaps out in evocative details," remarked Campbell.

Toward the end of the decade, Potok rewrote *The Chosen* as a musical. Potok felt the time-consuming project was worthwhile, even though it took over a year. As he told Mervyn Rothstein of the *New York Times,* it appeared "that there was potentiality for seriousness

here." Simultaneously, Potok felt that "it didn't have to be heavy-handed, because the novel itself is not heavy-handed." In theater script, Potok centered on "a sense of the way a particular core culture confronts the world outside, and the dimensions of that confrontation," Rothstein reported. Many theater critics, however, found the production disappointing. *New York Times* contributor Mel Gussow noted that "the relationship between Reuven and Danny moves perilously close to a love that dare not speak its name ... one that would clearly contradict the author's intent."

As a sequel to *My Name Is Asher Lev,* Potok wrote *The Gift of Asher Lev.* The author picks up the narrative many years after the first book. Lev has left New York and the Hasidic world to live with his family on the Côte d'Azur. A funeral brings the Lev family back to Asher's old home. Matters become complicated when Lev's wife and son prefer the tight-knit Hasidic community to life on the Mediterranean. In the end, Lev's father resolves the conflict. As the elderly Rebbe's successor, Lev's father turns his attention to Asher's son, Avrumel. The older man decides that Avrumel shall take his father's place and continue the dynasty. The sad conclusion is that "the price of Lev's restoration to his people is his physical and personal exclusion," noted Brian Morton in the *Times Literary Supplement.* "Much as Christ was a sacrificed 'missing generation' between God and mankind, Lev's self-sacrificing art is a personal crucifixion.... [it also guarantees] that the tradition will pass on."

In 1993, *The Tree of Here,* Potok's first picture book for young children, appeared. Jason—the book's main character—finds his life shaken when his parents plan to move. The boy believes he sees a face in the craggy bark of the large tree that grows in his backyard and concludes that the tree listens to him. In turn, Jason trusts the tree to whisper its own "secret feelings." Wanting to ease Jason's unhappiness, a gardener gives him a dogwood sapling to plant at his new home.

Potok also completed a second picture book for young readers, *The Sky of Now,* in 1995. In this work, almost ten-year-old Brian relates his fear of heights during a visit to the Statue of Liberty. When his uncle gives him a ceramic statue of a pilot, and later, a ride over New York City in a glider for his birthday, Brian's fear surfaces once again. By using his imagination, however, Brian overcomes his anxiety and enjoys his uncle's special present. *Booklist* contributor Julie Corsaro called the work "well-crafted," containing an "eloquently expressed story line."

In *Zebra and Other Stories,* Potok's 1998 collection of six short tales, the author tackled another age group— young adults. Each story features a teenage protagonist in transition, like B. B., whose father leaves the family the same day the teen's mother goes into labor; or Isabel, whose widowed mother marries a widowed man with a daughter the same age as she. "All the stories are thought-provoking and gripping," wrote Susan Scheps in *School Library Journal.* "The characters and their personal dilemmas" added the reviewer, "will linger with readers."

In her *Dictionary of Literary Biography* essay, Kremer summarized the general response to Potok's body of work by noting that the criticism "ranged from denunciation to acclaim." Some critics have called the author's approach, plots, and characters narrow and dry, pointing to a sometimes labored style and pompous narrative tone; these reviewers also write that Potok's brilliant theology students often seem too good to be true. Other assessors, however, note the author's thoughtful, careful deliberation of important issues. Potok has likewise received praise for his piercing visions into Orthodox Jewish life and culture. (By comparison, many contemporary Jewish authors appear topical in their treatment of the variety of Jewish experience.)

Overall, Potok sees as his mission to bring meaning to a nonsensical world. He once commented that doing this "specifically ... is the task of the artist." In his interview with Rothstein, Potok clarified, "You deal with a small and particular world.... You dig into that world with as much honesty as you can, and if you do it honestly and skillfully enough, somehow you're going to bridge the gap."

Works Cited

Abramson, Edward A., *Chaim Potok*, Twayne, 1986.

Bandler, Michael J., "Faith's Long Journey," *Christian Science Monitor*, December 16, 1969, p. 13.

Campbell, Patty, review of *Davita's Harp, Wilson Library Bulletin*, June, 1985, pp. 688-89.

Review of *The Chosen, Commentary*, September, 1967, p. 107.

Corsaro, Julie, review of *The Sky of Now, Booklist*, January 1, 1996, p. 848.

Gussow, Mel, "Theater: *The Chosen* As a Musical," *New York Times*, January 7, 1988.

Review of *In the Beginning, Time*, November 3, 1975, p. 94.

Irwin, Michael, "A Full-Time Condition," *Times Literary Supplement*, April 9, 1976, p. 413.

Kaplan, Johanna, "Two Ways of Life," *New York Times Book Review*, October 11, 1981, pp. 14-15, 28.

Kremer, S. Lillian, "Chaim Potok," *Dictionary of Literary Biography*, Volume 28: *Twentieth-Century American-Jewish Fiction Writers*, Gale, 1984, pp. 232-43.

Merkin, Daphne, "Why Potok Is Popular," *Commentary*, February, 1976, pp. 73-75.

Milch, Robert J., review of *My Name Is Asher Lev, Saturday Review*, April 15, 1972, pp. 65-66.

Morton, Brian, "Banished and Banished Again," *Times Literary Supplement*, November 2, 1990.

Nissenson, Hugh, "My Name Is David Lurie," *New York Times Book Review*, October 19, 1975.

Nissenson, review of *The Promise, New York Times Book Review*, September 14, 1969.

Nissenson, "The Spark and the Shell," *New York Times Book Review*, May 7, 1967, pp. 4-5, 34.

Potok, Chaim, essay in *Literature and Urban Experience: Essays on the City and Literature*, edited by M. C. Jaye and A. C. Watts, Rutgers University Press, 1981.

Rothstein, Mervyn, "Crafting a Musical from *The Chosen*," *New York Times*, January 3, 1988.

Scheps, Susan, review of *Zebra and Other Stories, School Library Journal*, September, 1998, p. 208.

Review of *Wanderings: Chaim Potok's History of the Jews, Maclean's*, January 1, 1979, p. 47.

For More Information See

BOOKS

Authors in the News, Gale, Volume 1, 1976, Volume 2, 1976.

Contemporary Literary Criticism, Gale, Volume 2, 1974, Volume 7, 1977, Volume 14, 1980, Volume 26, 1983, Volume 112, 1999.

Dictionary of Literary Biography Yearbook: 1984, Gale, 1985.

PERIODICALS

Booklist, February 1, 1990, p. 1050; April 1, 1992, p. 1413; November 1, 1996, p. 480.

Kirkus Reviews, April 1, 1992, p. 423; September 15, 1996, p. 1383.

New York Times, December 1, 1996, p. 33.

Publishers Weekly, March 30, 1992, p. 89; November 27, 1995, p. 69; July 20, 1998, p. 222.

School Library Journal, October, 1993, p. 108.

*   *   *

PRIOR, Natalie Jane 1963-

Personal

Born November 10, 1963, in Brisbane, Australia; married, husband's name Peter. *Education:* University of Queensland, graduated, 1984. *Hobbies and other interests:* Reading, gardening, going to the theatre.

Addresses

Home—Brisbane, Australia. *Agent*—c/o Margaret Connolly and Associates, P.O. Box 945, Wahroonga, New South Wales, 2076, Australia.

Career

Writer. Has also worked as a librarian.

Awards, Honors

Honour Book, Picture Book of the Year Award, Children's Book Council of Australia, 1994, for *The Paw;* shortlisted for Eve Pownall Award, 1995; shortlisted for numerous other writing awards.

Writings

The Amazing Adventures of Amabel, Allen & Unwin (St. Leonards, Australia), 1990.

Amabel Abroad—More Amazing Adventures, Allen & Unwin, 1991.

The Paw, illustrated by Terry Denton, Allen & Unwin, 1993.

Bog Bodies, Mummies and Curious Corpses, Allen & Unwin, 1994.

Mysterious Ruins: Lost Cities and Buried Treasure, Allen & Unwin, 1994.

Dance Crazy: Star Turns from Ballet to Belly Dancing, Allen & Unwin, 1995.

Yesterday's Heroes, University of Queensland Press, 1995.

Tasha's Witch, University of Queensland Press, 1995.

The Paw in Destination: Brazil, illustrated by Terry Denton, Allen & Unwin, 1995.

The Demidenko Diary, Mandarin (Port Melbourne, Australia), 1996.

Caves, Graves and Catacombs: Secrets from Beneath the Earth, Allen & Unwin, 1996.

West End Shuffle, University of Queensland Press, 1996.

London Calling, University of Queensland Press, 1997.

The Loft, Hodder Headline (Sydney, Australia), 1997.

Cleopatra, Last Queen of Egypt: An Extraordinary Life, Omnibus Books (Norwood, South Australia), 1998.

Nero, Evil Emperor of Rome: An X-rated Extraordinary Life, Omnibus Books, 1998.

The Paw in the Purple Diamond!, illustrated by Terry Denton, Hodder, 1998.

Lily Puench, Hodder, 1999.

Contributor of short story "Collecting the Mail" to the anthology *Nightmares in Paradise,* edited by Robyn Sheahan, University of Queensland Press.

Sidelights

Australian novelist Natalie Jane Prior specializes in writing fiction and nonfiction for children and young adults. Three of her books for primary graders, *The Paw, The Paw in Destination: Brazil,* and *The Paw in the Purple Diamond!,* feature Leonie, a schoolgirl by day and a cat burglar by night. Dubbed the "Paw" because she carries out her capers in a loose-fitting cat costume, Leonie is a latter-day Robin Hood, stealing caviar from the rich and feeding it to stray cats. "Leonie is a cross between [Maurice] Sendak's Max and [Louise] Fitz-hugh's Harriet the Spy as she slinks through her nocturnal outings boldly and mischievously," asserted Heather McCammond-Watts of the *Bulletin of the Center for Children's Books. The Paw in Destination: Brazil* features an ecological theme, as Leonie travels to Brazil to foil the plot of villains scheming to capture the world's last sabre-toothed puma. "The Paw is back," enthused Jo Goodman of *Magpies* in a review of the story, "to the delight of everyone except those humourless police chiefs who objected so persistently to her first adventure." Goodman also praised illustrator Terry Denton's pictures, asserting: "Prior and Denton have done it again!"

For adolescent readers, Prior has written two books about Amabel, an adventurer. Part spoof and part adventure yarn, *The Amazing Adventures of Amabel* and *Amabel Abroad—More Amazing Adventures* take the

Natalie Jane Prior's book of stories and anecdotes about dance describes how a ballet company operates; relates tales of famous dancers; and discusses dance fashion, spirited and magical dances, and other related topics. (Cover photo by Jeff Busby.)

eponymous heroine on a series of quests, including a search for the Great White shark in the first book and for the Loch Ness monster in the latter story. Don Matthews, reviewing the earlier title in *Magpies,* called it a "very talented little book," adding that the story and language are demanding but "certainly an interesting challenge." *Magpies* contributor Neil Mackenzie, reviewing *Amabel Abroad,* asserted: "This is an entertaining novel-cum-diary of Amabel and her will to experience the new and unusual."

For older students Prior has written more conventional novels, among them *Yesterday's Heroes, West End Shuffle,* and *London Calling. Yesterday's Heroes* is a coming-of-age tale about Marie, a normal teen trying to cope with life as her parents rehearse for a comeback tour of the rock band they were members of in their youth. "Natalie Jane Prior has got a lot of things right in this contemporary novel," maintained Carmel Ballinger, writing in *Magpies*. Ballinger called *Yesterday's Heroes* a "satisfying novel ... with a believable set of characters and a familiar setting," and praised Prior for "a wonderful control of dialogue resulting in an accurate portrayal of teenagers' speech and attitudes." *West End Shuffle* incorporates some of the same characters as *Yesterday's Heroes,* but this time the narrative focuses on Marie's friend Carmen as she copes with her first love. Prior followed *West End Shuffle* with *London Calling,* in which Carmen, whose father has recently died, decides to pursue her dream of performing in a musical on the London stage.

Prior has also penned a number of nonfiction studies for children. These include such efforts as *Bog Bodies, Mummies and Curious Corpses, Mysterious Ruins: Lost Cities and Buried Treasure, Dance Crazy: Star Turns from Ballet to Belly Dancing,* and *Caves, Graves and Catacombs: Secrets from Beneath the Earth.* Reviewing *Caves, Graves and Catacombs* in *Kliatt,* Barbara Jo McKee maintained that Prior's collection of "strange but true stories," such as the poet Dante Rossetti having had his wife's grave opened to recover some poetry he had written, will "fascinate almost anyone." *Dance Crazy,* a book of stories and anecdotes written in similar format, describes how a ballet company operates, relates stories of famous dancers, and offers "a motley collection of information about such things as belly dancing, dancing fashions over the centuries, the birth of the Australian ballet, and magical dance, which amongst other things mentions Aboriginal secret dancing," noted reviewer Anne Hanzl in *Magpies*. Hanzl added: "The chatty writing style and interesting stories and information makes this a book that most young readers with an interest in dance would enjoy dipping into."

Prior has also written a memoir, *The Demidenko Diary,* about her part in an Australian literary scandal. Writer Helen Demidenko achieved fame for her prize-winning autobiographical account *The Hand That Signed the Paper,* detailing her parents' war crimes during World War II in the Ukraine. However, it was eventually revealed that the events in the book never happened. Helen Demidenko's real name turned out to be Helen Darville and she had made up the personae from which she wrote the book. Prior had known Helen as Helen Demidenko back in high school. When her secret was uncovered, Helen came to Prior for emotional support. Prior's theory is that Helen Darville actually believed she *was* Helen Demidenko. Peter Craven wrote in the *Australian Book Review* that "the story Prior tells is riveting."

Works Cited

Ballinger, Carmel, review of *Yesterday's Heroes, Magpies,* September, 1995, p. 33.

Craven, Peter, "A Kind of Boswell," *Australian Book Review,* February-March, 1996, pp. 14-17.

Goodman, Jo, review of *The Paw in Destination: Brazil, Magpies,* September, 1995, p. 27.

Hanzl, Anne, review of *Dance Crazy: Star Turns from Ballet to Belly Dancing, Magpies,* March, 1996, pp. 42-43.

Mackenzie, Neil, review of *Amabel Abroad—More Amazing Adventures, Magpies,* March, 1993, p. 31.

Matthews, Don, review of *The Amazing Adventures of Amabel, Magpies,* May, 1991, p. 32.

McCammond-Watts, Heather, review of *The Paw, Bulletin of the Center for Children's Books,* September, 1995, pp. 25-26.

McKee, Barbara Jo, review of *Caves, Graves and Catacombs: Secrets Beneath the Earth, Kliatt,* September, 1997, p. 39.

For More Information See

PERIODICALS

Australian Book Review, June, 1996, pp. 60-61; June, 1997, p. 59.

Magpies, July 1993, p. 23; March, 1994, p. 28; March 1996, pp. 42-43.

OTHER

The Paw Page, http://www.home.gil.com.au/~dragon/paw-main.html (April 30, 1998).

*   *   *

PUTNAM, Peter B(rock) 1920-1998

OBITUARY NOTICE—See index for *SATA* sketch: Born June 11, 1920, in Fort Ogelthorpe, GA; died of lymphoma, September 23, 1998, in Princeton, NJ. Educator, executive in nonprofit organizations, author. Putnam found his life's calling when a suicide attempt at the age of twenty left him alive but blind. He went on to complete his bachelor's degree at Princeton University, where he had been studying, and received a doctorate in Russian literature from the same institution in 1950. He taught history at Princeton from 1944 until 1955, and spent the remainder of his career writing and working for various nonprofit organizations, including the Unitarian Universalist Association, Recording for the Blind, the Princeton Alumni Council, and many others. Although he published several works of Russian history, Putnam's best known writings are his two volumes of autobiography, *Keep Your Head Up, Mr. Putnam!,* published in 1952, and *Cast off the Darkness,* which was published by Harcourt in 1957. Putnam also penned two works of nonfiction for younger readers: *The Triumph of the Seeing Eye* (1963) and *Peter, The Revolutionary Tsar* (1973), although the latter, which Putnam once described as an attempt to explain Peter and his period "from the ground up," was categorized with a juvenile label that the author felt had "restricted readership needlessly."

OBITUARIES AND OTHER SOURCES:

PERIODICALS

New York Times, September 28, 1998, p. B7.

R

REGER, James P. 1952-

Personal

Born June 2, 1952, in Buckhannon, WV; son of Robert H. (a salesman) and Gwen (a homemaker; maiden name, Finlayson) Reger; married Pamela Gray (a hospital administrator), May 21, 1983; children: Grayson William. *Education:* West Virginia University, B.A. in psychology (magna cum laude), 1975; National University, M.A. in education, 1990. *Politics:* Democrat. *Religion:* Protestant. *Hobbies and other interests:* History, books, computers, travelling, reenacting military eras, collecting military miniatures.

James P. Reger

Addresses

Home—4703 Caminito Eva, San Diego, CA 92130.

Career

Special education teacher, San Diego, CA, 1985—.

Writings

FOR YOUNG ADULTS; NONFICTION

The Battle of Antietam, Lucent, 1997.
Life in the South during the Civil War, Lucent, 1997.
The Rebuilding of Bosnia, Lucent, 1997.
Life among the Indian Fighters, Lucent, 1998.
Civil War Generals of the Confederacy, Lucent, 1999.

Work in Progress

When War Was Glory, "historical fiction set in the early months of the American Civil War (Fort Sumter through the First [battle of] Manassas)"; research on the early American Civil War.

Sidelights

James P. Reger told *SATA:* "I hail from a West Virginia family whose history parallels that of America itself. Delaware Indians captured one of my ancestors as a young girl and hatcheted her mother to death before her eyes. The girl lived with the Indians in Ohio as a slave 'wife' until released by treaty several years later, whereupon she married a member of George Washington's Continental Army. A roadside marker outside of my hometown, Buckhannon, commemorates the deeds of another ancestor, a professional Indian scout who ran one hundred twenty-five miles in just twenty-four hours to warn the settlement of an impending Indian attack and then set up an ambush that routed the attackers.

"During the Civil War, my great-grandfather rode with Confederate cavalry legend J. E. B. Stuart; another relative fought with 'Stonewall' Jackson's Southern infantry. Still another, an older civilian incarcerated for espousing his secessionist views to a Unionist crowd, died in a Northern prison camp. One grandfather, a Scottish immigrant, wrote books; the other coursed the wilderness as a lumberjack. My father and mother survived the Great Depression. My father survived the European Theater of World War II. One of my three older brothers did not survive Vietnam.

"Against this backdrop, I grew up listening to ancestral lore passed down by parents and grandparents whose own parents and grandparents had either lived through or heard from their parents and grandparents true and thrilling adventure stories ranging through all the epochs of American history: Colonial, Revolutionary, pioneer, Civil War, Reconstruction, World War I, the Depression, World War II, and Vietnam. I heard firsthand and up-close how Americans met their challenges, their hardships, and, in most cases, survived them.

"For this reason, and certainly others, I have long immersed myself in reading, writing, and, whenever possible, reliving history. I have reenacted and performed living history portrayals as a Revolutionary soldier, an Indian fighter, Confederate and Union soldier, and many more. I subscribe to the notion that truth is not only stranger than fiction but infinitely more exciting as well.

"I share my passion for writing history with a passion for teaching it. I now reside in San Diego, California, where I enjoy my third great passion: my wife and young son."

Reger has written several histories for young adult readers that have garnered praise for a lively narrative style that draws readers by focusing on details of the daily lives of ordinary people. In his first book, *The Battle of Antietam,* which covers one of the most famous battles of the American Civil War, Reger opens with a brief account of the causes of the war and the events leading up to the battle. He then focuses on various actions within the battle, specifically those occurring on September 17, 1862, the day of the most intense fighting. Sidebars report the activities of Captain Oliver Wendell Holmes, Jr., who later became a justice of the Supreme Court, William McKinley, who later became president of the United States, and other participants of historical interest. "These human-interest stories bring this episode alive," observed Elizabeth M. Reardon in a *School Library Journal* review. Reardon also praised Reger's text as "well written and easy to follow."

Reger's next book, *Life in the South during the Civil War,* begins with an account of the rich, planter class, incorporating material from letters and journals of the era to provide information about the everyday lives of those comprising this Southern society. He then concentrates on the Southern middle classes, who formed the primary part of the Confederate forces, and whose lives contrasted greatly with those of the wealthy planters. "On the whole, a balanced account of life before Reconstruction that should fill a gap in many collec-

tions," Reardon declared in another *School Library Journal* review.

Reger shifts his focus to the twentieth century in his third book, *The Rebuilding of Bosnia,* in which he "provides a lucid account of the Yugoslav War and the peace process," according to Elizabeth Talbot in *School Library Journal.* The author opens with an account of the shocking murder of a teenage couple, one of the young people an Orthodox Serb and the other a Bosnian Muslim. Reger then backtracks to introduce the context of this incident, surveying fifteen hundred years of conflict, the peace process of the 1990s, and the work of recovering from this latest outbreak of hostilities in the Balkan peninsula. Throughout, "Reger delivers a lively, carefully balanced, vividly written account of the recent war in Bosnia," asserted *Booklist* commentator John Peters.

Works Cited

Peters, John, review of *The Rebuilding of Bosnia, Booklist,* September 1, 1997, p. 104.

Reardon, Elizabeth M., review of *Life in the South during the Civil War, School Library Journal,* March, 1997, p. 207.

Reardon, Elizabeth M., review of *The Battle of Antietam, School Library Journal,* July, 1997, p. 111.

Talbot, Elizabeth, review of *The Rebuilding of Bosnia, School Library Journal,* August, 1997, p. 174.

*   *   *

RESNICK, Michael D(iamond) 1942-
(Mike Resnick)

Personal

Born March 5, 1942, in Chicago, IL; son of William (a salesman) and Gertrude (a writer; maiden name, Diamond) Resnick; married Carol L. Cain (a writer and kennel owner), October 2, 1961; children: Laura L. *Education:* Attended University of Chicago, 1959-61, and Roosevelt University, 1962-63. *Politics:* Independent. *Hobbies and other interests:* Travel, reading, Africana, breeding and exhibiting purebred collies.

Addresses

Home and office—10547 Tanager Hills Dr., Cincinnati, OH 45249. *Agent*—Spectrum Literary Agency, 111 East 8th Ave., Suite 1501, New York, NY 10011. *Electronic mail*—Resnick@delphi.com.

Career

Full-time freelance writer, 1966—. Santa Fe Railroad, Chicago, IL, file clerk, 1962-65; National Features Syndicate, Chicago, editor of *National Tattler,* 1965-66, and *National Insider,* 1966-69; Oligarch Publishing, Libertyville, IL, editor and publisher, 1969-70; *Collie Cues Magazine,* Hayward, CA, columnist, 1969-80; Briarwood Pet Motel, Cincinnati, OH, co-owner with wife, 1976—. *Speculations,* columnist, 1975—; *Magazine of Fantasy and Science Fiction,* columnist, 1997-98, Science Fiction and Fantasy Writers of America (SFWA) *Bulletin,* columnist, 1998—. *Member:* Science Fiction Writers of America.

Awards, Honors

Best Short Fiction award, American Dog Writers Association, 1978, for "The Last Dog," and 1979, for "Blue"; Browning Award finalist for Best SF Humorist, 1993 and 1994; Hugo Award nominations for best editor, 1994 and 1995; Hugo Awards for best short story, for "Kirinyaga," "The Manamouki," "Seven Views of Olduvai Gorge," and "The 43 Antarean Dynasties"; Hugo Award nominations for "For I Have Touched the Sky," *Bully!,* "Winter Solstice," "One Perfect Morning, with Jackals," "The Lotus and the Spear," "Mwalimu in the Squared Circle," "Barnaby in Exile," "A Little Knowledge," "Bibi," "When the Old Gods Die," and "The Land of Nod"; Nebula Award for "Seven Views of Olduvai Gorge"; Nebula nominations for "Kirinyaga," "For I Have Touched the Sky," *Ivory,* "The Manamouki," *Bully!,* "Bibi," and "When the Old Gods Die"; Skylark Award for Lifetime Achievement in Science Fiction; HOMer Awards for "The Manamouki," "Song

of a Dry River," "Mwalimu in the Squared Circle," "Seven Views of Olduvai Gorge," "Bibi" and "When the Old Gods Die"; HOMer nominations for *Bully!,* "Bwana," "How I Wrote the New Testament, Brought Forth the Renaissance, and Birdied the 17th Hole at Pebble Beach," *Oracle,* "The Lotus and the Spear," *Purgatory,* "The Pale Thin God," "Birdie," "Barnaby in Exile," *A Miracle of Rare Design,* and "A Little Knowledge"; *SF Chronicle* Poll awards for "Kirinyaga," "For I Have Touched the Sky," *Bully!,* "The Manamouki," "Seven Views of Olduvai Gorge," and "Bibi"; Universitat Politecnica de Catalunya Novella Contest winner for "Seven Views of Olduvai Gorge"; Hayakawa SF award (Japan), for "For I Have Touched the Sky"; Hayakawa SF award finalist for "Song of a Dry River," "Posttime in Pink," and "Kirinyaga"; Alexander Award, AT&T, for "Winter Solstice"; Golden Pagoda Award for "The Manamouki"; Clarke nomination (England) for *Ivory;* Ignotus Award (Spain) for "Seven Views of Olduvai Gorge"; Futura Poll Winner (Croatia), for "Seven Views of Olduvai Gorge"; Nowa Fantastyka Poll Winner (Poland) for "Kirinyaga"; SFinks Award (Poland) for "For I Have Touched the Sky" and "When the Old Gods Die"; Seiun-Sho nomination (Japan) for "For I Have Touched the Sky," "Bwana," *Ivory,* "Posttime in Pink," and *Santiago; Locus* Poll Winner for "When the Old Gods Die"; Science Fiction Weekly Poll Winner for "When the Old Gods Die" and "The 43 Antarean Dynasties"; Asimov's Readers Poll Winner for "The 43 Antarean Dynasties"; Year's Best SF Anthology awards for "Kirinyaga," "For I Have Touched the Sky," "Mwalimu in the Squared Circle," "Seven Views of Olduvai Gorge," "The Land of Nod," and "One Perfect Morning, with Jackals."

Writings

SCIENCE FICTION

The Forgotten Sea of Mars (novella), Camille E. Cazedessus, Jr. (Baton Rouge, LA), 1965.
The Goddess of Ganymede, illustrated by Neal MacDonald, Jr., Grant (West Kingston, RI), 1967.
Pursuit of Ganymede, Paperback Library (New York City), 1968.
Redbeard, Lancer (New York City), 1969.
(With Glen A. Larson) *Battlestar Galactica Number Five: Galactica Discovers Earth,* Berkley, 1980.
The Soul Eater, Signet, 1981.
Birthright: The Book of Man, Signet, 1982.
Walpurgis III, Signet, 1982.
The Branch, Signet, 1984.
Adventures, Signet, 1985.
Santiago: A Myth of the Far Future, Tor, 1986.
Stalking the Unicorn: A Fable of Tonight, Tor, 1987.
The Dark Lady: A Romance of the Far Future, Tor, 1987.
Ivory: A Legend of Past and Future, Tor, 1988.
Paradise: A Chronicle of a Distant World, Tor, 1989.
Second Contact, Tor, 1990.
Through Darkest Resnick with Gun and Camera, Washington Science Fiction Association, 1990.
Bully!, illustration by George Barr, Axolotl Press, 1990.

Michael D. Resnick

(With Jack L. Chalker and George Alec Effinger) *The Red Tape War,* Tor, 1991.

Bwana [and] *Bully!* (two novellas), Tor, 1991.

Stalking the Wild Resnick, NESFA, 1991.

Will the Last Person to Leave the Planet Please Shut Off the Sun?, Tor, 1992.

Lucifer Jones, Warner/Questar, 1992.

Purgatory: A Chronicle of a Distant World, Tor, 1993.

Inferno: A Chronicle of a Distant World, Tor, 1993.

A Miracle of Rare Design: A Tragedy of Transcendence, Tor, 1994.

Return of the Dinosaurs, DAW, 1997.

A Hunger in the Soul, Tor, 1998.

Kirinyaga: A Fable of Utopia, Del Rey, 1998.

Also author of *An Alien Land,* Dark Regions; "Seven Views of Olduvai Gorge," Axolotl Press; *Solo Flights through Shared Worlds,* Dark Regions; *Exploits,* Wildside Press; *Encounters,* Wildside Press; *The Alien Heart,* Pulphouse; *Pink Elephants and Hairy Toads,* Wildside Press; and *The Outpost.*

"TALES OF THE GALACTIC MIDWAY" SCIENCE FICTION SERIES

Sideshow, Signet, 1982.

The Three-Legged Hootch Dancer, Signet, 1983.

The Wild Alien Tamer, Signet, 1983.

The Best Rootin' Tootin' Shootin' Gunslinger in the Whole Damned Galaxy, Signet, 1983.

Tales of the Galactic Midway (contains all four books), Farthest Star (Alexander, NC), 1998.

"TALES OF THE VELVET COMET" SCIENCE FICTION SERIES

Eros Ascending, Phantasia Press, 1984.

Eros at Zenith, Phantasia Press, 1984.

Eros Descending, Signet, 1985.

Eros at Nadir, Signet, 1986.

"THE ORACLE" TRILOGY

Soothsayer, Ace, 1991.

Oracle, Ace, 1992.

Prophet, Ace, 1993.

"THE WIDOWMAKER" TRILOGY

The Widowmaker in Spring, Bantam, 1996.

The Widowmaker Reborn, Bantam, 1997.

The Widowmaker Unleashed, Bantam, 1998.

MYSTERIES

Dog in the Manger, Alexander Books, 1995.

Also editor of mystery *The Compleat Chance Perdue,* by Ross Spencer, Alexander Books.

EDITOR

Shaggy B.E.M. Stories, Nolacon Press (New Orleans, LA), 1988.

Alternate Kennedys, Tor, 1992.

Whatdunnits, DAW, 1992.

Aladdin: Master of the Lamp, DAW, 1992.

Alternate Presidents, Tor, 1992.

More Whatdunnits, DAW, 1993.

Alternate Warriors, Tor, 1993.

(With Martin H. Greenberg) *Christmas Ghosts,* DAW, 1993.

(With Gardner Dozois) *Future Earths: Under African Skies,* DAW, 1993.

(With Gardner Dozois) *Future Earths: Under South American Skies,* DAW, 1993.

(With Martin H. Greenberg) *By Any Other Fame,* DAW, 1994.

(With Loren D. Estleman and Martin H. Greenberg) *Deals with the Devil,* DAW, 1994.

Alternate Outlaws, Tor, 1994.

Arthur H. Neumann, *Elephant Hunting in East Equatorial Africa,* St. Martin's, 1994.

(With Anthony R. Lewis) *The Passage of the Light: The Recursive Science Fiction of Barry N. Malzberg,* NESFA, 1994.

Witch Fantastic, DAW, 1995.

(With Martin H. Greenberg) *Sherlock Holmes in Orbit,* DAW, 1995.

Alternate Tyrants, Tor, 1997.

Girls for the Slime God, Obscura Press, 1997.

Also editor of *Inside the Funhouse,* Avon; *Alternate Worldcons,* Axolotl Press; *Again, Alternate Worldcons,* WC Press; (with Patrick Nielsen Hayden) *Alternate Skiffy,* Wildside; (with Martin H. Greenberg) *Dinosaur Fantastic,* Daw; (with Greenberg) *Return of the Dinosaurs,* DAW. Series editor for "The Library of African Adventure," St. Martin's Press; "The Resnick Library of African Adventure," Alexander Books, "The Resnick Library of Worldwide Adventure," Alexander Books, and (co-editor with Carol Resnick) "The Resnick Library of Travelers' Tales," Alexander Books.

OTHER

Official Guide to Fantastic Literature, photographs by Larry Reynolds, House of Collectibles (Florence, AL), 1976.

Official Guide to Comic Books and Big Little Books, House of Collectibles, 1977.

Gymnastics and You: The Whole Story of the Sport, Rand McNally, 1977.

Official Guide to Comic and Science Fiction Books, House of Collectibles, 1979.

Unauthorized Autobiographies and Other Curiosities (collection of short fiction), Misfit Press (Detroit, MI), 1984.

The Inn of the Hairy Toad (short stories), Delta Con (New Orleans, LA), 1985.

(Contributor) *The Gods of War,* Baen, 1992.

Author of screenplay adaptations, with wife, Carol, of *Santiago* and *The Widowmaker.* Author of introduction to Edgar Rice Burrough's *The Land that Time Forgot,* University of Nebraska Press, 1999. Also author of many other novels and stories under various pseudonyms; contributor of reviews to periodicals. Resnick's works have been published in Germany, Japan, Italy, Poland, Bulgaria, Russia, Czech Republic, Spain, Holland, England, Sweden, France, Hungary, Romania, and Lithuania.

Adaptations

Several of Resnick's books have been optioned for movies, including *Eros Ascending, Santiago, Stalking the Unicorn, Ivory, Second Contact, Soothsayer, Oracle, Prophet, The Widowmaker, The Widowmaker Reborn, The Widowmaker Unleashed, The Outpost,* and *Dog in the Manger.* A number of his stories have been recorded on audiocassette. Gaming rights to *Santiago* have also been sold to Editions De Noel in France.

Work in Progress

The Mike and Nick Show, for Old Earth Books; *An Ambiguous Clay,* for Tor.

Sidelights

Michael D. Resnick has had a long and prolific career as an author—mostly of science fiction—that dates back to the 1960s. However, it was not until the 1980s that he began to come into his own as a writer. His science-fiction stories since then have varied from comical adventures to tales of alternate universes to Western-esque sagas of rough and rugged gunslingers. But Resnick has become most noted for setting stories in the future that have themes relevant to the continent and people of Africa. Of these, his utopian short story "Kirinyaga" has become one of the most awarded works in science fiction history. "I've been writing science fiction most of my life," Resnick told *SATA.* "The short story is still very much alive and well in science fiction, and I like writing short stories. Humor is still marketable in science fiction, and I write a lot of humor. Twice-told tales are frowned upon at the highest levels of science fiction, and creativity and imagination are rewarded. I find that artistically both challenging and satisfying."

Resnick earned a comfortable living early on with his writing. He worked for newspapers and periodicals, as well as churning out literally hundreds of books under a variety of pseudonyms. He wrote so quickly that his output was not of the highest quality, the author confesses. "For dozens of years, from 1964 until 1976, I was—I freely admit—a pseudonymous hack writer ...," he once said. "I wrote every word of seven monthly newspapers—that's about 175,000 words a month—in addition to the never-ending stream of more than two hundred junk books. Finally, the stream did end.... In late 1976 I took my ill-gotten literary gains (and they were munificent) and invested them in the largest and most luxurious boarding and grooming kennel then extant. I stopped writing almost completely for about four years while turning the business around, and then, totally secure financially for the rest of my life, I returned to my typewriter, albeit at a far slower pace, to see what I could do now that my writing didn't have to put bread on the table.

"All those books which have appeared since mid-1981 have been written during this period, and it is on these that I would like to be judged. I am still getting used to the luxury of rewriting and polishing, of not having to

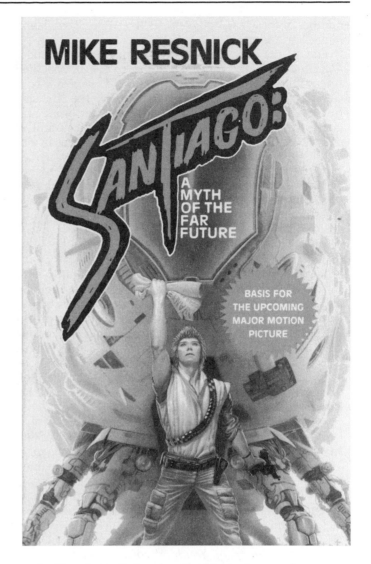

In his science-fiction novel with western undertones, Resnick pits a legendary criminal named Santiago against several colorful bounty hunters who are motivated by reasons ranging from fame to personal redemption. (Cover illustration by Michael Whelan.)

churn out fifty pages a day, of occasionally not completing even one page a day. I feel guilty about it— old habits die hard—but I suspect my books are about three thousand percent better for it, and for their author being completely free from the demands of the market-place.

"Most of my recent output has been labelled science fiction, though I sometimes wonder if 'moral parable' isn't a more proper category. I am not concerned with aliens (I have never met one), telepaths (ditto), invading extra-terrestrial armadas (still ditto). I am concerned, to borrow from Mr. Faulkner, with the human heart in conflict with itself—and far from proving a hindrance to such a quest, science fiction, with all of time and space to draw from, seems especially fitting for it."

Resnick's early 1980s sci-fi works are adventure tales that nevertheless often have serious undertones. A number of these works have a distinctive Western flavor, including *Santiago: A Myth of the Far Future* and his "Tales of the Galactic Midway" series, which includes *Sideshow, The Three-Legged Hootch Dancer, The Wild Alien Tamer,* and *The Best Rootin' Tootin' Shootin' Gunslinger in the Whole Damned Galaxy.* The "Galactic Midway" stories all involve characters who work at a circus called the Ahasuerus and Flint Traveling Carnival and Sideshow. The books can be quite violent, as in *The Wild Alien Tamer,* in which an animal tamer named Jupiter Monk takes turns playing a wild beast with a batlike alien, depending on which world the circus is performing. But the pact between human and alien deteriorates into a contest of who can stand being tortured the most without giving in.

In *The Best Rootin' Tootin' Shootin' Gunslinger in the Whole Damned Galaxy,* Billybuck Dancer proves himself to be an unbeatable shot, facing down and beating any opponent—human or alien—that challenges him at the circus. While his performances are extremely profitable, Billybuck is depressed because he has met no one who poses a true challenge to his skills. But the circus boss, Thaddeus Flint, comes up with a brainstorm: he gets an android to play Doc Holliday, Billybuck's idol, thus managing to satisfy both the gunslinger and his entertainment-hungry audiences.

In what a *Publishers Weekly* critic called a "pleasing adaptation of the Wild West to outer space," *Santiago: A Myth of the Far Future* pits a legendary criminal named Santiago against several colorful bounty hunters who are out to get him for reasons ranging from money to fame to art to personal redemption. Critics applauded Resnick's ending, calling it both surprising and satisfying. "Highly recommended for all readers," concluded David Snider in a *Voice of Youth Advocates* review.

Resnick's more recent *Prophet*—part of the "Oracle" trilogy—is also replete with Westernesque elements. It's the story of a hired gun called "Gravedancer" who is after the dangerous Penelope Bailey, known as "the Prophet." The Prophet has the ability to change the future just by moving her body in certain ways. The Prophet is also being hunted, however, by a cult leader with designs on ruling the universe. Despite the laser weapons and spaceships, the feel of the novel is highly reminiscent of classic Westerns, with gunfighters pacing down dusty streets toward frontier saloons, and other similar scenes. "If you [librarians] . . . have patrons who enjoy both science fiction and westerns," wrote Vicky Burkholder in *Voice of Youth Advocates,* "this is definitely the book for them."

What distinguishes these novels from other similar adventure tales, according to Don D'Ammassa in *Twentieth-Century Science Fiction Writers,* is that Resnick pays more attention to characterization than many other authors in the genre, thus "providing a greater depth to the stories." D'Ammassa made a similar observation about other Resnick books, such as *The Branch, Birthright,* and *Walpurgis III.* "Although primarily adventure stories," remarked the critic, "there

was an underlying seriousness missing in many similar books, concerns about the future of humanity, and the nature of power and government."

Walpurgis III portrays a battle between Conrad Bland, a mass murderer who has literally destroyed the populations of entire planets, and Jericho, an assassin hired by the government to kill him once and for all. But because Jericho is given license to do anything he needs to to execute Bland, including killing anyone in his way, the question becomes who is the worse monster, Bland or the unscrupulous government bent on his destruction. "Violent SF, this is graphic but well-written, with an unexpected ending," attested Barb Kerns in *Voice of Youth Advocates.*

Resnick tackles religious themes with his 1984 work, *The Branch,* but he does so with a definite twist. The book, set in the year 2047 in Chicago, is about the Second Coming of the Messiah, who takes on the very unexpected form of a gangster. When "Jeremiah the B" starts horning in on crime boss Solomon Moody Moore's territory, Moore tries to off the new competition. This proves impossible when "J the B" shows himself to be impervious even to bullets. Taking a growing crowd of followers with him to Jerusalem, Jeremiah writes a new gospel and thwarts his attackers. *The Branch* received some mixed reviews. A *Publishers Weekly* critic felt that Resnick wrote "himself into a dead end about halfway through the book," finding only the first half of interest. However, John M. Landsberg, a reviewer for *Kliatt,* was impressed that the author had "done his religious homework," creating a believable scenario that "makes the reader think more than the average SF adventure."

What would become a major concern in Resnick's more recent writing begins to reveal itself as early as his 1982 book, *Birthright: The Book of Man. Birthright* is an ambitious collection of stories that traces the story of human civilization over a 17,000 year period. The stories follow humanity's progression from planet colonizer, to empire builder, to decline, and finally destruction. While obviously admiring humanity's ingenuity and determination, Resnick also clearly illuminates mankind's many flaws as humans establish brutal and destructive reigns over the various alien races they conquer. In the end, it is these same alien races that eventually unite to destroy the last of the humans. *Voice of Youth Advocates* contributor Pat Pearl called *Birthright* a "cold-eyed, cleverly-conceived, wry view of our potential future," and Dennis A. Hinrichs, writing in *Kliatt,* described the novel as "an impressive work that will have strong appeal to the mainline SF fan."

The concern Resnick shows for man's cruelty when it comes to colonizing lands already inhabited by other people stems from his interest in Africa, a continent he has visited several times. "It has been noted that almost all of my more famous and popular science fiction deals with Africa," Resnick told *SATA,* "or at least with African themes transferred to other times and worlds. The answer to that is really quite simple: I think just about everyone believes that if we can ever reach the stars, we're going to colonize them ... and that if we colonize enough of them, sooner or later we're going to come into contact with a sentient alien race. Africa offers fifty-one separate, distinct, and devastating examples of the effects of colonization on both the colonized and the colonizers. And if fiction holds a mirror up to life, then science fiction holds a funhouse mirror up to it. My mirror just happens to be set in Africa more often than not."

Resnick stories with themes relating to Africa and colonialism include *Paradise: A Chronicle of a Distant World, A Hunger in the Soul,* the novella *Bully!,* and his award-winning short story "Kirinyaga." While books such as *Paradise* illustrate the adverse effects of colonization on native peoples, Resnick shows that the converse is also true in *Bully!* and *A Hunger in the Soul.* "*Paradise* is a barely concealed portrayal of the pillage of the African wilderness by outside powers," wrote D'Ammassa. As the story begins, Planet Peponi is a beautiful paradise, but when human colonists arrive, the land is soon raped of its natural resources and its people oppressed. Eventually, after years of struggle, the native people manage to force the humans to give them back their world, but Peponi's inhabitants have already had their way of life destroyed. "Resnick avoids stock solutions; there is no magical reconciliation in the final chapter," commented D'Ammassa. "Beautifully handled, engrossing, and thought provoking ... [this is] top-notch science fiction," declared a *Kirkus Reviews* critic. Resnick repeated this performance with *Purgatory: A Chronicle of a Distant World,* in which the natives of the planet Karimon experience the same fate as those on Peponi.

In works such as *A Hunger in the Soul, Bully!,* and *A Miracle of Rare Design,* the author shows the negative effects of colonialism on the colonizers themselves. Adapting the well-known historical tale of H. M. Stanley's search for Dr. David Livingstone after he has disappeared into the jungles of Africa, Resnick reconfigures the story in *A Hunger in the Soul* as journalist Robert Markham's search for Dr. Michael Drake, who had gone missing on another planet. Markham gathers together a team of humans and a group of aliens—called "Orange-Eyes"—to serve as porters. Markham brutalizes the aliens—both on the planet and on his own team—and leads most of his team's members to their deaths in his single-minded pursuit of the doctor. Finding Drake, he learns the doctor has discovered a cure for a horrible plague, but Drake is unwilling to give it to Markham. Markham decides to kill Drake, and returns home triumphant. Markham's descent into his own brutal nature clearly shows the "civilized" actions of colonialists in a grim light. "With finesse, discernment, and splashes of vitriol," as a *Kirkus Reviews* contributor put it, "Resnick continues to expose colonialism and its vicious attitudes."

Resnick accomplishes this with more subtlety in his novella *Bully!,* whose main character is President Theodore Roosevelt. Set in an alternate history, the story follows Roosevelt, after he has left office, and his efforts to create a democratic nation in Africa. "Roosevelt is Resnick's most fully realized character," observed D'Ammassa, "earnest and sincere on one hand, flawed by egotism and an inability to recognize the reality of his situation on the other. Although he makes great strides toward his goal, it is ultimately doomed to failure because the historical basis for such a rapid alteration of the social climate doesn't exist."

A Miracle of Rare Design offers a more bizarre twist on colonization's effects on the colonizers. Xavier William Lennox accepts the opportunity to have his body surgically manipulated to resemble that of various aliens, whereupon he is sent to other worlds to persuade the natives to allow various human businesses and other interests to infiltrate their worlds. After a number of these procedures, Xavier begins to lose track of his human identity, and eventually decides to never go back to his original human form. In this way, Resnick uses the overt alteration of the physical appearance of his main character to illustrate the loss of people's humanity through the exploitation of others. A *Kirkus Reviews* critic called this entry into Resnick's ongoing exploration of a theme "low-key, thoughtful, [and] absorbing," and *Booklist* reviewer Carl Hays described the novel as "insightful as well as entertaining."

Among all his stories and novels with African themes, Resnick's "Kirinyaga" stories have garnered the most awards and acclaim, including two Hugo Awards for "Kirinyaga" and "The Manamouki." Originally published separately in various science fiction magazines, the stories were collected in 1998's *Kirinyaga: A Fable of Utopia.* Resnick got his idea of African people settling a terraformed world from fellow novelist Orson Scott Card. The central figure of these stories is the witch doctor—or *mundumugu*—named Koriba. Koriba is the spiritual leader of the people who settle Kirinyaga. He is a wise but very strict leader, forbidding his people from emulating European culture in any way and forcing them to live a primitive, traditional lifestyle. While there are many positive sides to this way of life, there are also drawbacks. For example, in one story a young girl with a fervent desire to learn how to read commits suicide after Koriba forbids this education because it is a Western practice. "Koriba is in fact a fanatic ...," remarked a *Publishers Weekly* critic. "Yet throughout, as Resnick's superb use of first-person narration makes clear, Koriba remains a man of integrity and vision, and a gifted storyteller." *Booklist* reviewer John Mort felt that the stories were more effective before they were published in a collection, where they get a bit repetitive, but, overall, Mort proclaimed the book an "extraordinary work."

With numerous awards to his credit for both his short and long fiction, Resnick has contributed much to his chosen genre by providing his readers with both entertaining and thought-provoking stories. The author told *SATA,* "For years science fiction has been sneered at by the 'literary establishment' as being nothing but trashy pulp literature, teenaged power fantasies in clumsy disguise. But while the litcrits were busy sneering, the science fiction writers were busy working at their craft, to the point where not only isn't science fiction the mainstream's poor relation any longer, but the very best writing around can actually be found in science fiction." Resnick is likely to continue contributing to the growing respectability of science fiction, too. "Many of the writers I know hate writing, but love having written," he said. "Not me. I love the act of writing, of pushing nouns up against verbs, of looking at the day's output and deciding that it was pretty much what I intended to say when I sat down to work."

Works Cited

Review of *The Branch, Publishers Weekly,* December 23, 1983, pp. 55-56.

Burkholder, Vicky, review of *Prophet, Voice of Youth Advocates,* October, 1993, pp. 232, 234.

D'Ammassa, Don, "Mike Resnick," *Twentieth-Century Science Fiction Writers,* St. James Press, 1991, pp. 660-61.

Hays, Carl, review of *A Miracle of Rare Design, Booklist,* November 1, 1994, p. 482.

Hinrichs, Dennis A., review of *Birthright: The Book of Man, Kliatt,* spring, 1982, p. 20.

Review of *A Hunger in the Soul, Kirkus Reviews,* April 15, 1998, p. 538.

Kerns, Barb, review of *Walpurgis III, Voice of Youth Advocates,* April, 1983, p. 46.

Review of *Kirinyaga: A Fable of Utopia, Publishers Weekly,* January 26, 1998, p. 73.

Landsberg, John M., review of *The Branch, Kliatt,* spring, 1984, p. 12.

Review of *A Miracle of Rare Design, Kirkus Reviews,* October 1, 1994, p. 1318.

Mort, John, review of *Kirinyaga: A Fable of Utopia, Booklist,* February 15, 1998, p. 990.

Review of *Paradise: A Chronicle of a Distant World, Kirkus Reviews,* April 15, 1989, p. 592.

Pearl, Pat, review of *Birthright: The Book of Man, Voice of Youth Advocates,* August, 1982, p. 40.

Review of *Santiago: A Myth of the Far Future, Publishers Weekly,* January 10, 1986, p. 83.

Snider, David, review of *Santiago: A Myth of the Far Future, Voice of Youth Advocates,* June, 1986, p. 90.

For More Information See

PERIODICALS

Booklist, April 1, 1990, p. 1532; November 1, 1991, p. 496; July, 1992, p. 1925; February 1, 1993, p. 972.

Kirkus Reviews, June 15, 1992, p. 753; January 1, 1993, p. 29; January 15, 1998, p. 88.

Kliatt, September, 1990, p. 22; April, 1991, p. 21; March, 1993, p. 18; July, 1993, pp. 18, 20; September, 1993, p. 22; January, 1995, p. 19.

Library Journal, February 15, 1998, p. 173.

Publishers Weekly, July 27, 1992, pp. 52-53; January 18, 1993, p. 465.

School Library Journal, August, 1990, p. 177; March, 1993, pp. 234, 236; March, 1999, p. 231.

Voice of Youth Advocates, February, 1993, p. 357; February, 1995, p. 346.

—*Sketch by Kevin S. Hile*

* * *

RESNICK, Mike
See RESNICK, Michael D(iamond)

* * *

ROBESON, Kenneth
See JOHNSON, (Walter) Ryerson

* * *

ROTTMAN, S(usan) L(ynn) 1970-

Personal

Born July 12, 1970, in Albany, GA; married Arthur E. Wickberg (member of the United States Air Force); children: Arthur "Paul" Wickberg. *Education:* Colorado State University, B.A. (in English, with teacher certification for secondary education), 1992. *Hobbies and other interests:* White-water rafting, swimming, downhill skiing, watching sit-coms.

Career

Widefield School District #3, Colorado Springs, CO, English teacher, 1993-96, 1998—; Deer Creek Schools, Edmond, OK, English teacher, 1996-98.

Awards, Honors

Oklahoma Book Award, young adult/children's category, 1998, Books for the Teen Age citation, New York Public Library, 1998, Best Books for Young Adults, Young Adult Library Services Association (YALSA) of the American Library Association, 1999, all for *Hero;* Quick Pick for Reluctant Readers, YALSA, 1999, for *Rough Waters.*

Writings

Hero, Peachtree (Atlanta, GA), 1997.
Rough Waters, Peachtree, 1998.
Head above Water, in press, 1999.

Sidelights

S. L. Rottman told *SATA:* "The first story I remember writing (that I liked) was when I was in the sixth grade. I continued to write for my own enjoyment through high school, and received a creative writing scholarship from Colorado State University for a short story. I never dreamed I would sell my first novel before I turned thirty, but I've already sold three and I've still got a couple years left!"

S. L. Rottman

S. L. Rottman's first novel, *Hero*, garnered considerable attention as a moving account of a young man's transformation from a troublemaking outsider to one who has learned to give and receive help from others. "*Hero* had me laughing out loud on page three and nearly crying several times thereafter," wrote Cynthia L. Blinn in a *Voice of Youth Advocates* review. The novel centers on Sean, a fifteen-year-old who has learned to mistrust all adults based on his experience with his own parents: his alcoholic mother is both physically and emotionally abusive, while his father's presence is known only through a monthly support check. "Sean is a likable loner—tough as nails—with a survivor's sense of humor," remarked a reviewer for *Publishers Weekly*, "and his message is a powerful one for adolescents."

During a week's suspension from school for fighting, Sean breaks curfew for a fourth time and is sentenced to a week of community service on World War II veteran Dave Hassler's farm. There he learns that hard work has its rewards in increased self-confidence. Mr. Hassler helps Sean express and work through his feelings of abandonment and neglect by having him help birth a foal that bonds with Sean after being abandoned by its mother. The author also resolves Sean's conflict with a school bully, reintroduces him to his father, and arranges

for the disappearance of the abusive mother into a hospital, though some reviewers contended that Rottman avoids an easy ending. "Through Sean, [Rottman] gives readers a convincing and difficult protagonist and a fresh perspective on what it means to be a hero," observed Carolyn Lehman in *School Library Journal.*

"Along with reading and writing," Rottman continued to *SATA*, "I count white-water rafting, swimming, downhill skiing, and watching sit-coms among my hobbies. Although I was born in Georgia and have lived in Oklahoma, I consider Colorado my true home."

Works Cited

Blinn, Cynthia L., review of *Hero, Voice of Youth Advocates,* December, 1997, p. 320.
Review of *Hero, Publishers Weekly,* August 18, 1997, p. 93.
Lehman, Carolyn, review of *Hero, School Library Journal,* December, 1997, p. 130.

For More Information See

PERIODICALS

Booklist, December 1, 1997, p. 638.
Bulletin of the Center for Children's Books, January, 1998, p. 175.
Kirkus Reviews, September 15, 1997, p. 1462.

*   *   *

RUSSO, Marisabina 1950-

Personal

Born May 1, 1950, in New York, NY; daughter of Michele Russo (a naval architect) and Sabina Neuman Russo Wedgewood (a businesswoman); married Whitney W. Stark (a teacher), October 4, 1975; children: Hannah, Samuel, Benjamin. *Education:* Mount Holyoke College, B.A., 1971. *Politics:* Independent. *Hobbies and other interests:* Photography, swimming, scuba diving.

Addresses

Electronic mail—russostar@aol.com.

Career

Author and illustrator of children's books. *Exhibitions:* Biennale Illustrations, Bratislava, Czech Republic, 1989; exhibition of picture books edited by Susan Hirschman, Itabashi Art Museum (Tokyo), Shizuoka, and Hiroshima, Japan, June-September, 1990; "The Original Art," Society of Illustrators' Museum of American Illustration, New York, NY, 1992 and 1993; "Happily Ever After: Children's Book Illustrations," Fine Arts Gallery, Westchester Community College, New York, June-July, 1993; "The Magic of Storybook Art: Original Illustrations from Children's Literature," Rye Arts Center, October-November, 1996; "Illustrations Past and Present," from the Permanent Collection of the Society of Illustrators' Museum of American Illustration, July-August, 1997.

Awards, Honors

Children's Choice Award, International Reading Association, 1986, for *The Line Up Book;* Fanfare List, *Horn Book,* 1989, for *Waiting for Hannah;* Washington Irving Children's Choice Book Award, 1994, for *A Visit to Oma;* National Parenting Publications Book Award, 1994, for *Time to Wake Up!;* Children's Choice, International Reading Association-Children's Book Council, 1994, for *Trade-In Mother;* Best Books of the Year citation, Bank Street College, 1998, for *Under the Table.*

Writings

AUTHOR AND ILLUSTRATOR

The Line Up Book, Greenwillow, 1986.
Why Do Grown-Ups Have All the Fun?, Greenwillow, 1987.
Only Six More Days, Greenwillow, 1988.
Waiting for Hannah, Greenwillow, 1989.
Where Is Ben?, Greenwillow, 1990.
A Visit to Oma, Greenwillow, 1991.
Alex Is My Friend, Greenwillow, 1992.
Trade-In Mother, Greenwillow, 1993.
Time to Wake Up!, Greenwillow, 1994.
I Don't Want to Go Back to School, Greenwillow, 1994.
Grandpa Abe, Greenwillow, 1996.
Under the Table, Greenwillow, 1997.
When Mama Gets Home, Greenwillow, 1998.
Hannah's Baby Sister, Greenwillow, 1998.

ILLUSTRATOR

Nikki Giovanni, *Vacation Time: Poems for Children,* Morrow, 1980.
Elizabeth Burton Brown, *Vegetables: An Illustrated History with Recipes,* Prentice-Hall, 1981.
Mary and Dewey Blocksma, *Easy-to-Make Spaceships that Really Fly,* Prentice-Hall, 1983.
Nancy Van Laan, *The Big Fat Worm,* Knopf, 1987.
Helen Plotz, editor, *A Week of Lullabyes,* Greenwillow Books, 1988.
Susi Gregg Fowler, *When Summer Ends,* Greenwillow Books, 1989.
Stephanie Calmenson, *It Begins with an A,* Hyperion, 1993.
Susan Straight, *Bear E. Bear,* Hyperion, 1995.
Kevin Henkes, *Good-Bye, Curtis,* Greenwillow Books, 1995.
Eve Rice, *Swim!,* Greenwillow Books, 1996.

The Line Up Book and *Under the Table* have been translated into Japanese, and *The Big Fat Worm* has been translated into French.

Work in Progress

Mama Talks Too Much and *The Big Brown Boy,* both picture books, both for Greenwillow.

Marisabina Russo

Sidelights

Marisabina Russo is the author and illustrator of more than a dozen picture books that focus on childhood situations: from what to do with jumbled up blocks to counting the days until a birthday or to a sibling's thoughts while waiting for the birth of a new baby. Russo keeps her storylines simple and direct and blends them with colorful gouache illustrations that she fills to the brim with background detail. In both illustration and writing, Russo deals with the familiar to imbue her books "with a reassuring aura of love, understanding, and acceptance," according to Sandra Ray in *Children's Books and Their Creators.*

Russo grew up in Queens, New York, the daughter of a single parent and with siblings much older than she. A shy child, she spent much of her time alone; drawing and writing kept her occupied. Art lessons from a neighbor encouraged a natural proclivity, and visits to New York's museums introduced her to the possibilities of art in all its guises. From an early age, Russo was determined to become an artist. In the sixth grade she first read *The Diary of Anne Frank,* and this experience moved her to keep her own journal. Encouragement from a seventh-grade English teacher set her to writing short stories, one of which was published in her junior-high literary magazine.

As high-school graduation neared, Russo had dreams of attending an art school, but her mother persuaded her to go to a liberal-arts institution, Mount Holyoke College, instead. However, she still majored in studio art, a field of study that sct hcr apart from the mainstream on the campus. After graduation, Russo went on to study lithography at the Boston Museum School and life drawing at the Art Students League in New York. Freelance illustrating jobs and marriage both came about in the mid-1970s. Early illustration assignments included spot drawings and covers for *The New Yorker* as well as illustrations for cookbooks, two of which were award-winners. Babies arrived, as well, and it was only after her third was born that Russo began writing and illustrating picture books, following a meeting with Susan Hirschman at Greenwillow Books.

Russo's first picture book, *The Line Up Book,* was published in 1986 and set the tone for much of her subsequent work. It was inspired by her son, Sam, who was obsessed with lining up objects in the house. In the book, Sam dumps his blocks on the floor when his mother calls him to lunch. Sandra Ray noted in *Children's Books and Their Creators* that "Russo taps into a child's logic to provide an amusingly satisfactory way for Sam to play with his blocks while wending his way from bedroom to kitchen." In fact, he uses objects in the house, including blocks, books, and boots, to make a line from the bedroom to kitchen. Lying down on the kitchen floor, Sam becomes the last "object" in line.

"The reassurance of [the mother's] reaction and Sam's pride in his innovative route combine to create a warm, satisfying feeling," Lauralyn Persson remarked in *School Library Journal.* "A charming book," Persson added. A *Publishers Weekly* contributor remarked that the "paintings have a folk-art look and are full of homey touches: a checked tile floor, family photos and a simple lunch of soup and sandwiches," while *Horn Book* reviewer Mary M. Burns commented on "the illustrator's skill in developing striking graphic patterns from the juxtaposition of ordinary household artifacts." Burns also drew attention to the text, "paced well for picture-book programs," and concluded that *The Line Up Book* is "remarkable for its thoughtful design" and "especially notable as the author-artist's first book of her own." The winner of a Children's Choice Award from the International Reading Association, Russo's inaugural book got her new career off to a good start.

A child's fantasies about how wonderful it would be to stay up late are at the heart of Russo's second picture book, *Why Do Grown-Ups Have All the Fun?* Young Hannah, the protagonist, imagines her parents eating ice cream, working with play dough, and constructing towers out of blocks. "The beauty of this book lies in its simple story line, in the charm of the ingenious protagonist, and in Russo's graphic illustrations," commented David Gale in a *School Library Journal* review. Again Russo employed gouache paintings in two-dimensional blocks of color along with a simple, child-centered text. *Booklist* commentator Denise M. Wilms concluded that "the story's gentle handling of a child's sleep problems is nice to see and the pictures ... echo the story's quiet sensibility."

Expectation is the inspiration for several Russo titles, including *Only Six More Days, Waiting for Hannah, When Mama Gets Home,* and *Hannah's Baby Sister.* A mother's memory of waiting for the birth of her child one summer forms the storyline for *Waiting for Hannah,* a "tender story that captures the love and expectancy of birth far better than most books written on the topic," according to Ilene Cooper in a starred *Booklist* review. Leda Schubert, writing in *School Library Journal,* noted that "children rarely tire of hearing this kind of tale; it should be particularly successful in one-on-one reading." *Hannah's Baby Sister* is something of a reprise of this idea, with young Hannah now waiting for the birth of a baby sister—which, in the event, turns out to be a baby brother. Pam Gosner remarked in *School Library Journal* that this "loving family is warmly portrayed in both text and in the cheerful childlike paintings with Russo's signature use of flat areas of color and pattern."

Expectation takes the form of waiting for a birthday in *Only Six More Days,* and in *When Mama Gets Home,* a little girl eagerly expects her mother home from work so she can tell her all about her day. Ben is the birthday boy in the former title. There are only six more days until his fifth birthday and he begins counting down, but older sister Molly is getting tired of the whole subject and decides to boycott the party until Mother comes to the rescue. *Booklist* contributor Ilene Cooper concluded that the "party scene featuring a multiracial group has warm appeal." *When Mama Gets Home* provides a "realistic

When she cannot understand her great-grandmother's foreign language, Celeste fashions her own stories from the old woman's narratives in this tale of a warm intergenerational relationship.

A young girl eagerly anticipates her mother's arrival in **When Mama Gets Home,** *written and illustrated by Russo.*

glimpse into family life where children are often home before their parents," according to Lisa Gangemi Krapp in *School Library Journal.* Mama is bombarded by stories, questions, and requests when she finally gets home, but wears a smile through it all. "The dreamy quality of the narrative is extended in flat gouache paintings in muted colors," according to a critic in *Kirkus Reviews.* Hazel Rochman concluded in *Booklist* that "Russo captures the drama of a small child's day with immediacy and feeling and without condescension."

Other Russo themes and situations include visits to members of the extended family and a child's rebellion. In *A Visit to Oma,* Celeste visits her great-grandmother, receives a warm welcome, and listens to stories she cannot understand because Oma does not speak English. Celeste fashions her own story about Oma in a "perceptive glimpse of a child's imaginative concept of her elder's past," according to a *Kirkus Reviews* contributor. Ellen Fader remarked in *Horn Book* that "Russo's story

will engage young readers with its warmth, love, and mysterious sense of personal history." *Grandpa Abe,* on the other hand, is "a sensitive, caring story of a young girl's relationship with her grandfather, and of how her family deals with his death," according to *School Library Journal* contributor Janet M. Blair. Maeve Visser Knoth concluded in a *Horn Book* review that "*Grandpa Abe* celebrates the special connection between a grandparent and a child."

A trio of books celebrates something very different from intergenerational connections. *Trade-In Mother, Time to Wake Up!,* and *I Don't Want to Go Back to School* all explore childhood rebellion against authority in a loving and humorous manner. In *Trade-In Mother,* Max blames Mama for his frustrating day and finally wishes he could trade her in, until he thinks he might get a mom who would trade him in. A *Kirkus Reviews* critic noted that Russo's "attractive illustrations ... reinforce the realistic story's warmth and sense of security." Ben does not want to return to school at the end of summer in *I Don't*

Want to Go Back to School, and his parents offer reassurances, while his big sister Hannah tells horror stories of her own school years. Jacqueline Elsner, writing in *School Library Journal,* called this an "all-around superior picture book."

Russo captures a common childhood playtime activity in *Under the Table.* The young protagonist of this picture book brings her dolls, crayons, books, and even the dog to her special hiding place. One day she begins to draw pictures on the underside of the table, which her parents discover upon moving the furniture. Fortunately, Mom and Dad are understanding, and make things right in a gentle way. "Many kids will see themselves in this pleasing tale," wrote *Booklist*'s Ilene Cooper.

To create her picture books, Russo employs incidents from her own childhood as well as observations of her children. Indeed, the main characters of her stories often bear her children's names. Reviewers of her works repeatedly point to the simple, direct language she employs, as well as the two-dimensional gouache paintings full of strong, bold colors that work together to create warm effects. Russo has noted that the paintings are the most fun for her—they come naturally. She continues to illustrate books for other writers. Regarding the writing of the text, "the initial idea is usually the easy part," Russo has commented, "but giving it shape, rhythm, and a climax is much more difficult." Nevertheless, Russo continued, "There is no other job I would want. Every day when I sit down to work in my studio ... I feel very lucky and very happy."

Works Cited

Blair, Janet M. review of *Grandpa Abe, School Library Journal,* July, 1996, p. 72.

Burns, Mary M. review of *The Line Up Book, Horn Book,* November-December, 1986, p. 739.

Cooper, Ilene, review of *Only Six More Days, Booklist,* March 1, 1988, p. 1185.

Cooper, Ilene, review of *Under the Table,* April 1, 1997, p. 1339.

Cooper, Ilene, review of *Waiting for Hannah, Booklist,* September 15, 1989, pp. 189-90.

Elsner, Jacqueline, review of *I Don't Want to Go Back to School, School Library Journal,* July, 1994, p. 88.

Fader, Ellen, review of *A Visit to Oma, Horn Book,* March-April, 1991, pp. 195-96.

Gale, David, review of *Why Do Grown-Ups Have All the Fun?, School Library Journal,* March, 1987, p. 150.

Gosner, Pam, review of *Hannah's Baby, School Library Journal,* September, 1998, p. 180.

Knoth, Maeve Visser, review of *Grandpa Abe, Horn Book,* May-June, 1996, p. 328.

Krapp, Lisa Gangemi, review of *When Mama Gets Home, School Library Journal,* April, 1998, p. 108.

Review of *The Line Up Book, Publishers Weekly,* July 25, 1986, p. 184.

Persson, Lauralyn, review of *The Line Up Book, School Library Journal,* November, 1986, p. 83.

Ray, Sandra, essay on Russo in *Children's Books and Their Creators,* Houghton Mifflin, 1995, p. 566.

Rochman, Hazel, review of *When Mama Gets Home, Booklist,* March 1, 1998, pp. 1141-42.

Russo, Marisabina, comments in a publicity release for Greenwillow Books, 1996.

Schubert, Leda, review of *Waiting for Hannah, School Library Journal,* November, 1989, pp. 92-93.

Review of *Trade-In Mother, Kirkus Reviews,* February 15, 1993, p. 233.

Review of *A Visit to Oma, Kirkus Reviews,* May 1, 1991, p. 609.

Review of *When Mama Gets Home, Kirkus Reviews,* February 15, 1998, p. 274.

Wilms, Denise M., review of *Why Do Grown-Ups Have All the Fun?, Booklist,* April 15, 1987, p. 1294.

For More Information See

PERIODICALS

Booklist, April 15, 1991, p. 1648; May 1, 1992, p. 1610; March 1, 1993, p. 1237; September 1, 1994, p. 54; March 15, 1995, p. 1338; October 15, 1995, p. 411; May 15, 1996, p. 1593; August, 1996, p. 1908.

Bulletin of the Center for Children's Books, April, 1987, p. 154; December, 1990, p. 100; May, 1992, pp. 248-49; May, 1997, p. 344.

Horn Book, May-June, 1993, p. 325; July-August, 1994, p. 444.

Kirkus Reviews, March 15, 1994, p. 403; August 15, 1994, p. 1138.

School Library Journal, October, 1988, pp. 127-28; October, 1990, p. 100; April, 1992, p. 100; May, 1994, p. 102; July, 1994, p. 88; June, 1995, p. 96; October, 1995, p. 104; September, 1996, p. 189; April, 1997, p. 116.

—Sketch by J. Sydney Jones

S

Will Shetterly

1955-

My Life, So Far

Foreword

Autobiographies would be much more fun to write if you could choose your subject.

Well, I thought that was funny.

When asked what sort of writer I am, I tend to say that I'm a novelist, but that's only because I'm afraid I'll sound pompous if I say I'm a fantasist. I make up stories. Some have been called fantasy; some, science fiction; some, children's stories; some, comic books; some, screenplays; but they're all fantasies.

As a fantasist, I know one thing: Art is mystery. What can be known is the stuff of science, and I have as much respect for scientists as I have for artists, but I'm interested in things that ultimately cannot be known: Why do we love who we love? What happens after we die? Why is it more important to do what's right than what's practical?

Because an element of mystery is essential to all art, I'm not sure storytellers should write about themselves. Like magicians, we're afraid you won't respect us if you learn how our tricks are done.

But I know two things: Artists must share what they know, and artists must be bold. So here is a sketch of my life. Make of it what you will.

My Family

Seven Shetterly brothers came to North America before the American Revolution. I think I heard that somewhere, but I may have made it up. I like the idea of seven brothers coming to a new land—though it makes me wonder about their sisters, and what land they left, and why.

That's the stuff of story: a notion that intrigues a writer for reasons the writer may not ever know. The truth of the notion is not especially relevant: there's an emotional truth to the idea that my family came here in time to be part of the birth and shaping of a nation.

Yet the fact is that I don't know whether one Shetterly or many came here, or when they came, or whether they were fleeing something or seeking something. Family legend has it that a Shetterly served under Light-Horse Harry Lee during the Revolutionary War. A genealogy put together by a distant relative claims that an Andrew Shetterly was born in Pennsylvania in 1763. Other records show Shetterlys in America in the 1780s and '90s. All we know is that Shetterlys have probably been in the United States for as long as the country has existed.

One family legend says we come from the Alsace-Lorraine, that territory between France and Germany that has, over the centuries, been claimed by both of them. That's a satisfying notion: The Shetterlys I know are fond of a good argument. It's nice to think we come from a place where people have quarreled for ages.

Another legend says we came here in debtors' prison. That also has an emotional truth. Shetterlys appear to have been a lower-class lot who survived as farmers or, my father suggests, horse thieves. Over half of the Europeans in the British colonies were sent there as prisoners (Australia only became Britain's penal dumping ground after the Revolution closed off North America); it's certainly likely that we came as prisoners, too. Perhaps the first Shetterlys made their way from Germany to England, were jailed for debt or some other minor crime, and then were shipped away from a land that didn't want them.

Our name doesn't give us any clues to our past. "Shetterly" has a superficially British appearance—the similarity to "Chatterley" must explain why the most common misspelling of the name comes from adding an extra "e" in the last syllable. But my family pronounces the name as though that first "e" was a "u," as though the name was "Shutterly," and some members of the family have speculated that this is a hangover from an older, Germanic form of the name.

That's plausible. Emigrants often anglicized their names. Yet the true origin of our name may be something that no one has guessed. Perhaps the first Shetterly needed a name and invented one that he—or perhaps, she, if she gave that name to an illegitimate son—thought sounded good.

I can speak more confidently about Shetterlys in the latter part of the nineteenth century. We moved west with the expanding nation, following newly available farmland and having large families in which the name William repeated frequently from generation to generation.

My great-grandfather, a William Shetterly, had a farm in the midwest. When his wife ran away with another man, that William Shetterly found the couple on a train, killed the man with a shotgun, then hung himself in jail.

One of his children was Ross Shetterly, who married a woman named Bess Hoover. They settled on a farm near Oklee, a tiny farming town in northern Minnesota. They stood out in that community—the Shetterlys were English-speaking, dark-haired and dark-skinned, and not especially tall. Northern Minnesota was mostly settled by German, Swedish, and Norwegian immigrants—tall, fair people who spoke their native tongue at home. But the Shetterlys got along with their neighbors, and they were respected. Grandpa Ross was elected to a local office or two, his daughters married well, and while his sons may have had a reputation for being a bit wild, they were also known for working as hard as they played.

I don't remember Grandpa Ross. He died when I was a baby. There's a picture of me sitting on his lap that I like, because we're both laughing. I know that he was a hard man who came through hard times—Dad once apologized for spanking me by saying that Grandpa Ross had been beaten with a whip when he had misbehaved, while Dad had been beaten with a razor strap, a comparatively less brutal tool, whereas I was only punished with a bare palm or a belt. I also know that Ross's family liked and respected him, so I'm inclined to think I would've, too.

I know less about Grandma Bess, though she visited my family often. She was a fat, dark, cheerful woman who was never more cheerful than when she was telling you about her medical history and what was happening on the soap operas that she adored. She told one story that I liked, about crossing a river in a covered wagon when she was a girl and watching the water come up through the cracks in the floorboards.

Ross and Bess had six children: Millie, Harry, Wilma, Howard (whose first name was William, though he was never called that), Bob, and Ben. A gap of a few years separated Bob and Ben from the older children. Harry left

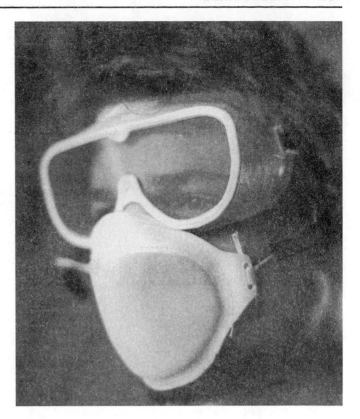

"The Ultimate Anonymous Author's Photo," about 1980.

home early, so Uncle Howard served as the younger boys' older brother, role model, and hero.

The part was a natural fit for Howard, a tall and handsome youth. He drove a fast car, and he was captain of the football team. He was popular with the girls, and though he got into fights with the boys, he was popular with them, too. How he was with other children, I do not know, but he was patient with Bob. When he thought Bob had been wronged, he stood up for him. Howard was, perhaps, the closest thing Bob had to a champion.

Howard must have only grown larger in Bob's eyes when he became a pilot during World War II. Returning from a mission, he was shot down over Italy by "friendly fire"—the enemy could not kill him, but his own side could.

There is a stone with William Howard Shetterly's name on it in a Minneapolis cemetery, but no one in the family knows whether Howard's body lies under it. Bob, too young to join the army, had joined the merchant marine. As a radioman, he overheard a report about the sinking of a ship carrying war victims about the time that Howard's body was being sent back to the states. The public was never informed, so far as Bob knew. Why give more trouble to grieving families who only expect a headstone and the assurance that someone they love lies under it?

Whether Howard's body lies under his marker, where the government says he is, none of the Shetterlys especially care. We have no affection for hallowed ground. If I could choose, I would prefer that he sank with the corpse ship, that the sea took back as many of her own as she could.

Bob saw much of the world in the merchant marine. When he came home after several years, he got a cabin on a lake, bought a sports car, and lived as wild a life as one could in northern Minnesota. He and his siblings put together a water-skiing show. As he approached the age of thirty, he was tending bar at the local hot spot, a club called the Nitehawk, and there he met Joan (pronounced "Jo-Ann") Mary Fikkan.

The Fikkan family came from Norway. Grandpa Amos was the town druggist in Roseau, Minnesota, a few miles from the Canadian border. He served as a medical aide in World War I, and had a letter of commendation from one of General Pershing's aides. He was a man who loved children, and I loved him very much.

Grandma Irene was a Kuster, distantly related to General George Armstrong Custer, which impressed me as a boy obsessed with cowboys. She was a quiet woman who liked order. Her idea of presents for children were clothes, not toys.

Their daughter Joan was a pretty woman whose light brown hair was always short and curly. She played in the band in high school and went off for a year of college before she dropped out to be a nurse in the navy. After the war, she drove down to Mexico with three girlfriends and travelled, flirting and drinking and dancing with the men that they met. She had at least one fiance before she met Bob Shetterly, but the men that she knew were staid, solid sorts with simple dreams. She had never known anyone with Bob's fierce passion for the possibilities of life.

They were as unalike as two people from the same land can be. She was a Republican; he was a Democrat. She was fair-haired and fair-skinned; he was black-haired and tanned. She was the daughter of the town druggist, one of the richest men in the county; he was the son of farmers. They came together because she was looking for excitement, and he was looking to settle down, and each thought the other offered something that they had never had. And perhaps they were right.

When they married, the Korean War was ending, but the Cold War continued. Their plans for a honeymoon were upset by the government: though most World War II veterans were exempt from the draft, those who had served in the merchant marine were not. So, with a new wife and a child on the way, Bob was sent south to serve his country again.

The Child

I was born on August 22, 1955, in an army hospital in Columbia, South Carolina. Dad said Mom could name their other kids; I would be William Howard Shetterly, like the brother he had loved.

They called me Billy. I was a large, healthy baby with curly red hair. We lived in a small trailer house in a trailer park with other married servicemen. It may not have been the beginning of married life that Mom had expected, but there are many photos from that time—I was the first child, and the Fikkans' first grandchild, so there are *many* pictures of me—and in all of them, Mom looks happy, and Dad looks proud, and I look like I think the world is a strange and funny place.

Dad wasn't in the army long. World War III failed to erupt, so the nation no longer needed every potential warrior. I went along on my parents' honeymoon, on an ocean steamer that cruised along the coast of South America.

By November of 1956, when my sister, Elizabeth Irene, was born, we were living on a farm in northern Minnesota, and Dad worked part-time as a butcher at the local grocery.

By February of 1958, when my brother, Michael Amos, was born, we were living in a pink house in the suburbs of Lexington, Kentucky. Dad divided his time between selling insurance and training horses. That year, the Shetterlys were as close to the American ideal as they ever would be: a hard-working husband, a cheerful housewife, and three children in a newly-built house with all the modern conveniences.

My oldest memories are of Lexington. I remember the power going out on the TV set, or perhaps someone simply turned it off. I remember running along a curving sidewalk near our house. Mom says that, wanting to keep us from soft drinks, she gave us orange juice in Coca-Cola bottles, which satisfied us until we tasted a neighbor's soft drink—I want to say I remember that, but I think I only remember the story.

When we left Lexington, someone bought our swing set. I couldn't understand why strangers were carrying it away. I think I ran crying after it, and the boys on the truck thought that was funny, but those details may only be a storyteller's embellishments.

We left Lexington because Dad had a dream. He would build a tourist attraction with over a hundred breeds of dogs on display, and it would be called Dog Land. He almost bought land near a small town called Orlando, where Disney World was built ten years later, but he decided to build on Route 19 within a mile of the Suwanee River.

The land was the site of a motel whose rooms had burned down. The only buildings that remained were the restaurant and the manager's unit, a cinder-block building that consisted of two bedrooms connected by a small bathroom. Whether my mother cried when she saw what she had gotten in exchange for the pink house, I don't know. She could be unhappy about many of the things that my father did, but she was rarely unhappy for long.

Mom and Dad lived in one room, Mike and Liz and I lived in the other, and we ate in the restaurant. Mike and I shared a bed, and Liz had one of her own, which hardly seemed fair since I was the oldest. But, as Dad pointed out, the world wasn't fair; that's why you should do what you can to make it fair.

Dog Land grew steadily for several years. We built kennels, and then a gift shop beside the restaurant. Many of the dogs were borrowed from breeders who were happy to provide dogs in exchange for signs on their kennels telling where they had come from. If Dad could not borrow a dog, he bought one. My favorite was Captain the Norwegian Elkhound, but I also loved the Pug and the Basenji and, well, all of them, even if the whippet and the greyhound were too skittish, and the Dalmatian too quick to bark, and the Doberman a bit frightening with his lean, black frame and long, white teeth.

Dog Land was in Levy County, but the nearest town with a kindergarten was Trenton, in Dixie County. At the beginning of the day, Mom or Dad would drive me to the

Will Shetterly at age three, "Early manifestations of an odd imagination."

gas station across the county line, where I would wait for the bus with the old man who ran the pumps.

One day, the old man gave me a tiny gray kitten. I named him Tiger, because he had black stripes and deserved a good name. Tiger hunted the woods around our house for many years, and always let me act as though I owned him.

I loved kindergarten. I loved going off to school and being complimented for drawing and coloring and cutting with scissors. I loved playing with other kids. I especially loved recess, when the girls would chase the boys and kiss the ones they caught, while we boys ran screaming away and vigorously rubbed the cooties from our faces whenever a girl kissed us.

A small, dark-haired girl and I were chosen to be crown-bearers at the high school prom. Our parents dressed us in miniature evening clothes. I walked across the gymnasium floor with a tinsel crown balanced on a velvet pillow, and I didn't trip.

First grade came as quite a shock. I had to transfer to Chiefland, the nearest town in Levy County. The bus ride was long, since we were near the end of the route, but that didn't bother me. My disappointments were that the girls did not chase the boys in first grade, and I was in the slowest reading group in my class.

But Chiefland's school had other virtues. There was an enormous tree in the playground with thick limbs low enough for first graders to climb. I made friends on the bus, Ronnie and Johnny and Pam and Roxie. Every morning, Mom drilled me with flashcards, and my reading improved until I was in the fastest reading group.

One reason that I loved Grandpa Amos was that he often sent packages of items from his drugstore, some useful, some frivolous. My favorites were comic books. I loved them before I could read them. The pictures told stories about amazing things and unusual people. I knew that the balloons had words in them—Mom read them to me, when she wasn't too busy—but I didn't mind that I couldn't read them.

One day, the word balloons made sense. Looking back, I should've been ecstatic or smug, but I think I was just happy. The universe offers a million wonders every day. Being allowed into the hidden world of words was only one.

Comic books may have sparked my love of science fiction. I adored Superman as much as any of them: the exploding planet, the child sent by loving parents in a rocket ship to a new world—comic books showed me a way that I could tell stories. I could draw. I could print. So I drew my own superheroes and spacemen and cowboys fighting supervillains and aliens and Indians with word balloons above their heads to explain the action: "You missed me!" "Ow! I'm dying!"

The concerns of the greater world came into Dog Land when a well-dressed black man knocked at the door of the restaurant and asked whether we had colored rest rooms. Most businesses in the South then had three rest rooms, for "Men," "Women," and "Colored." A few had four, so black men and women didn't have to share the same toilet. But the restaurant at Dog Land had two. Dad told the man, "Yes, they're pink." Word spread in the black community that blacks were welcome in Dog Land. Word spread in the white community, too.

Though the Supreme Court had ordered schools to integrate, many defied the law. Chiefland's classes were all white. Black children attended a small school that did not have enough text books for its children. Mom would save our magazines to give to the black school, so those children would have reading material.

I grew up with the same awareness of politics that some children have of football. Dad talked about his political beliefs, and he wrote letters to the local newspaper. He knew that wise business people hide their beliefs to avoid offending customers, but he never thought making money should be the whole of a person's purpose.

He was a liberal, though he never thought his views were extreme. He thought they were simply American: he believed people should be free to think and live as they please. Many Americans disagreed with him. Dog Land lost some business from local whites, but so long as U.S. 19 was the most popular road to Miami, we did not need the local trade to thrive—construction, however, had begun on I-75, which would by-pass us.

I became an atheist in second grade. The South was not interested in the separation of church and state; Florida's schools included prayer and Bible-reading. I would come home and tell my parents what I had learned each day. On the day that I told Dad the story of Samson setting fire to the foxes' tails to burn the fields of the Philistines, he asked me what the foxes had done to deserve being burnt. I thought about that and about the dinosaurs that I loved that weren't in the Bible, and atheism seemed my only option.

My love for science fiction grew deeper. My favorite TV show was *Fireball XL-5,* a puppet show about an explorer named Steve Zodiac who had a furry alien friend, a beautiful girlfriend, a robot companion, and a wise old man to advise him. I would convince my friends to play the characters, and we would race our imaginary space ships across the playground.

That might also be the year that I discovered I could tell stories with words. When we were assigned words and told to use them in sentences, I used them to tell simple stories about cowboys and space monsters.

Third grade was especially wonderful because I was in love with my teacher, the patient and pretty Mrs. Moore. Dad had bought an old riverboat that we used for trips on the Suwanee. We invited Mrs. Moore to come with us one afternoon. I was delighted, then disappointed when she brought her husband. I had plans to marry her when I grew up.

President Kennedy was killed that year. Many Southerners hated him, and kids tend to share their parents'

Portrait of an actor, about 1979.

Will Shetterly with his wife Emma Bull at a book signing, about 1985.

politics. A boy in my class cheered when the news was announced. Mrs. Moore cried.

That year I discovered science fiction books in the library. They had rocket ships on their spines, which made them easy to find in the fiction section. Twenty-five years later, Pamela Dean asked me the name of the first science-fiction book that I read. The answer was Heinlein's *Rocket Ship Galileo.* I'm sure I've known how Galileo's name was pronounced since I was a teenager, but on the day when Pamela asked, I pronounced it "Gah-*lil*-ee-oh." She laughed, and so did I, when I realized what had happened. Billy Shetterly read a book that I can never reread, a book whose title he carefully deciphered, and it stayed *Rocket Ship Ga-LIL-ee-oh* until I had a reason to recall it.

The summer after third grade, I worked every morning hosing down the dog pens. In the afternoons, I would drive the riding mower or pick up litter or do some other chore. I was paid a quarter a day, a fortune to me. On Thursday afternoons, I would pedal my bicycle ten miles into town to buy the new comic books. Mom worried that I was too young to go alone, and maybe Dad did, too, but he thought it was my pay, and if I was willing to go to that effort to spend it, that was my decision.

Fourth grade's most notable incident happened on the playground. In very Christian Levy County, atheism was extremely shocking to children. One asked me if I was really an atheist. I said I was. The kid asked if I would tell that to the teacher supervising the playground. I said I

would. While several kids ran to fetch the teacher, I hid in the boy's bathroom.

But someone came into the bathroom and found me, so I had to face the teacher. Our conversation began with her quite amused and me quite afraid. It went something like this:

"You're the boy who doesn't believe in God?"

"Yes, ma'am."

"Then who do you think made the world?"

Very aware of the kids watching, I said, "I don't know, and I don't care."

She made me sit in the sun for the rest of recess and watch the other children play. I was supposed to think about the reason for existence, but mostly I considered the arbitrary nature of power.

In 1965, Dad took us out of school for a few weeks to go to the New York World's Fair. Mom stayed behind to run Dog Land. We drove in our station wagon and camped along the way. Dad hated the crowds and traffic of New York, so we only stayed for a couple of days. I believe the hotels were full because of the fair, so Dad parked our station wagon each night at a gas station, and we slept in our sleeping bags in the car and used the gas station's rest rooms.

We visited pavilions dedicated to the world of the future, and we ate exotic Asian food, but the main thing I remember is that I was entrusted with a camera to take pictures for Mom and Grandpa. I backed up to get the shot

The Scribblies: (from left) Terri Windling, Valerie Smith, Steven Brust, Kara Dalkey, Nate Bucklin,
Will Shetterly, Emma Bull, and Pamela Dean, about 1988.

that I wanted, of Mike and Liz in front of a statue or a building that impressed me, and I stepped into a reflecting pool. My cowboy boots were soaked, so I spent the day walking barefoot on the hot cement sidewalks.

Fifth grade was taught by the teacher who had made me sit in the sun. I don't remember any trouble with her—even if I was, like my father, a Yankee atheist who believed in integration, I was a polite boy who loved to learn.

Halfway through fifth grade, Dad took us out of school. I did not know then how bad things had gotten because of his involvement in the civil rights movement. The *Gainesville Sun* published an article about him titled "The Only Liberal in Levy County." We received hate mail and anonymous phone calls. Dog Land could not get fire insurance because the word was out that the Ku Klux Klan would burn us down.

Mike and Liz and I went to live with Aunt Millie and Uncle Orlo in Oklee. We arrived in the middle of the Minnesota winter. In Florida, the kids thought I spoke like a Yankee, but in Oklee, they thought I sounded like a southerner. I was never especially interested in sports, but since I couldn't ice skate or play hockey, I spent most afternoons after school watching TV and eating toast with cinnamon sugar.

When Mom and Dad came to get us, I was fat. Dad addressed the matter as he addressed all matters: directly. As we drove from National Park to National Park in a Volkswagen van that he had outfitted with camping gear, he would stop and make me run beside the van each afternoon.

Dad sold Dog Land, and we moved to Gainesville. He entered the University of Florida as a forty-year-old freshman, Mom got a job as a secretary at the U.'s medical school, and I entered Miss Larson's sixth grade class at Myra Terwilliger Elementary School. (I have no idea who Myra Terwilliger was, but I have always loved the sound of her name.)

Miss Larson was young, slender, dark-haired, and unmarried. My crush on her may have been as great as the one on Mrs. Moore, or it may have been greater, since at the age of twelve, my body was beginning to change. I still remember my disappointment at learning she had a boyfriend.

Our home on Northwest 55th Terrace was a small cinder-block house in a blue-collar neighborhood. It had a carport instead of a garage, three small bedrooms, a bathroom, and a combination living room-dining room next to a galley kitchen. Mike and I had a room that we did not have to share with Liz. But the odd thing about it—there always seemed to be something odd about the places Dad found to live—was the bomb shelter in the backyard. The entrance to it had buckled, so no one knew what was down there when we bought it. (When we finally dug it out, the answer was disappointing: a lot of water and a few typed pages of someone's pornographic fantasy.)

In Gainesville, Dad continued to be active in politics. He walked at the head of Gainesville's first march against the Vietnam War, and I rode my bicycle. Long-haired men and girls in bell-bottomed jeans decorated my bicycle with flowers and little American flags. Though people screamed that we were Commies and traitors, the protest felt like a celebration, and I suppose it was: a celebration of peace.

I made a trip, perhaps through the local Unitarian Church, to the town of Belle Glade and saw the conditions that migrant workers lived under. Black families lived in shacks with no running water or working toilets. The shacks were rented to them by the company that employed them under classic "company store" policies: The only place for the workers to buy goods was at the company store, where the prices were very high; once they were in debt to the company, it was impossible to leave. I had known that economic injustice existed in the United States, but that was the first time that I saw the price some people paid for other people's prosperity.

I decided to lose weight that year. I rode my bicycle to school instead of taking the bus, ate sandwiches with one slice of bread instead of two, and quit indulging in the occasional sugarfest—my favorite treat was to buy a frozen chocolate ice box pie and eat the whole thing in one sitting.

Grandpa Amos died around this time. We kids went with Mom to Minnesota for the funeral. One night, I went alone into the basement where his workshop had been, and though I knew that men were not supposed to cry, I did.

As a sixth grader at elementary school, I was one of the oldest students, but entering Westwood Junior High as a seventh-grader made me one of the youngest. I remember the embarrassment of the locker room after physical education classes, when everyone found out who had gone through puberty and who had not.

Mike and Liz and I helped Dad enclose the carport to make another room for the house. He built a bookcase out from the wall to divide the room, with the back half for a bedroom and the front half for an office. Mom and Dad moved into the new room, and, feeling like a king of infinite space, I took over their old room.

In eighth grade, I studied karate at the local recreation center and was delighted to find a sport that I enjoyed. Knowing I wanted to be a writer, I took typing, where I may have been the only boy in a class full of girls—in the days before home computers, typing was a skill for secretaries, and secretaries were invariably women.

Dad bought an old bread truck, a Chevrolet step-van, and converted it into a camper. He built a bed across the back, installed a small refrigerator, bolted aluminum beach chairs on either side of the van that unfolded into beds, then painted the outside red, Mom's favorite color. We took several long summer vacations in the red van. That may have been the summer that we drove the long, unpaved road to Alaska. The van was put to another use, as well: Pa drove us kids around in the afternoons after he and we were done with school, and Mike and Liz and I would go door-to-door, selling tins of potato chips to earn pocket money.

Both Grandmothers lived with us for a while in Gainesville. Grandma Bess was poor, so she stayed in our house. Grandma Irene was rich, so she rented an apartment nearby. At best, I tolerated them. I was interested in comic books, science fiction, rock and roll, and girls; I didn't think I could talk about any of those things with them.

The Youth

In ninth grade, I was again one of the oldest students. Buchholz Junior High opened that year. Its students had

gleaming new facilities and a sense that we were shaping a school's spirit. I wrote for the school newspaper, and I practiced my typing by writing stories that I gave to my friends to read. I grew my hair long, which meant a great deal in those days: once when I was bicycling, a man in a truck yelled "Hippie!" and threw a bottle at my head, only missing by a foot or two. I smoked marijuana for the first time—the mother of the boy who gave me my first joint said I could not hang out with her son, because I was a bad influence.

Dad let me skip school for a few days so we could drive with some college students to the Moratorium, a major war protest. Tens of thousands of people marched past the White House. I had too little sleep, but I felt like I had participated in history.

Mom took me to see *Easy Rider,* an R-rated film that I badly wanted to see. It confirmed my desire to become a hippie—I thought there could be nothing better in life than to have long hair and a motorcycle.

I ran away from home that year. I don't remember what I had done to be punished. Since I was too old to be spanked, Dad told me to dig a large hole in the backyard and fill it up again. I screamed at him, calling him every foul word I could remember. Then I turned and ran into the woods.

I had less than a dollar in my pocket. But Mom had given me a charge card at a local department store, so I hitchhiked to the store and bought a blanket that I could wear like a cloak and use to sleep in. I went to the university's student center and watched television in the lounge—if I ever write a story about this, I'll have the runaway watch *Star Trek,* but I honestly don't remember

Wife Emma Bull

what was on. I spent the night sleeping on the grass in a park.

The next day, I called a girl I had a crush on. I said, "Guess who ran away from home?" and was quite disappointed when she didn't guess me. She convinced me to go home again. I had to dig the hole three times, which seemed fair enough, especially since the subsequent times were easier once the dirt had been loosened.

I wanted more freedom than I had at home, and Dad found a solution. Grandpa Amos had left enough money to send me away to private school. The family was going to move to Washington, D.C., where Dad would teach high school while taking night classes at George Washington Law School. Since I would be leaving my friends at Gainesville whether I went away to school or not, boarding school seemed like a good deal to me.

I went through a book on private schools and found several that I liked: liberal, co-ed schools. Dad also sent an application to one that he liked: Choate, the school John F. Kennedy graduated from after being expelled from several others. It did not admit girls then, so I wasn't interested, but when Choate accepted me, I saw how proud Dad was of me, and I agreed to go.

Shortly before we left Gainesville, I met Beth Davis, my first girlfriend. I had always been shy around girls I found attractive, but knowing that I was leaving made me bold. I can't remember whether Mom or Dad drove us to *Anne of the Thousand Days,* the movie that was our first date. I do remember that we saw very little of it in the back row of the theatre, and I felt very mature when our ride came to pick us up.

Dad drove the red camper to Mexico in the summer of 1970. We went deep-sea fishing, and I caught a fish that weighed two-thirds as much as I did. Dad and I and a Mexican guide set out to climb Mt. Popocatepetl while Mom, Mike, and Liz stayed below. Perhaps half a mile from the top, Dad's breathing grew short. He told me to go on to the top without him, so I did. I wasn't proud of either of those events—I never liked killing anything with a face, and I didn't think a few thousand feet made much difference in what was a great view either way—but Dad was proud of them, and that made me proud.

My favorite parts of the summer in Mexico were the week we spent at a campground near Acapulco, then another week at Zihuatanejo, which was then a small fishing town. I spent days swimming, and walking along the beach, and lying in hammocks under palm-covered shelters reading science fiction and fantasy paperbacks.

Most of the boys at Choate were wealthy New Englanders and New Yorkers. The classes were small, the teachers were excellent, and I felt as if I were in prison. I had to cut my hair to meet the dress code. Most of our day was accounted for: assigned tables for meals, classes in the early part of the day, sports in the afternoon, study halls, nondenominational chapel, and an early lights-out.

Students and prisoners escape the same way: with drugs. A boy in my house had plenty to sell, so I experimented with hashish, amphetamines, mescaline, and LSD. Another friend liked to spray Right Guard into a plastic bag and inhale the freon, which provided brief, hallucinogenic effects by depriving the brain of oxygen.

On vacations, I took the train to D.C., a long day's trip. I never felt as if I lived at the house on T Street, so I often

Author Will Shetterly

stayed at Choate for short vacations like Thanksgiving to read or write or do drugs.

For Easter break, I took a bus down to Florida to visit my friends. A girl my age got on the bus. At fifteen, she was leaving an abusive husband and going home. We talked through the night, huddled under a blanket together. In Florida, I flirted with one girl, made out with another, then got back together with Beth. A group of us went to a house in the country and dropped acid. Someone shot squirrels for dinner. Skinned and decapitated, they looked like tiny headless humans, but tasted delicious.

One reason I had agreed to go to Choate was that it would merge with Rosemary Hall, a girls' school, in another year. That spring, a small group of girls came from Rosemary Hall to take classes with the boys. I loved to walk in the woods close to where they were building the girls' campus. One day, I saw a beautiful blonde girl in the Rosemary Hall white blouse and plaid skirt, lying perfectly still in a clearing. I felt as if I had come upon a sleeping princess. I learned her name and wrote bad love poems for her, but nothing came of that.

A loner at Choate, I was free to befriend social outcasts, such as a boy who dressed in black and claimed to be both homosexual and a witch. I decided the first was no reason to avoid him, and the second was a good reason to seek him out. But if there was any depth to his study of magic, he did not share it with me. At the mandatory chapel services, I would whisper the Lord's Prayer backward because that was supposed to deconsecrate the ground. I'm sure I was neither the first nor the last boy to do that. At least I was using the place for something like a spiritual matter, which seemed to me to be more than anyone else did there. I was interested in magic the way I was interested in folklore and mythology. I remained an atheist or, at least, an agnostic. Magic was fun, but it was not an answer.

Drugs might be, I thought. I had read Aldous Huxley's *Doors of Perception* and Tom Wolfe's *The Electric Kool-Aid Acid Test,* as well as science fiction by writers like Phillip K. Dick and Roger Zelazny in which reality was rarely what it seemed. I was prepared to believe that there was a truth to the world that I had not seen, and I thought drugs might reveal it to me.

My second year at Choate was better than the first because the girls of Rosemary Hall moved into their new campus. But I was still shy, there were twice as many Choate boys as Rosemary Hall girls, and the girls did not think Choaties were as cool as boys from other prep schools. I became the confidant of several girls that I adored with the pure love of a romantic sixteen-year-old; they liked me because they could talk to me "as a friend."

I increased my use of drugs until, finally, drugs rejected me. One acid trip went horribly wrong. I became convinced that I could break through the false world that I perceived by throwing myself out a third-story window. In my mind's eye, I saw very clearly that my body would hit the ground, but my soul would hurtle onward. And if I found myself in another false reality, I could kill myself

With Brain Damage, "The best cat in the universe," about 1990.

again and again, until finally the illusions would break down and I would arrive at the truth.

My practical streak saved me. I decided that these things were too hard to consider when I was tired, so I went to sleep confident that I could always kill myself the next day.

I tripped twice more after that, hoping that drugs would be good to me again. Those trips were every bit as bad. Worse, I suffered minor flashbacks when time seemed to slow and the fabric of reality grew thin. The bad acid trips spoiled other drugs for me, too: even the dreamlike experience of marijuana came too close to an eerie timelessness that presaged the unveiling of some truth about reality that I knew I did not want to learn.

I decided to remake myself. I quit doing all banned drugs. Fond of symbolic gestures, I cut my hair. I had smoked cigarettes for a few months; this may be when I quit tobacco, too. I don't know if I worked harder at schoolwork, but my grades did not suffer, and I finished the year expecting to return to Choate.

I had to stay over for a few days after graduation because I had accumulated demerits for minor offenses like tardiness and skipped classes that had to be worked off in manual labor, doing things like cleaning the grounds or painting the boathouse. A group of us went into the woods to celebrate the end of the year. Someone bought beer. My resolve to go straight did not include socially condoned drugs like alcohol.

A teacher found us. I was expelled for drinking. My parents were disappointed, and so was I. I had endured two hard years at Choate. I was looking forward to the relative freedom of being a senior, and maybe finally finding love with one of the many girls I liked.

But being expelled turned out well. I moved back in with my family and found it much easier to live with them as a seventeen-year-old. To graduate from Western High School, where Dad taught, I only needed one more credit than I had gotten at Choate, so I took a few classes in the morning for three months, then, in the spring, began classes at George Washington University. In the afternoons, I worked at a head shop, where we sold pipes and bongs and rolling paper, black light posters, underground comix—all the paraphernalia of the counter-culture, which was becoming increasingly mainstream by 1972.

I returned to Choate one weekend to visit old friends and met Barbara Friedman, a girl my age who had transferred to Rosemary Hall for her senior year. She was beautiful and clever, a talented painter and a voracious reader, and, for reasons I never completely understood, quite taken with me.

That summer, Dad sold the house in Washington. Instead of using his newly acquired law degree, he bought a trading post at Rat Rapids, near New Osnaburgh, an Ojibwe reservation in northern Ontario. At the time, you reached it by driving north from the Trans-Canada Highway for a hundred and fifty miles on a gravel road. Tired of cities, Dad found a place where he could live simply. The original buildings were the store, which had an office, and a small cabin with two bedrooms. He bought two ancient generators to provide electricity. No television signals reached that far north. The place was beautiful, with its clear lakes and tall pines, but it was no place I wanted to be.

I spent part of the summer at Cornell University with Barbara, then she came with me to work at Rat Rapids. In the fall, we went our separate ways, she to Beloit College in Wisconsin, me to New College in Sarasota, Florida.

New College was an experimental school with a three-year course; its quarters were the equivalent of semesters at other schools. Its students did not have to have a major, which appealed to me: I wanted to take classes that interested me, and not what someone thought I needed to take.

Barbara transferred to New College to be with me. We took a semester abroad, staying at Angers in France and with her parents near Monaco, but mostly we travelled by student rail through France, Spain, Italy, Germany, and Britain.

When New College merged with the Florida state system and no one knew what would happen to it, we both transferred to Beloit. The only drawback was that Beloit required its students to choose majors. I discovered that I had one more credit in English than in history, so I became an English major.

I met Emma Bull at Beloit. Barbara saw her reading a science fiction book, told her that her boyfriend read science fiction, and asked if it was any good. Barbara dragged me to meet a tall, dark-haired woman who loved the same books that I loved, who played folk songs on her guitar and sang beautifully, who also wanted be a writer.

Emma and I became best friends. We started a literary magazine together, *The Beloit Tri-Weekly*. We formed a branch of the Society for Creative Anachronism, and threw the best Medieval feast that we could afford on students' budgets. We took creative writing courses together, and we went to the Coughy House, the campus hangout, to drink beer and talk about art and our respective love lives.

Barbara and I graduated in 1976 and drove east. She wrecked my car, but neither of us were hurt, so I bought a used car for $300 and we continued to Providence, Rhode Island, where she entered the Rhode Island School of Design. I found an apartment near the campus and tried to write the traditional sensitive young artist's semi-autobiographical first novel, and discovered I had nothing to say that I thought anyone would want to hear.

Barbara and I parted that fall, and I moved to New York City.

The Man

In New York, I found a cheap apartment in the east nineties where I worked as the building manager for an owner who was so paranoid that he tried to hide his real name from his renters. I got a job as an editorial assistant

Shetterly beside his uncle's tombstone, about 1990.

Shetterly and Emma in their kitchen in Minnesota, about 1994.

for Berkley Books, a paperback publishing house. At editorial meetings, the publisher would pick scabs from the palms of his hands and eat them while no one commented. The woman I worked for was hardly that odd, but she needed a more experienced assistant, so the company offered me the chance to transfer. I quit instead and became a production aide for John Wiley & Sons, a textbook publisher.

I moved from the east nineties to the west eighties, then found a studio on West Seventy-third for a $125 a month, an incredible deal even then. I painted it myself, then scrubbed the floor and polyurethaned it. And I set up my typewriter and kept trying to write.

I quit John Wiley to spend a year as an actor. I took classes, modelled for the covers of a few romance magazines, had a part in an off-off-Broadway play, and appeared briefly in a terrible movie called *Toxic Zombies.* It was often fun, but it was not a career, and it did not look like it would become one.

In 1980, I moved back to live with my family in Northern Ontario. I liked it better then: the business had expanded, and I could appreciate a simpler life. Dad had built a new store with an apartment above it, so I lived in the old house.

The work was hard, seasonal, and satisfying. In the fall, the Ojibwe people harvested wild rice. Dad and another man would fly small planes out to their camps, land on the water, and load the planes with one-hundred-pound bags of wild rice. I met them at the dock, unloaded the bags, and carried them up to a storage shed.

Dad built a small plant to process the wild rice. Four giant steel cylinders rotated night and day above wood fires. You shovelled in wet, green wild rice, let it parch in the cylinder, then dumped it out and shovelled in more while keeping the fire hot and making sure the rice didn't burn. The work area filled with smoke, so we wore goggles and breathing masks—see the picture that I always wanted to use as an author's bookjacket photo.

After six months in Ontario, I saved enough money to travel. I went to Minneapolis to visit Emma and her boyfriend. I liked the city and her friends in Minn-stf, the local science fiction club. I took an apartment, found a girlfriend, and decided to write a fantasy novel.

Then Emma and I became lovers as well as best friends. We moved into an apartment together and bought an Apple II+ computer. We married in 1981 in the bar of a St. Paul hotel where Scott and Zelda Fitzgerald once danced in the fountain.

For the next couple of years, we spent part of our time in Ontario helping with the family business and the rest of our time in Minneapolis, where Brain Damage, the Best Cat in the Universe, found us on the street one day. Though his previous owners had declawed him, he was fearless. What we mistook for stupidity was his pure delight in life. He loved to ride on people's shoulders, and he adored cantaloupe. He softened us up for cat ownership, so we acquired Chaos, who probably deserved Brain Damage's name.

In 1983, Emma and I bought a house and started SteelDragon Press. In the next thirteen years, SteelDragon published novels by Steven Brust, Larry Niven, Jane Yolen, and Barry Longyear; three compact discs of music by Cats Laughing and the Flash Girls, bands that Emma sang and played guitar in; and twenty-two comic books, including twelve issues of one that I wrote: *Captain Confederacy*, the story of a superhero in a world where the American South seceded. One of SteelDragon's first publications was *SteelDragon Stories*, a comic book with two stories that I wrote, one of which was illustrated by Emma. We thought we might have a career doing comic books together, but then our prose began to sell.

In 1981, we had helped form a writing group that eventually included Pamela Dean, Patricia C. Wrede, Steven Brust, Nathan Bucklin, and Kara Dalkey. When the group formed, none of us had been published. Then Pat finished her first book and sold it to Terri Windling at Ace Books through agent Valerie Smith. Steve did the same. And so did Emma and Pamela and Kara and I. We originally had no formal name for our group, but when Ace Books wanted to promote us, we became the Interstate Writers Workshop, a.k.a. the Scribblies.

I wrote six novels in Minneapolis and, with Emma, edited five anthologies.

I began *Cats Have No Lord* in Ontario. Realizing that whenever I attempted to write something ambitious, I eventually grew frustrated and quit, I decided to write something fun, something like the swashbuckling fantasies that I loved as a teenager. I didn't have a plan when I began: I wrote four chapters about other characters before Lizelle the thief and her telepathic horse, Darkwind, showed up and let me know that the book was about them. So I reshaped it accordingly. When the first draft was done, I realized that one of the minor characters was stealing attention from Lizelle, so I cut him out of the book entirely.

Witch Blood was an attempt to combine heroic fantasy with the tough-guy voice of detective writers like Raymond Chandler and Robert B. Parker. I had writer's block, so I decided to write something that I could plot as I wrote by alternating scenes of violence and sex, and if the story turned out badly, I could try to sell it under a pseudonym. But, as I wrote, I found themes of identity and redemption that interested me, so I worked hard on the subsequent drafts to make it look as if I knew what I was doing all along.

The Tangled Lands was an attempt to fuse heroic fantasy with cyberpunk. It takes two very different stories and weaves them into one. I think it's my least successful book, but it has things in it that I like.

Elsewhere and *Nevernever* were published in hardcover as young adult novels and in paperback as fantasy. Publishers decide categories for books; writers merely write them. These are stories about a boy who runs away to Bordertown, a place invented by Terri Windling for a shared-world anthology series. Bordertown is a city between the world we know and the lands of Faerie, a city where magic and science work erratically, and runaways go to learn about life.

Dogland is a semi-autobiographical fantasy about a boy whose father builds a tourist attraction with over a hundred breeds of dogs. It owes a great deal to my life at Dog Land, and I sometimes wonder if I should have written it as an autobiography, but I'm a fantasist, not an essayist. I believe *Dogland* is the finest thing I've written—but writers are often wrong about their work; Arthur Conan Doyle thought his Sherlock Holmes stories were his least important writing.

I've written two stories that I feel inexpressibly fortunate to have written: "Dreamcatcher," which is in Terri Windling's *The Armless Maiden,* and "The Princess Who Kicked Butt," which appeared in Michael Stearns's *A Wizard's Dozen* and *Cricket* magazine. When I read them to an audience, the first can be counted on to bring a few tears, and the second, a few laughs.

Once most of the Scribblies had sold a novel or two, Terri Windling asked us to create a shared-world anthology, a collection of stories by different writers using the same setting and some of the same characters. We discussed what would make a good setting for all of us, and so we created the city of Liavek. We invited other writers to join us, people like Jane Yolen, Gene Wolfe, Megan Lindholm (who also writes as Robin Hobb), Charles de Lint, and Walter Jon Williams, and eventually published five volumes.

Emma and I became vegetarians early in the 1990s for all the usual reasons, with an emphasis on health and morality. My sense of fairness says that you shouldn't eat anything that wouldn't try to eat you, and my sense of integrity says you shouldn't eat anything that you wouldn't be willing to kill yourself.

I ran for governor of Minnesota in 1994 as the candidate of the Grassroots Party and came in third out of a field of six. I never hoped to win. I merely wanted to talk about issues that the Democrats and the Republicans had agreed not to raise, like the madness of the war on drugs. I suppose my politics might best be described as democratic libertarian socialism: I believe in a government that stays out of its citizens' private affairs while helping them in public matters like education and health care.

In 1996, Emma and I sold our house and most of our possessions. We retraced old Route 66 most of the way to Los Angeles. Since arriving here, we've sold a screenplay and a couple of TV scripts. Brain Damage died, but Chaos is still healthy at the age of seventeen, and we've acquired an Angeleno cat who came with the name of Buddha, though he's singularly unenlightened. We've become active in the Unitarian Church. We study Tai Chi. And we write.

I'm working on a science fiction detective novel tentatively titled *Chimera;* it's loosely based on the comic book story that I wrote and Emma drew so many years ago. I think my next novel will be *The Secret Academy*, a sequel to *Dogland*. Whether we'll continue seeking work in Hollywood, I don't know. Show business is a business that requires a great willingness to accept compromise, and I've never been good at that. And I do know that the pursuit of happiness and the pursuit of wealth are often at odds with each other. I can imagine worse epitaphs than "He chose happiness."

Writings

FICTION

Cats Have No Lord, Ace Books, 1985.
Witch Blood, Ace Books, 1986.
The Tangled Lands, Ace Books, 1989.
Elsewhere, Harcourt Brace, 1991.
(With Emma Bull) *Double Feature* (short story collection), NESFA Press, 1993.
Nevernever, Harcourt Brace, 1993.
Dogland, Tor Books, 1997.

OTHER

Contributor of short stories to numerous collections, including *Xanadu 2,* 1993, *Starfarer's Dozen,* 1995, *Immortal Unicorn,* 1995, *The Armless Maiden,* 1995, *The Sandman Book of Dreams,* 1996, and editor of the "Liavek" series with Emma Bull, Ace Books. Also creator of comic books and graphic albums, including "Home Is a Hard Place," *Open Space #3,* Marvel Comics, 1990, and *Captain Confederacy,* Epic/Marvel Comics, 1991. Nonfiction articles have appeared in the *Utne Reader, Year's Best Fantasy and Horror,* and *Artpaper.* A science fiction screenplay, co-authored with Emma Bull, has been purchased for development by Perfect World Entertainment.

SHULEVITZ, Uri 1935-

Personal

Given name pronounced *oo*-ree; born February 27, 1935, in Warsaw, Poland; immigrated to United States in 1959; naturalized during the 1960s; son of Abraham and Szandla (Hermanstat) Shulevitz; married Helene Weiss (an artist) June 11, 1961 (divorced). *Education:* Teacher's College, Israel, teacher's degree, 1956; attended Tel-Aviv Art Institute, 1953-55, and Brooklyn Museum Art School, 1959-61. *Religion:* Jewish. *Hobbies and other interests:* Art, music, movies, old tales and parables of eastern traditions, yoga and tai-chi-chuan, ballroom dancing.

Addresses

Home—New York, NY.

Career

Kibbutz Ein Geddi (collective farm), Israel, member 1957-58; art director of youth magazine in Israel, 1958-59; illustrator of children's books, 1961—; author of children's books, 1962—; School of Visual Arts, New York City, instructor in art, 1967-68; Pratt Institute, Brooklyn, NY, instructor in art, 1970-71; New School for Social Research, New York City, instructor in art and in writing and illustrating of children's books, 1970—; Hartwick College, Oneonta, NY, director of summer workshop in writing and illustrating children's books, 1974—. *Exhibitions:* Work has been exhibited in numerous galleries and museums, including Tel Aviv Museum, A. M. Sachs Gallery, New York City, Metropolitan Museum of Art, and New York Public Library. *Military service:* Israeli Army, 1956-59. *Member:* Authors Guild, Authors League of America (member of children's

books committee), Society of Children's Book Writers and Illustrators, American Society of Contemporary Artists.

Awards, Honors

Children's Book Awards, American Institute of Graphic Arts, 1963-64, for *Charley Sang a Song,* 1965-66, for *The Second Witch,* 1967-68, for *One Monday Morning,* and Certificate of Excellence, 1973-74, for *The Magician* and *The Fools of Chelm and Their History,* and 1979, for *The Treasure;* American Institute of Graphic Arts Children's Books (AIGACB) citations, 1967-68, for *One Monday Morning,* 1973-74, for *The Fools of Chelm and Their History* and *The Magician,* and 1980, for *The Treasure;* American Library Association (ALA) Notable Book citations, 1967, for *One Monday Morning,* 1968, for *The Fool of the World and the Flying Ship,* 1969, for *Rain Rain Rivers,* 1974, for *Dawn,* and 1982, for *The Golem; Horn Book* honor list citations, 1967, for *One Monday Morning,* 1969, for *Rain Rain Rivers,* and 1979, for *The Treasure;* Certificate of Merit, Society of Illustrators (New York), 1965, for *Charley Sang a Song;* books displayed at Children's Book Exhibition, New York Public Library, 1967, 1968, 1969, 1972, 1973, and 1974, and at International Biennale of Illustrations, Bratislava, Czechoslovakia, 1969; Caldecott Medal, ALA, 1969, for *The Fool of the World and the Flying Ship; The Fool of the World and the Flying Ship* included in American Booksellers 1969 Gift to the Nation from the Library of the White House; Children's Books of the Year honors, Child Study Association of America, 1969, for *Rain Rain Rivers,* 1972, for *Soldier and Tsar in the Forest: A Russian Tale,* 1974, for *Dawn,* and 1976, for *The Touchstone;* Bronze Medal, Leipzig International Book Exhibition, 1970, for *Rain Rain Rivers; Book World*'s Children's Spring Book Festival Picture Book honor, 1972, for *Soldier and Tsar in the*

Uri Shulevitz

Forest: A Russian Tale; Book World's Children's Spring Book Festival Award for Younger Children and *New York Times* Outstanding Books of the Year, both 1973, and Children's Book Showcase, Children's Book Council, 1974, all for *The Magician; New York Times* Outstanding Books of the Year, 1974, Christopher Award, 1975, Children's Book Showcase, Children's Book Council, 1975, Honor List, International Board on Books for Young People, 1976, and Brooklyn Art Books for Children citations, 1976, 1977, and 1978, all for *Dawn; New York Times* Best Illustrated Books citations, 1978, for *Hanukkah Money,* and 1979, for *The Treasure;* certificate, Graphic Arts Awards of the Printing Industries of America, 1979, and Caldecott Honor Book, ALA, 1980, both for *The Treasure; New York Times* Outstanding Book and *School Library Journal*'s Best Books, both 1982, and Parents' Choice Award for Literature, Parents' Choice Foundation, 1983, all for *The Golem;* Sydney Taylor Book Award, 1992, for *The Diamond Tree: Jewish Tales from around the World;* Best Books, *Publishers Weekly* and *School Library Journal,* and Editors' Choice, *Booklist,* all 1998, Blue Ribbon citation, *Bulletin of the Center for Children's Books,* Notable Books for Children, ALA, Charlotte Zolotow Award, Cooperative Children's Book Center of the University of Wisconsin, Certificate of Excellence, *Parenting* Magazine, Golden Kite Award book, Society of Children's Book Writers and Illustrators, and Caldecott Honor Book, ALA, all 1999, all for *Snow.*

Writings

AUTHOR AND ILLUSTRATOR

The Moon in My Room, Harper, 1963.
One Monday Morning, Scribner, 1967.
Rain Rain Rivers, Farrar, Straus, 1969.
(Adapter) *Oh What a Noise!* (text based on "A Big Noise" by William Brighty Rands), Macmillan, 1971.
(Adapter) *The Magician,* Macmillan, 1973.
Dawn, Farrar, Straus, 1974.
The Treasure, Farrar, Straus, 1979.
Writing with Pictures: How to Write and Illustrate Children's Books, Watson-Guptill, 1985.
The Strange and Exciting Adventures of Jeremiah Hush, Farrar, Straus, 1986.
Toddlecreek Post Office, Farrar, Straus, 1990.
The Secret Room, Farrar, Straus, 1993.
(Reteller) *The Golden Goose,* Farrar Straus, 1995.
Snow, Farrar, Straus, 1998.

ILLUSTRATOR

Charlotte Zolotow, *A Rose, a Bridge, and a Wild Black Horse,* Harper, 1964.
Mary Stolz, *The Mystery of the Woods,* Harper, 1964.
H. R. Hays and Daniel Hays, *Charley Sang a Song,* Harper, 1964.
Sulamith Ish-Kishore, *The Carpet of Solomon,* Pantheon, 1964.
Jack Sendak, *The Second Witch,* Harper, 1965.
Molly Cone, *Who Knows Ten? Children's Tales of the Ten Commandments,* Union of American Hebrew Congregations, 1965.
Jacob Grimm and Wilhelm Grimm, *The Twelve Dancing Princesses,* translated by Elizabeth Shub, Scribner, 1966.
Mary Stolz, *Maximilian's World,* Harper, 1966.
Jean Russell Larson, *The Silkspinners,* Scribner, 1967.
Dorothy Nathan, *The Month Brothers,* Dutton, 1967.
John Smith, editor, *My Kind of Verse,* Macmillan, 1968.
Jan Wahl, *Runaway Jonah and Other Tales,* Macmillan, 1968.
Arthur Ransome, adapter, *The Fool of the World and the Flying Ship: A Russian Tale,* Farrar, Straus, 1968.
Jan Wahl, *The Wonderful Kite,* Delacorte, 1971.
Yehoash Biber, *Treasure of the Turkish Pasha,* translated from Hebrew by Naruch Hochman, Blue Star Book Club, 1971.
Alexander Afanasyev, *Soldier and Tsar in the Forest: A Russian Tale,* translated by Richard Lourie, Farrar, Straus, 1972.
Isaac Bashevis Singer, *The Fools of Chelm and Their History,* Farrar, Straus, 1973.
Robert Louis Stevenson, *The Touchstone,* Greenwillow, 1978.
Sholem Aleichem, *Hanukah Money,* translated and adapted by Shulevitz and Elizabeth Shub, Greenwillow, 1978.
Richard Kennedy, *The Lost Kingdom of Karnica,* Sierra Club, 1979.
Isaac Bashevis Singer, *The Golem,* Farrar, Straus, 1982.
Howard Schwartz, *Lilith's Cave: Jewish Tales of the Supernatural,* Harper, 1988.

Howard Schwartz and Barbara Rush, *The Diamond Tree: Jewish Tales from around the World,* HarperCollins, 1991.

Ehud Ben-Ezer, *Hosni the Dreamer: An Arabian Tale,* Farrar, Straus, 1997.

OTHER

Contributor to *Horn Book.*

Adaptations

One Monday Morning (film), Weston Woods, 1972, (filmstrip), 1973; *The Treasure* (film), Weston Woods, 1980; *Dawn* (filmstrip with cassette), Weston Woods, 1982. Also, *The Fool of the World and the Flying Ship* (filmstrip).

Work in Progress

What is a Wise Bird Like You Doing in a Silly Tale Like This?, for Farrar, Straus.

Sidelights

Encouraged by his artistic parents, author and illustrator Uri Shulevitz began drawing before the age of three, and has been creating stories and pictures from his fertile imagination ever since. Embarking upon a career as an author and illustrator of children's books with his first published work, *The Moon in My Room,* Shulevitz has also distinguished himself by providing pictures for the works of such celebrated writers as Arthur Ransome, Isaac Bashevis Singer, Charlotte Zolotow, Robert Louis Stevenson, and the Brothers Grimm. His illustrations, which have been characterized as "evocative" and "timeless" by a *Kirkus Reviews* critic, have garnered a host of accolades, including the 1969 Caldecott Medal for *The Fool of the World and the Flying Ship.*

Shulevitz was born February 27, 1935, in Warsaw, Poland. When he was four years old, Warsaw was attacked by Nazi invaders. Shulevitz retains vivid memories of burning buildings and of a bomb falling into the very building where he and his family lived. "I recall people carrying water from the Vistula [river] to drink and to wash in, and the complete paralysis of most public services, including electricity," he added.

Shulevitz and his family fled Poland in 1939, eventually settling in Paris after the conclusion of the war. In his newly adopted country, Shulevitz attended French grammar school and frequented book stores. He became fascinated with French comic books, and soon he and a friend were creating their own, with Shulevitz serving as artist. His talents were further encouraged when he won first prize in a grammar school drawing contest. After moving to Israel with his family in 1949, Shulevitz was honored as the youngest member to participate in a drawing exhibition at the Museum of Tel Aviv.

In 1953 Shulevitz attended the Teachers Institute and studied at the Art Institute in Tel Aviv. When the Sinai War broke out in 1956 he went into basic training with

Shulevitz provided ten paintings full of humor and animation for **The Diamond Tree,** *a collection of Jewish folk and fairy tales selected and retold by Howard Schwartz and Barbara Rush.*

the Israeli army, then joined a group of his friends in forming a *kibbutz,* or communal farm, located near the Dead Sea. While there he made his first attempt at designing graphics, creating a Passover Haggadah containing the narrative of the Exodus read at Seder. While still in army service, Shulevitz also worked as art director of a magazine for teenagers, becoming a freelance artist when his military tour of duty was complete.

In 1959, twenty-four-year-old Shulevitz came to New York City and studied painting at the Brooklyn Museum Art School. His first illustrating job was for a New York publisher of Hebrew books for children. "I was strictly supervised and permitted only to work from sketches given to me," Shulevitz later recalled to *SATA.* "Still, this experience improved my pen and brush techniques." Interestingly, it was while working in this structured, controlled atmosphere that Shulevitz developed what would become his unique illustration style.

Shulevitz's first published book for children, *The Moon in My Room,* was released in 1963. Written and illustrated under the guidance of two editors at Harper & Row, the book allowed Shulevitz to come to terms with his own feelings of inadequacy as a speaker of English. "I eventually understood that my initial reaction, my fear that I could not write, was based on a preconception," he later explained. "A preconception that writing was strictly related to words and to spoken language. That it was essential to use many words in a skillful way. I was overlooking what was of primary importance—*what* I had to say; and I was caught in a secondary consideration—*how* to say it. That secondary concern has nothing to do with writing, but I was allowing it to take over the primary one."

In creating his stories, Shulevitz begins by focusing on the action of the story, first visualizing it and then figuring out how to express it in words. He tries to express the action as simply as possible, using a pictorial approach. For example, the story about a young, imaginative boy who explores the world without leaving his room in *The Moon in My Room* "unfolded in my head like a movie," Shulevitz stated. "I was the camera seeing the action conveyed by pictures. The few words necessary to communicate the story fell into place on their own. It was all so simple and natural." Shulevitz dubbed this technique "writing with pictures," maintaining that this method can also enhance the ability to visualize for writers who do not have a background in art. "Visual thinking can also avoid excessive wordiness in writing in general," Shulevitz added. "In this way my visual approach evolved—an approach based on my writing and teaching experience."

With the success of his first book, Shulevitz was quickly provided more opportunities to "write with pictures," and in 1969 he earned enduring renown as a recipient of the coveted Caldecott Medal, awarded for his work on Arthur Ransome's retelling *The Fool of the World and the Flying Ship,* a traditional folk tale imbued with moral undertones. The book was Shulevitz's first full-color project, and preparing its dummy took him six months. The author was honored again the following year with a Bronze Medal at the International Book Exhibition in Leipzig for his *Rain Rain Rivers.* "I first had the idea for my own picture book *Rain Rain Rivers* about five years before actually starting on the illustrations," Shulevitz recalled. "[The idea] came and imposed itself on me in an unmistakable way. One evening I heard the patter of rain and simultaneously saw a series of images—impressions of which I immediately wrote down. This was the beginning. I thought that it was raining outside, since I could actually hear it. But when I looked out of the window, there was a clear night sky over the Greenwich Village rooftops. All this happened in a flash, and it was the seed of the future book."

In 1975 Shulevitz received the Christopher Award for *Dawn,* which was also selected to represent the United

When Hosni the shepherd has one gold dinar to spend, he makes an inspired choice that saves his life and secures his ***fortune.*** *(From* Hosni the Dreamer: An Arabian Tale, *written by Ehud Ben-Ezer and illustrated by Shulevitz.)*

A small boy and his dog eagerly anticipate the big snowfall that they feel must surely follow the first few flakes. (*From* Snow, *written and illustrated by Shulevitz.*)

States on the International Honor List at the Congress of the International Board on Books for Young People. In *Dawn,* like *Rain Rain Rivers* a book written and illustrated by Shulevitz, the author employs both picture book and story book concepts. As he once explained: "Early in the book there is a picture of a mountain by a lake before dawn. The text simply: 'Still.' Without the picture, you would not know what 'still' referred to. This is characteristic of the picture book concept.

"Later, however, I describe how 'Under a tree by a lake an old man and his grandson curl up in their blankets.' The picture here shows them curled up in their blankets. This approach is characteristic of the story book concept. Although the words help guide the reader to where to focus in the picture, the words could be understood without the picture."

Reviewers have consistently praised Shulevitz's self-illustrated books for their thoughtful storylines and engaging illustrations. Reviewing his picture book *Toddlecreek Post Office, School Library Journal* contributor Carolyn Vang Schuler noted that "Shulevitz's fresh, orderly, yet angular, watercolors . . . are just right for group sharing," and *Booklist*'s Ilene Cooper praised

his "as always, striking" artwork. The story centers on a small post office where everything from lamp-mending to button-sewing is performed by the helpful and underworked local postmaster. Eventually, however, the regional postal inspector visits and decides to shut the office down. Betsy Hearne of the *Bulletin of the Center for Children's Books* called *Toddlecreek Post Office* a "fable about society's decline of humane concern."

Shulevitz's adaptation of *The Golden Goose* was dubbed "a fun version of a traditional tale" by *School Library Journal* contributor Donna L. Scanlon. The critic praised Shulevitz's use of contrast, as well as his "vibrant watercolor paintings, full of blocky angular characters and quirky off-kilter buildings" that "enhance the story." Characterizing the author's rhythmic text as a "challenging chant," *Bulletin of the Center for Children's Books* reviewer Elizabeth Bush opined that *The Golden Goose* "should attract a new generation of listeners." *Booklist* reviewer Susan Dove Lempke described Shulevitz's illustrations as "bursting with a bouncy vitality that fits the amusing story well."

One of Shulevitz's more recent efforts, his self-illustrated picture book *Snow,* has also been widely praised.

Featuring a spare text and detailed illustrations that capture "the transforming power of a snowstorm," *Snow* demonstrates the author's belief that "the true picture book, with its inevitable melding of words and art, is a distinct genre," according to *Horn Book* reviewer Mary M. Burns. A *Publishers Weekly* critic called the book "pure enchantment from start to finish," noting that Shulevitz "works a bit of visual alchemy as the tale progresses, gradually transforming the chilly gray watercolor washes with flecks of snow, until his cityscape is a frozen fairyland." The story, told primarily in pictures, centers on a small boy who, with his dog, eagerly anticipates the big snowfall that must surely follow those first few flakes. "Here [snow] becomes a metaphor for the faith young children possess in the face of an adult world lacking in vision and understanding," asserted Betsy Groban, writing in the *New York Times Book Review*. Groban also cited Shulevitz's pictures as the source of a wealth of thoughtful and illuminating detail in the book. For instance, the Mother Goose bookstore, the most distinctive building in the cityscape, introduces elements of the fantastic found nowhere in the text, as the boy and his dog dance in the accumulating snow with Mother Goose characters who emerge from a storefront display to join in the festive celebration.

In addition to his success at bringing his own story ideas to life by writing with pictures, Shulevitz has also received praise for his success in interpreting the works of other authors. Commenting on *The Diamond Tree: Jewish Tales from around the World*, *Horn Book* reviewer Hanna B. Zeiger hailed the illustrator's watercolor renderings, noting that these "add just the right touch of wit and fantasy" to the text by Howard Schwartz and Barbara Rush. "Shulevitz's illustrations evoke a strong sense of place," asserted Robin Tzannes in her review of Ehud Ben-Ezer's *Hosni the Dreamer* for the *New York Times*. "Pictures and text work together to create a portrait of a humble and compassionate hero that young readers should love."

Because he has illustrated a wide variety of books over his career, Shulevitz continually changes his methods of illustrating, incorporating such media as pen and ink, watercolor, Japanese reed pen, and Chinese brush. "My own working procedure has changed since I first began illustrating books," the illustrator once explained to *SATA*. "For my first book I made several actual-size, finished dummies; for subsequent books I made small, rough dummies and storyboards and small, rough dummies as necessary and go back and forth from one to another as I plan the book. I prefer to start by making a storyboard, however, and I recommend that beginners start this way too."

Once the storyboard is created, Shulevitz must present it to the book's editor for review. "Sometimes, after having made a storyboard and a rough thumbnail dummy for my own use, I paste down the final sketches (or photocopies of them) with masking tape onto an actual-size dummy to show to the editor or the designer. In any case, I find that a readable dummy is the most helpful tool for communicating how you see the book.

For picture books, which rely so much on the visual aspect, some editors require it before giving you a contract. They also want to see how you are progressing. On many occasions, I show my dummies to the editor to convey how I envision the book. The editor can then give me criticism, which in turn enables me to go back and work on my book idea further."

Shulevitz encourages would-be illustrators to discard the idea of a "perfect flawless picture" and to concentrate on making each picture come alive instead. "All too often there is a loss of emotion and freshness during the progression from first rough sketch to final illustration," he stated. "The finished picture may be more resolved, polished, and readable, but the spontaneity of the first sketch has almost disappeared. Readability is essential to good illustration, and some compromises to achieve it are justified. If, however, the price of readability is lifelessness, the result can be viewed as a failure." Shulevitz offers the following advice to his students. "When asked why they want to write children's books, many people reply, 'I love children.' Sentimentality, unfortunately, is no help; in fact it is a hindrance. Sentimentality does not replace the craft that is essential in making good children's books. Your first obligation is to the book, not the audience. Only by understanding the book's structure—including its mechanical structure—and how it functions can you make a good book."

"A picture book is not a silly little plaything," Shulevitz maintained in an essay published in *The Illustrator's Notebook*. "It is much more. Sometimes it can be everything to a child. A picture book can be a messenger of hope from the outside world. Its message, written in coded language, reaches the child in his prison, is understood by him while often hidden from the adult or parent who is unwilling to listen to its true content or is simply insensitive to it." The key to that prison is a life-affirming attitude. "Children are very sensitive to this, because their lives depend upon it. A destructive, life-negating attitude will not do. Neither will a saccharine approach. A picture book does not have to be deep, but it does have to be alive—whether it offers pleasure, joy, or sadness. I believe this point of view is essential to anyone interested in the field."

Works Cited

Burns, Mary M., review of *Snow, Horn Book,* January-February, 1999, pp. 55-56.

Bush, Elizabeth, review of *The Golden Goose, Bulletin of the Center for Children's Books,* January, 1996, p. 171.

Cooper, Ilene, review of *Toddlecreek Post Office, Booklist,* November 15, 1990, pp. 666-67.

Groban, Betsy, review of *Snow, New York Times Book Review,* January 17, 1999, p. 26.

Hearne, Betsy, review of *Toddlecreek Post Office, Bulletin of the Center for Children's Books,* January, 1991, p. 129.

Lempke, Susan Dove, review of *The Golden Goose, Booklist,* November 15, 1995, p. 562.

Scanlon, Donna L., review of *The Golden Goose, School Library Journal,* December, 1995, p. 97.

Schuler, Carolyn Vang, review of *Toddlecreek Post Office, School Library Journal,* January, 1991, p. 80.

Shulevitz, Uri, essay in *The Illustrator's Notebook,* edited by Lee Kingman, Horn Book, 1978.

Shulevitz, Uri, "Writing with Pictures," *Horn Book,* February, 1982, pp. 17-22.

Review of *Snow, Kirkus Reviews,* October 15, 1998, p. 1537.

Review of *Snow, Publishers Weekly,* August 31, 1998, p. 75.

Tzannes, Robin, review of *Hosni the Dreamer, New York Times,* November 16, 1997, p. 42.

Zeiger, Hanna B., review of *The Diamond Tree: Jewish Tales from around the World, Horn Book,* January-February, 1992, pp. 83-84.

For More Information See

BOOKS

Children's Literature Review, Volume 5, Gale, 1983.

Hopkins, Lee Bennett, *Books Are by People: Interviews with 104 Authors and Illustrators of Books for Young Children,* Citation Press, 1969.

Schmidt, Suzy, essay on Shulevitz in *Children's Books and Their Creators,* edited by Anita Silvey, Houghton, 1995, pp. 599-601.

Third Book of Junior Authors, H. W. Wilson, 1972.

PERIODICALS

Booklist, November 1, 1997, p. 478; January 1, 1999, p. 785.

Horn Book, March-April, 1994, p. 211.

Kirkus Reviews, October 1, 1995, p. 1428.

Publishers Weekly, October 11, 1993, p. 85.

School Library Journal, March, 1992, p. 252; December, 1997, p. 81; December, 1998, p. 92.

* * *

SILVERSTEIN, Herma 1945-

Personal

Born February 21, 1945, in TX; daughter of Benjamin Ellman (a jeweler) and Tobia (a homemaker; maiden name, Miller) Ellman; children: Lawrence Jr., Benjamin. *Education:* Sophie Newcomb College, B.A., 1967; attended University of Madrid, 1964, University of California-Los Angeles, 1978-80. *Religion:* Jewish.

Addresses

Agent—Andrea Brown Literary Agency, P.O. Box 371027, Montara, CA 94037.

Career

Author of children's books, 1978—. Instructor of writing for children; lecturer. Breeder of Tibetan terriers. Volunteer for Pediatric AIDS Foundation, Los Angeles, Horizon Women's Shelter, and National Council of Jewish Women. *Member:* Society of Children's Book Writers and Illustrators, Authors' Guild, Southern Cali-

Herma Silverstein

fornia Council on Literature for Children and Young People.

Awards, Honors

Quick Picks for Reluctant Young Adult Readers, American Library Association (ALA), 1988, for *Mad, Mad Monday;* Books for the Teen Age, New York Public Library, 1994, for *Date Abuse,* and 1996, for *Threads of Evidence: Using Forensic Science to Solve Crimes;* Nonfiction Honor Book designation, *Voice of Youth Advocates,* 1996, for *Threads of Evidence: Using Forensic Science to Solve Crimes,* and 1997, for *Kids Who Kill;* award for best article, *Highlights for Children,* for "Mother Teresa And The Poorest of The Poor."

Writings

(With Caroline Arnold) *Anti-Semitism: A Modern Perspective,* Simon & Schuster, 1985.

Mary Lou Retton and the New Gymnasts, F. Watts, 1985.

(With Caroline Arnold) *Hoaxes That Made Headlines,* Simon & Schuster, 1986.

Scream Machines: Roller Coasters Past, Present, and Future, Walker, 1986.

Mad, Mad Monday (fiction), Dutton, 1988.

Spies among Us: The Truth about Modern Espionage, F. Watts, 1988.

David Ben-Gurion, F. Watts, 1988.

Teenage and Pregnant: What You Can Do, Simon & Schuster, 1988.

Teen Guide to Single Parenting, F. Watts, 1989.

Alcoholism, F. Watts, 1990.

Teenage Depression, F. Watts, 1990.

The Alamo, Dillon Press, 1992.

Date Abuse, Enslow, 1994.

(With Terry Janson Donnahoo) *Baseball Hall of Fame,* Crestwood House, 1994.

(With Donnahoo) *Basketball Hall of Fame,* Crestwood House, 1994.

(With Donnahoo) *Pro Football Hall of Fame,* Crestwood House, 1994.

Yearbooks in Science: 1990 and Beyond, Holt, 1995.

Threads of Evidence: Using Forensic Science to Solve Crimes, Holt, 1996.

Kids Who Kill, Holt, 1997.

Contributor to periodicals, including *Highlights for Children* and *The Friend.*

Work in Progress

Other nonfiction works; picture books; middle-grade novels.

Sidelights

Giving her natural curiosity full rein has been the key to Herma Silverstein's success as a children's author. With a number of nonfiction titles, as well as the novel *Mad, Mad Monday,* to her credit, Silverstein focuses in particular on topics of vital interest to today's teens, ranging from date rape to coping with teen pregnancy to understanding depression. Her books have been characterized as "well crafted" and "competent addition[s] to the genre" by *Voice of Youth Advocates* contributor Margaret Galloway, and her ability to confront controversial issues head-on has also been appreciated by reviewers.

Silverstein includes interviews with actual teen mothers in her 1988 book *Teenage and Pregnant: What You Can Do,* which is geared toward the young woman who wants to understand both her changing body and her options upon becoming pregnant. The author's *Teen Guide to Single Parenting,* dubbed "a sensible primer on child care" by *Bulletin of the Center for Children's Books* critic Betsy Hearne, contains information on nutrition and finance and instructions on how to build support systems, in addition to its routine discussion of child care and development. Focusing on its diagnosis and treatment as a disease, *Alcoholism* received praise from Cathy Welgarz in her *Voice of Youth Advocates* review for "its clear presentation of a complicated theory and Silverstein's sensitive style which never preaches or condescends to the reader." And in *Kids Who Kill,* the author examines the rash of juvenile murders that have captured media attention in recent years. Calling the book "an important addition to the body of socially relevant nonfiction for young adults," *School Library Journal* contributor Joan Soulliere praised Silverstein for

handling the often chilling subject "in an evenhanded, intelligent manner," noting that the author "documents extensive research and is not prone to personal commentary or bias."

"Reading has always been my passion," Silverstein told *SATA.* "Books can take you anywhere you want to go, to have any experience you desire. My favorite books are mysteries. And I love anything to do with medical science. Putting these two interests together, it was only natural that I would think of writing about forensic science." The result: *Threads of Evidence: Using Forensic Science to Solve Crimes,* which *Booklist* contributor Stephanie Zvirin called "a reassuring perspective on law enforcement." Exploring the up-to-date techniques used by pathologists, toxicologists, ballistics experts, and other criminologists, Silverstein explains to readers how the police gather and analyze evidence. From mad bombers to secretive murderers, *Threads of Evidence* emphasizes "ingenuity and deductive reasoning" on the part of medical experts, noted *Science Books and Films* contributor Jacques Wallach, "as well as the careful, painstaking, meticulous, difficult, and time-consuming labor that is involved in the collection and analysis of possible clues." While disappointed by the book's lack of illustrations, Jonathan Betz-Zall praised *Threads of Evidence* in *School Library Journal:* "In a crowded field of books on forensic science, this one stands out for effective writing, up-to-date coverage, and gory details."

Other books that reflect Silverstein's personal interests include *Hoaxes That Made Headlines,* which follows the dubious careers of such individuals as the purported surviving son of the murdered Czar Nicholas II of Russia; various forgers, masqueraders, long-lost heirs; and even "Piltdown Man," the partial skeletal remains that were eventually revealed to be those of an orangutan. The lifestyles of the cloaked and daggered are explored in *Spies among Us: The Truth about Modern Espionage,* as several spy cases—including the Rosenbergs, Kim Philby, and Gary Powers—from the 1960s through the 1980s, as well as advances in surveillance technology, are described in detail. While remarking that Silverstein's factual details provide "thin" documentation, *Booklist* contributor Hazel Rochman commented that "the stories of individual spy cases ... will fascinate readers."

Although she primarily writes nonfiction, Silverstein attests to the fact that much of what she writes has "bits and pieces" of her own life woven in. "Each year," she recalled to *SATA,* "I eagerly awaited the arrival of the Texas State Fair. Totally fearless, I would run for the highest, fastest, scariest ride on the midway. Hence my book *Scream Machines,* on the history of roller coasters." Being a tomboy broadened Silverstein's childhood experience, providing her with fertile ground for ideas when she later became a writer. "Living on a street that overlooked the zoo offered grand opportunities to play make-believe," she explained. "One of my favorite pastimes was pretending to explore African territory—in reality, the woodsy trails leading from across my street downhill into the elephant pen. In fact, every night from

Exploring the up-to-date techniques used by pathologists, toxicologists, ballistics experts, and other criminologists, Silverstein explains how the police gather and analyze evidence in her informational book for teen readers.

my bedroom window I would hear the lions and tigers growl for their midnight feeding. My friends and I thought nothing of jumping the fence into the mountain goat habitat and rock-climbing the boulders with the goats.... From those memories came a story I wrote about woodsy trails by—who else?—a young girl who lived over the zoo."

Her novel *Mad, Mad Monday* also has its source in events from Silverstein's childhood. "I hate to admit it, but when I was growing up television was in its infancy," the author recalled. "One of my favorite early sitcoms was *Topper,* about a family who buys a house inhabited by a couple of ghosts. Recalling how only Mr. Topper could see the ghosts, and how he had to quickly think of explanations to his wife for their pranks, I wondered, 'What if a young girl was suddenly visited by a teenage ghost who lived during the 1950s?' Hence my novel, *Mad, Mad Monday.*"

Mad, Mad Monday finds fourteen-year-old Miranda Taylor totally smitten with high school heartthrob Stormy Kinkaid; but how to make him notice a middle-schooler when he is surrounded by all those high school girls? Miranda decides to try magic, but goofs on the recipe and ends up with a teen ghost named Michael instead. Allowed to roam the earth for two weeks, Michael is glad for the opportunity to revenge himself on his old girlfriend—she is in fact almost fifty years old, as Michael has been dead for three decades—and uses Miranda's plight to get even in a novel that a *Kirkus Reviews* critic called "Pleasant, romantic, [and] lightweight." *School Library Journal* contributor Deborah Locke declared, "*Mad, Mad Monday* is totally unbelievable and lots of fun."

Like many authors who travel to schoolrooms to talk to their readers, Silverstein has often been asked when it was that she first realized she wanted to be a writer. Her answer, as she told *SATA:* "When my two sons were in elementary school. They were having the common arguments most siblings do, and I thought, 'I should write a story for kids about two brothers who can't get along.' So I enrolled in the University of California-Los Angeles Writers Program to take courses on writing books for children. And the rest, as they say, is history."

But it took more than just sitting down and writing to make Silverstein *feel* like a real, honest-to-goodness writer. That feeling didn't come until part-way through her book, *Hoaxes That Made Headlines,* which she co-wrote with Caroline Arnold. "While researching the chapter on literary hoaxes, specifically whether Shakespeare was an imposter, I remembered that in high school I had written a term paper on that very subject. It was then that I realized I had been heading toward a writing career all my life, especially nonfiction. I would lose myself all day in the library hunting for even the tiniest scrap of information. Searching through old periodicals became a treasure hunt, with facts on the Shakespeare 'impostors' the treasure. I recalled how much I loved doing research, not only that term paper but all the others I was assigned in school."

One evening, while Silverstein was looking through some family scrapbooks, she came across one of the stories she had written in first grade. "It was about a young boy who was very curious," she explained. "Although written in the elementary style of a six-year-old, the tale had the three necessary ingredients of a story: a beginning, middle, and end, including a 'moment of despair,' in which the hero thinks there is no way out of his predicament." The story reminded Silverstein of the many hours she had spent daydreaming as a child, "making up all kinds of adventurous stories in my head, with me being the star of those adventures, of course. A pen pal crossed my mind, to whom I had written long letters filled with detailed descriptions of what I was doing and my feelings about everything from my family, teachers, and friends to my pet goldfish. In truth, I had been a writer all my life and just never knew it."

Silverstein recalls the relief she felt when she finally realized that she was a writer. "Friends constantly ask, 'When will you take a vacation from writing?' I always answer, 'But writing *is* my vacation.' Writing books gives me so much pleasure I can't imagine a day not putting some thought on paper."

Works Cited

Betz-Zall, Jonathan, review of *Threads of Evidence, School Library Journal,* February, 1997, p. 125.

Galloway, Margaret, review of *Teenage and Pregnant: What You Can Do, Voice of Youth Advocates,* August, 1989, p. 178.

Hearne, Betsy, review of *Teen Guide to Single Parenting, Bulletin of the Center for Children's Books,* July-August, 1989, p. 284.

Locke, Deborah, review of *Mad, Mad Monday, School Library Journal,* February, 1988, p. 74.

Review of *Mad, Mad Monday, Kirkus Reviews,* December 15, 1987, p. 1738.

Rochman, Hazel, review of *Spies among Us: The Truth about Modern Espionage, Booklist,* December 1, 1988, p. 638.

Soulliere, Joan, review of *Kids Who Kill, School Library Journal,* January, 1998, p. 132.

Wallach, Jacques, review of *Threads of Evidence: Using Forensic Science to Solve Crimes, Science Books and Films,* March, 1997, p. 44.

Welgarz, Cathy, review of *Alcoholism, Voice of Youth Advocates,* February, 1991, p. 382.

Zvirin, Stephanie, review of *Threads of Evidence: Using Forensic Science to Solve Crimes, Booklist,* December 1, 1996, p. 657.

For More Information See

PERIODICALS

Booklist, January 1, 1986, p. 688; October 1, 1986, p. 275; January 1, 1987, p. 704; April 1, 1988, p. 1353; March 15, 1989, p. 1273; December 15, 1997, p. 690.

Bulletin of the Center for Children's Books, March, 1986, p. 137; April, 1987, p. 156; December, 1987, p. 76; November, 1988, p. 83; December, 1990, p. 101.

Kirkus Reviews, February 1, 1994, p. 150.

Publishers Weekly, January 15, 1988, p. 97.

School Library Journal, January, 1987, p. 80; February, 1987, pp. 94-95; May, 1988, p. 120; November, 1988, p. 139; August, 1990, p. 172; June, 1991, p. 133; August, 1994, p. 162.

Voice of Youth Advocates, October, 1988, p. 104; October, 1989, p. 239; December, 1990, p. 320; August, 1994, p. 171; February, 1998, p. 406.

*   *   *

SIMMIE, Lois (Ann) 1932-

Personal

Born June 11, 1932, in Edam, Saskatchewan, Canada; daughter of Edwin Maurice (a pool elevator agent) and Bessie Margaret (a homemaker; maiden name, Thomson) Binns; married (divorced); children: Odell, Leona, Anne, Scott. *Education:* Attended Saskatchewan Business College, 1951-52, and University of Saskatchewan, 1973-77.

Addresses

Home—1501 Cairns Ave., Saskatoon, Saskatchewan S7H 2H5, Canada.

Career

Novelist, short-story writer, poet, and author of children's books. Saskatoon Public Library, writer-in-residence, 1987-88; Saskatoon Summer School of the Arts, University of Saskatchewan Extension Department, fiction instructor; instructor at community colleges. *Member:* Saskatchewan Writers' Guild, Canadian Children's Book Center, Writers Union of Canada, Association of Canadian Television and Radio Artists.

Awards, Honors

Award for short-story collection, Saskatchewan Department of Culture and Youth, 1976; artist's grant, Saskatchewan Arts Board, 1983; award for book-length story collection, Saskatchewan Writers' Guild, 1983; various awards from Saskatchewan Writers' Guild; Saskatchewan Book Award for Children's Literature, 1995, for *Mister Got to Go: The Cat That Wouldn't Leave;* Saskatchewan Book Award shortlist, 1995, for *The Secret Lives of Sgt. John Wilson: A True Story of Love and Murder.*

Writings

FOR CHILDREN; ILLUSTRATED BY DAUGHTER ANNE SIMMIE

Auntie's Knitting a Baby (poems), Western Producer Prairie Books (Saskatoon, SK), 1984, Orchard, 1988.

An Armadillo Is Not a Pillow (poems), Western Producer Prairie Books, 1986.

What Holds Up the Moon?, Coteau (Regina, SK), 1987.

Who Greased the Shoelaces? (poems), Stoddart (Toronto, ON), 1989.

FOR CHILDREN

Oliver's Chickens, illustrated by Kim LaFave, Douglas & McIntyre (Toronto, ON), 1992.

Mister Got to Go: The Cat That Wouldn't Leave, illustrated by Cynthia Nugent, Red Deer College Press (Red Deer, AB), 1995, published in the United States as *No Cats Allowed,* Chronicle Books, 1996.

FOR ADULTS

Ghost House (short stories), Coteau (Moose Jaw, SK), 1976.

They Shouldn't Make You Promise That (novel), New American Library of Canada (Scarborough, ON), 1981.

Pictures (short stories), Fifth House (Saskatoon, SK), 1984.

Betty Lee Bonner Lives There (short stories) Douglas & McIntyre (Vancouver, BC), 1993.

The Secret Lives of Sgt. John Wilson: A True Story of Love and Murder (nonfiction), Greystone (Vancouver, BC), 1995.

Contributor to numerous anthologies, including *Best of Grain, Sundogs, Saskatchewan Gold, Number One Northern, Canadian Short Fiction Anthology Two, Western Moods,* and *Inquiry into Literature.* Editor of *Julie,* 1985, *The Doll,* 1987, and *A Gift of Sky,* 1988. Contributor to periodicals, including *Saturday Night* and *McCall's.*

They Shouldn't Make You Promise That and *The Secret Lives of Sgt. John Wilson: A True Story of Love and Murder* were recorded on audio cassette by the Library Services Branch, Province of British Columbia, 1985 and 1998, respectively. *Auntie's Knitting a Baby* was recorded on audio cassette by Kid's Records, 1988.

Adaptations

The short story "Red Shoes" was adapted as a feature film, directed by Allan Kroeker, produced by Susan A'Court and William Weintraub, Atlantis Films and National Film Board of Canada, 1986.

Sidelights

Canadian fiction writer Lois Simmie has spun a career that includes novels, short-story collections, and an award-winning true-crime book for adults, in addition to several volumes of prose and verse for children. She is considered by many to be one of Canada's top poets for children. Joan McGrath, writing in *Quill & Quire,* described Simmie as "a very funny, original, and empathetic writer for children and adults."

Simmie's first work for children, *Auntie's Knitting a Baby,* met with immediate success. Here, Simmie presents a whimsical collection of fifty-two poems, mostly humorous and some of them gruesome as well, in the vein of Shel Silverstein and Jack Prelutsky. A *Publishers Weekly* reviewer and *School Library Journal* critic Barbara S. McGinn were among those who enjoyed the poems' energetic, dark humor. Praise was also bestowed upon the book's illustrations, which were done by Simmie's daughter, Anne Simmie, who had majored in painting at the Alberta College of Art.

Her next collection of poetry, *An Armadillo Is Not a Pillow,* also received applause from critics. Consisting of fifty-three poems, *An Armadillo Is Not a Pillow* features verses which, noted McGrath, "hum along, conjuring up a cockeyed world as seen through a child's imagination." In *Who Greased the Shoelaces?,* Simmie filled the pages with poems ranging from dinosaurs to everyday frustrations typically experienced by children. Jacqueline Reid Walsh, writing in *Canadian Children's Literature,* noted that Simmie relates "the joys and irritations of life … with gusto." *Canadian Materials* contributor Fran Newman found many of Simmie's poems, including the Murphy poems, "totally delightful." She was a little disappointed though in the way some of the poems

Set in the grand old Sylvia Hotel in Vancouver, Lois Simmie's tale involves a cat who wanders into the establishment and the inhabitants who find themselves becoming increasingly, reluctantly attached to her. (From Mister Got to Go: The Cat That Wouldn't Leave, *illustrated by Cynthia Nugent.)*

flow, suspecting that perhaps they contained "untidy rhyme." But overall, Newman felt that "much of this book is good."

A recipient of several literary awards, Simmie received the Saskatchewan Book Award in 1995 for the picture book *Mister Got to Go: The Cat That Wouldn't Leave* (published in the United States as *No Cats Allowed*). Set in the grand old Sylvia Hotel in Vancouver, the story concerns a cat who enters the hotel to get out of the rain. The manager maintains that the cat must leave when the rain stops. But in Vancouver, the rain rarely stops; and as the cat lingers, he gains the affection of staff and guests, including the manager himself. *School Library Journal* contributor Kathy Piehl predicted that "*Mister Got to Go* will win listeners and readers as surely as he convinced Mr. Foster to let him stay." Phil Hall, a *Books in Canada* reviewer, was grateful to Simmie's book for providing him an enjoyable evening with his own daughter. A *Kirkus Reviews* critic praised the picture book as a "cozy tale of coming home, executed with an edge that makes it interesting."

Simmie once told *SATA:* "Although I always intended to write, I didn't actually get serious until I saw forty looming on the horizon. A late starter has some advantages—all that life experience and years of writing in your head plus all those good and bad books you've read. The good ones fill you with longing and the bad ones make you say I can write a better book than that! (You can only say this so often before you have to put up or shut up). Your apprenticeship is shorter, and you don't struggle with developing a voice or style; your voice is simply who you have become.

"When I write for children I write with one aim in mind, to entertain the child. I hate message plays, books, songs, for children. What's wrong with just making them laugh? In a wonderful children's book, like *Charlotte's Web,* there is a message but never at the expense of the story. Though I write to entertain, I take writing for children very seriously. We must take it seriously. What we can't take too seriously is ourselves."

Works Cited

Review of *Auntie's Knitting a Baby, Publishers Weekly,* September 9, 1988, p. 135.

Hall, Phil, review of *Mister Got to Go: The Cat That Wouldn't Leave, Books in Canada,* November, 1995, p. 40.

McGinn, Barbara S., review of *Auntie's Knitting a Baby, School Library Journal,* December, 1988, p. 102.

McGrath, Joan, review of *An Armadillo Is Not a Pillow, Quill & Quire,* December, 1986, p. 15.

Newman, Fran, review of *Who Greased the Shoelaces?, Canadian Materials,* November, 1989, p. 268.

Review of *No Cats Allowed, Kirkus Reviews,* November 15, 1996, p. 1675.

Piehl, Kathy, review of *Mister Got to Go: The Cat That Wouldn't Leave, School Library Journal,* January, 1996, p. 96.

Walsh, Jacqueline Reid, review of *Who Greased the Shoelace, Canadian Children's Literature,* Number 61, 1991, p. 79.

For More Information See

PERIODICALS

Books in Canada, November, 1993, p. 42.

Canadian Children's Literature, Number 46, 1987, pp. 99-100.

Canadian Materials, July, 1988, p. 147.

Edmonton Journal, March 21, 1987; May 29, 1994, p. B5.

Kirkus Reviews, August 1, 1988, p. 1157.

Los Angeles Times Book Review, January 16, 1983, p. 5.

Quill & Quire, July, 1981, p. 58; June, 1984, p. 32; August, 1992, p. 27; January, 1994, p. 27; August, 1995, p. 36; November, 1995, p. 30.

School Library Journal, April, 1997, p. 117.*

SIS, Peter 1949-

Personal

Born May 11, 1949, in Brno, Moravia, Czechoslovakia (now Czech Republic); immigrated to United States, 1982, naturalized citizen, 1989; son of Vladimir (a filmmaker and explorer) and Alena (an artist; maiden name, Petrvalska) Sis; married Terry Lajtha (a film editor), October 28, 1990; children: Madeleine, Matej. *Education:* Academy of Applied Arts, Prague, Czechoslovakia, M.A., 1974; attended Royal College of Art, London, England, 1977-79.

Addresses

c/o Farrar, Straus and Giroux, 19 Union Square W., New York, NY 10003.

Career

Artist, animator, illustrator, stage designer, and writer. Worked as a disc jockey while in art school. Teacher of art classes at schools in Los Angeles, CA, and New York City. *Exhibitions:* Group shows include Interama, Berlin, 1975; Best of British Illustrators, London, England, 1979; Magical Mystery Tour, Los Angeles, CA, 1982; Expo Art and Metropole, Montreal, Canada, 1984; Bienalle of Illustrations, Japan, 1985; University

Peter Sis

of Oregon School of Art, Portland, OR, 1986; International Gallery, San Diego, CA, 1986; Henry Feiwel Gallery, New York City, 1990-91; Stedelijk Museum Schiedam, Holland, 1992; Santa Monica Heritage Museum, Santa Monica, CA, 1992-93; New York Public Library, New York City, 1994; Gallery MB ART, Stuttgart, 1995; Storyopolis, Los Angeles, 1996; Chrysler Museum, Norfolk, VA, 1996-97; Salon du Livre de Jeunesse, Montreuil-Paris, 1997-98; Katonah Museum of Art, Katonah, NY, 1998; International Youth Library, Blutenburg Castle, Munich, Germany, 1998; Okresni Muzeum a Galerie, Jicin, Czech Republic, 1998; Columbia College Center for Book and Paper Arts, Chicago, IL, 1998; Bohemian Gallery, Astoria-Queens, New York City, 1998; "Le immagini della fantasia," Sarmede, Italy, 1998-99; Salon du Livre de Jeunesse, Montreuil-Paris, 1998-99; Tibet House, New York City, 1998-99. One-man shows at Gallery Klostermauer, St. Gallen, Switzerland, 1975; Gallery Ploem, Delft, Netherlands, 1977; Gallery Martinska, 1977, and Gallery Rubin, 1979, both in Prague, Czechoslovakia; Gallery Vista Nova, Zurich, Switzerland, 1980; Gallery Medici, London, 1980; Ohio University School of Art, Athens, OH, 1990; Gallery Zeta, Olten, Switzerland, 1990; New York Public Library, New York City, 1992; James Cummins Gallery, New York City, 1994; Gallery Paseka, Prague, 1995; International Youth Library, Blutenburg Castle, Munich, 1995; Swiss Children's Book Institute and Johanna Spyri Foundation, Zurich, 1995-96; Books & Co., New York City, 1996; Salon du Livre de Jeunesse, Montreuil-Paris, 1996-97; Prague Castle-Riding School, Prague, 1997-98; Embassy of the Czech Republic in collaboration with Smithsonian Associates, Washington, D.C., 1999. *Military service:* Czechoslovak Army, graphic designer with army's symphony orchestra, 1975-76. *Member:* Association Internationale du Film d'Animation, American Institute of Graphic Arts, Graphic Artists Guild.

Awards, Honors

Golden Berlin Bear for best short film, Berlin International Film Festival, 1980, for *Heads;* Grand Prix Toronto, 1981, for short film *Players;* CINE Golden Eagle Award, Council on International Non-Theatrical Events, 1983, for *You Gotta Serve Somebody;* "Ten Best Illustrated Children's Books for the Year," *New York Times,* 1987, for *Rainbow Rhino,* and 1990, for *Beach Ball;* Caldecott Honor Book, American Library Association (ALA), 1997, for *Starry Messenger: Galileo Galilei,* and 1999, for *Tibet: Through the Red Box;* Notable Books for Children, ALA, 1999, for both *Fire Truck* and *Tibet: Through the Red Box;* Children's Books of Distinction, *Riverbank Review,* 1999, for *Tibet: Through the Red Box.*

Writings

AUTHOR AND ILLUSTRATOR

Rainbow Rhino, Random House, 1987.
Waving: A Counting Book, Greenwillow, 1988.
Going Up!: A Color Counting Book, Greenwillow, 1989.
Beach Ball, Greenwillow, 1990.

Follow the Dream: The Story of Christopher Columbus, Knopf, 1991.
An Ocean World, Greenwillow, 1992.
Komodo!, Greenwillow, 1993.
A Small Tall Tale from the Far Far North, Knopf, 1993.
The Three Golden Keys, Doubleday, 1994.
Starry Messenger: Galileo Galilei, Farrar, Straus & Giroux, 1996.
Fire Truck, Greenwillow, 1998.
Tibet: Through the Red Box, Farrar, Straus & Giroux, 1998.
Trucks, Trucks, Trucks, Greenwillow, 1999.
Ship Ahoy!, Greenwillow, 1999.
Faust, Carl Hanser Verlag (Munich), 1999.

Starry Messenger was recorded on audio cassette by Recorded Books, 1997.

ILLUSTRATOR

Eveline Hasler, *Hexe Lakritze und der Buchstabenkoenig,* Benziger (Zurich, Switzerland), 1977.
Eveline Hasler, *Hexe Lakritze und Rhino Rhinoceros,* Benziger, 1979.
Milos Maly, reteller, *Tales of the Amber Ring* (Baltic fairy tales), Artia (Prague, Czech Republic), 1981, Orbis, 1985.
Max Bolliger, *Eine Zwergengeschichte* (title means "Little Singer"), Bohem (Zurich), 1982.
George Shannon, *Bean Boy,* Greenwillow, 1983.
Shannon, *Stories to Solve: Folktales from around the World,* Greenwillow, 1985.
Sid Fleischman, *The Whipping Boy,* Greenwillow, 1985.
Julia Cunningham, *Oaf,* Knopf, 1986.
Caron Lee Cohen, *Three Yellow Dogs,* Greenwillow, 1986.
Myra Cohn Livingston, *Higgledy-Piggledy: Verses and Pictures,* Atheneum, 1986.
Jean and Claudio Marzollo, *Jed and the Space Bandits,* Dial, 1987.
Monica Mayper, *After Good-Night,* Harper, 1987.
Eve Rice, *City Night,* Greenwillow, 1987.
Sid Fleischman, *The Scarebird,* Greenwillow, 1988.
Kate Banks, *Alphabet Soup,* Knopf, 1988.
Caroline Feller Bauer, editor, *Halloween: Stories and Poems,* Harper, 1989.
Sid Fleischman, *The Ghost in the Noonday Sun,* Greenwillow, 1989.
Louis Decimus Rubin, *The Algonquin Literary Quiz Book,* Algonquin, 1990.
Sid Fleischman, *Midnight Horse,* Greenwillow, 1990.
George Shannon, *More Stories to Solve: Fifteen Folktales from around the World,* Greenwillow, 1991.
Jack Prelutsky, *The Dragons Are Singing Tonight,* Greenwillow, 1993.
Christopher Noel, *Rumpelstiltskin,* Simon & Schuster, 1993.
George Shannon, *Still More Stories to Solve: Fourteen Folktales from around the World,* Greenwillow, 1994.
Sid Fleischman, *The 13th Floor: A Ghost Story,* Greenwillow, 1995.
Jack Prelutsky, *Monday's Troll,* Greenwillow, 1996.
Miriam Schlein, *Sleep Safe, Little Whale: A Lullaby,* Greenwillow, 1997.
(With Cliff Nelson) Madeleine L'Engle, *Many Waters,* Bantam Doubleday Dell, 1998.

Jack Prelutsky, *Gargoyles on the Roof,* Greenwillow, 1999.

Also illustrator of *Fairy Tales of the Brothers Grimm,* Albatros (Prague, Czech Republic), Volume 1, 1976, Volume 2, 1977; *Zizkov Romances,* CSS (Prague), 1978; and *Poetry,* CSS, 1980. Contributor of illustrations to *American Illustration, New York Times, New York Times Book Review, Atlantic Monthly, Time, Newsweek, House & Garden, Esquire, Forbes, Connoisseur,* and *Print. Rumpelstiltskin* was also released on audiocassette by Rabbit Ears, 1995.

SHORT FILMS

Mimikry, Academy of Applied Arts (Prague, Czech Republic), 1975.
Island for 6,000 Alarm Clocks, Kratky Film, 1977.
Heads, Kratky Film, 1979.
Players, Halas & Batchelor (London, England), 1981.
Hexe Lakritze (ten parts; title means "Little Witch Licorice"), televised in Zurich, Switzerland, 1982.
You Gotta Serve Somebody, Fine Arts (Los Angeles, CA), 1983.
Aesop's Fables, (two films), Helicon Video, 1984.
Twelve Months, Billy Budd Films, 1985.
Rumpelstiltskin, Rabbit Ears Productions (Westport, CT), 1992.

Heads and *Island for 6,000 Alarm Clocks* are part of the permanent film collection of the Museum of Modern Art in New York City.

Also creator of the CD-ROM "Eskimo Welzl" about the Czechoslovakian inventor, storyteller, adventurer, and explorer Jan Welzl. Creator of posters for theater, film, institutions and festivals, including the film *Amadeus,* The Metropolitan Transportation Authorities in New York City, the Children's Book Council, and the International Jazz Festival in Rennes, France.

Work in Progress

Madelenka and *Lighthouse* (tentative title), both for Farrar, Straus & Giroux; and *Dinosaur* (tentative title), with Jack Prelutsky, for Greenwillow.

Sidelights

Peter Sis is a distinguished illustrator and writer recognized internationally for his contributions to children's literature. Since the mid-1970s, he has made more than half a dozen short films, illustrated nearly twenty-five books for other authors, and written over a dozen of his own self-illustrated children's books. Stephen Fraser, writing in *Five Owls,* noted that Sis "remains one of the truly distinctive picture-book creators today—quirky, sophisticated, and imaginative."

Born into an artistic family in 1949, Sis grew up Czechoslovakia at a time when the former Soviet Union ruled his homeland. Because both of his parents were artists (his father was a filmmaker and explorer and his mother, an artist), Sis was surrounded by art as a child. As early as age four or five, Sis began drawing pictures,

and within a few years he became quite serious about his craft. "I was already illustrating regularly by the time I was eight or nine," Sis once told *SATA.* "My father and my mother would give me certain assignments, and I remember I would even have deadlines." Sis credits his parents with providing an appropriate environment to foster his growth as an artist. His talents flourished in an atmosphere that balanced creative freedom with a certain amount of structure and discipline. Above all, he was challenged intellectually as a youth by his parents.

When he had reached his early teens, Sis was convinced that he wanted to pursue a career as a professional artist. Once in formal art school, however, Sis began to experience some frustration in his quest. His family's interest in contemporary art clashed with the traditional ideals of formal artistic training. In spite of these difficulties, Sis earned his master's degree from the Academy of Applied Arts in Prague in 1974 and later attended the Royal College of Art in London, England. He credits his so-called "soft technique," which is still evident in his works, to his traditional art education.

Sis first became involved with animated films in the 1960s, and he considers famous Czechoslovakian illustrator, animator, and teacher Jiri Trnka to have been an important role model. By the early 1980s, Sis was already a popular artist and filmmaker in Europe. "Film for me was the passport to the whole world," he once told *SATA.* His short animated film *Heads* earned the Golden Bear at the 1980 Berlin International Film Festival. He was then invited to design and paint illustrations for a Swiss television series called *Hexe Lakritze* ("Little Witch Licorice"). Sis also worked on another film in London. Then, in 1982, he traveled to Los Angeles—the site of the 1984 Olympic Games—to do a film that tied in the theme of the liberation of humanity with the Olympics. However, following the Soviet Union's decision to boycott the 1984 Olympics, other eastern and central European countries, including Czechoslovakia, also withdrew from the competition. The Olympic film project was canceled, but Sis remained in Los Angeles to pursue his career in art.

At first, Sis found life on the West Coast quite challenging. As he once explained to *SATA,* "It was very hard to find my way around in Los Angeles because all of a sudden things were completely different than what I was used to in Europe—the palm trees and lifestyle and everything. I felt completely misplaced and strange." Although Sis had difficulty obtaining film and illustration jobs, he did find work teaching classes in illustration in Los Angeles. In addition, he illustrated two of Aesop's fables for television.

At about the same time, Sis took the advice of a friend who suggested that he send a sample of his work to famous American children's writer and illustrator Maurice Sendak. Sis never expected to get a response, but Sendak was impressed enough with the young artist's work to call him personally and discuss his career aspirations. Several months later, Sendak called again while attending the 1984 American Library Association

Sis's funny black-and-white illustrations enhance Sid Fleischman's story of the lively adventures of Jemmy, an orphan who must take the whippings for a spoiled prince. (From The Whipping Boy.*)*

convention, which was held in Los Angeles. He invited Sis to join him at the convention and introduced him to Ava Weiss, art director of Greenwillow Books, a New York City-based publisher. Sis broke into the American book illustration market on the spot, agreeing to illustrate George Shannon's *Bean Boy.*

Following *Bean Boy* and a move to New York City, Sis illustrated two more books for Greenwillow, Sid Fleischman's juvenile novel *The Whipping Boy,* which won the Newbery Medal in 1985, and *Stories to Solve: Folktales from around the World,* by Shannon. Not long afterwards, Sis became a regular contributor of illustrations to the *New York Times Book Review* and began to write and illustrate his own work. His first self-illustrated work, *Rainbow Rhino,* was listed among the *New York Times* top ten best illustrated children's books of 1987.

By 1991, Sis was well-known in the children's book industry. He had already illustrated almost two dozen works by other authors and created six of his own, including the well-received *Follow the Dream: The Story of Christopher Columbus. School Library Journal* contributor Jean H. Zimmerman deemed *Follow the Dream* a "fascinating artistic representation of the discovery of the New World." Excitement surrounding this work stemmed partly from the 500-year anniversary of Columbus's discovery of America and partly from Sis's experimentation with both color and composition. Using oil colors on special plaster-like backgrounds, the artist achieved a textured, authentic old-world look of fifteenth-century paintings. Sis was inspired in part by his continuing fascination with his father's exploration and travels and his own journey from a Soviet-dominated country to the new world. He once explained to *SATA,* "I realized coincidental things with my own life

or with somebody who wants to break free from certain situations. With determination and persistence, a person can do it."

Over the next few years, Sis's works, such as *Komodo!,* the 1993 story of boy who travels to Indonesia to visit a famous dragon, and *A Small Tall Tale from the Far Far North,* a story based on the Czech legend of traveler Jan Welzl, also met with success. He then added to his repertoire *The Three Golden Keys,* published in 1994. In this fairy tale, a young man is led by a cat through the city of Prague to find his childhood home, and eventually, the three keys that help him enter it. Writing and illustrating *The Three Golden Keys* proved to be quite intriguing for Sis, and critics and readers applauded the book. While *School Library Journal* contributor Julie Cummins felt the work was suited more for older children and adults, she decided that overall, "the book is intriguing, with visual and textual subtleties interconnecting with cultural and historical ties." Mary Burns, commenting in *Horn Book,* also categorized the book as one for an older audience, but praised the book for its "[d]azzling design, opulent production, [and] meticulous execution," not to mention its "elegantly crafted, breathtaking fine line illustrations."

Turning his attention to biography once again, Sis wrote and illustrated *Starry Messenger: Galileo Galilei,* which the American Library Association named a Caldecott Honor Book in 1997. Like Christopher Columbus in *Follow the Dream,* Galileo set out to prove that the Earth was not what people thought it was—in this case the center of the universe. Unlike Columbus, however, the famous astronomer could only prove it with his theories. In this picture book Sis conveys the finer and darker periods of Galileo's life, with simple descriptions in large type for younger readers and more detailed notes in

A picture-book portrait of a young girl's day at the beach, Sis's self-illustrated **Beach Ball** *teaches very young readers about shapes, colors, numbers, animals, and more.*

In his picture-book biography of Galileo, Sis conveys the finer and darker periods of the astronomer's life with simple descriptions in large type for younger readers and more detailed notes in smaller type for older readers. (From Starry Messenger, *written and illustrated by Sis.)*

smaller type for older ones. Reviewing this work in the *New York Times Book Review*, Elizabeth Spires commended Sis on how he "manages to tell the relatively complicated story of Galileo in such a simple, straightforward way, accompanied by some of the most gorgeous illustrations imaginable." Wendy Lukehart, writing in *School Library Journal*, added that the "pathos, the painstaking copies of Galileo's famous sketches of the heavens, and the attention to current scholarship make this book a fascinating find."

Sis wrote about the adventures of another explorer—this time his father—in the 1998 work *Tibet: Through the Red Box.* In the 1950s, the Chinese government recruited Vladimir Sis to record on film the construction of the first highway leading from China into Tibet. While fulfilling his duties, Vladimir witnessed the horrors of China's invasion of Tibet, which ultimately lead to the removal of the Dalai Lama. It was during this two-year

period away from home that Vladimir kept a diary. When he returned home, the elder Sis kept the diary locked in a red box, passing on stories about his journey orally to his son. In 1994, Vladimir wrote a note to his son saying the diary was his. Sis, in turn, decided to share his father's diary and oral tales with the world by creating a "groundbreaking, creative" picture book, as described by *School Library Journal* contributor Shirley Wilton. Similarly, a *Publishers Weekly* reviewer wrote that the "luminous colors of the artwork, the panoramas of Tibetan topography and the meticulous intermingling of captivating details ... make this an extraordinary volume." Caldecott Medal committee members also thought the book was extraordinary, awarding the work a Caldecott Honor in 1999.

Also published in 1998 was Sis's picture book for preschoolers, *Fire Truck.* In this short story, a young boy wakes up to find that he has become a fire truck. He relishes in his newly formed body until the smell of pancakes brings him back to reality. "Sis blends simple text with bold pictures to give insight into one boy's vivid imagination," wrote Torrie Hodgson in *School Library Journal.* Two more works that feature things of interest to many children are Sis's *Ship Ahoy!* and *Trucks, Trucks, Trucks,* both published in 1999.

Sis once expressed to *SATA* that through his work, he aims to cultivate free and open thought among children. He firmly believes that an artist's work should challenge a child's imagination. Especially intriguing to him is the wonder and innocence of early elementary-school students. "I really like talking to second graders," he said. "The young kids are wonderful because their minds are completely open. And the feelings children have here are probably the same as children have all over the world. It's amazing to see—in Asia, Thailand, Indonesia, or wherever—how similar the children are, whether they play with a piece of wood, or they play with a very sophisticated computer."

Sis also added: "I think children should have choices, and I would like to participate in their growth." Indeed, Sis advises young readers who aspire to a career as an artist to persevere and "not be intimidated by anybody." He believes that artistic talent should develop naturally, and a child should be left to "create freely—without any pressure to achieve commercial success."

Works Cited

Burns, Mary, review of *The Three Golden Keys, Horn Book,* March-April, 1995, pp. 189-90.

Cummins, Julie, review of *The Three Golden Keys, School Library Journal,* December, 1993, p. 87.

Fraser, Stephen, review of *Komodo!, Five Owls,* May-June, 1993, pp. 113-14.

Hodgson, Torrie, review of *Fire Truck, School Library Journal,* September, 1998, p. 182.

Lukehart, Wendy, review of *Starry Messenger: Galileo Galilei, School Library Journal,* October, 1996, p. 118.

Spires, Elizabeth, "Stars Were Always on His Mind," *New York Times Book Review,* November 10, 1996, p. 32.

Review of *Tibet: Through the Red Box, Publishers Weekly,* August 10, 1998, p. 365.

Wilton, Shirley, review of *Tibet: Through the Red Box, School Library Journal,* October, 1998, p. 160.

Zimmerman, Jean H., review of *Follow the Dream: The Story of Christopher Columbus, School Library Journal,* September, 1991, p. 249.

For More Information See

BOOKS

Children's Literature Review, Volume 45, Gale, 1998, pp. 153-77.

Sixth Book of Junior Authors & Illustrators, edited by Sally Holmes Holtze, H. W. Wilson, 1989, pp. 279-81.

PERIODICALS

Booklist, March 15, 1991, p. 468; January 15, 1995, p. 907; October 15, 1996, p. 423; April 15, 1996, p. 1437.

Bulletin of the Center for Children's Books, May, 1991, p. 226; January, 1995, p. 177; November, 1996, p. 115; January, 1999, p. 183; May, 1999, p. 328.

Five Owls, September-October, 1991, pp. 1-3.

Horn Book, September-October, 1991, pp. 614-15; January-February, 1997, pp. 79-80; September-October, 1998, pp. 601-02.

Kirkus Reviews, April 1, 1999, p. 538.

New York Times Book Review, June 2, 1996, p. 25; April 11, 1999, p. 32.

Publishers Weekly, August 10, 1990, p. 443; November 14, 1994, p. 26; April 26, 1999, p. 81.

*   *   *

SLADE, Arthur G(regory) 1967-

Personal

Born July 9, 1967, in Moose Jaw, Saskatchewan, Canada; son of Robert (a farmer) and Anne (a writer; maiden name, Shea) Slade; married Brenda Baker (a singer and writer), August 16, 1997. *Education:* University of Saskatchewan, B.A. (with honors), 1989. *Hobbies and other interests:* Biking, t'ai chi, hockey.

Arthur G. Slade

Addresses

Home—404 Tenth St. E., Saskatoon, Saskatchewan, Canada S7N 0C9. *Electronic mail*—arthur-slade@geocities.com.

Career

Advertising copywriter in Saskatoon, Saskatchewan, 1990-95; writer, 1995—. *Member:* Canadian Society of Children's Authors, Illustrators, and Performers (CANSCAIP), Writers Union of Canada, Saskatchewan Writers Guild.

Writings

Draugr (young adult novel), illustrated by Ljuba Levstek, Orca Books (Victoria, British Columbia), 1997.
The Haunting of Drang Island (young adult novel), Orca Books, 1998.

Author of the comic book series "Hallowed Knight."

Work in Progress

The Fenrir Wolf, a young adult suspense novel.

Adaptations

Slade's stories have been recorded for the collection *Up There There Are Only Birds: Stories from the Edge,* released by Shea Publishing (Saskatoon, Saskatchewan) in 1994.

Sidelights

Arthur G. Slade began writing at quite a young age and finished his first novel when he was eighteen. He has averaged a novel every year since then, though not all have been published. As a child he was a voracious reader of comic books and science fiction and fantasy novels. He also read every book on Norse mythology that he could get his hands on. Later he studied Icelandic literature and Norse mythology in university. This laid the groundwork for his series of young adult novels, "Northern Frights," which are based on Norse myths. "I love putting a new twist on all the old stories that the Vikings used to tell by the firelight," Slade told *SATA*.

Slade took the title for his first book *Draugr,* pronounced draw-ger, from Norse mythology and the old Icelandic name for those whose hate prevents them from resting after death. Three young Americans, visiting their grandfather in Manitoba, are caught in a frightening series of events that involve empty graves, strange disappearances, supernatural connections, and a touch of romance. John Wilson, writing in *Quill and Quire,* declared: "*Draugr* sits solidly in the preteen horror genre yet stands above much of its competition in writing and plot development."

Slade has also written "Hallowed Knight," a comic book series that is sold worldwide. He is currently working on several different series of books for young adults.

Works Cited

Wilson, John, review of *Draugr, Quill and Quire,* January, 1998, p. 38.

For More Information See

PERIODICALS

Canadian Materials, November 14, 1997.
School Library Journal, October, 1998, pp. 146-47.

*   *   *

SLOAT, Teri 1948-

Personal

Born June 24, 1948, in Salem, OR; daughter of Paul (a millworker) and Myrtle (a secretary; maiden name, McClay) Smith; married Robert Sloat (a general contractor), March 14, 1970; children: Matt, Carrie, Becky. *Education:* Oregon State University, B.A. (with honors), 1970; graduate study at Sonoma State University and Oregon College of Education.

Addresses

Home—5841 Lone Pine Rd., Sebastopol, CA 95472. *Agent*—Kendra Marcus, 67 Meadow View Dr., Orinda, CA 94563.

Career

Elementary school teacher in rural villages in Alaska, 1970-75; developer and illustrator of bilingual materials used in classrooms, 1975-81; free-lance textbook developer and illustrator in Alaska, 1981-83; teacher of sixth grade and art in Sebastopol, CA, 1984-87; free-lance writer and illustrator, 1988—. Oregon College of Education, teacher's aide training instructor, 1981-83 (summers). *Member:* Society of Children's Book Writers and Illustrators.

Awards, Honors

New York Times best picture book of the year selection, 1989, for *From Letter to Letter;* Pick of the Lists, American Booksellers Association, 1995, for *The Thing That Bothered Farmer Brown.*

Writings

The Thing That Bothered Farmer Brown, illustrated by Nadine Bernard Westcott, Orchard, 1995.
Really, Really Bad Monster Jokes, illustrated by Mike Wright, Candlewick, 1998.
There Was an Old Lady Who Swallowed a Trout!, illustrated by Reynold Ruffins, Holt, 1998.

Farmer Brown Goes Round and Round, illustrated by Nadine Bernard Westcott, DK, 1999.

SELF-ILLUSTRATED

From Letter to Letter, Dutton Children's Books, 1989.

(Reteller) *The Eye of the Needle: Based on a Yup'ik Tale Told by Betty Huffmon,* Dutton Children's Books, 1990.

(Contributor) *The Big Book of Peace,* Dutton Children's Books, 1990.

From One to One Hundred, Dutton Children's Books, 1991.

(Illustrated with husband, Robert Sloat) *The Hungry Giant of the Tundra,* Dutton Children's Books, 1993.

(Author and illustrator with husband, Robert Sloat) *Rib-Ticklers: A Book of Punny Animals,* Lothrop, Lee & Shepard, 1995.

Sody Sallyratus, Dutton Children's Books, 1997.

Patty's Pumpkin Patch, Putnam, 1999.

ILLUSTRATOR

Jane Howard, *When I'm Hungry,* Dutton Children's Books, 1992.

Barbara Winslow, *Dance on a Sealskin,* Alaska-Northwest Books (Anchorage, AK), 1995.

Charlotte Armajo, *Desert Dance,* Addison-Wesley Educational, 1995.

OTHER

(With Susan Henry) *Early Action: Developmental Activities for the Dynamic Early Learning Classroom,* Mariswood Educational Resources, 1990.

Sidelights

Teri Sloat once told *SATA:* "My mom ... reminded me that I have been writing as well as drawing since I was very small, like many other children. When I was in college, a required class in children's literature made me feel so excited about books for younger people that I think I have steered myself in that direction ever since.

"I have always been interested in other cultures and in new ways of looking at the same idea. While I was growing up, my dad often watched travel adventures on television and would talk to me about how other people lived. My mom would let me talk and talk and would always say 'I never looked at it that way' or 'what makes you able to think of those things?' She made me feel that I had a special ability. My first stories were typed in my mom's office after school.

"Like so many other children, I began drawing by copying Walt Disney characters. I was an only child and drawing also became my way of being sure that I was never bored—as did writing poems. When I started to teach and had access to so many children's books, embellishing the stories that I read or spinning off into new stories became a hobby."

Sloat's picture books first garnered praise for the colorful, detailed, and humorous illustrations; later works were equally admired for the energy of the stories, often told in rhyme and employing repetition, making them exemplary read-aloud material. Like many children's book authors and illustrators, Sloat began her career with an alphabet book. She once told *SATA:* "In 1991, I finished *From One to One Hundred,* a counting book. I made it as a companion book for *From Letter to Letter.* I really wanted to have fun with the idea that numbers are all around us in every imaginable setting. I also like to put things in an illustration that may not be noticed the first time. Trying to add just one more idea to an illustration is part of the reason it takes me longer to do a book than I would like." Both *From One to One Hundred* and *From Letter to Letter* were warmly received by book reviewers, who consistently praised Sloat's clever incorporation of numbers and letters in her colored-pencil illustrations. After listing several examples, Judith Gloyer of *School Library Journal* concluded her review of *From One to One Hundred* saying: "There are tons of other clever details worked in throughout the book." Calling *From Letter to Letter* "a delight," a *Kirkus Reviews* critic noted that the "links between the upper- and lower-case letters on each page are especially creative and amusing." In both cases, reviewers recommended these books for children a bit older than the usual ABC and counting-book audiences because the illustrations are so filled with visual information that they reward close and repeated examination. For instance, *Booklist* reviewer Denise Wilms called *From Letter to Letter* "a rich but quiet lesson for independent browsers or children sharing this with adults."

Sloat's first venture into the realm of retelling traditional tales produced *The Eye of the Needle,* a Yupik Eskimo legend about a boy who is sent out to hunt for food by his grandmother. The boy is so hungry that instead of bringing the food back home, he eats everything in sight, from a small fish to a giant whale. Returning empty handed and ashamed to his grandmother's hut, the overstuffed boy discovers that he cannot squeeze through the front door. But grandmother's magic needle releases all the fish, enough to feed the whole village community. "This tall tale, simply told in an oral style, should have wide appeal," predicted Karen James in *School Library Journal.* Critic Betsy Hearne also praised the energy of Sloat's illustrations in her review in *Bulletin of the Center for Children's Books.* Hearne concluded: "However true this may or may not be to the Yupik tradition, it's a jolly celebration of the oral stage."

Like *The Eye of the Needle,* Sloat's retelling of *The Hungry Giant of the Tundra* was recommended for reading aloud. In *The Hungry Giant,* a group of children play out on the Alaskan tundra later than their parents have warned them is safe and are captured by Akaguagankak the Giant. With the help of two birds, they are saved by their wits and good luck. In her review in *School Library Journal* Roz Goodman called this "a masterful retelling that combines rich, lively language ... and colorful, detailed illustrations."

Sloat collaborated with her husband, Robert, on the illustrations for *The Hungry Giant of the Tundra,* and the two teamed up again for both text and illustrations with

Rib-Ticklers: A Book of Punny Animals. Essentially a joke book, *Rib-Ticklers* was praised for its superior artwork and interesting layout, which organizes the text into fifteen two-page spreads, each replete with jokes, puns, and riddles, as well as visual humor on a particular animal. Describing the illustrations as "subtly humorous rather than cartoonishly wacky," Steven Engelfried, a reviewer for *School Library Journal,* claimed that "kids will enjoy perusing the pages." Julie Yates Walker, a contributor to *Booklist,* added: "Young jokesters should pick up quite a bit of information amid giggles."

Like her earlier retellings of traditional Yupik legends, Sloat's rendition of *Sody Sallyratus,* a tall tale from the Appalachian region, garnered praise for what *Booklist* reviewer Julie Corsaro dubbed "engaging humor, rhythm, and repetition," elements that, in the reviewer's opinion, make this an ideal choice for reading aloud. In this story, an Appalachian family with a yen for biscuits but short on sody sallyratus—baking powder—goes one by one to the store to buy some. However, each family member encounters a hungry black bear who eats them before they reach the store. Luckily, a loyal pet squirrel outwits the bear, freeing the undigested family.

Taking off from the story about the old lady who swallowed a fly, then a spider, then a bird, cat, dog, cow, and finally a horse, Sloat created the picture book story *There Was an Old Lady Who Swallowed a Trout!,* illustrated by Reynold Ruffins. In Sloat's version, set in the Pacific Northwest, the old lady of the title swallows a variety of ocean wildlife before consuming the entire ocean itself, only to regurgitate the whole mess and survive the ordeal—unlike the old lady who swallowed a horse, as *School Library Journal* reviewer Tom S. Hurlburt noted. Sloat's version was commended for its "simple but satisfying rhymes" and "cheery humor" by a reviewer for *Publishers Weekly.*

Sloat illustrated her first book for another author with *When I'm Hungry* by Jane Howard. Of the title, Sloat once told *SATA:* "This has been a book for me to relax with, as I love to draw animals. It has given me an excuse to spend wonderful research hours learning more about a variety of animals and how they eat." Sloat also provided the illustrations for Barbara Winslow's account of a young Yupik Eskimo girl's coming-of-age ritual in *Dance on a Sealskin.* Winslow tells of the mix of emotions felt by Annie as she prepares for her first ceremonial dance, emphasizing the involvement of her

A frustrated farmer keeps the whole farm awake with his relentless pursuit of a pesky insect. (From The Thing That Bothered Farmer Brown, *written by Teri Sloat and illustrated by Nadine Bernard Westcott.)*

family and community. *Booklist* reviewer Kay Weisman praised Sloat's illustrations as "particularly effective in showing the mix of modern and traditional elements in the Yupik culture." Roz Goodman, who reviewed *Dance on a Sealskin* for *School Library Journal,* also commented favorably on the realism of Sloat's illustrations, adding: "This book ... combines powerful writing and vivid illustrations to capture the joy of giving and sharing among the Yupik Eskimos."

Featuring illustrations by Nadine Bernard Westcott, *The Thing That Bothered Farmer Brown* follows a farmer who wakes up the whole farm pursuing a pesky mosquito. However, for all the racket, the frustrated farmer never manages to catch the insect. *School Library Journal* reviewer Beth Tegart called the book "a rousing story-hour offering that's frivolous and fun." A sequel, *Farmer Brown Goes Round and Round,* offers more mayhem, as a twister hits the farm with unexpected results: no injuries, but when the whirling cast of characters returns safely to the ground, they find that their languages have been completely mixed up. "The clever and expertly written story will tickle the funny bones of the nursery-school set," asserted a *Kirkus Reviews* commentator. *School Library Journal* contributor Heide Piehler also offered a favorable assessment of the book, concluding: "Pair it with Bernard Most's *Cock-a-Doodle-Moo!* and score a 10 on the storytime giggle meter."

Works Cited

Corsaro, Julie, review of *Sody Sallyratus, Booklist,* December 15, 1996, p. 730.

Engelfried, Steven, review of *Rib-Ticklers, School Library Journal,* July, 1995, p. 75.

Review of *Farmer Brown Goes Round and Round, Kirkus Reviews,* February 15, 1999, p. 306.

Review of *From Letter to Letter, Kirkus Reviews,* August 15, 1989, p. 1251.

Gloyer, Judith, review of *From One to One Hundred, School Library Journal,* December, 1991, p. 112.

Goodman, Roz, review of *The Hungry Giant of the Tundra, School Library Journal,* January, 1994, p. 111.

Goodman, Roz, review of *Dance on a Sealskin, School Library Journal,* December, 1995, p. 110.

Hearne, Betsy, review of *The Eye of the Needle, Bulletin of the Center for Children's Books,* January, 1991, p. 130.

Hurlburt, Tom S., review of *There Was an Old Lady Who Swallowed a Trout!, School Library Journal,* November, 1998, p. 96.

James, Karen, review of *The Eye of the Needle, School Library Journal,* November, 1990, p. 108.

Piehler, Heide, review of *Farmer Brown Goes Round and Round, School Library Journal,* April, 1999, p. 109.

Tegart, Beth, review of *The Thing That Bothered Farmer Brown, School Library Journal,* March, 1995, p. 187.

Review of *There Was an Old Lady Who Swallowed a Trout!, Publishers Weekly,* October 19, 1998, p. 79.

Walker, Julie Yates, review of *Rib-Ticklers, Booklist,* June 1 & 15, 1995, p. 1780.

Weisman, Kay, review of *Dance on a Sealskin, Booklist,* August, 1995, p. 1958.

Wilms, Denise, review of *From Letter to Letter, Booklist,* October 15, 1989, p. 464.

For More Information See

PERIODICALS

Booklist, December 1, 1993, pp. 695-96.
Bulletin of the Center for Children's Books, September, 1991, p. 22.
Horn Book, July, 1993, p. 110; March-April, 1999, p. 202.
Publishers Weekly, July 12, 1991, p. 64; March 27, 1995, p. 85.
School Library Journal, November, 1989, pp. 99-100.

* * *

SNYDER, Midori 1954-

Personal

Born January 1, 1954, in Santa Monica, CA; daughter of Emile Snyder (a poet and professor of African languages and literature) and Jeanette Lebaron (an ethnomusicologist and Tibetan scholar); married Stephen Haessler (an educator), June 16, 1979; children: Carl, Taiko. *Education:* Attended the University of Wisconsin (European social history and East Asian literature); graduate studies in African languages and literature, specializing in Arabic and Swahili oral narrative traditions; pursuing degree in Italian studies. *Hobbies and other interests:* Building masks for theatre productions, playing classical and folk mandolin, Shotokan karate instructor, fan of movies produced by Hong Kong Cinema.

Addresses

Agent—Howard Morhaim, Morhaim Literary Agency, 841 Broadway, Suite 604, New York, NY 10001; c/o Tor Books, 175 Fifth Ave., New York, NY 10010.

Career

Writer.

Writings

FANTASY NOVELS; FOR CHILDREN

Dinotopia, Hatchling, Random House, 1995.

OTHER FANTASY NOVELS

Soulstring, Ace, 1987.
The Flight of Michael McBride, Tor, 1994.
The Innamorati, Tor, 1998.

FANTASY NOVELS; "QUEEN'S QUARTER" SERIES

New Moon, Ace, 1989, Unwin Paperbacks (London), 1989.
Sadar's Keep, Unwin Paperbacks, 1990, Tor, 1991.
Beldane's Fire, Tor, 1993.

OTHER

Contributor of novellas and stories to anthologies, including the *Borderlands* anthologies, edited by Terri Windling, published by Signet; and *The Year's Best*

Fantasy and Horror, edited by Ellen Datlow and Terri Windling, published by St. Martins Press.

Work in Progress

Zizola's Proposal, a sequel to *The Innamorati.*

Sidelights

Midori Snyder is the author of several fantasy novels. Her first, *Soulstring,* is a Gothic, high-fantasy novel based on the British folk song *Tamlin.* Since then she has penned a trilogy known as the "Queen's Quarter" series, a western cowboy fantasy novel called *The Flight of Michael McBride,* a contribution to Jim Guerney's *Dinotopia* world with the juvenile novel *The Hatchling,* and an Italianate fantasy, *The Innamorati.* She has also collaborated with comic book artist Charles Vess in writing the script for "Barbara Allen" in the acclaimed series, *Book of Ballads and Sagas.* Snyder is a founding member of the popular shared-world anthology, *Borderlands,* edited by Terri Windling, and has published three novellas in the series. In addition, she has contributed short stories to numerous anthologies, some of which have been reprinted in *Year's Best Fantasy and Horror,* edited by Ellen Datlow and Terri Windling.

Soulstring tells the tale of a young woman who inherits her sorcerer father's talents for magic. Instead of being delighted, the father is enraged that his magic has passed to a female instead of a male child. Unable to kill her until she is grown, he bides his time and uses a great deal of cunning to keep her from marrying or finding any other form of escape. When she is finally taken away by the man of her dreams, the sorcerer complicates things by changing that man into a deer—making the sorcerer's pursuit of the loving couple even more harrowing. Citing "some well realized minor characters" in a positive assessment of *Soulstring,* a reviewer for *Science Fiction Chronicle* asserted that "fantasy and gothic romance mix well" in the pages of this story.

The Flight of Michael McBride combines Irish myth and legend with a Wild West setting. Centering on the experiences of an Irish immigrant family in the eastern part of the United States, the tale opens as Michael McBride and his father play cards while Michael's mother lies dying. Upon her death, the fairy curse that has been upon her all her life is transferred to Michael, and he soon finds himself fleeing all manner of beings straight out of Irish legend—most notably a demon known as Red Cap. Michael flees to the American West, where he makes friends with the half-Apache Jake Talking Boy and others. When Michael falls in love with a young woman named Annie May, however, he realizes he must face his supernatural enemies or risk endangering his loved ones. *Voice of Youth Advocates* contributor Janet G. Polacheck admired the novel's characterization, citing Annie May in particular as "believably delicate and attractive" despite her "Ozark country accent." Tom Easton of *Analog* hailed *The Flight of Michael McBride* as "a charming tale of growing up under fire." Easton concluded: "Snyder shows considerable talent here. She

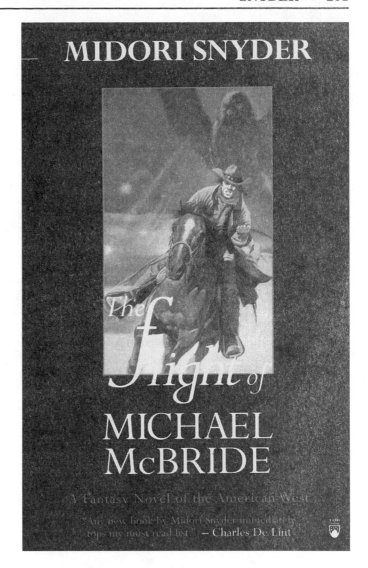

In Midori Snyder's fantasy novel combining Irish myth and legend with a Wild West setting, Michael McBride, an Irish immigrant to the United States, inherits a fairy curse when his mother dies, and flees to the frontier West in an attempt to escape his affliction.

is a strong, vivid storyteller, and fantasy fans will not be disappointed."

Snyder followed *The Flight of Michael McBride* with *The Innamorati,* a fantasy inspired by a one-year sojourn she took to Milan, Italy, with her husband and children. The story centers on four companions who travel to the Italian city of Labirinto during the Renaissance period. The four have come seeking a maze, which, according to legend, holds the power to purge the curses of all who can successfully reach its center. The characters arrive at the maze, each hoping to unburden themselves of a particular worry or problem. Among them are an actor who cannot stop stuttering, a muted siren who is forced to live in exile from the island of her birth, and a duelist who wants to stop living by the sword. Throughout the book the characters encounter fantastic creatures and figures from Greek and Roman mythology. Jackie Cassada, writing in *Library Journal,* called the book "a dreamlike novel [that] resonates with overtones of the commedia dell'arte as [Snyder's] characters confront mythical creatures and nightmarish visions." A *Publishers Weekly* critic declared, "It's fairly miraculous how Snyder pulls all this off.... The hybrid of street theater and fantasy seems to spin itself into existence before the reader's eyes. Farts, decapitations and sirens' songs are equally likely and equally delightful in this amazing story."

Works Cited

Cassada, Jackie, review of *The Innamorati, Library Journal,* July, 1998, p. 141.

Easton, Tom, review of *The Flight of Michael McBride, Analog,* May, 1995, p. 166.

Review of *The Innamorati, Publishers Weekly,* June 22, 1998, p. 88.

Polacheck, Janet G., review of *The Flight of Michael McBride, Voice of Youth Advocates,* June, 1995, p. 110.

Review of *Soulstring, Science Fiction Chronicle,* April, 1988, p. 56.

For More Information See

PERIODICALS

Library Journal, October 15, 1994, p. 90.

Locus, April, 1991, p. 44; October, 1994, p. 33; January, 1995, p. 51; February, 1995, p. 39.

Magazine of Science Fiction and Fantasy, February, 1995, pp. 33-34.

Publishers Weekly, November 14, 1994, p. 57.

*   *   *

SULLIVAN, Paul 1939-

Personal

Born June 10, 1939, in Trenton, NJ; son of Paul Jacob Sullivan (in real estate) and Anna K. Sullivan (maiden name, Muller; present surname, Johnson); married Dorothy A. Dutton (in retail management), December 27, 1958; children: Paul Stephen Sullivan.

Career

Has worked as a foreman and production manager in the chemical industry since 1970.

Writings

Legend of the North, Royal Fireworks Press, 1995.
Keewatin, Royal Fireworks Press, 1996.
The Unforgiving Land, Royal Fireworks Press, 1996.
The Spirit Walker, Royal Fireworks Press, 1997.

Work in Progress

A novel set in the mountains of Peru.

Paul Sullivan

Sidelights

Paul Sullivan told *SATA:* "I try to write books that can be enjoyed by a person of any age. Never to write above or below them. And I think a writer owes it to the reader to tell a good story honestly. To have something worth saying.

"I believe that if a book can wake the curiosity of a child to the world for even a few hours, then all the writing is worth it. That's what the whole thing is about. A child fascinated by a wolf or polar bear in the Arctic or an elephant in Africa. Asking a question. Reading and asking another question. I believe the four novels *The Spirit Walker, Legend of the North, Keewatin,* and *The Unforgiving Land* do this at least in a small way. And I thank all the people at Royal Fireworks Press for giving them the chance."

In his first book, *Legend of the North,* Paul Sullivan interweaves the legend of Amitok, a white wolf, and the story of Tukarra, an elderly Inuit man, "making vivid points about man's interference with the Arctic natural and spiritual world," according to Diane P. Tuccillo in a *Voice of Youth Advocates* review. Although born a runt, through determination and intelligence Amitok survives to become a leader of his pack. With the guidance of Kivvik, the spirit of his grandfather, Amitok fights a polar bear, becomes separated from his pack, is rescued from a fox trap by another lone wolf, and in turn rescues Tukarra from an attack by a wolverine. Writing in *Booklist,* Frances Bradburn drew positive comparisons between Sullivan's personification of a wolf pack and that found in Whitley Strieber's *Wolf of Shadows,* calling *Legend of the North* "equally well done." Further, Bradburn claimed that readers would willingly suspend disbelief in order to listen to the voices of these wolves, a point made by Tuccillo as well. "There is just too much good character development, both human and animal, and exciting action to keep readers from wanting to finish," Tuccillo claimed. Bradburn recommended *Legend of the North* as "an exciting, satisfying read for that special young adult."

Works Cited

Bradburn, Frances, review of *Legend of the North, Booklist,* January 1, 1996, p. 818.

Tuccillo, Diane P., review of *Legend of the North, Voice of Youth Advocates,* April, 1996, p. 30.*

T–U

TAKAYAMA, Sandi 1962-

Personal

Born November 6, 1962, in Honolulu, HI; daughter of Frank (a retired computer analyst) and Jessie (a retired preschool teacher) Ginoza; married Layne Takayama (a financial consultant), August 18, 1990; children: Jordan, Joelle, Reece. *Education:* University of Hawaii at Manoa, B.Ed., 1985, Professional Diploma, 1986, M.L.I.S., 1990. *Religion:* Christian.

Sandi Takayama and family.

Career

Elementary school teacher in Hawaii, 1987-90; elementary school librarian in Hawaii, 1991—. *Member:* Hawaii Association of School Librarians.

Awards, Honors

Recognition for excellence in children's books, Hawaii Book Publishers Association, for *The Musubi Man.*

Writings

The Musubi Man: Hawaii's Gingerbread Man, illustrated by Pat Hall, Bess Press (Honolulu, HI), 1996.
Sumorella: A Hawaii Cinderella Story, illustrated by Esther Szegedy, Bess Press, 1997.
The Prince and the Li Hing Mui: Hawaii's Princess and the Pea, illustrated by Szegedy, Bess Press, 1998.

Sidelights

Sandi Takayama told *SATA:* "As a child I always enjoyed writing stories and making up my own endings to familiar tales. When I'm in the middle of a story, my head is filled with the characters and their situations. I think about them whenever I have a free moment—at a stop light, while waiting at the doctor's office, even late at night when I'm rocking my baby to sleep. Some of my best ideas come to me while I wash the dishes or fold the laundry.

"With a fulltime job and three young children, my greatest challenge is actually getting the words down on paper without sacrificing any precious family time. I usually compose the entire story in my head, then spend a week or two scribbling in notebooks at odd hours of the night."

*   *   *

TAYLOR, Margaret 1950-

Personal

Born May 30, 1950, in Campbell River, British Columbia, Canada; daughter of Clarence Richard (a pulp and paper mill supervisor) and Ruth (a schoolteacher; maiden name, Butler) Hulme; married Paul Taylor (a millwright), December 11, 1970; children: Michael, Andrew, Warren. *Education:* Attended Simon Fraser University. *Politics:* "Left of center." *Religion:* United Church of Canada. *Hobbies and other interests:* Reading, boating, hiking, knitting.

Addresses

Home—P.O. Box 64, Heriot Bay, British Columbia, Canada V0P 1H0. *Electronic mail*—marg.taylor@ sd72.bc.ca.

Career

School District 72, Campbell River, British Columbia, library technician and clerk, 1987—; also worked as a school secretary. Past director of a local youth soccer group. *Member:* Canadian Union of Public Employees, British Columbia Federation of Writers.

Awards, Honors

"Our Choice" Award, Canadian Children's Book Centre, for *Three Against Time.*

Writings

Three Against Time, illustrated by Ljuba Levstek, Orca Book Publishers (Custer, WA), 1997.

Work in Progress

Research on the "Nisga'a treaty, the Nass Valley, and the volcanic eruption."

Sidelights

Margaret Taylor told *SATA:* "My eldest son was a reluctant reader, so I decided to write a story for him. He was my first 'proofreader,' and I soon had him waiting impatiently for the next chapter to come out of the typewriter! Throughout the project, I kept my sights on two goals: write something that would appeal to a reluctant reader, and impart a bit of history at the same time. I avoided emotion-wrangling because I wanted my history lesson to be fun and because, basing the characters of my 'story boys' on the lives of my sons, I decided that, as long as they were all together, the boys could survive quite well without Mom and Dad. They tended to get engrossed in adventures and to forget they had parents who might be worried about them. From this, *Three Against Time* was born.

"My work habits are atrocious, just like my spelling! I like to get so totally engrossed in writing that the world around me ceases to exist. Unfortunately, that can't happen at present, so I haven't started on another project.

"There are so many good children's writers being published today. I wish I'd had access to such a variety when I was young. I can't resist Monica Hughes, Kit Pearson, Margaret Buffie, or Gary Paulsen. Still, Lucy Maud Montgomery is number one. For anyone trying to break into print, my advice is: be patient and don't give up. Learn from rejections. Edit, revise, rewrite, and be open to suggestions."

UNGERER, (Jean) Thomas 1931-
(Tomi Ungerer)

Personal

Born November 28, 1931, in Strasbourg, France; came to the United States in 1957; son of Theodor (an astronomical clock manufacturer) and Alice (Essler) Ungerer; married Nancy White, 1957 (marriage was dissolved); married Miriam Lancaster, 1959 (marriage was dissolved); married Yvonne Deborah Wright, 1971; children: Phoebe Alexis, Aria, Pascal, Lukas. *Education:* Attended Ecole des Arts Decoratifs, Strasbourg. *Hobbies and other interests:* botany, mineralogy, anatomy, geology, carpentry, collecting antique toys, and making kites.

Addresses

Home—Ungerer divides his time between Strasbourg, France, and County Cork, Ireland; he has also lived in the United States and Canada. *Office*—c/o Diogenes Verlag, 8 Sprecher Strasse, Zurich, Switzerland 8030.

Career

Freelance writer and illustrator; also painter, cartoonist, and graphic artist. Worked in advertising and as a commercial artist in New York City. Founder of Wild Oats Film Co. and Culture Bank in Strasbourg, France. The imprint "TomiCo" was created for him by American publisher Roberts Rinehart, 1997. *Exhibitions:* Exhibitor at the Musee des Arts Decoratifs (retrospective), Paris, 1981; at Royal Festival Hall (retrospective), London, 1985; and in numerous one-man shows in Europe and New York City. *Military service:* French Desert Police, Camel Corps; Attache de Mission, French Ministry of Culture, and French Ministry of Foreign Affairs for French-German cooperation, 1987—. Member of the Franco-German interministerial commission, 1993—.

Awards, Honors

Spring Book Festival honor book, 1957, for *The Mellops Go Flying;* Children's Spring Book Festival Award, *New York Herald Tribune,* 1958, for *Crictor,* and 1967, for *Moon Man;* Notable Book citation, American Library Association (ALA), 1958, for *Crictor;* Best Illustrated Children's Books of the Year, *New York Times,* 1962, for *The Three Robbers,* 1971, for *The Beast of Monsieur Racine,* 1974, for *A Storybook from Tomi Ungerer,* and 1978, for *The Great Song Book;* Notable Book citation, ALA, and Honor List citation, *Horn Book,* both 1963, both for *The Three Robbers;* Society of Illustrators Gold Medal, 1969; American Institute of Graphic Arts Award, 1969, for *The Hat,* and 1973-74, for *No Kiss for Mother;* American Institute of Graphic Arts fifty books of the year citation, 1971, for *The Beast of Monsieur Racine; I Am Papa Snap and These Are My Favorite No Such Stories* and *Oh, That's Ridiculous!* both chosen for the American Institute of Graphic Arts Children's Book Show, 1971-72; Children's Book Showcase choices, 1972, for *The Beast of Monsieur*

Racine, and 1975, for *Allumette;* Brooklyn Arts Books for Children Citation, 1973, for *Moon Man,* and 1975, for *The Beast of Monsieur Racine;* Emily Award, 1973, for the film version of *Moon Man;* Ragnazzi Award, Bologna Children's Book Fair, 1998, for *Flix.* Ungerer has also received several awards for his body of work, including the Hans Christian Andersen Medal, International Board on Books for Young People (IBBY), 1998, for lifetime achievement; he was also named a highly commended illustrator by the Hans Christian Andersen awards committee in 1980. Ungerer has been honored three times by the French government: in 1985, he was made Commandeur des Arts et des Lettres; in 1990, he was made a Chevalier de la Legion d'Honneur; and in 1995, he received the Grand Prix National des Arts Graphiques from the French cultural minister. Ungerer received the Jacob Burckhart Prize in 1983, and in 1993 was awarded a German prize, the Deutscher Bundesverdienstkereusz.

Writings

FOR CHILDREN; AUTHOR AND ILLUSTRATOR; AS TOMI UNGERER; PICTURE BOOKS AND STORIES, EXCEPT AS NOTED

Crictor, Harper, 1958.
Adelaide, Harper, 1959, reissued by Roberts Rinehart, 1999.
Emile, Harper, 1960.
Rufus, Harper, 1961.
Snail, Where Are You? Harper, 1962.
The Three Robbers, Atheneum, 1963, reissued by Roberts Rinehart, 1998.
(With Miriam Ungerer) *Come into My Parlor,* Atheneum, 1963.
One, Two, Where's My Shoe? (verse), Harper, 1964.
Orlando the Brave Vulture, Harper, 1966.
Moon Man, Whiting & Wheaton (London), 1966, Harper, 1967, reissued by Roberts Rinehart, 1998.
(With Andre Hodeir) *Warwick's Three Bottles,* Grove, 1966.
Basil Ratski, Diogenes Verlag (Zurich), 1967.
Zeralda's Ogre, Harper, 1967, reissued by Roberts Rinehart, 1999.
Ask Me a Question, Harper, 1968.
(With Andre Hodeir) *Cleopatra Goes Sledding,* Grove, 1968.
(With Barbara Shook Hazen) *The Sorcerer's Apprentice,* Lancelot Press, 1969.
The Hat, Parents' Magazine Press, 1970.
The Beast of Monsieur Racine, Farrar, Straus, 1971.
I Am Papa Snap and These are My Favorite No Such Stories, Harper, 1971, reissued by Roberts Rinehart, 1999.
No Kiss for Mother, Harper, 1973, reissued by Roberts Rinehart, 1998.
Allumette: A Fable, with Due Respect to Hans Christian Andersen, the Grimm Brothers, and the Honorable Ambrose Bierce, Parents' Magazine Press, 1974.
(Compiler and contributor) *A Storybook from Tomi Ungerer,* Watts, 1974.
Flix, Roberts Rinehart, 1998.

Tortoni Tremolo the Cursed Musician, Roberts Rinehart, 1998.

Tomi: A Childhood under the Nazis (autobiography), Roberts Rinehart, 1998.

FOR CHILDREN; AUTHOR AND ILLUSTRATOR; AS TOMI UNGERER; "MELLOPS" SERIES; PICTURE BOOKS

The Mellops Go Flying, Harper, 1957.

The Mellops Go Diving for Treasure, Harper, 1957, reissued by Roberts Rinehart, 1999.

The Mellops Strike Oil, Harper, 1958, reissued by Roberts Rinehart, 1999.

Christmas Eve at the Mellops, Harper, 1960, reissued by Roberts Rinehart, 1998.

The Mellops Go Spelunking, Harper, 1963, reissued by Roberts Rinehart, 1998.

FOR CHILDREN; ILLUSTRATOR; AS TOMI UNGERER

Millicent E. Selsam, *Seeds and More Seeds,* Harper, 1959.

Bennett Cerf, compiler, *Riddle-De-Dee: 458, Count Them, 458 Riddles Old and New, for Children from Twelve to 112,* Random House, 1962.

Mary Stolz, *Fredou,* Harper, 1962.

John Hollander, *A Book of Various Owls* (poems), Norton 1963.

William Cole, *Frances Face-Maker: A Going-to-Bed Book,* World, 1963.

Jeff Brown, *Flat Stanley,* Harper, 1964.

Jerome Beatty, *The Clambake Mutiny: An Undersea Story,* Young Scott Books (New York), 1964.

Barbara Brenner, *Mr. Tall and Mr. Small,* W. R. Scott, 1966.

Miriam Ungerer, *The Too Hot to Cook Book,* Walker, 1966.

William Cole, *What's Good for a Four-Year-Old?,* Holt, 1967.

Jean B. Showalter, *The Donkey Ride: A Fable,* Doubleday, 1967.

Edward Lear, *Lear's Nonsense Verses,* Grosset, 1967.

William Cole, *That Pest Jonathan,* Harper, 1970.

Donnarae MacCann and Olga Richard, *The Child's First Books,* Wilson, 1973.

Anne Diekmann, *Das Grosse Liederbuch: 204 deutsche volksund kinderlieder* (songbook), Diogenes Verlag, 1975.

Johanna Spyri, *Heidi Kann brauchen, was es gelernt hat,* Diogenes Verlag, 1978.

Spyri, *Heidis lehr-und wunderjahre,* Diogenes Verlag, 1978.

Timothy John, editor, *The Great Song Book,* Doubleday, 1978.

Johanna Spyri, *Tomi Ungerer's Heidi: The Classic Novel,* translated by Helen B. Dole, 1990, reissued by Roberts Rinehart, 1997.

FOR CHILDREN; ILLUSTRATOR; AS TOMI UNGERER; COMPILED BY WILLIAM COLE

Beastly Boys and Ghastly Girls, World, 1964.

Oh, What Nonsense! (poems), Viking, 1966.

A Case of the Giggles, World, 1967, published in England as *Limerick Giggles, Joke Giggles: Collected by William Cole,* Bodley Head, 1969.

The Book of Giggles, World, 1970.

Oh, How Silly! (poems), Viking, 1970.

Oh, That's Ridiculous! (poems), Viking, 1972.

FOR ADULTS; AUTHOR AND ILLUSTRATOR; AS TOMI UNGERER

Inside Marriage: Wedding Pictures, Grove, 1958.

Horrible: An Account of the Sad Achievement of Progress, Atheneum, 1960.

Der schonste Tag: achtundvierzig Hochzeitsbilder, Diogenes Verlag, 1960.

Der Herzinfrakt: ein Stundenbuch fur Geschaftsleute, Diogenes Verlag, 1962.

A Television Notebook, CBS, 1963.

(With William Cole) *A Cat Hater's Handbook, or, The Ailurophobe's Delight,* Dial, 1963.

The Underground Sketchbook of Tomi Ungerer, Viking, 1964.

The Party, Paragraphic Books, 1966.

(Editor and compiler) *Nicht wahr? Text from Kaputt,* by Curzio Malaparte, Paragraphic Books, 1966.

Fornicon, Rhinoceros Press, 1969, Grove, 1970.

Compromises, Farrar, Straus, 1970.

Portfolio, Diogenes Verlag, 1970.

The Poster Art of Tomi Ungerer, edited by Jack Rennart, Darien House, 1970.

Der Sexmaniak, Diogenes Verlag, 1973.

Der Spiegelmensch, Diogenes Verlag, 1973.

America: Zeichnungen, 1956-1971, Diogenes Verlag, 1974.

Adam and Eve: A Collection of Cartoons, Diogenes Verlag, 1974, W. Heyne (Munich), 1974.

Freut Euch des Lebens, Diogenes Verlag, 1975.

Das grosse Liederbuch, Diogenes Verlag, 1975.

Das kleine Liederbuch, Diogenes Verlag, 1975.

Hopp Hopp Hopp (erotica), privately printed, 1975.

Totempole: Erotische Zeichnungen 1968-1975, Diogenes Verlag, 1976.

Babylon, Diogenes Verlag, 1979.

(With Robert Putz and Alfred Limbach) *Abracadabra: Das Ideenbuch,* Argos Verlag (Cologne), 1979.

Politricks, Diogenes Verlag, 1979.

Der Furz, Argos Verlag, 1980.

(With Daniel Keel and others) *Das Tomi Ungerer Bilder- und Lesebuch: mit Essays, Zeugnissen und Zeichnungen von und uber Tomi Ungerer,* Diogenes Verlag, 1981.

Tomi Ungerer: Ausstellung, Exposition, Exhibition, Argos, 1981.

Symptomatics, Diogenes Verlag, 1982.

Das Kamasutra der Frosche, Diogenes Verlag, 1982, published as *The Joy of Frogs,* Grove Press, 1985.

Here Today—Gone Tomorrow (autobiography), Diogenes Verlag, 1983, published as *Far Out Isn't Far Enough,* Grove Press, 1984.

Slow Agony, Diogenes Verlag, 1983.

1911 (erotica), Diogenes Verlag, 1983.

Rigor Mortis, Diogenes Verlag, 1983.

Once in a Lifetime, Cape (London), 1984.

Tomi Ungerer's Frauen, Diogenes Verlag, 1984.

Femmes Fatale, Diogenes Verlag, 1984.

Testament: A Collection of Satirical Drawings 1960-80, Cape, 1985.

Frisch, Frosch, Frohlich, Frei, Diogenes Verlag, 1985.

Warteraum, Diogenes Verlag, 1985.

Schutzengel der Holle, Diogenes Verlag, 1986.

Derby, Diogenes Verlag, 1987.

L'Alsace en torts et de travers, Ecole des Loisirs, 1988.

Schnip Schnap, Diogenes, 1989.

33 spective, Musees de la Ville de Strasbourg, 1990.

Das grosse Buch vom Schabernack, Diogenes, 1990.

Tin leben, Diogenes, 1990.

Fatras, Vent d'Ouest, 1991.

A la Guerre Comme a la Guerre: dessins et souvenirs d'enfance, Nuee Bleue (Strasbourg), 1991.

Tomi Ungerer: Catalogo a cura di Paola Vassalli, Edizioni Carte segrete (Rome), 1991.

Tomi Ungerer: eine Retrospektive, Diogenes Verlag, 1991.

Tomi Ungerer im Gesprach fur Europa, Elster (Baden-Baden, West Germany), 1992.

Tomi Ungerer, Photographie, 1960-1990, Editions Braus (Heidelberg), 1993(?).

Schmuck Stucke, Gunther Krauss, 1994.

Tomi Ungerer: das Spiel ist aus: Werkschau, 1956-1995, Jonas Verlag (Marburg), 1995.

Das Grone Katzenbuck, Diogenes, 1995.

Cats as Cats Can, Roberts Rinehart, 1997.

Europolitain, Anstett, 1998.

Mon Alsace, Nuee Bleue, 1998.

FOR ADULTS; ILLUSTRATOR; AS TOMI UNGERER

Art Buchwald, *The Brave Coward*, Harper, 1957.

James Agee, *Agee on Film*, two volumes, McDowell, Obolenksy, 1958-60.

Paul Rothenhaeusler, *Amerika fuer anfaenger: Einschnelkurs fuer Europaeer* (travel book), Diogenes Verlag, 1960.

Dick West, *The Backside of Washington*, Doubleday, 1961.

Bergen Evans, *Comfortable Words*, Random House, 1962.

David Newman and others, editors, *Esquire's Book of Gambling*, Harper, 1962.

Jerome Beatty, *The Girls We Leave Behind: A Terrible Scientific Study of American Women at Home*, Doubleday, 1963.

Saul Maloff and others, editors, *All About Women*, Harper, 1963.

Henry Slesar, *Erlesene verbrechen und makellose mord*, Diogenes Verlag, 1964.

Tait Trussell and Paul Hencke, editors, *Dear NASA: Please Send me a Rocket*, foreword by Wernher von Braun, Dutton, 1964.

Herbert Feuerstein, *New York Fuer anfaenger*, Diogenes Verlag, 1969.

Archie W. Troelstrup, *The Consumer in American Society: Personal and Family Finance*, 4th edition, McGraw-Hill, 1970 (Ungerer was not associated with earlier editions).

Jack Rennert, editor, *The Poster Art of Tomi Ungerer*, Darien House, 1971.

Rainer Brambach and Frank Geerk, *Kneipenlieder*, Diogenes Verlag, 1974.

Ben Witter, *Liebesdienste: Anweisungen zum toeten, ein unzerreissbares bilderbuch fuer erwachsene*, Hoffman & Campe (Hamburg), 1976.

Alfred Limbach, *Der Furz: zusammengestellt und kommentiert von Alfred Limbach*, Argos Press (Koln), 1980.

Tomi Ungerer: Ausstellung, Exposition, Exhibition (text in English, French, and German), Argos, 1981.

Tony Schneider and others, *La cuisine alsacienne*, Bueb & Reumaux (Strasbourg), 1985.

Adrien Finck, *Fremdsprache: kritische Lyrik*, Olms (New York), 1988.

Bernard Lassahn, *Das grosse Buch der kleinen Tiere: elf Gute-Nacht-Geschichten*, Diogenes Verlag, 1989.

Patrick Hamm, *Les cartes postales de Tomi Ungerer*, Editions du Rhin (Mulhouse, France), 1991.

Eva Demski, *Eva Demskis Katzenbuch*, Frankfurter Verlagsanstalt (Frankfurt), 1992.

Jacques Bank, *Het beest van Monsieur Racine: voor een sprekende pianist en dia projectie (ad libitum), 1990-1991*, Donemus (Amsterdam), 1992.

Collection des jouets mecaniques metalliques: donation Tomi Ungerer, Editions Les Musess de la Ville de Strasbourg, 1993.

Dave Page, *Marianne Moore*, Creative Education (Mankato, MN), 1994.

OTHER

Also illustrator of *Games, Anyone?* by Robert Thomson, 1964, *A Collection of French Poetry*, 1966, *School Life in Paris*, 1970, a retelling of Johanna Spyri's *Heidi* by Rosemary Harris, 1983, and translated works by Ambrose Bierce and H. G. Wells. Contributor to numerous magazines, including *Holiday, Esquire, Fortune, Harper's, Sports Illustrated, McCall's, Show, Life*, and the *Village Voice*. Ungerer is also the creator of the film *The Electric Circus: The Ultimate Legal Entertainment Experience*, 1969, and numerous posters. In addition, he has done work for the Canadian Broadcasting Corporation and the State of New York. Ungerer's works have been translated into thirty languages and have prompted spin-off products that have been issued in Europe. His papers are housed in a permanent collection at the Free Library, Philadelphia. The Centre Tomi Ungerer at the Musees de Strasbourg houses over seven thousand original drawings, and all posters, limited editions, archives, sculptures, prints, and postcards.

Adaptations

Weston Woods released four of Ungerer's works as animated films: *The Three Robbers* in 1972, *The Beast of Monsieur Racine* in 1974, *Moon Man* in 1981, and *The Hat* in 1982. Weston Woods also produced a film about Ungerer, *Tomi Ungerer: Storyteller*, directed by Gene Deitch, in 1981. *The Beast of Monsieur Racine* was released on video and audio cassette by Weston Woods; *Crictor* was released as an audio cassette; *The Three Robbers, Moon Man*, and *The Hat* were released on video in both English and Spanish. *The Three Robbers* also appears as part of *What's Under My Bed? And Other Creepy Stories*, a video released by Children's Circle in 1990. In 1993, Weston Woods released *The Tomi Ungerer Library*, a video collection including *The Three Robbers, Moon Man, The Beast of Monsieur Racine*, and the documentary *Getting to Know Tomi Ungerer*.

Sidelights

An internationally recognized illustrator and author who creates books for children and adults in English, French, and German, Ungerer is regarded as an innovative artist and writer as well as one of the most controversial social satirists in contemporary literature. A prolific author and illustrator as well as a painter, cartoonist, sculptor, poster artist, and publisher, he uses his works to present sharp, unsentimental views of humanity, from its most violent aspects to its most gentle. Ungerer is a black humorist, a self-designed "agent provocateur," as he calls himself, whose darkly satiric words and pictures use personal symbols and biting wit to provide, according to Michael Scott Joseph of *Bookbird,* "a coherent vision, a penetrating and honest glimpse of human society." His works for adults, which include books on politics, relationships, and death as well as collections of cartoons and erotica, often reflect the author's more graphic and sardonic side. In his works for children, characteristically picture books that feature child and animal characters, Ungerer is equally open about the vagaries of the human condition but tempers many of his books with a playful humor and sense of fun as well as a respect for both the innocence and self-sufficiency of children.

Like the rest of the author's oeuvre, Ungerer's books for children are considered unusual works that reflect a particularly European sensibility. In these books, he takes characters of questionable nature—a vulture, a boa constrictor, a giant, a group of robbers—and shows their inherent goodness while skewing the conventions of the folk and fairy tale. The works also contain a strong moral core and address themes such as the triumph of good over evil, the difficulties of being an outsider, and the importance of tolerance. As an artist, Ungerer is celebrated as, in the words of Joe Flaherty of the *New York Times Book Review,* "one of the most brilliant illustrators at work today." Working in strong line and bright colors, Ungerer is acknowledged for creating bold, sophisticated pictures filled with detail, movement, and humor. As a literary stylist, the author favors spare prose filled with large, vocabulary-stretching words and punlike names that underscore the wit of his pictures. Ungerer's books for both children and adults have occasionally been described as subversive, tasteless, and overly grotesque. However, most reviewers laud the author as a true original, a gifted writer and artist whose irreverence masks his underlying concern for humanity. Writing in *Children's Books and Their Creators,* Mary Brigid Barrett commented, "His heroes are boa constrictors, bats, vultures, robbers, moon men, and octupi. His supporting cast is Dickensian. His style is both tender and satiric. His illustrations are both charming and frightening. He is not sweet. He is never pretty. He is, at the very least, Jean de Brunhoff and Eugene Ionesco, together, in one body . . . . He can draw blood with an incisive stroke of the pen, but he also displays a keen understanding of, and affection for, the human condition." Writing in the *Spectator,* Kevin Crossley-Holland noted that Ungerer "has unquestionably established himself amongst the small company capable of producing text and illustration worthy of one another," while

Joan McGrath of *Twentieth Century Children's Writers* concluded, "Ungerer's is an unprejudiced eye, able to discover admirable qualities in unlikely places, and, better still, he is able to make his readers do the same."

Born in Strasbourg, France, Ungerer lost his father, a manufacturer of astronomical clocks, at the age of three; he told Selma G. Lanes of *New York Times Magazine,* "Every child who loses a father very young will be both insecure and angry." Ungerer grew up in a home that included his mother, brother, and two much older sisters. In an interview with Lanes in the *Atlantic Monthly,* Ungerer noted, "My sisters taught me to draw, my brother taught me to think, and my mother taught me to use my imagination." As a child, Ungerer was a voracious reader, enjoying books such as Wilhelm Busch's *Max und Moritz* and Heinrich Hoffman's *Der Struwwelpeter* that were later to influence his own works. He also discovered music and painting; his early artistic influences included the German painters Mathias Grunewald, Albrecht Durer, and Martin Schongauer as well as the Alsatian illustrators Hansi and Schnugg. The Depression forced Ungerer's mother to move the family into his grandmother's house in Colmar, a city adjacent to Strasbourg. He told Lanes in *New York Times Magazine,* "My worst nightmares, still, are about being stranded somewhere without any money. To me, poverty is synonymous with powerlessness."

With the advent of World War II, Ungerer's life took another profound turn. When the Germans occupied

Crictor, a friendly boa constrictor, is the pet of Madame Bodot and a favorite of the neighborhood. (From Crictor, *written and illustrated by Thomas Ungerer.)*

Alsace, the French province where his family lived, Ungerer was forced to receive a German education from the ages of eight to thirteen. His home in Colmar was occupied by Nazi troops and the factory across the street was turned into a camp for prisoners of war. Everything French-related was banned: for example, those caught wearing berets were jailed. However, Ungerer's mother charmed the Nazis into letting her family speak French at home. In school, Ungerer was taught Nazi ideals, but he learned to lead a double life. He told Michael Patrick Hearn of the *Riverbank Review,* "[A]ll the time there was the clash between the anti-Nazi drawings at home and the schoolwork." He told Lanes in *New York Times Magazine,* "My whole childhood was a schooling in relativity, in figuring out for myself who were the good guys and who were the bad. As schoolchildren we were given pushcarts and told to bring from home any books written in French so that they could be burned. What a fox I became, and, of course, to be a good fox you must look like a lamb." During the last three months of the war, Ungerer and his family lived in their basement after their house was bombed. He told Lanes, "One thing I learned then. There is nothing in this life so stupid, so empty and devoid of meaning, as the dead body of a human being.... A human carcass is the most desolate thing in the world." Summarizing his wartime experience, Ungerer concluded, "There was plenty to see and remember, and my taste for the macabre certainly finds its roots there."

In 1998, Ungerer wrote a memoir of his early years, *Tomi: A Childhood under the Nazis.* Originally published in French and German, this work, directed at children and young adults, is described by a critic in *Kirkus Reviews* as a "lively, sardonic account of the multiple occupations of his native Alsace...." The book, which is based on Ungerer's boyhood journal and illustrated with cartoons, photographs, postcards, advertisements, stamps, posters, childhood drawings, school assignments, and propagandist literature, reflects both the absurdity and tragedy of the time. While addressing such aspects as anti-Semitism and prison camps as well as the general horror of his experience, the author, according to *Kirkus Reviews,* "serves up more tributes here than indictments—and by looking for the humor, or at least the irony, in every situation, he effectively demonstrates the triumph of spirit over circumstance." In an interview with Michael Patrick Hearn, Ungerer noted, "For this book I had the greatest compliment in my life. A mother told me that her little boy slept with it under his pillow ... because of my childhood drawings, you see. In the text there might be some jokes, some plays on words that escape a child, but basically it is clear. And there is no exaggeration." He concluded, "That's exactly the way it was—everybody, everything. I wouldn't do it otherwise."

After the end of World War II and the return of the French to Alsace, Ungerer became disillusioned by his teachers, who would, he told Lanes, "laugh at our German accents and punish us for all the French grammar we'd forgotten. They treated us as if we were second-class citizens—even collaborators." Ungerer

Kitten Piper Paw is disruptive at school and disobedient at home in protest against his mother's doting attention. (From No Kiss for Mother, *written and illustrated by Ungerer.)*

dropped out of school and began traveling across Europe, mainly on foot. In 1953, he joined the French Camel Corps in Algeria, but was discharged after coming down with a bad case of pleurisy. When he returned to Strasbourg, Ungerer studied for a year at the Ecole des Arts Decoratifs. However, as he stated in the film *Tomi Ungerer, Storyteller,* "I feel that the greatest part of my education came from my travels through Europe, walking and hitchhiking, earning my way by odd jobs, and, of course, painting, drawing, and working in the graphic arts." Inspired by the writings of F. Scott Fitzgerald, William Faulkner, and John Steinbeck and harboring the desire to meet *New Yorker* cartoonist Saul Steinberg, Ungerer emigrated to New York City in 1956 with just sixty dollars and his portfolio. He worked in advertising, as a magazine and book illustrator, and as a designer for television commercials, rapidly earning a reputation as one of the top graphic artists in America. During the 1960s, he produced several posters in support of American civil rights and against the war in Vietnam; the latter were acclaimed internationally, garnering Ungerer comparisons with such artists as William Hogarth and Honore Daumier.

While working in the graphic arts, Ungerer began writing and illustrating his own books. His first work,

The Mellops Go Flying, is a story for children that introduces a family of French pigs. In the five-volume series, Ungerer describes the porcine adventurers as they dive for treasure, strike oil, enjoy Christmas, and explore an underground cavern. In a review of the fourth volume, *The Mellops Go Spelunking,* George A. Woods of the *New York Times Book Review* queried, "What child wouldn't want to be a member of Tomi Ungerer's resourceful Mellops family?... No one can resist turning the pages to see if the Mellops come out on top." *Crictor,* the story of a friendly boa constrictor, is often considered among the most successful of Ungerer's

early books for children. Writing in the *Lion and the Unicorn,* R. A. Siegel commented, "The best of these earlier books is *Crictor,* which, like the Mellops series, has affinities with Babar." In her *American Picturebooks from Noah's Ark to the Beast Within,* Barbara Bader stated, "Ungerer is a comic artist of delicate ease and Crictor is—snake and book—an exquisite creation." In 1963, Ungerer published another of his most well-received books for children, *The Three Robbers.* Written in a style reminiscent of classic fairy tales, the narrative depicts a trio of plundering bandits whose lives are changed when they abduct a little orphan girl, Tiffany.

As a dog born to cat parents, Flix finds it hard to fit in, but he eventually earns the respect of the bigoted residents of Cattown. (From Flix, *written and illustrated by Ungerer.)*

Having discovered that when his music was played on tape the notes poured out of loudspeakers, he went into mass production.

Musician Tortoni Tremolo is cursed by a fortune teller, but finds a way to build a business on his misfortune. (From Tortoni Tremolo: The Cursed Musician, *written and illustrated by Ungerer.)*

The innocence, goodness, and pluck of the little girl reform the robbers, who use their stolen treasure to support an entire village of children. A reviewer in the *Junior Bookshelf* concluded that the book, which is the first of Ungerer's works to be illustrated with bold paintings instead of line and watercolor drawings, is a "beautifully comical nonsense story told by a master of simplicity."

In 1966, Ungerer produced one of his signature books, *Moon Man,* which describes what happens when Jean, the man in the moon, comes to earth to make friends. Greeted by a militaristic society, he is arrested and jailed. Jean escapes by reducing to his third-quarter size and slipping through the bars of his cell. Rocketed back to the moon by a scientist, Jean learns to accept his distance from the world of humans. Michael Scott Joseph of *Bookbird* commented that Ungerer's "central account of the 'blue' moon exhibits romanticism and a sense of adolescent emotional vulnerability not antici-pated in his previous works," while a reviewer in *Kirkus Reviews* concluded, "This has some of the sting of *Dr. Strangelove*—but tenderized, the contemporary charisma of *Where the Wild Things Are;* it's great." Soon after *Moon Man,* Ungerer wrote and illustrated another of his most popular works, *Zeralda's Ogre.* In this book, an ogre dines on little children stolen from a nearby village until he is converted by the culinary gifts of little Zeralda. Feeling sorry for the hungry giant, Zeralda feeds him so well that he hires her to run the kitchen of

his castle. At the end of the story, Zeralda—now grown—marries the ogre and raises a family. However, the final illustration reveals some potential trouble: one of their children holds a knife and fork while gazing intently at a newborn sibling. R. A. Siegel of the *Lion and the Unicorn* called *Zeralda's Ogre* "the first of Tomi Ungerer's own works for children to fully employ the grotesque tradition." Writing in *Children's Book Review,* John A. Cunliffe predicted, "Most children, from about six to eight, will take the gruesome humor in their stride, and find this book hilarious, but it is not for the over-sensitive." The critic concluded that *Zeralda's Ogre* is "an excellent picture-book, made with energy and wit, with a direct appeal to children."

In 1970, Ungerer and his third wife moved from New York City to Nova Scotia. The couple, who moved to Canada to protest the involvement of the United States in Vietnam, ran a farm for five years before moving to Europe. Ungerer wrote and illustrated *Here Today—Gone Tomorrow,* a memoir of his experience for adults that was published in the United States and Canada as *Far Out Isn't Far Enough.* A year after moving to Nova Scotia, Ungerer published *The Beast of Monsieur Racine,* a story for children that is considered among his best. In this work, the lonely bachelor Monsieur Racine, a retired French tax collector, finds his prize pears gone. He catches the culprit, a floppy beast with socks for ears, and takes it to an exhibit in Paris. While at the exhibit, scientists discover that the beast is in fact two mischievous children. Despite their hoax, Racine decides to share his pears with them. A critic in *Kirkus Reviews* described *The Beast of Monsieur Racine* as "funny and bright and immediate on lots of levels, a sort of rare tour de farce for the whole family," while a reviewer in the *Junior Bookshelf* declared, "If [Ezra Jack] Keats is the sanest of contemporary American artists, Tomi Ungerer is the craziest.... Some parents may be distressed by the sickness, but probably their children will be moved only to delighted laughter." R. A. Siegel of the *Lion and the Unicorn* stated that *The Beast of Monsieur Racine* "is arguably the best of Tomi Ungerer's picture books to date, a delicious blend of droll fantasy and the comic grotesque."

In 1973, Ungerer created *No Kiss for Mother,* a picture book that is perhaps his most controversial book for children. In this work, kitten Piper Paw, feeling that his masculinity is being compromised by the constant kisses of his doting mother, tells her that he no longer wants to be kissed. Piper sasses his mother, rumples his carefully ironed clothes, and disrupts school with a peashooter and stink bombs. During one of his tantrums, Mrs. Velvet Paw smacks Piper across the face. When Piper realizes that his rebuff of her affections has hurt his mother's feelings, he buys her a bouquet of roses. At the end of the story, Piper apologizes to his mother but also asks that she honor his request not to kiss him. Writing in *New York Times Book Review,* Judith Viorst claimed, "Certainly no naughtier kid (in this case a sour-pussed kitten ...) has appeared between the covers of a picture book." Viorst concluded, "Piper's disgraceful, outrageous behavior will make toes curl with horrified delight and his ooey-gooey, overprotective, over-indulgent ma is bound to make young readers feel smugly superior.... What kid could resist?" Some reviewers found the book distasteful: for example, Zena Sutherland of *Bulletin of the Center for Children's Books* noted that *No Kiss for Mother* has "no humor to relieve the acid depictions of the female characters and a climax that seems to indicate that he who gets slapped sees reason," while Valerie Alderson of *Children's Book Review* stated that there is "an elusive nastiness behind the story." However, most observers found the book— described by Ungerer in his *Atlantic Monthly* interview as his most autobiographical work as well as "a kind of *Portnoy's Complaint* of children's books"—a humorous yet pointed look at mother-son relationships. Lanes called Piper "the orneriest, most self-centered and willful hero to hit kids' picture books since the mid-nineteenth-century heyday of *Struwwelpeter* ... Part of Ungerer's charm in this forty-page tantrum is his instinctive grasp of the anger of impotence that grips all small children during large chunks of their early lives. It is a rage directed at the limitations of childhood itself." Lanes concluded that *No Kiss for Mother* "strikes, with therapeutic clout, at the very heart of family relationships."

From the mid-1970s to the late 1990s, Ungerer was absent from the field of children's literature. Remarried, he had three children, relocated to County Cork, Ireland, alternately living there and in Strasbourg, joined the Roman Catholic Church, and published a diverse range of works for adults. In 1998, Ungerer reappeared on the children's book scene with *Flix,* the story of a pug dog born to a cat couple. The dog is raised lovingly, becomes a popular student in Dogtown, and, after rescuing a cat from drowning, is respected in Cattown. Later, Flix marries a French poodle and goes into politics, forming the party CDU (Cats and Dogs United) before being elected Lord Mayor of both Cattown and Dogtown. As the story ends, Flix's wife gives birth to a kitten. Writing in *Horn Book,* Selma G. Lanes noted, "Flix might be considered a sort of spiritual offspring of Thomas Mann's *Buddenbrooks.*" Jane Yolen in the *New York Times Book Review* commented, "It is clear that Ungerer is going for a Picture Book with Meaning. Which means that readers of whatever age need to look at it with as clear and unsentimental an eye as Ungerer himself has had in the past." Calling *Flix* "a delightfully witty and lighthearted look at race relations," a reviewer in *Publishers Weekly* concluded, "Ungerer's return to the field will be welcomed by all who discover this charming addition to his oeuvre, but will be especially appreciated by children growing up in more than one cultural tradition."

In addition to *Flix* and *Tomi: A Childhood under the Nazis,* Ungerer published another picture book, *Tortoni Tremolo the Cursed Musician,* in 1998. In this work, Ungerer features a talented musician who offends his neighbor, fortune teller Madame Abrah Kadabrah, with his practicing. Madame puts a triple curse on Tortoni so that all of his notes turn into olive-like nuggets that make a mess when they hit the floor. Tortoni discovers that the notes are good to eat and that different kinds of music produce different tastes. He becomes an entrepreneur and opens a note factory, but when he appears on television, the notes jam up and explode, emitting a foul odor. At the end of the story, Tortoni sells the factory and goes back to music, opening a symphony hall. Calling *Tortoni Tremolo the Cursed Musician* "a sly poke at television, among other things," GraceAnne A. DeCandido of *Booklist* concluded, "The illustrations are properly weird, with acid colors and exaggerated gestures. The last line notes that curses can take their own course: indeed, as Tortoni conducts his symphony, alert children will note that the horns have some thick orange and green stuff where the notes should be coming out."

Evaluating his artistic goals in the film *Tomi Ungerer, Storyteller,* Ungerer said, "I want to amuse myself and then in the same process amuse ... children. I use a lot of satire because I find satire more digestible and I think it has less hypocrisy." The author concluded, "I would say that my books have been labeled subversive and I would say that, if they are subversive, it's because I am subversive and I do take quite some pleasure in being subversive. It's a kind of sport like any other sport, and I think it's a realistic sport and I think, too, it eliminates a great deal of hypocrisy in life and I think that children are subversive. In every one of my books I can find myself. Every book is a mirror of several aspects of either my life or personality. This makes them very selfish books because I do these books for myself, not for children. They happen to be children's books and have been labeled children's books but they are my books for my own pleasure and, I would say, for the child in me." Interviewed by Selma G. Lanes in *Horn Book,* Ungerer noted that he considers himself "a documentalist, a chronicler of the absurd. Our world, our children, our aspirations are all absurd. If my books teach children anything, it's to make fun of adults, especially those who are taking themselves too seriously!"

Works Cited

Alderson, Valerie, review of *No Kiss for Mother, Children's Book Review,* spring, 1975, p. 36.

Bader, Barbara, *American Picturebooks from Noah's Ark to the Beast Within,* Macmillan, 1976, pp. 544-52.

Barrett, Mary Brigid, essay on Ungerer in *Children's Books and Their Creators,* edited by Anita Silvey, Houghton Mifflin, 1995, pp. 658-69.

Review of *The Beast of Monsieur Racine, Kirkus Reviews,* August 1, 1971, p. 806.

Crossley-Holland, Kevin, review of *The Hat, Spectator,* November 13, 1971.

Cunliffe, John A., review of *Zeralda's Ogre, Children's Book Review,* February, 1971, p. 16.

DeCandido, GraceAnne, review of *Tortoni Tremolo the Cursed Musician, Booklist,* January 1, 1999, p. 892.

Flaherty, Joe, review of *I Am Papa Snap and These Are My Favorite No Such Stories, New York Times Book Review,* February 20, 1972, p. 8.

Review of *Flix, Publishers Weekly,* June 1, 1998, p. 62.

Hearn, Michael Patrick, "Wartime Childhoods: Tomi Ungerer," *Riverbank Review,* Fall, 1998, pp. 18, 20, 22.

Joseph, Michael Scott, "The Illustrator as 'Agent Provocateur,'" *Bookbird,* fall, 1996, pp. 11-15.

Lanes, Selma G., "Peck's Bad Boy of Art," *New York Times Magazine,* May 24, 1981.

Lanes, "Tomi Ungerer's Reluctant Heroes," *Atlantic Monthly,* January, 1974, pp. 87-90.

Lanes, "Tomi Ungerer—The *Enfant Terrible* Grows Up—Or Is It Down?," *Horn Book,* November-December, 1998, pp. 682-86.

McGrath, Joan, essay on Ungerer in *Twentieth Century Children's Writers,* 4th edition, edited by Laura Standley Berger, St. James Press, 1995, pp. 974-76.

Review of *Moon Man, Kirkus Reviews,* January 15, 1967, p. 55.

Siegel, R. A., "The Little Boy Who Drops His Pants in a Crowd: Tomi Ungerer's Art of the Comic Grotesque," *Lion and the Unicorn,* volume 1, number 2, pp. 26-32.

Sutherland, Zena, review of *No Kiss for Mother, Bulletin of the Center for Children's Books,* September, 1973, p. 19.

Review of *The Three Robbers, Junior Bookshelf,* July, 1962, p. 120.

Review of *Tomi: A Childhood under the Nazis, Kirkus Reviews,* November 15, 1998, p. 1673.

Ungerer, Tomi, in the film *Tomi Ungerer: Storyteller,* directed by Gene Deitch, Weston Woods, 1981.

Viorst, Judith, review of *No Kiss for Mother, New York Times Book Review,* June 24, 1973, p. 8.

Woods, George A., review of *The Mellops Go Spelunking, New York Times Book Review,* May 12, 1963, p. 4.

Yolen, Jane, "Look What the Cats Brought Home," *New York Times Book Review,* August 16, 1998, p. 15.

For More Information See

BOOKS

Children's Literature Review, Volume 3, Gale, 1978, pp. 195-205.

Tomi Ungerer: Ausstellung, Exposition, Exhibition (text in English, French, and German), Argos, 1981.

Twentieth-Century Children's Writers, Fourth edition, St. James Press, 1995, pp. 974-76.

PERIODICALS

School Library Journal, September, 1998, pp. 184-85; March, 1999, p. 228.

—*Sketch by Gerard J. Senick*

*   *   *

UNGERER, Tomi
See UNGERER, (Jean) Thomas

V–W

VASILEVA, Tatiana
See WASSILJEWA, Tatjana

      *   *   *

VASILIEVA, Tatiana
See WASSILJEWA, Tatjana

      *   *   *

WASSILJEWA, Tatjana 1928-
(Also transliterated as Tatiana Vasilieva; Tatiana Vasileva)

Personal

Born January 12, 1928, in Leningrad, U.S.S.R. (now St. Petersburg, Russia); daughter of Peter and Evfalia (Berkul) Vasiliev; divorced; children: Vladimir Tyminsky. *Education:* Attended Pedagogic Institute, 1951-55. *Religion:* "I believe in conscience."

Addresses

Home—Warshawskaya St. 108, Apt. 281, St. Petersburg 196066, Russia. *Agent*—Charlotte Larat, Beltz & Gelberg, Verlagsgruppe Beltz, Postfach 10 01 54, 69441 Weinheim, Germany.

Career

High school teacher in the polar region of what is now Russia, 1955-60; guide and interpreter in Leningrad, U.S.S.R. (now St. Petersburg, Russia), 1961-84.

Writings

Hostage to War, published in Russian, 1990, English translation, Scholastic Inc. (New York City), 1997.

Work in Progress

Books for adults, including *Russian Teacher* and *Russia Today.*

Sidelights

Tatjana Wassiljewa told *SATA:* "I was born in Leningrad in 1928. My father, a former nobleman, died of hunger during World War II. My teenage years were hard. I was twelve when the Nazis occupied the place where we

Tatjana Wassiljewa

lived. There was hunger; people ate cats and dogs. Then I was taken to Germany to work at a factory in Magdeburg. I was released from the work camp by American troops, whom I write about with gratitude. After returning to my native land I graduated from high school and university. Then I moved to the far north to work as a teacher. In 1961 I returned to Leningrad, where I worked as a teacher, guide, and interpreter.

"I retired in 1985 and wrote my first book. The beginning of *perestroika* was a hard time. I began to write in order to help the youngsters bear the difficulties, just as the stories of Jack London had helped me in my teenage years. Then I also had an opportunity to thank all the people who had helped me to survive—Russians, the French, Germans, and Americans. My book was published in St. Petersburg, then it was translated and published in Germany, Denmark, the Netherlands, Japan, Taiwan, England, and the United States.

"In 1990 I visited the United States, where I enjoyed the spirit of freedom. Later, in St. Petersburg, I published an article titled 'View of the Rocky Mountains' in the local newspaper. Now I am writing two manuscripts, the notes of a young teacher and a work about present-day Russia. My stories are autobiographical. They oppose war and fascism and promote morality and friendship among people. I am happy to know that my book *Hostage to War* was acknowledged in the United States for its social importance."

Wassiljewa's memoir recounts the true story of Soviet citizens taken captive by Nazi invaders and used to replace Germany's industrial labor force during World War II. "The picture of German society during wartime is chilling: German citizens accepted slave labor as their due, and most ignored the hunger that kept Wassiljewa and her fellow prisoners weak and sick," noted a *Kirkus Reviews* commentator, who concluded *Hostage to War* a "harrowing, uplifting story." Wassiljewa describes vividly the terrible plight she and other Soviet prisoners endured during the war years, adding that, for many, returning home was not a joyful event either, as Soviets under Stalin's regime often viewed those taken prisoner to other nations as traitors. "This story has the distance and perspective of a memoir, but is related with an immediate candor," maintained Lauren Adams of *Horn Book*. Adams added: "Tatjana's experience raises uneasy questions about our expectations of humanity, both in and out of war." Betsy Hearne, writing in the *Bulletin of the Center for Children's Books*, noted: "The suffering of Russians during World War II is scarcely documented in children's literature, and this individualistic memoir takes a long step toward closing the gap."

Works Cited

Adams, Lauren, review of *Hostage to War*, *Horn Book*, May-June, 1997, p. 330.

Hearne, Betsy, review of *Hostage to War*, *Bulletin of the Center for Children's Books*, April, 1997, p. 299.

Review of *Hostage to War*, *Kirkus Reviews*, January 15, 1997, p. 146.

WATSON, James 1936-

Personal

Born November 8, 1936, in Darwen, Lancashire, England; son of James (a wages clerk) and Miriam (a clerk; maiden name, Arnold) Watson; married Catherine Rose Downey (a nurse), July 6, 1963; children: Rosalind, Miranda, Francesca. *Education:* University of Nottingham, B.A. (honors), 1958; University of Sussex, Brighton, M.Ed., 1979. *Hobbies and other interests:* The arts, archaeology, exploring old castles and churches, soccer, cricket, travel.

Addresses

Home—9 Farmcombe Close, Tunbridge Wells, Kent TN2 5DG, England. *Office*—West Kent College, Tunbridge Wells, Kent, England.

Career

British Council, Milan, Italy, teacher of English, 1960-61; *North East Evening Gazette*, Middlesbrough, Yorkshire, England, journalist and art critic, 1961-63; Dunlop Co., London, education officer and editor of educational literature, 1963-65; West Kent College, Tunbridge Wells, Kent, England, lecturer in communication and media studies, 1965—. *Military service:* British Army,

James Watson

Royal Army Educational Corps, National Service Officer, 1958-60. *Member:* Amnesty International, Association for Liberal Education, Tunbridge Wells and West Kent College Film Society.

Awards, Honors

Other Award, Children's Rights Workshop, 1983, for *Talking in Whispers;* Walter Hines Page scholarship, 1987; Buxtehude Bulle Prize (Germany), 1987, and Carnegie Medal commendation, both for *Talking in Whispers.*

Writings

FOR CHILDREN

Sign of the Swallow, Thomas Nelson, 1967.
The Bull Leapers, Gollancz, 1970, Coward, McCann, 1970.
Legion of the White Tiger, Gollancz, 1973.
The Freedom Tree, Gollancz, 1976.
Talking in Whispers, Gollancz, 1983, Knopf, 1983.
Where Nobody Sees, Gollancz, 1987.
Make Your Move (short stories), Gollancz, 1988.
No Surrender (also see below), Gollancz, 1991.
The Noisy Ducks of Buxtehude, Verlag an der Erte (Buxtehude, Germany), 1992.
Ticket to Prague, Gollancz, 1994.
Justice of the Dagger, Puffin (London), 1998.

OTHER

Liberal Studies in Further Education, National Foundation for Educational Research, 1973.
The Loneliness of a Long-Distance Innovation: General Studies in a College of Further Education, Association for Liberal Education, 1980.
(With Anne Hill) *A Dictionary of Communication and Media Studies,* Edward Arnold, 1984, 2nd edition, 1989, 3rd edition, 1993.
What Is Communication Studies?, Edward Arnold, 1985.
Media Communication: An Introduction to Theory and Process, St. Martin's Press, 1998.

Author of the radio plays *Gilbert Makepeace Lives!,* British Broadcasting Corp., 1972; *Venus Rising from the Sea,* 1977; *A Slight Insurrection,* 1980; *What a Little Moonlight Can Do,* 1982; and *No Surrender* (adapted by the author from his novel of the same name), 1993.

Contributor to periodicals, including the London *Times, Guardian, Studio,* and *Arts Review.*

Sidelights

British novelist James Watson has been characterized by several reviewers as a writer whose primary interest is politics, but "one who, in his most important work, is able to display this political feeling in a powerful and telling manner," according to *Twentieth-Century Children's Writers* essayist Keith Barker. With the novels *The Freedom Tree, No Surrender, Talking in Whispers,* and *Justice of the Dagger* to his credit, Watson has combined his lifelong love of history with a developing political consciousness that condemns the violent juntas

that have erupted throughout South America, Eastern Europe, and Asia, while "still [leaving] room for hope." In *School Librarian,* contributor Dennis Hamley praised Watson's contribution to children's literature, calling him "an author who cannot have too much influence" on readers poised to "take on the vigilance that maintenance of freedoms in our own society more and more needs."

Born in 1936, Watson was raised in Lancashire, England. "As a child, in addition to wandering the Lancashire moors, playing football in the street, and gathering wood for Guy Fawkes' Night, I was chiefly interested in puppets and magazines," Watson once told *SATA.* "I made my own hand puppets and eventually my own string puppets and marionette theatre. I started magazines of one sort or another and told people I wanted to be a jet pilot or a journalist." Instead, Watson ended up "a word-pilot, taking flights of fancy on the printed page. There have been some long and perilous journeys, both in time and space," he commented on his writing career.

Watson never considered writing for children until one day, during his military service, he read how mystery novelist Georges Simenon could write a novel in fourteen days. "I was stationed in Anglesey, a bare, sea-swept isle swilled by the wild Irish Sea, and there was little call on my services as an education officer. I was looking back, rather forlornly, on three years at university reading history. I'd obtained a degree but ceased to enjoy history. Three years of intensive academic study had rubbed off every dewdrop of curiosity or romance: it seemed such a waste." So, with Simenon's example before him, he sat down and in two weeks had completed an entire first draft of an historical novel for children—the book would later be published as *Sign of the Swallow.* "I relished the experience and the challenge," Watson confided, "yet it was a year at least before I really got the story right. Since then, though I may have become more technically adept at writing for the younger reader, the books have taken me longer and longer to research and complete."

"If history has a continuing relevance, then sooner or later the author chooses a period which has a particular [personal] relevance," Watson once commented to *SATA.* He noted that his novel *The Freedom Tree,* which takes place during the 1930s against the backdrop of the Spanish Civil War, "amounts to a declaration of faith, or taking sides" on the part of its author. The fictitious villains of Watson's earlier books are in this work embodied by the political evil perpetrated by Spain's fascist government. The novel finds sixteen-year-old English orphan Will Viljoen joining the Republican forces against the Fascists in the 1936 war, partly to avenge the recent death of his father at the hands of the fascist army. While the Republican volunteers fight bravely, they are no match for their well-trained opposition, and Will, serving with the International Brigade as a stretcher-bearer, witnesses his army's ultimate destruction during the bombardment of the Spanish town of Guernica. Calling the novel "hard-hitting" and "notably honest," *Growing Point* critic

Margery Fisher commended the book's overall message as "one of optimism simply because of the generous, whole-hearted way the various characters offer themselves in the never-ending fight for freedom." Again praising Watson's novel during its 1986 reissue in commemoration of the war's fiftieth anniversary, Fisher added that in *The Freedom Tree,* "The warnings of the Spanish Civil War, ignored so widely at the time, are emphasised," thereby supplying "a link between fictional accounts of the two world wars."

Political violence is also the focus of *Talking in Whispers.* In this work, Andres Larreta, the sixteen-year-old son of a folksinger, Juan, escapes capture after his father and other members of his musical troupe are arrested by a military junta in his native Chile. Vowing never to forget his father, rather than have him join the ranks of "the disappeared," Andres aligns himself with others speaking out against the junta, despite his own fear of capture. *Horn Book* reviewer Nancy C. Hammond praised Watson's depiction of Andres's "moral conflict between self-preservation and political protest and his more subtle questioning of whether inaction equals collaboration." *School Library Journal* contributor Hazel Rochman maintained that *Talking in Whispers* "has immediacy combined with the appeal of World War II stories about totalitarian regimes, in which death squads murder innocent victims and young people must survive without adults." Remarking on the novel's reference to the ongoing political upheaval in Latin America, *Booklist* reviewer Sally Estes maintained that *Talking in Whispers* "stands up as an exciting, moving, and timely political thriller."

Of all the books he has written, one of Watson's favorites is *The Bull Leapers.* "A life-long fascination for things Greek had set me writing an imaginary historical reconstruction of the tale of Theseus and the Minotaur," he recalled of the inspiration for his second novel. "I'd been to Crete with my wife and returned enchanted by the ruins of the palace of Knossos. An aunt then revealed to me that my grandfather had been similarly interested in Greek archeology and that he had visited Knossos in 1900 when the discoverer of the palace, Arthur Evans, was excavating there. My Aunt Muriel gave me some fragments of Minoan pottery which my grandfather had brought back with him—and a book on Crete." Inside the cover of that book Watson discovered a penciled note describing how his grandfather had been present at the unearthing of the famous painting "The Boy with the Drinking Cup." Archeologist Evans had also given Watson's grandfather a tour of the excavation site, and then invited him to tea. "The hidden dimensions of history were never more alive in me as I read those neatly written notes. From that point on, writing fiction set in history restored for me the infinite variety and richness of the past; and attempting to give history the 'livingness' of fiction helped to highlight the ongoing validity of man's experience, whether he existed in 500 B.C. or 2000 A.D."

Commenting on his more recent efforts, Watson told *Twentieth-Century Children's Writers:* "After beginning my writing career with books exploring my interest in history, I moved to themes that stirred interest but also a more involved concern .... *Where Nobody Sees* returns me to home ground, telling the story of two teenagers who discover the illegal dumping of nuclear waste and the peril this places them in when they attempt to make the matter public. My first collection of stories, *Make Your Move,* ranges from a tale set in the Chaco War in Bolivia to the kind of problems faced by teenagers in modern Britain. *No Surrender* is set in the forgotten war in Angola, while in *Ticket to Prague* Amy Douglas meets a forgotten Czech poet in an English mental hospital. Their friendship transforms them both, he to a poet reborn and returning to the land of his birth, she discovering a new world in herself and one reborn in the enchanting and enchanted city of Prague."

Commentators responded favorably to *Make Your Move* and *Ticket to Prague,* works offering a thought-provoking exploration of the theme of social justice. Of the nine stories comprising *Make Your Move,* Marcus Crouch noted in *Junior Bookshelf* that "Watson ranges wide in subject and mood, but the common factor in all [the stories] is justice." Crouch added: "The world [Watson] writes of is a hard one, and he has no illusions about the existence of intolerance and viciousness on both sides of the social divide. He should find an audience among the young, especially those not usually given to reading, because he knows and respects them and speaks out in their defence with a tough eloquence." *School Library Journal* contributor Laura McCutcheon maintained that the stories in *Make Your Move* "explore the darker, less pleasant characteristics of modern-day, 'civilized' people; and yet with a great deal of cleverness and humor they somehow manage to celebrate the essential goodness and nobility of spirit that mark humankind."

Ticket to Prague was lauded as an outstanding achievement by Watson. The novel centers on the relationship that develops between Amy, who has been sent to perform community service in an English psychiatric hospital, and a Czech exile named Josef, a patient in the hospital who hasn't communicated with anyone for some two decades. *School Librarian* contributor Caroline Axon called the work "an intense story dealing with Amy's reactions to the situations surrounding her and the injustice and cruelty of the world." Marcus Crouch, writing in *Junior Bookshelf,* commented favorably on the characterizations of Amy and Josef, asserting that "there can be little but praise" for what he called a "splendid novel." Crouch concluded: "Immensely readable, *Ticket to Prague* is deeply thought-provoking, dealing as it does with real personal and political problems and wisely leaving most of the answers to the individual reader."

Works Cited

Axon, Caroline, review of *Ticket to Prague, School Librarian,* May, 1994, p. 74.

Barker, Keith, essay on Watson in *Twentieth-Century Children's Writers,* 4th edition, St. James Press, 1995, pp. 1003-04.

Crouch, Marcus, review of *Make Your Move, Junior Bookshelf*, April, 1989, p. 85.

Crouch, Marcus, review of *Ticket to Prague, Junior Bookshelf*, February, 1994, p. 40.

Estes, Sally, review of *Talking in Whispers, Booklist*, June 15, 1984, p. 1470.

Fisher, Margery, review of *The Freedom Tree, Growing Point*, July, 1976, p. 2905.

Fisher, Margery, review of *The Freedom Tree, Growing Point*, May, 1986, p. 4623.

Hamley, Dennis, review of *The Freedom Tree, School Librarian*, December, 1986, p. 371.

Hammond, Nancy C., review of *Talking in Whispers, Horn Book*, September-October, 1984, p. 601.

McCutcheon, Laura, review of *Make Your Move, School Library Journal*, March, 1991, p. 218.

Rochman, Hazel, review of *Talking in Whispers, School Library Journal*, April, 1984, p. 128.

Watson, James, comments in *Twentieth-Century Children's Writers*, 4th edition, St. James Press, 1995, p. 1003.

*   *   *

WESLEY, Valerie Wilson 1947-

Personal

Born November 22, 1947; married Richard Wesley (a screenwriter and playwright); children: two daughters. *Education:* Howard University, received undergraduate degree; Graduate School of Journalism, Columbia University, M.A.; Bank Street College of Education, M.A.

Addresses

E-mail—Valwilwes@aol.com. *Agent*—c/o Putnam Berkley Publishing Group, 200 Madison Ave., New York, NY 10016.

Career

Scholastic News, former associate editor; *Essence* Magazine, New York City, contributing editor, formerly executive editor.

Awards, Honors

Griot Award, New York chapter of National Association of Black Journalists; Best Books for Reluctant Young Adult Readers, American Library Association, 1994, for *Where Do I Go from Here?;* named author of the year, Go On, Girl Book Club, a national African-American reading society.

Writings

FOR YOUNG PEOPLE

(With Wade Hudson) *Afro-Bets Book of Black Heroes from A to Z: An Introduction to Important Black Achievers for Young Readers,* Just Us Books (East Orange, NJ), 1988.

Where Do I Go from Here? (young adult novel), Scholastic (New York City), 1993.

Freedom's Gifts: A Juneteenth Mystery, illustrated by Sharon Wilson, Simon & Schuster (New York City), 1997.

FOR ADULTS; "TAMARA HAYLE" MYSTERY NOVELS

When Death Comes Stealing, Putnam (New York City), 1994.

Devil's Gonna Get Him, Putnam, 1995.

Where Evil Sleeps, Putnam, 1996.

No Hiding Place, Putnam, 1997.

Easier to Kill, Putnam, 1998.

OTHER

Contributor of fiction to periodicals, including *Essence, New York Times, Ms., Family Circle, Creative Classroom,* and *TV Guide.*

Sidelights

Valerie Wilson Wesley is the author of the popular "Tamara Hayle" mystery novels featuring black private investigator Hayle, a single parent and ex-cop from the tough streets of Newark, New Jersey. Wesley has also written several well-received works for young people. A former executive editor for *Essence* Magazine, she published her first book, a collection of biographical sketches entitled *Afro-Bets Book of Black Heroes from A-Z: An Introduction to Important Black Achievers for Young Readers,* with coauthor Wade Hudson for Just Us Books. Wesley further explores the experiences and history of African Americans in two works of fiction for young readers, *Where Do I Go from Here?* and *Freedom's Gifts: A Juneteenth Mystery.*

Where Do I Go from Here? tells the story of Nia, a young black girl who receives a scholarship to a prestigious white boarding school and struggles to find acceptance there. When a racially based fight results in a two-week suspension for Nia, she returns home to Newark, contemplating the plight of her friends there and comparing the alternatives afforded her at school. *Voice of Youth Advocates* contributor Kim Carter, who commended the "easy readability" of the novel and its "smooth progression of events," asserted: "*Where Do I Go from Here?* ... succeeds in portraying the human similarities that cross racial and economic distinctions. While the main theme is the classic adolescent search for identity and direction, an important sub-theme is that of human interdependence." Tim Rausch, writing in *School Library Journal,* maintained: "This book is about being an outsider, the effects of everyday decisions on the future, and the importance of educational opportunities." Rausch added that the novel's themes are "positive but not preachy" and its characters "believable and interesting," noting that the authentic contemporary dialogue and touch of mystery in the book would appeal greatly to young-adult readers.

Wesley shares with primary graders an important and unique bit of history in *Freedom's Gifts: A Juneteenth Story.* In this work, set in 1943, the author explores a small Texas town's celebration of the Juneteenth holiday, which commemorates the day in 1865 when slaves

Nia, feeling totally lost at Endicott Academy, where most of the students are white and rich, sets out to find her own identity and self-worth in Valerie Wilson Wesley's novel.

in Texas were notified of their legal emancipation. Young African American cousins June and Lillie listen attentively as their great-great-aunt offers first-hand memories of her early days in slavery. Praising Wesley's "forthright treatment of a sensitive and important subject," a *Publishers Weekly* commentator called *Freedom's Gift* a "resonant" book that "offers a penetrating perspective on the degree of liberation the holiday commemorated in the pre-civil rights South." Judith Constantinides, writing in *School Library Journal,* also offered a favorable assessment of the work, declaring *Freedom's Gift* "a beautiful effort, of special interest to Texans, but sure to enrich any library collection because of its subject matter and its quality."

Works Cited

Carter, Kim, review of *Where Do I Go from Here?*, *Voice of Youth Advocates,* February, 1994, p. 375.

Constantinides, Judith, review of *Freedom's Gifts: A Juneteenth Story, School Library Journal,* June, 1997, pp. 102-03.
Review of *Freedom's Gifts: A Juneteenth Story, Publishers Weekly,* March 31, 1997, p. 75.
Rausch, Tim, review of *Where Do I Go from Here?*, *School Library Journal,* November, 1993, pp. 126-27.

For More Information See

PERIODICALS

American Visions, April-May, 1997, pp. 18-21.
Black Enterprise, August, 1982, pp. 39-44.
Booklist, December 15, 1993, p. 748; May 1, 1997, p. 1468.
Bulletin of the Center for Children's Books, June, 1997, p. 378.
Children's Book Review Service, February, 1994, p. 121; spring, 1997, p. 145.
Kirkus Reviews, December 1, 1993, p. 1531; August 1, 1997, p. 1164.
Los Angeles Times Book Review, August 14, 1994, p. 7.
New York Times Book Review, June 22, 1997, pp. 102-103.
Publishers Weekly, November 8, 1993, p. 79.
School Library Journal, December, 1988, p. 117.

*   *   *

WINTERS, Paul A. 1965-

Personal

Born April 3, 1965, in San Diego, CA; son of Robert E. and Alma C. (Chavannes) Winters; married Julie S. Bacchus, May 8, 1999. *Education:* University of California, Los Angeles, B.A., 1988; University of California, Davis, M.A., 1991.

Addresses

Home—1327 Clubhouse Dr., Aptos, CA 95003.

Career

University of California, Los Angeles, Oral History Program, editorial assistant, 1988-89; Getty Art History Information Program, Santa Monica, CA, assistant editor, 1989; University of California, Davis, teaching assistant, 1989-91; Greenhaven Press, Inc., San Diego, CA, editor, 1993-97; Enslow Publishers, Inc., Springfield, NJ, editor, 1997—.

Awards, Honors

New York Public Library Books for the Teen Age citation, 1995, for *Crime and Criminals: Opposing Viewpoints,* and 1997, for *America's Victims: Opposing Viewpoints.*

Writings

EDITOR

Islam: Opposing Viewpoints, Greenhaven Press, 1995.

At Issue: Policing the Police, Greenhaven Press, 1995.

Crime and Criminals: Opposing Viewpoints, Greenhaven Press, 1995.

Interventionism, Greenhaven Press, 1995.

(With Charles P. Cozic) *Gambling,* Greenhaven Press, 1995.

Hate Crimes, Greenhaven Press, 1996.

Urban Terrorism, Greenhaven Press, 1996.

Race Relations: Opposing Viewpoints, Greenhaven Press, 1996.

At Issue: The Media and Politics, Greenhaven Press, 1996.

Voting Behavior, Greenhaven Press, 1996.

America's Victims: Opposing Viewpoints, Greenhaven Press, 1996.

Death Penalty: Opposing Viewpoints, Greenhaven Press, 1997.

Welfare: Opposing Viewpoints, Greenhaven Press, 1997.

Paranormal Phenomena: Opposing Viewpoints, Greenhaven Press, 1997.

Death and Dying: Opposing Viewpoints, Greenhaven Press, 1997.

Teen Addiction, Greenhaven Press, 1997.

Computers and Society, Greenhaven Press, 1997.

Crime, Greenhaven Press, 1998.

Cloning, Greenhaven Press, 1998.

Child Sexual Abuse, Greenhaven Press, 1998.

The Collapse of the Soviet Union, Greenhaven, 1998.

Sidelights

Editor Paul A. Winters organizes and presents explorations of contemporary issues and events in his many series of nonfiction titles for Greenhaven Press. Among the best known of his early efforts is the "Opposing Viewpoints" series, which *Kliatt* contributor Shelley A. Glantz noted "has long been known by librarians, teachers, and students for its consistent quality and constantly expanding list of titles." One of the first books in the series, *Crime and Criminals,* is divided into chapters that contain essays addressing various questions from differing perspectives. Among the issues covered are the causes of crime, gun control, programs for young criminals, and whether or not genetics plays a factor in crime. "Having undertaken the daunting task of providing a comprehensive overview of opposing viewpoints to some basic questions about crime, this text has performed admirably," asserted Cynthia L. Blinn in *Voice of Youth Advocates.*

Other books in the "Opposing Viewpoints" series have also garnered favorable assessments from critics. *Islam* explores "the religion, culture, and politics of Islam and its significance for the West," according to *Booklist* reviewer Hazel Rochman, who maintained that "classroom units on contemporary world politics will find a lot to discuss here." *America's Victims* discusses topics ranging from the civil rights movement and the criminal justice system to talk shows and the notion of political correctness. *Booklist*'s Frances Bradburn described the compilation as "a dense but engaging resource" and a "truly fascinating volume that explores the rise of victimhood in America." *Paranormal Phenomena,* another "Opposing Viewpoints" title, examines the science of the paranormal. "The selection of opinions is balanced and the accompanying bibliographic material make this an excellent starting place for exploring these mysterious issues," asserted *School Library Journal* contributor Ann G. Brouse.

The concerns over current police culture in the United States is a highlight of one in another series of young adults works edited by Winters. The subject is addressed by several prominent criminal justice commentators in *At Issue: Policing the Police.* The history of police from their early beginnings as a group of civic minded citizens to what is now a highly organized modern system is presented in this study. Marilyn Makowski, writing in *School Library Journal,* maintained that "Winters does a good job of presenting various points of view in a readable, interesting context," and concluded that the volume makes a complex subject "thoroughly comprehensible and nonthreatening." Other subjects explored in Winters's "At Issue" series include *Voting Behavior, The Media and Politics, Cloning,* and the more recent *Child Sexual Abuse.*

Works Cited

Blinn, Cynthia L., review of *Crime and Criminals: Opposing Viewpoints, Voice of Youth Advocates,* April, 1995, p. 43.

Bradburn, Frances, review of *America's Victims, Booklist,* December 15, 1996, p. 715.

Brouse, Ann G., review of *Paranormal Phenomena, School Library Journal,* September, 1997, p. 238.

Glantz, Shelley A., review of *Crime and Criminals* and others, *Kliatt,* January, 1995, pp. 33-34.

Makowski, Marilyn, review of *At Issue: Policing the Police, School Library Journal,* September, 1995, p. 230.

Rochman, Hazel, review of *Islam, Booklist,* June 1, 1995, p. 1744.

For More Information See

PERIODICALS

School Library Journal, April, 1998, p. 157; May, 1998, p. 160; December, 1998, p. 144; January, 1999, p. 157.

Voice of Youth Advocates, August, 1996, p. 181; December, 1996, p. 292; February, 1997, p. 342; December, 1997, pp. 336-37.

*   *   *

WOODRUFF, Elvira 1951-

Personal

Born June 19, 1951, in Somerville, NJ; daughter of John (a truck driver) and Francis G. (a nurse; maiden name, Giasullo) Pirozzi; married David Woodruff (divorced); children: Noah, Jess. *Education:* Attended Adelphi University, 1970-71, and Boston University, 1971-72.

Addresses

Office—c/o Holiday House, 425 Madison Ave., New York, NY 10017.

Career

Writer. Worked variously as janitor, gardener, baker, window decorator, ice-cream truck driver, storyteller, and library aide; owned toy, clothing, and miscellany store in Clinton, NJ.

Writings

Awfully Short for the Fourth Grade, illustrated by Will Hillenbrand, Holiday House, 1989.

Tubtime, illustrated by Sucie Stevenson, Holiday House, 1990.

The Summer I Shrank My Grandmother, illustrated by Katherine Coville, Holiday House, 1990.

The Wing Shop, illustrated by Stephen Gammell, Holiday House, 1991.

Show and Tell, illustrated by Denise Brunkus, Holiday House, 1991.

Back in Action, illustrated by Will Hillenbrand, Holiday House, 1991.

Mrs. McClosky's Monkeys, illustrated by Jill Kastner, Scholastic, 1991.

George Washington's Socks, Scholastic, 1991.

The Disappearing Bike Shop, Holiday House, 1992.

Dear Napoleon, I Know You're Dead, But—, illustrated by Noah and Jess Woodruff, Holiday House, 1992.

The Secret Funeral of Slim Jim the Snake, Holiday House, 1993.

Ghosts Don't Get Goose Bumps, illustrated by Joel Iskowitz, Holiday House, 1993.

The Magnificent Mummy Maker, Scholastic, 1994.

Dear Levi: Letters from the Overland Trail, illustrated by Ruth Peck, Knopf, 1994.

A Dragon in My Backpack, illustrated by Denise Brunkus, Troll, 1996.

The Orphan of Ellis Island: A Time Travel Adventure, Scholastic, 1997.

Dear Austin: Letters from the Underground Railroad, illustrated by Nancy Carpenter, Knopf, 1998.

The Christmas Doll, Scholastic, 1998.

The Memory Coat, illustrated by Michael Dooling, Scholastic, 1998.

Can You Guess Where We're Going?, illustrations by Cynthia Fisher, Holiday House, 1998.

The Ghost of Lizard Light, Knopf, 1999.

Sidelights

Elvira Woodruff is the author of numerous novels and picture books for young readers, many of which deal with history and combine magic and fantasy in equal dollops. A *Publishers Weekly* reviewer noted of her *The Summer I Shrank My Grandmother,* "Woodruff seems to know all the tricks for holding a middle grade audience: blending elements of magic, fast-paced action and a dab of levity, she produces an irresistible tale." Her best works, such as *Awfully Short for the Fourth Grade,*

Tubtime, The Disappearing Bike Shop, Dear Napoleon, I Know You're Dead, But—, Dear Levi, and *The Orphan of Ellis Island,* use this formula to create stories suitable for read-alouds as well as for middle-grade novels.

"Becoming a writer has been one of the most pleasant surprises I've had in my life," Woodruff once told *SATA.* "I have always enjoyed reading and especially writing, though I never seriously considered it as a profession until I was well into my thirties."

Born in Somerville, New Jersey, Woodruff grew up on the East Coast. She wrote her first poem at age nine: "I can remember sitting at the dining room table with my pencil and paper and feeling as if I had just discovered something really wonderful," Woodruff once told *SATA.* "I had. It was the joy of creating. It was the same feeling I had when I completed my first piece of embroidery, planted my first garden, painted my first picture."

Woodruff attended both Adelphi University and Boston University, and then worked for fifteen years at all manner of odd jobs, from janitor to library aide. Married, she had two sons, and began reading children's books to them. It was at this time that she became interested in writing her own children's books. "It was like coming back to an old love," she told *SATA.* Her cousin, the author and illustrator Frank Asch, gave her a helping hand with both manuscript preparation and with finding a publisher. "He looked over my work, offered suggestions, and basically held my hand through the births of those first efforts." When it was finished, this first manuscript was shown to Asch's editor at Scholastic, who purchased it. Though it was her first book, *Mrs. McClosky's Monkeys,* a picture book, ultimately was published only after several other Woodruff titles had hit the shelves.

Meanwhile, Woodruff was still working part time at the library and "baking pies, sewing curtains, weeding my garden, and looking after my boys, who were in school by then. It was a nice life." However, the sale of another manuscript convinced her that perhaps there was a living to be made in children's books. She converted her sewing table to a desk and exchanged her sewing machine for a computer. Woodruff the children's author was born.

Woodruff's picture books include the popular *Tubtime, The Wing Shop, Mrs. McClosky's Monkeys,* and *Show and Tell.* Of the first of these, *Tubtime,* Ilene Cooper wrote in *Booklist* that "bath time has never been more fun." Three little sisters are taking a bath together after a mud fight. As she talks on the telephone downstairs, their mother keeps yelling up to the children to see if they are doing all right. Meanwhile, the girls have begun blowing bubbles with all the soap, and magically stuffed inside each bubble is an animal: a chicken, a frog, even an alligator. "The fantastic happenings in the bathroom ... escalate with impunity," Cooper added, concluding that the book is "bubbling over with good cheer." In a *School Library Journal* review, Liza Bliss called this first creation a "lighthearted book," and the fantasy

Matthew finds it easier to accept his new home when he has a chance to view the neighborhood from the air. (From The Wing Shop, *written by Elvira Woodruff and illustrated by Stephen Gammell.*)

element signalled a motif that would be repeated in many of Woodruff's later works.

More fantasy is served up in *The Wing Shop,* the story of Matthew, who has just moved into a new neighborhood and is not too happy about it. Led to Featherman's Wing Shop by a passing pigeon, Matthew tries on a plethora of wings which are for rent, though none seem to make him take wing as intended. Aided in his shopping by little Lucy, the granddaughter of the owner, he finally finds his Icarus apparatus in the shape of old biplane wings which set him adrift for a bird's eye view of his new neighborhood. Suddenly, from this perspective, his new house begins to look more like home. *Horn Book* contributor Nancy Vasilakis commented that the "simple story, with its reassuring theme of change and acceptance, is filled out and given added meaning by Stephen Gammell's exuberant and wildly improbable illustrations." Eve Larkin, writing in *School Library Journal,* noted that "there's more than a touch of Icarus in this tale."

In *Show and Tell,* Andy never has anything really exciting to share with his kindergarten class. His favorite fork and an old shoelace are definitely duds; but when Andy finds a bottle of bubbles in the grass, he is well on his way to the best show-and-tell ever. One of the

bubbles lands on his teacher and shrinks her down to the size of a dust mote blown about the room. Soon the rest of the class is joining her in the airborne adventure, floating out the window on an air draft. The teacher and classmates, once they are safely on ground again, are eager for Andy's next show-and-tell adventure. "Any kid who has ever brought a dopey item for show-and-tell ... will relish Andy's success," remarked Ilene Cooper in a *Booklist* review.

With *Tubtime* there were the three O'Mally sisters; in *Mrs. McClosky's Monkeys,* there are the three McClosky brothers going ape over the approach of summer vacation. After one very silly day, the three actually begin changing into monkeys, and as their behavior deteriorates, so too do their Darwinian fortunes: they become literally more and more apelike. Finally they decide to go live in the zoo, but when that proves too boring, they return home, and change back into humans, "albeit retaining some simian aspects," according to Ruth Semrau in *School Library Journal.*

Woodruff is perhaps even better known and has a wider readership for her middle-grade novels. In the first of these, *Awfully Short for the Fourth Grade,* young Noah finds a packet of magic dust in the gumball machine, and surprisingly, the dust actually works, making him shrink to the size of his plastic toy figures. Once lilliputian in size, Noah joins his toys in an adventure, proving how treacherous the school yard can be if you're a little guy. Noah and his companions have several close shaves involving the school bully and a rapacious hamster before he is ultimately returned to normal size. A critic for *Kirkus Reviews* noted that "Woodruff wins some chuckles with her humorous depiction of grade-school subcultures ... and her topic will be dear to the heart of any child who collects little plastic creatures." Elaine Fort Weischedel concluded in *School Library Journal* that "this is pleasant fare and a promising debut for Woodruff," while *Booklist* reviewer Denise Wilms dubbed the book a "breezy adventure, with particular appeal for boys."

The sequel to *Awfully Short for the Fourth Grade* came in *Back in Action,* in which nine-year-old Noah still enjoys making up dramas for his plastic action figures. This time, however, he brings another human friend, Nate, along on his adventures. Unfortunately, the shrinking powder brings Nate's toy monster to life, as well, and it is out for blood. Noah must learn some fast leadership skills to deploy his action figures to battle the monster. Elaine E. Knight, writing in *School Library Journal,* noted that Woodruff affirms "the value of individual initiative and cooperative effort in this light-fantasy adventure." Linda Callaghan remarked in *Booklist* that "Woodruff's blend of fantasy and action is ripe with clever plot action, excitement, and humor," while Kathryn Pierson Jennings of the *Bulletin of the Center for Children's Books* commented that Woodruff "knows boys' fantasies—endless candy, a working space station and plane to fly in, and a real army."

Grisha refuses to part with the tattered coat his mother made for him before she died, even though the rest of his family fears a bad impression will jeopardize their inspection at Ellis Island. (From The Memory Coat, *written by Woodruff and illustrated by Michael Dooling.*)

Time travel and history combine in many of Woodruff's books. *George Washington's Socks* takes the reader back to the American Revolution when Matthew, his sister, and three friends board an old rowboat and are transported back in time. Matthew's sister Kate receives the socks of the title from Washington himself to keep her feet warm. Bruce Anne Shook noted in *School Library Journal* that Woodruff's book "will be most useful where such stories can support curricular needs in American history." Leonardo da Vinci plays a supporting role in Woodruff's *The Disappearing Bike Shop,* in which Tyler and his best friend, Freckle, grow suspicious over a bike shop that seems to disappear and reappear on a vacant lot. Finally building up their courage, they enter the shop and encounter the strange owner, Quigley, who has a secret room full of inventions and amazing drawings. Later, working on a school report on Leonardo da Vinci, Tyler becomes convinced that Quigley is the reincarnation of the Italian inventor/artist. *School Library Journal* contributor Jana R. Fine noted that "Woodruff's story combines mystery, suspense, and an element of danger into a rollicking good adventure." Fine added that "readers will be drawn into the smoothly building plot and find that the past can be truly exciting."

Napoleon Bonaparte plays a walk-on role in *Dear Napoleon, I Know You're Dead, But—*, a story centered on another school assignment. Writing letters to historical figures can be boring—until they begin to respond. And this is exactly what happens to Marty, whose letter, relayed through his crusty but lovable grandfather, receives a response postmarked from Paris—from the Emperor himself. Marty thinks it's one of Grandfather's tricks, until the old man dies, and after the death Marty receives a letter from Van Gogh. Todd Morning, reviewing the novel in *School Library Journal,* felt that throughout the book, "a nice balance is maintained between the story's serious elements and the humorous, fantastic parts," and went on to conclude that the "affectionate relationship between Marty and his grandfather is particularly well rendered."

History takes on another time-travel aspect in *The Orphan of Ellis Island,* in which Dominic has no heritage to share in his fifth-grade discussion on family backgrounds, for he has spent much of his life in foster care. A visit to Ellis Island with his class results in a trip back in time to Italy of 1908. Dominic is befriended by orphaned brothers en route to America and shares their adventures in this "enjoyable and informative tale," according to Susan L. Rogers in *School Library Journal.*

More conventional history is served up in the companion books, *Dear Levi: Letters from the Overland Trail* and *Dear Austin: Letters from the Underground Railway*. In both, Woodruff employs the epistolary format to tell historical tales. *Dear Levi* follows the trail of a twelve-year-old orphan as he sets out in 1851 for the Oregon Territory. Austin Ives writes to his brother in Pennsylvania about the adventures he has on his pioneering trip. *Booklist* reviewer Deborah Abbott concluded that the book makes for "solid reading," while Elizabeth Bush noted in *Bulletin of the Center for Children's Books* that "Woodruff presents a bounty of information in a format that will be especially valued as a classroom readaloud." Levi writes to his brother Austin in *Dear Austin,* telling of his escapades in Pennsylvania helping with the escape of slaves through the Underground Railroad. "This carefully researched and vividly imagined novel presents the emotional and gripping tale of one boy's confrontations with the issue of slavery and its significance in American history," concluded Janet Gillen in a *School Library Journal* review.

Whether writing lighthearted fare about the shrinking adventures of a fourth-grader, or more hard-hitting stories of young people caught in the maw of history, Woodruff employs a keen observer's eye and a continual sense of humor. "I've found that writing is an organic process, unfolding from one's life," Woodruff once told *SATA.* "What you have to do as a writer is feel, look, and listen. Your stories then become a celebration of these observations."

Works Cited

Abbott, Deborah, review of *Dear Levi: Letters from the Overland Trail, Booklist,* July, 1994, p. 1949.

Review of *Awfully Short for the Fourth Grade, Kirkus Reviews,* September 1, 1989, p. 1335.

Bliss, Liza, review of *Tubtime, School Library Journal,* July, 1990, p. 66.

Bush, Elizabeth, review of *Dear Levi: Letters from the Overland Trail, Bulletin of the Center for Children's Books,* September, 1994, pp. 28-29.

Callaghan, Linda, review of *Back in Action, Booklist,* January 15, 1992, p. 941.

Cooper, Ilene, review of *Show and Tell, Booklist,* September 15, 1991, pp. 167-68.

Cooper, Ilene, review of *Tubtime, Booklist,* April 1, 1990, p. 1561.

Fine, Jana R., review of *The Disappearing Bike Shop, School Library Journal,* May, 1992, p. 117.

Gillen, Janet, review of *Dear Austin: Letters from the Underground Railway, School Library Journal,* October, 1998, p. 148.

Jennings, Kathryn Pierson, review of *Back in Action, Bulletin of the Center for Children's Books,* January, 1992, p. 142.

Knight, Elaine E., review of *Back in Action, School Library Journal,* December, 1991, pp. 119-20.

Larkin, Eve, review of *The Wing Shop, School Library Journal,* November, 1991, p. 109.

Morning, Todd, review of *Dear Napoleon, I Know You're Dead, But—, School Library Journal,* October, 1992, pp. 123-24.

Rogers, Susan L., review of *The Orphan of Ellis Island: A Time Travel Adventure, School Library Journal,* May, 1997, p. 140.

Semrau, Ruth, review of *Mrs. McClosky's Monkeys, School Library Journal,* June, 1991, p. 93.

Shook, Bruce Anne, review of *George Washington's Socks, School Library Journal,* November, 1991, p. 125.

Review of *The Summer I Shrank My Grandmother, Publishers Weekly,* November 2, 1990, p. 74.

Vasilakis, Nancy, review of *The Wing Shop, Horn Book,* May-June, 1991, p. 327.

Weischedel, Elaine Fort, review of *Awfully Short for the Fourth Grade, School Library Journal,* November, 1989, p. 116.

Wilms, Denise, review of *Awfully Short for the Fourth Grade, Booklist,* January 1, 1990, p. 922.

For More Information See

PERIODICALS

Booklist, January 15, 1991, p. 1059; March 15, 1992, pp. 1380-81; December 15, 1992, p. 739; January 15, 1994, p. 931.

Bulletin of the Center for Children's Books, December, 1992, p. 128; February, 1994, p. 205; March, 1997, pp. 261-62.

Horn Book, September-October, 1994, p. 592.

Kirkus Reviews, March 1, 1991, p. 325; May 15, 1994, p. 710; January 15, 1997, p. 147.

New York Times Book Review, June 16, 1991, p. 25.

Publishers Weekly, April 27, 1990, p. 60; March 22, 1991, p. 80; May 10, 1991, p. 281; July 8, 1996, p. 85; February 9, 1998, p. 98.

School Library Journal, March, 1999, p. 188.

—Sketch by J. Sydney Jones

*   *   *

WORMSER, Richard 1933-

Personal

Born in 1933. *Education:* Bucknell University, graduated 1955.

Addresses

Office—Videoline Productions, 1697 Broadway, Room 901, New York, NY 10019.

Career

Documentary filmmaker and writer of nonfiction for young adults. Also worked as a logger in the Pacific Northwest, a translator of French film treatments, a newspaper salesman in Paris, a longshoreman in London, and as a journalist for the *Shamokin Citizen,* Shamokin, PA. *Member:* PEN.

Writings

NONFICTION; FOR YOUNG ADULTS

Pinkerton: America's First Private Eye, Walker, 1990.
Lifers: Learn the Truth at the Expense of Our Sorrow, Simon & Schuster, 1991.
Countdown to Crisis: A Look at the Middle East, Simon & Schuster, 1992.
Three Faces of Vietnam, Franklin Watts, 1993.
The Iron Horse: How Railroads Changed America, Walker, 1993.
Growing Up in the Great Depression, Atheneum, 1994.
Hoboes: Wandering in America, 1870-1940, Walker, 1994.
Juveniles in Trouble, Simon & Schuster, 1994.
American Islam: Growing Up Muslim in America, Walker, 1994.
The Titanic, Explorer Books, 1994.
American Childhoods: Three Centuries of Youth at Risk, Walker, 1996.

Wormser has also written and produced over forty documentary films.

Work in Progress

Separate and Unequal: Jim Crow in the American South (working title), for Atheneum; *Defense Lawyers* (working title), for Franklin Watts; *Whistle-Blowers* (working title), for Franklin Watts.

Sidelights

Richard Wormser is a filmmaker turned writer who has published several works of nonfiction for young adult readers on such varied topics as teens at risk, Vietnam, hoboes, railways, American Islam, and even a biography of Allan Pinkerton, the first private investigator in America. Wormser's writings generally have a social slant, and he often chooses to feature those who, "having experienced the worst that life has to offer, are able to pick themselves up, tumble forward, and move out of the darkness of their lives into some light," as Wormser wrote in an essay for *Something about the Author Autobiography Series* (*SAAS*).

Born in 1933, Wormser was a child of the Great Depression, and a great fan of baseball, partly because Babe Ruth lived only two blocks away from his home. Playing hooky to go to a Yankees game, he was later caught by his father and spent a "long period of confinement to my room without allowance," the author noted in *SAAS*. Reading came easily to the young Wormser, who devoured "comic books, boy's adventure stories of super-macho idiotic heroes who speak in near-grunts or single-syllable words," and of course baseball stories. Writing, however, was another matter; penmanship was a perennial problem for Wormser and he spent tortured hours in the second grade trying to master cursive handwriting. But it was not simply the mechanical aspect that bothered him; content proved difficult as well. "Writing remains hard for me," Wormser admitted in *SAAS*. "I never seem to say exactly what I want to say in the way I want to say it. The nuances of feelings I

Richard Wormser's nonfiction account focuses on the culture and habits of America's wandering laborers.

want to express elude me. Trying to capture the right word is like trying to catch butterflies."

Prep school was a trial for Wormser, who was smaller and less mature than the other boys. He turned to books during these years and soon graduated from "junk" reading to novels and history. His first years in college, however, almost extinguished this light, until a sociology course awoke intellectual passion in him. He also began reading the works of the Beat generation, including Jack Kerouac's novel *On the Road,* which became Wormser's "Bible." Wormser explored America between his junior and senior years, riding Greyhound buses and talking to everyone he met. In California he stayed with friends for a time, taking odd jobs, then travelled on to the Southwest and Denver, where he drove a dealer's car to Seattle. During these travels he first came into contact with that mobile class of itinerant workers, the hoboes who hitchhiked and rode the rails from one job to the next. The experience of meeting these men would later come to fruition in a book on hoboes.

In Washington state, Wormser worked for a time as a choker setter on a logging crew, one of the most dangerous jobs in the woods. Back at school, Wormser graduated in 1955, then went on to law school, which he ultimately quit, and then to graduate school. In 1959 he left for Paris, where he intended to pursue his doctorate at the Sorbonne; in the event, he attended the school of life in that city, staying on for two years during the turbulent era of the Algerian-French conflict. In Paris he met some of the Beat poets and writers such as Allen Ginsberg and William Burroughs and began his own attempts at writing.

Returning to the U.S. in 1961, Wormser took a job for a time at a small weekly newspaper in Pennsylvania, where he covered everything from city politics to the coal mines which employed most of the local population. This work provided him with valuable experience in journalism and photography, and as the 1960s got into full swing, he began to discover his own creative voice. Visiting an institution for retarded children in Pennsylvania, he decided that the only way he could do justice to the story of such children was by making a documentary film about them. He had never made a film nor shot footage, but managed to find funding and learned as he went along. Once finished, his first film won a number of awards. He also helped to make a film about the 1968 Democratic Convention in Chicago when the police force literally ran riot against demonstrators. Suddenly Wormser saw what he wanted to do with film: to make movies about "the past and present struggles of people to win the political, civil, and human rights denied them by their fellow Americans, politicians, police, and courts," as the author put it in *SAAS*.

In the 1970s and 1980s Wormser travelled far and wide documenting lives throughout the Middle East and Egypt as well as in the United States. As the 1990s approached, and Yippie—"those opposed to the killing in Vietnam"—was replaced by Yuppie—"those in favor of making a killing on Wall Street"—Wormser found it increasingly difficult to produce his social and political documentaries, and turned to writing instead. His first title resulted from a failed film project about the life of Allan Pinkerton, the founder of the Pinkerton Agency, whose name is often associated with strike breaking. Wormser discovered, however, that far from being a social conservative and tool of the ruling class, Pinkerton was a labor radical in his native Scotland and had to emigrate to the United States to avoid arrest. A staunch abolitionist, Pinkerton helped slaves escape from the South and put his new agency at the service of the Union during the Civil War.

In a review for *School Library Journal,* Jacqueline Elsner described Wormser's debut book, *Pinkerton: America's First Private Eye,* as an account "told with exciting pacing and engrossing anecdotes." Elsner concluded that "readers are treated to a fast-paced, absorbing look at this complex, unique man and to a vivid view of U.S. history during his lifetime." Leone McDermott, writing in *Booklist,* noted that an "intriguing subject, lively prose, and in-depth analysis combine to make this a first-rate biography." Concluding a review for *Voice of Youth Advocates,* Pat Costello wrote that "history comes alive through the author's efforts and it is just this effect which should encourage more young people to sample the nonfiction genre."

Such a warm critical reception encouraged Wormser to continue with YA nonfiction. In *SAAS* Wormser wrote that he realized that "writing for the young adult market allows me to write about subjects I care about, and for which there is no longer a strong support for [in] documentary films.... Perhaps through my books I can reach an audience that is not yet indifferent to the plight of America's dispossessed—those for whom society seems to have no place."

Wormser's next book deals with crime and young people at risk. After a year's research at the East Jersey State Prison in New Jersey, and interviewing four men sentenced to life imprisonment, Wormser penned *Lifers: Learn the Truth at the Expense of Our Sorrow.* The book, rather than trying to scare adolescents away from a life of crime, simply presents the facts about life inside prisons. Wormser documents how these "lifers" got into trouble on the outside and why, and also looks at what impact prison has on their lives. "This includes graphic language and a tough, no-nonsense treatment ... to demonstrate the realities and brutalities of life in a maximum security facility," remarked Celia A. Huffman

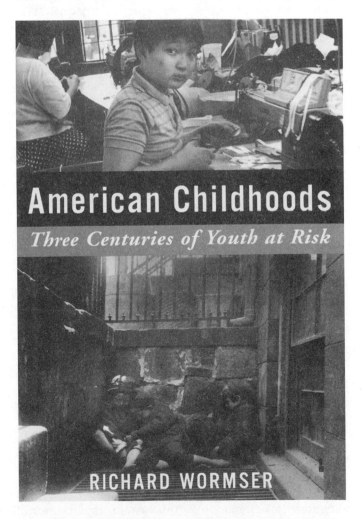

Wormser's historical view of American adolescence shows the grim realities of child labor and enforced military servitude, among other injustices. (Cover photos by Lina Pallotta, Impact.)

in a *School Library Journal* review. *Booklist* commentator Candace Smith called the book a "grim but perceptive look at the real horrors of prison—monotony, boredom, despair, and wasted lives."

In a similar vein are Wormser's *Juveniles in Trouble* and *American Childhoods: Three Centuries of Youth at Risk*, both dedicated to investigations of troubled and difficult adolescence, historical and contemporary. In *Juveniles in Trouble*, Wormser "describes the lives of young people who run away from home and live on the streets, who are addicted to drugs, who are in gangs, and who commit crimes," observed *School Library Journal* contributor Jacqueline Rose. Jeanne Triner commented in *Booklist* that "teens need more hard-hitting, factual information like this to help them understand how important the choices they make today are going to be for the rest of their lives."

In *American Childhoods,* Wormser does much the same for the historical view of adolescence, showing the grim realities of child labor and enforced military servitude, among other injustices. Deborah Stevenson, reviewing the book in *Bulletin of the Center for Children's Books*, commented that Wormser "pays particularly close attention to those groups that fared least well—immigrants, minorities, and the poor—and finishes each chapter with an extensive discussion of the contemporary situation."

Wormser has also turned his hand to historical issues such as the Vietnam conflict in *Three Faces of Vietnam*, the effect of railroads on America in *The Iron Horse*, the Great Depression in *Growing Up in the Great Depression*, and religion in America in *American Islam: Growing Up Muslim in America*. It is Wormser's gift to approach his subjects with an editorial slant as well as to come at them from a new and different angle. In *Three Faces of Vietnam,* for example, he presents the war "through the eyes of antiwar protestors, American GIs, and the Vietnamese people," according to Mary Mueller in *School Library Journal*, "attempting to capture the feelings and attitudes of that era." *Booklist* critic Sheilamae O'Hara concluded that Wormser's book "does effectively show the tragic marks the war left on both the Vietnamese and Americans." Of Wormser's book, *The Iron Horse*, a *Publishers Weekly* critic noted that it "provides an evenhanded history of the growth and impact of the railroads in 19th-century America," while Allison Rogers Hutchison declared in *Voice of Youth Advocates* that "this is such a good read for a nonfiction YA title that it comes highly recommended for any YA collection."

Wormser did not forget the effect that meeting hoboes and tramps had on him when he was a young man: in 1994 he wrote a book documenting their lives that spans seventy years of American history. His *Hoboes: Wandering in America, 1870-1940* focuses on the rules, literature, jokes, modes of life, customs, and politics of this class of wandering workers, similar to today's itinerant laborers. Hazel Rochman noted in a *Booklist* review that while "Wormser evokes the adventure of the hobo journey, the romance of the rugged individual ...

he's frank about the brutal reality of living on the edge in hard times—the hunger, the viciousness, the 'jungle' warfare." A *Kirkus Reviews* contributor called that same book an "engaging account of the penurious workers who crisscrossed America as 'internal refugees' from the Industrial Revolution," and concluded by calling Wormser's work "informative and fascinating."

Wormser is aware of the impression he wants to create; as with his films, he is seeking in his books to give voice to the silent in society, to illuminate today's concerns by examining yesterday's failures and successes. "I still write for young people," Wormser concluded in *SAAS*, "finding that the ideas and opinions of most adults are hopelessly set in concrete and are all but impossible to break through. In many young people, the concrete, though hardening, has not yet solidified in their brains. Some are still open to new experiences, willing to suspend judgment until they have more understanding of issues, and listen to different sides. So I write for those who can make a difference in the world, can change it, and help make it a place where all people can have a chance to live decent and productive lives."

Works Cited

Costello, Pat, review of *Pinkerton: America's First Private Eye, Voice of Youth Advocates,* December, 1990, pp. 323-24.

Elsner, Jacqueline, review of *Pinkerton: America's First Private Eye, School Library Journal,* December, 1990, p. 120.

Review of *Hoboes: Wandering in America, 1870-1940, Kirkus Reviews,* May 15, 1994, p. 710.

Huffman, Celia A., review of *Lifers: Learn the Truth at the Expense of Our Sorrow, School Library Journal,* December, 1991, p. 147.

Hutchinson, Allison Rogers, review of *The Iron Horse: How Railroads Changed America, Voice of Youth Advocates,* April, 1994, p. 55.

Review of *The Iron Horse: How Railroads Changed America, Publishers Weekly,* November 22, 1993, p. 65.

McDermott, Leone, review of *Pinkerton: America's First Private Eye, Booklist,* January 1, 1991, p. 920.

Mueller, Mary, review of *Three Faces of Vietnam, School Library Journal,* January, 1994, p. 143.

O'Hara, Sheilamae, review of *Three Faces of Vietnam, Booklist,* February 15, 1994, p. 1070.

Rochman, Hazel, review of *Hoboes: Wandering in America, 1870-1940, Booklist,* June 1 & 15, 1994, p. 1794.

Rose, Jacqueline, review of *Juveniles in Trouble, School Library Journal,* June, 1994, p. 158.

Smith, Candace, review of *Lifers: Learn the Truth at the Expense of Our Sorrow, Booklist,* September 15, 1991, p. 140.

Stevenson, Deborah, review of *American Childhoods: Three Centuries of Youth at Risk, Bulletin of the Center for Children's Books,* October, 1996, p. 81.

Triner, Jeanne, review of *Juveniles in Trouble, Booklist,* May 15, 1994, p. 1673.

Wormser, Richard, essay in *Something about the Author Autobiography Series,* Volume 26, Gale, 1998, pp. 271-85.

For More Information See

PERIODICALS

Booklist, October 15, 1994, p. 417; December 15, 1994, pp. 746-47.
Bulletin of the Center for Children's Books, December, 1991, p. 110; January, 1994, pp. 171-72; September, 1994, p. 29.

Kirkus Reviews, June 15, 1991, pp. 794-95; July 15, 1996, p. 1058.
Publishers Weekly, December 5, 1994, p. 78.
School Library Journal, July, 1994, p. 127; December, 1994, p. 129.
Voice of Youth Advocates, December, 1991, pp. 343-44; February, 1995, p. 366; December, 1996, p. 294.
Wilson Library Bulletin, March, 1992, p. 122.

—Sketch by J. Sydney Jones

Y

Ting-xing Ye

YE, Ting-xing 1952-

Personal

Given name is pronounced "Ting-sing;" born June 28, 1952, in Shanghai, China; immigrated to Canada, 1987; daughter of Rong-ting and Xiu-feng (Li) Ye; married William E. Bell (a writer and teacher); children: Qi-meng Zhao. *Education:* Beijing University, B.A., 1978;

Foreign Affairs College, Beijing, China, Post-Graduate Certificate, 1986.

Addresses

Home—21 Laurentian Lane, Orillia, Ontario, Canada L3V 7N8. *Electronic mail*—willbell@barint.on.ca.

Career

Da Feng Labor Camp, Jiang Su Province, China, 1968-74; Municipality of Shanghai, Shanghai, China, English translator in Foreign Affairs Office, 1978-87; worked in clerical positions in Toronto, Ontario, 1988-90; Canadian Manufacturers' Association, assistant editor of *Canadian Trade Index,* 1990-92; Harriett Todd Public School, Orillia, Ontario, library secretary, 1993-95; freelance writer, editor, and translator, 1995—. York University, visiting scholar, 1988.

Writings

Three Monks, No Water, illustrated by Harvey Chan, Annick/Firefly Books, (Toronto), 1997.
A Leaf in the Bitter Wind: A Memoir, Doubleday Canada (Toronto), 1997.
Weighing the Elephant, illustrated by Suzanne Langlois, Annick/Firefly Books, 1998.
Share the Sky, illustrated by Suzanne Langlois, Annick/Firefly Books, 1999.

Sidelights

Ting-xing Ye told *SATA:* "I was born in Shanghai, China, the fourth child of five. I was called 'Number Four' at home. My brothers and sisters were also called by number. My real name, or school name, is Ting-xing Ye. My last name means 'leaf' in Chinese, and that contributed the title of my autobiography, *A Leaf in the Bitter Wind.* It tells of my thirty-five years in China before I came to Canada.

"When I was six I started elementary school. My childhood was nothing like the nursery rhymes had described: they had called childhood a golden time. Mine was joyless and miserable. I lived in poverty and later became an orphan. I spent four years in high school but didn't graduate, due to the outbreak of the Cultural Revolution. At the age of sixteen, I was sent to work at a prison farm for six years, far away from home where, as the child of a 'capitalist,' I was continually subjected to humiliating psychological torture.

"My change of fortune came when I was accepted into Beijing University and eventually—consummate iro-ny—was offered a job with the Chinese Secret Police. Managing to get myself reassigned to the Foreign Ministry as a translator, I found myself translating for the delegations of such dignitaries as Queen Elizabeth, Ronald Reagan, and Imelda Marcos.

"As a child, I enjoyed reading Chinese classics and other 'thick' books, including the textbooks of my two older brothers. I found that the books sometimes helped me escape the tough real world I faced each day, and they gave me great satisfaction and pride whenever I finished one. (My mother attributed my early near-sightedness to my reading.) Nevertheless, my love of literature had never once inspired me to try to write on my own when I lived in China. I realized at an early age that writing, 'black character on white paper' as Chinese people put it, was dangerous and a curse. I witnessed people around me being punished, suppressed, or even executed, not for what they did, but for what they thought, believed,

said, and wrote. Writing was taboo, I concluded, and I'd better stay away from it.

"I came to Canada in August, 1987, as a visiting scholar to York University in Toronto. After living in the city for five years, I moved to Orillia, a small town north of Toronto. For months I couldn't find a job. One spring day in 1993, I found myself sitting in front of a word processor, trying to compose a story from an old Chinese saying which my mother often used when I was a child. 'Three monks, no water,' she said, whenever my siblings and I were trying to find excuses for not doing household chores, or passing the assignment among us like a baton in a relay.

"The acceptance of the story *Three Monks, No Water* turned out to be the beginning of my writing career. Soon thereafter, I started writing my memoirs, *A Leaf in the Bitter Wind.* Meanwhile, I wrote two more children's picture stories, *Weighing the Elephant* and *Share the Sky.* I plan to continue to write, a luxury to which not everyone in this world is entitled."

For More Information See

PERIODICALS

Booklist, February 1, 1998, p. 920.
Canadian Materials, February 27, 1998.
Maclean's, June 9, 1997, p. 69.
Quill and Quire, January, 1997, p. 13; October, 1997, p. 43.
School Library Journal, December, 1997, pp. 103-04.